NEW YORK
ITS LAND AND ITS PEOPLE

JAMES KILLORAN

STUART ZIMMER

MARK JARRETT

JARRETT PUBLISHING COMPANY

EAST COAST OFFICE
19 Cross Street
Lake Ronkonkoma, NY 11779

WEST COAST OFFICE
10 Folin Lane
Lafayette, CA 94549

516-981-4248 ❖ 1-800-859-7679
Fax: 516-588-4722
www.rwmg.com/jarrettpub

Copyright 1997 by Jarrett Publishing Company

All rights reserved. No part of this book may be reproduced in any form or by any means, including electronic, photographic or mechanical, or by any device for storage and retrieval of information, without the express written permission of the publisher.

ISBN 1-882422-26-0

Printed in Singapore
First Edition
10 9 8 7 6 5 4 3 2 1 97 98 99 00 01 02

ABOUT THE AUTHORS

James Killoran is a retired New York City Assistant Principal. He has written *Government and You;* and *Economics and You.* Mr. Killoran has extensive experience in test writing for the New York State Board of Regents in Social Studies and has served on the Committee for Testing of the National Council of Social Studies. His article on Social Studies testing has been published in *Social Education,* the country's leading Social Studies journal. In addition, Mr. Killoran has won a number of awards for outstanding teaching and curriculum development, including, "Outstanding Social Studies Teacher" and "Outstanding Social Studies Supervisor" in New York City. In 1993, he was awarded an Advanced Certificate for Teachers of Social Studies by the N.C.S.S.

Stuart Zimmer is a retired New York City Social Studies teacher. He has written *Government and You* and *Economics and You.* He served as a test writer for the New York State Board of Regents in Social Studies, and has written for the National Merit Scholarship Examination. In addition, he has published numerous articles on teaching and testing in Social Studies journals. He has presented many demonstrations and educational workshops at state and national teachers' conferences. In 1989, Mr. Zimmer's achievements were recognized by the New York State Legislature with a Special Legislative Resolution in his honor.

Mark Jarrett is a former Social Studies teacher and a practicing attorney at the San Francisco office of Baker and McKenzie, the world's largest law firm. Mr. Jarrett has served as a test writer for the New York State Board of Regents, and has taught at Hofstra University. He was educated at Columbia University, the London School of Economics, the Law School of the University of California at Berkeley, and Stanford University, where he is a doctoral candidate in history. Mr. Jarrett has won several academic awards, including Order of the Coif at Berkeley, and the David and Christina Phelps Harris Fellowship at Stanford.

ALSO BY KILLORAN, ZIMMER AND JARRETT

Global Studies
The Key To Understanding U.S. History and Government
Mastering Global Studies
Mastering U.S. History and Government
Comprende Tu Mundo: Su Historia, Sus Culturas
Historia Y Gobierno De Los Estados Unidos
Mastering Ohio's 9th Grade Citizenship Test
Mastering Ohio's
Los Estados Unidos: Su Historia, Su Gobierno
Nuestro Mundo: Su Historia, Sus Culturas
Ohio: Its Land and Its People
Ohio: Its Neighbors, Near and Far
Principios De Economia

ACKNOWLEDGMENTS

The authors wish to acknowledge the help of **Dr. Joel Fischer,** who provided some ideas for the activities. The authors also wish to thank **Lloyd Bromberg,** former Director of Social Studies, New York City Board of Education, for his many suggestions and advice regarding the needs of New York educators.

In addition, several New York teachers reviewed this book. Their comments, suggestions and recommendations proved invaluable. These teachers are:

- **Christine Antonio:** P.S. 26, Albany City School District.
- **Doreen Dell:** Dodge Elementary School, Williamsville School District.
- **Mary Duffin:** Moses DeWitt School, Jamesville DeWitt School District.
- **Deanna Washinsky:** P.S. 212, N.Y.C. Community School District 21.
- **Susan Wasserman:** Shaw Avenue School, Valley Stream School District.

We would also like to thank the following school administrators for their insights and suggestions:

- **Ann R. Flanagan:** Principal of Lynwood Avenue School, Sachem School District.
- **Dr. Michael Romano:** District Chairperson of Social Studies, Northport-East Northport U.F.S.D.

Finally, the authors would like to thank Julie Fleck and Hanna Kisiel for their many suggestions and insightful comments on the manuscript.

Cover design by Burmar Technical Corporation, Albertson, N.Y.
Artistic Illustrations by Ron S. Zimmer.
Maps and graphics by C.F. Enterprises and Burmar Technical Corporation.
Layout, maps/graphics and typesetting: Burmar Technical Corporation, Albertson, N.Y.

This book is dedicated to ...

my wife Donna, and my children Christian, Carrie, and Jesse. .... *James Killoran*
my wife Joan, and my children Todd and Ronald. .... *Stuart Zimmer*
my wife Goska, and my children Alexander and Julia. .... *Mark Jarrett*

TABLE OF CONTENTS

OPENING ACTIVITY
The image I have of New York State is ____?____ 1

UNIT 1: KEYS TO LEARNING WITH SUCCESS
Key 1: Visualizing Important Information 2
Key 2: Using Mnemonic Devices 4
Key 3: Answering Multiple-Choice Questions 6
Key 4: The Writing Process 8
Key 5: Pre-Reading Hints 10

YOUR SCHOOL YEAR PROJECT 11

UNIT 2: GEOGRAPHY
Unit Opener: Henry Hudson Searches for the Northwest Passage 14
Activity 2A: Can You Please Give Me Some Directions? 16
  Making Connections
    Exploring Beyond Your State: Learning to Use An Atlas 27
    Exploring Your Community: The Roadways of Your Community 29
Activity 2B: What Questions Might a Geographer Ask About Your School? 31
  Making Connections
    Exploring Beyond Your State: Applying the Five Themes to Cultures
      Around the World 35
    Exploring Your Community: Applying the Five Themes to Your Community 37
Activity 2C: What Role Does "Place" Play in People's Lives? 38
  Making Connections
    Exploring Beyond Your State: Geography and Its Effect on Where
      and How People Live 45
    Exploring Your Community: Describing the Physical Features of
      Your Community 46
Activity 2D: How Would You Map Your Community? 47
  Making Connections
    Exploring Beyond Your State: Learning About Latitude and Longitude 53
    Exploring Your Community: Creating a Map of Your Community 56
Activity 2E: What Does New York State "Look" Like? 57
  Making Connections
    Exploring Beyond Your State: Taking a Flight Across the United States 63
    Exploring Your Community: Taking a Helicopter Ride Over Your Community 65

Activity 2F: What Do New York's Regions "Look" Like?.. 66
   Making Connections
        Exploring Beyond Your State: Cultural Regions of the World........................... 80
        Exploring Your Community: Drawing or Writing About Where You Live 81
Activity 2G: Where Would You Locate Your Basketball Team?... 82
   Making Connections
        Exploring Beyond Your State: The Importance of Living Near Water.......................... 90
        Exploring Your Community: Reading Mileage Charts 91
Summarizing Your Understanding... 93
Information Sheet #1: Geography... 95

UNIT 3: AMERICAN HERITAGE

Unit Opener: New York Celebrates the Erie Canal.. 98
Activity 3A: How Would You Edit this Article?
   Making Connections
        Exploring Beyond Your State: The Native Americans of the United States 114
        Exploring Your Community: Stepping Into Your Community's Past............................ 116
Activity 3B: Are You a Good Historian of Colonial Times?... 117
   Making Connections
        Exploring Beyond Your State: Colonial America.. 120
        Exploring Your Community: Writing About Your Community's History 132
Activity 3C: Are You a Good Historian of Early New York State?
   Making Connections
        Exploring Beyond Your State: The Influence of Our Constitution 139
        Exploring Your Community: Researching Your Community's Past 140
Activity 3D: How Would You "Diagram" What You Read?... 142
   Making Connections
        Exploring Beyond Your State: The American Civil War.. 149
        Exploring Your Community: Taking a Field Trip to a Local Cemetery 151
Activity 3E: How Good Are You at Recognizing Different Types of Readings?...................... 153
   Making Connections
        Exploring Beyond Your State: The Rise of Industrial America.................................. 162
        Exploring Your Community: Interpreting Historic Photographs................................ 164
Activity 3F: What Effects Have Key Events Had on New York State?...................................... 165
   Making Connections
        Exploring Beyond Your State: America's Expanded Role in The World 172
        Exploring Your Community: Who Has Your Community Honored with
          a Monument?... 174

Activity 3G: What Was It Like Living Through World War II? 176
    Making Connections
        Exploring Beyond Your State: World War II and Its Aftermath 184
        Exploring Your Community: Community Veterans' Organizations 186
Activity 3H: How Would You Outline this Reading? 187
    Making Connections
        Exploring Beyond Your State: The World Following World War II 193
        Exploring Your Community: Becoming a Community Oral Historian 194
Summarizing Your Understanding 197
Information Sheet #2: History 199

UNIT 4: PEOPLE IN SOCIETY

Unit Opener: Why Do People Have Different Cultures? 202
Activity 4A: How Would You Categorize Yourself? 204
    Making Connections
        Exploring Beyond Your State: Some Major World Religions 211
        Exploring Your Community: Learning About People in Your Community 213
Activity 4B: What Generalizations Can You Make About New York's Ethnic Groups? 214
    Making Connections
        Exploring Beyond Your State: The United States: a Nation of Immigrants 229
        Exploring Your Community: Learning About Ethnic Groups in Your Community 230
Activity 4C: What Is Cultural Diffusion? 232
    Making Connections
        Exploring Beyond Your State: World Myths and Legends 236
        Exploring Your Community: Looking for Examples of Cultural Diffusion
           in Your Community 239
Activity 4D: Which Events Would You Place on the Timeline? 240
    Making Connections
        Exploring Beyond Your State: Creating a Picture Timeline 245
        Exploring Your Community: Creating a Community Timeline 247
Activity 4E: Who Would You Nominate to the New York Hall of Fame? 249
    Making Connections
        Exploring Beyond Your State: What Makes Someone a Hero? 254
        Exploring Your Community: Who Is a Hero in Your Neighborhood? 256
Activity 4F: How Would You Classify the Landmarks of New York? 258
    Making Connections
        Exploring Beyond Your State: Our Nation's Symbols 265
        Exploring Your Community: Creating a Pamphlet About Your Community 267
Summarizing Your Understanding 268
Information Sheet #3: People in Society 269

UNIT 5: ECONOMICS

Unit Opener: Professor Smith Visits a Factory 272
Activity 5A: How Would You Spend Your Money? 274
    Making Connections
        Exploring Beyond Your State: Different Types of Economic Groups 277
        Exploring Your Community: Consumption and Production in Your Community 280
Activity 5B: How Would You Illustrate the Factors of Production? 282
    Making Connections
        Exploring Beyond Your State: How Societies Meet Their Economic Needs 287
        Exploring Your Community: Goods and Services Produced in Your Community 290
Activity 5C: Would You Start Your Own Business? 291
    Making Connections
        Exploring Beyond Your State: Learning About Occupations in New York State 295
        Exploring Your Community: Reporting Your Local Economic News 298
Activity 5D: How Would You Promote the Economy of New York State? 300
    Making Connections
        Exploring Beyond Your State: The Resources of the United States 306
        Exploring Your Community: An Economic Profile of Your Community 308
Activity 5E: How Interdependent Are We With Foreign Countries? 309
    Making Connections
        Exploring Beyond Your State: Why Nations Trade with Each Other 313
        Exploring Your Community: Looking at Community Stores 317
Summarizing Your Understanding 318
Information Sheet #4: Economics 319

UNIT 6: GOVERNMENT

Unit Opener: A Young Author Struggles Through the Night 322
Activity 6A: What Rules Would You Make for Your Class? 324
    Making Connections
        Exploring Beyond Your State: The Rise of Governments 327
        Exploring Your Community: How Is Your School Governed? 329
Activity 6B: Who Represents You in the National Government? 330
    Making Connections
        Exploring Beyond Your State: Our Modern World of Nation-States 336
        Exploring Local Community: Who Is That Building Named After? 338
Activity 6C: Who Represents You at the State and Local Level? 339
    Making Connections
        Exploring Beyond Your State: The U.S. Constitution 349
        Exploring Your Community: Writing to Your Elected Official 349

Activity 6D: What Characteristics Make a Person a Good Leader? 352
    Making Connections
        Exploring Beyond Your State: Leaders Who Strengthened Democracy 358
        Exploring Your Community: Identifying a Person with Leadership Qualities 360
Summarizing Your Understanding 361
Information Sheet #5: Government 363

UNIT 7: CITIZENSHIP

Unit Opener: Jasiek Becomes an American Citizen 366
Activity 7A: How Would You Define a "Good" Citizen? 368
    Making Connections
        Exploring Beyond Your State: The Rights, Duties and Responsibilities
          of Citizenship 371
        Exploring Your Community: Learning About Community Newspapers 373
Activity 7B: You Be the Judge! 374
    Making Connections
        Exploring Beyond Your State: Human Rights in the Rest of the World 379
        Exploring Your Community: Community Organizations That Help People 380
Activity 7C: How Do People Participate in a Democracy? 382
    Making Connections
        Exploring Beyond Your State: Participating in a Democracy—Voting 388
        Exploring Your Community: What Would You Suggest for a Community
          Citizenship Project? 389
Activity 7D: How Would You Reduce Pollution in Your Community? 391
    Making Connections
        Exploring Beyond Your State: Changes in the Earth's Environment 396
        Exploring Your Community: Keeping a Journal About Community Problems 397
Activity 7E: Should We Limit the Amount Of Violence Shown on Television? 399
    Making Connections
        Exploring Beyond Your State: Important Issues Facing Americans Today 409
        Exploring Your Community: What Issues Divide Your Community? 409
Summarizing Your Understanding 411
Information Sheet #6: Citizenship 412

CLOSING ACTIVITY

The image I now have of New York State is _____?_____ 413

GLOSSARY 415

GAZETTEER 422

MAPS

Map of the United States	426
Map of New York State	427

INDEX 428

PHOTO CREDITS 433

SKILL BUILDERS

Using an Atlas	27
Learning to Interpret a Map	48
How to Find Information in an Almanac	84
Interpreting a Mileage Chart	91
Distinguishing Between Primary and Secondary Sources	176
Preparing to Become an Oral Historian	195
Interpreting Pie Charts	206
How Generalizations Are Formed	215
Timelines and Their Main Parts	240
Creating a Picture Timeline	245
How to Classify	260
Interpreting a Product Map	305
Interpreting Bar Graphs	348
Interpreting Line Graphs	385
An Approach to Problem Solving	393
The Five Steps to Making an Informed Decision	399

WRITING SKILLS

The "How To" Form of Writing	23
How to Write a Narrative Essay	183
How Outlines are Organized	187
How to Write a Descriptive Essay	257
Writing a Newspaper Article	299
Writing a Business Letter	350
Learning to Use a Dictionary	352
Creating and Keeping a Journal	398
Writing a Persuasive Letter or Essay	406

READING SKILLS

The Difference Between Facts and Opinions	100
What Does It Mean to Read Something	142
Three Types Of Readings: Problem-Solution, Sequential and Descriptive	153
Understanding Cause-and-Effect Relationships	165

SPECIAL FEATURES AND NOTES

Learning About Making Connections	26
Learning About Exploring Your Community	29
A Note About Long Island	76
A Note on Names	101
A Note On Some Countries in Western Europe	118
A Note on Turnpikes	136
Brainstorming	394
What Are Issues?	399

FAMOUS NEW YORKERS

George Boldt	68
Jackie Robinson	87
George W. Goethals	92
James Fenimore Cooper	102
Eli S. Parker	112
Benedict Arnold	132
Emma Lazarus	168
Theodore Roosevelt	174
Colin Powell	185
Fiorello LaGuardia	218
Irving Berlin	221
James Baldwin	224
A. Philip Randolph	231
Nathan Hale	257
Samuel Gompers	280
George Westinghouse	281
John Jacob Astor	284
Alfred E. Smith	302
George Pataki	342
Rudolph Giuliani	346

Robert Livingston 351
Eleanor Roosevelt 381
Franklin D. Roosevelt 387

REFERENCES

Almanac 84
Encyclopedia 113
Dictionary 353
Newspaper Editorial ....

HISTORIC DOCUMENTS

The Iroquois Constitution 110
The Declaration of Independence 125
A Declaration of Sentiments and Resolutions 144
"How the Other Half Lives" by Jacob Riis 159
New York's Constitution 343

MAPS

Route of Henry Hudson, 1609 15
Our Solar System 16
Our Planet: The Rotation of the Earth 17
Our Planet and its Hemispheres 17
Continents and Oceans 18
North America 19
Regions of the United States 20
United States 21
New York County Map 21
Physical Map of the United States 27
Political Map of the Northeast 28
Map Showing Anchorage, Manhattan and the Everglades 39
Map of Anytown 48
New York: Cities 50
Latitudes 53
Northern and Southern Hemispheres 53
Longitudes 54
Eastern and Western Hemispheres 54

xii

Quadrant Map of the Earth	55
New York State: Its Latitude and Longitude	55
City of Rochester: Congressional Districts	56
New York State: Physical Features	58
New York State: Upstate and Downstate	67
The St. Lawrence Lowlands Region of New York State	68
The Adirondack Mountain Region of New York State	69
The Great Plains Region of New York State	70
The Appalachian Plateau Region of New York State	71
The Hudson and Mohawk Valley Region of New York State	74
The New England Uplands Region of New York State	75
The Atlantic Coastal Plain Region of New York State	75
The World's Cultural Regions	80
New York and its Surrounding States	88
Outline Map of New York State	91
Erie, Oswego and Champlain Canals	98
Main Migration Routes to the Americas	101
Native American Tribes of New York State	107
Native American Tribes of Long Island	107
Countries of Western Europe	117
The British Plan for Taking New York	127
Colonial America	131
Path of the First New York State Turnpike: 1815	136
Path of the Erie Railroad: 1850	137
The Growth of U.S. Cities: 1865–1900	162
America's Pacific Colonial Possessions	173
The Caribbean Region	173
Location of Japanese-American Internment Camps: 1942–1945	182
Outline Map of the World	230
Outline Map of New York State	265
Outline Map of the United States	307
Outline Map of the World	312
The Levels of Government	313
Resources and International Trade	314
World Oil and Natural Gas Deposits: 1995	315
World Iron Ore Deposits	315
Members of the European Economic Community	316

xiii

Outline Map of the World	337
New York State Assembly District Map	340
New York State Senate District Map	341
County Map of New York State	344
Map of Local Levels of Government	344
Map of Poland	366
Map of the United States	426
Map of New York State	427

KEYS TO LEARNING WITH SUCCESS   1

OPENING ACTIVITY

THE IMAGE I HAVE OF NEW YORK IS ... ?

This school year you will learn about the state you live in: New York. You will also make connections between your community, your state, your country and the world. This book will involve you in many new and interesting activities, and the authors hope you enjoy your journey through its pages.

IMPORTANT NOTE
This is an interactive textbook. It asks you to participate in exciting activities as you learn new information. Even though there are empty spaces on many pages, **please do not write in this book.** Instead, do all of your writing on a separate piece of paper or in a notebook.

WHAT DOES "NEW YORK" MEAN TO YOU?

Before we start our journey together, let's find out what images or thoughts **you** have about New York. Millions of people around the world have an image of New York as a place with tall skyscrapers and crowded streets. When other people hear the words "New York" they may think of Niagara Falls. Still others think of New York as the Empire State—big and bold. But what does New York mean to **YOU**?

Niagara Falls

THINK ABOUT IT
List or draw the images and thoughts that "New York" brings to your mind.

When I think of New York, I think of ...

Next, compare your thoughts about New York with those of your classmates.

Now you are ready to begin your journey. The first unit of this book will give you some handy tools for studying and learning—making your trip a more pleasant and rewarding one. Later units will introduce you to the geography, history, culture, economy and government of New York State and its communities.

UNIT 1
KEYS TO LEARNING WITH SUCCESS

> Social Studies is exciting and fun because it teaches you about people and how they relate to one another. You also learn about the past and how we came to be the way we are today. In this book, you will learn about New York State and its connections to the United States and the world. There will be many facts and ideas for you to learn and understand. You will need to participate actively by reading, doing activities and studying. This unit focuses on the keys to becoming a successful student.

 ## 1: VISUALIZING IMPORTANT INFORMATION

Social Studies involves knowing about many important terms and ideas. To help you learn and remember them, you will be asked to complete two Vocabulary Cards at the end of each activity in this book.

Vocabulary Cards are index cards with information on them. They will help you remember important terms and ideas. As you go through the activities in this book, you should develop your own set of cards to use for studying. Each Vocabulary Card has two parts:

❖ **Front of the card.** This is for writing about the term or idea.
❖ **Back of the card.** This is used to create a "picture" of the term or idea.

THE FRONT OF THE CARD: WRITTEN INFORMATION

On the front of each card, you will be asked to describe or define a term or idea. Here are two examples:

When you have to learn a specific term, like the Declaration of Independence, you should describe it and explain why it is important. The Vocabulary Cards at the end of each activity will have questions about the term for you to answer.

Example #1

> <u>Declaration of Independence</u>
> <u>What is it?</u> (Description)
> A document written mainly by Thomas Jefferson in 1776. It announced to the world that America wanted to be independent from Great Britain.
> <u>Why Is It Important?</u> (Explanation)
> The document established the basic idea that governments are created to protect people's rights. It serves as a basis for our government.

When you learn about a new idea, like **democracy,** you will usually be asked to define the idea and to give an example of it.

Example #2

> <u>Democracy</u>
> <u>What is it?</u> (Definition)
> Democracy is a form of government in which citizens have a voice in the decisions that are made. This is usually done by citizens voting for people to represent them in their government.
> <u>Give An Example</u> (Example)
> The New York State government, whose members are elected by the voters of the state.

THE BACK OF THE CARD: VISUAL INFORMATION

Pictures are often easier to remember than words. On the back of each card, you will be asked to draw a picture about the information on the front. Making your ideas into pictures will help your understanding and your memory. Let's see what the information on these two Vocabulary Cards might look like when put into picture form.

4 NEW YORK: ITS LAND AND ITS PEOPLE

At the end of each activity in this book, you will find **two** terms or ideas to use for creating your own set of Vocabulary Cards. By the end of the book, you will have a complete set of cards to help you prepare for any test in fourth grade Social Studies.

2: USING MNEMONIC DEVICES

Another way to learn and remember factual information is to use mnemonic (*ne-mon-ik*) devices. **Mnemonic devices** are rhymes and other verbal "tricks" that help you to remember. They are especially useful when you have to learn a list of items—such as planets, continents, cities, rivers or important historical events.

THE PICTURE METHOD

With this method, you think of a picture for each name or word you must learn. For example, three cities in New York State that receive large amounts of snowfall are Buffalo, Rochester and Syracuse.

1. **Think of a word that rhymes with or reminds you of the name of each city:**
   * **Buffalo**–buffalo (both words start with "b")
   * **Rochester**–runs (both words start with "r")
   * **Syracuse**–snow (both words start with "s")

2. **Now visualize these words together as a picture that will help you to remember them. For instance:**

Buffalo → **runs** in the **snow.**

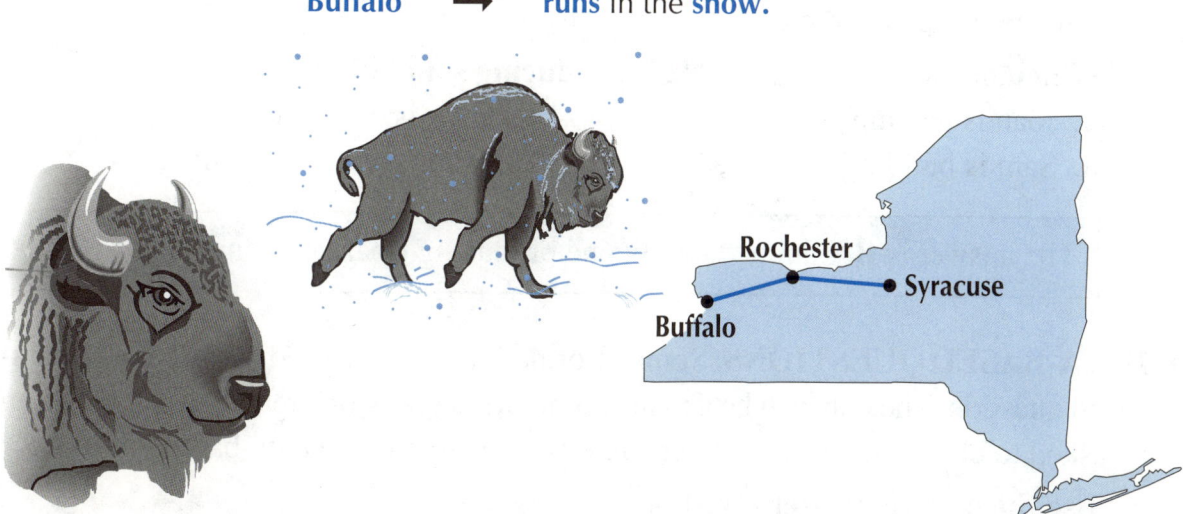

THE KEY SENTENCE METHOD

A third mnemonic technique is to take the first letter of each item you have to learn and to make a sentence or word with all the first letters.

States Bordering New York State
* **V**ermont
* **M**assachusetts
* **C**onnecticut
* **P**ennsylvania
* **N**ew Jersey

Creating a key sentence, such as "**V**ery **n**ice **p**eople **c**limb **m**ountains," helps you remember the five states that border New York.

Another helpful mnemonic is to form a word by using the first letter of each word on a list. For example, the word H-O-M-E-S might help you to remember the names of the five Great Lakes: **H**uron, **O**ntario, **M**ichigan, **E**rie and **S**uperior.

6   NEW YORK: ITS LAND AND ITS PEOPLE

3: ANSWERING MULTIPLE-CHOICE QUESTIONS

Taking tests is something that all students must do. Many tests will have multiple-choice questions. Here are some hints that will help you to answer them.

WHAT THE QUESTION WILL LOOK LIKE

Multiple-choice questions are usually followed by a list of four possible answers. Only one of the answers will be correct. The others are wrong. You must choose the correct answer. There are two kinds of multiple-choice questions: general questions and data-based questions.

❖ **GENERAL QUESTIONS.** These questions test your knowledge of specific information. Here is an example:

1. **Which of the following people is producing something?**
   A. Joan is playing with her cat.
   B. Sam is building a house.
   C. John is eating lunch.
   D. Fran is watching a movie.

> The answer is **B.** Sam is the only one producing (making) something.

❖ **DATA-BASED QUESTIONS.** Some information *(data)* is used to introduce a data-based question. The data can be a map, a timeline, a graph or a reading. You will then be asked to choose the right answer. Here is an example of a data-based question.

2. **Use the map to answer question 2.**
   If you lived in Buffalo, and wanted to visit your aunt in Albany, in which direction would you need to travel?
   A. north
   B. south
   C. east
   D. west

> The answer is **C.** To travel from Buffalo to Albany, you must go east.

MAIN SUBJECTS OF MULTIPLE-CHOICE QUESTIONS
Most multiple-choice questions will be about the following:

❖ **RECOGNIZING TERMS, IDEAS AND PEOPLE.** This type of question tests your knowledge of a term, idea or person. The following is an example:

3. One of the main powers of the Governor of New York State is to
   A. make national laws
   B. enforce state laws
   C. interpret city laws
   D. make state laws

> The answer is **B.** The main power of the Governor of New York State is to enforce the laws of the state.

To help you recognize main terms, ideas and people, these are presented in **bold print** throughout the book. Key words in each activity appear in a blue box.

❖ **RECOGNIZING CAUSES AND EFFECTS.** Cause-and-effect questions test your understanding of how two or more events are related. The *cause* is the event that happened first. The *effect* is what happened as a result of the first event. In other words, the cause is the reason for the *effect.* Here is an example of this type of question:

4. Buffalo is one of the most important economic centers in New York. A major reason why Buffalo has become an economic center is that it
   A. is located near Lake Erie
   B. is the capital of New York
   C. has tall buildings
   D. is the oldest city in New York

> The answer is **A.** Buffalo is located near Lake Erie. Being close to a large body of water and at the end of the Erie Canal brought trade and business to Buffalo. This helped make Buffalo an important economic center.

To help you answer cause-and-effect questions, important causes and effects are identified in each unit of the book. **Activity 3F** also examines cause-and-effect relationships in greater detail. Here are some key words or phrases to look for when answering cause-and-effect questions:

Causes	Effects
❖ Because of	❖ This a resulted in ....
❖ A main reason for	❖ This led to ....
❖ On account of	❖ This affected ....

4: THE WRITING PROCESS

Often you know the right information to complete an assignment. To do well you also need to know how to organize your thoughts and write them down.

STEPS IN THE WRITING PROCESS

The writing process is not one step, but several. It takes practice and skill to be a good writer. Let's take a look at each of the steps in the writing process:

- **Step 1: Prewriting.** In this first step, ask yourself, "Why am I writing this?" Your answer will determine *what* and *how* you write. Decide whether the purpose of the writing is to *inform, persuade, describe* or to *tell about* an event.

- **Step 2: Drafting.** Putting ideas on paper is similar to an architect following a blueprint when building a house. Your "blueprint" is your first draft or preliminary writing. Imagine your first draft resembles a "cheeseburger," with a top bun, a slice of cheese, patties of meat and a bottom bun. The top bun is your beginning, the cheese is your lead-in, the meat is the middle and the bottom bun is the end of your essay.

- **Step 3: Revising and Proofreading.** This is the most important part of the writing process. You need to read over your work to see if you have included all your main ideas. Some writers like to read their work aloud to see how it "sounds." Re-reading also allows you to edit your essay for grammar, punctuation and spelling.

APPLYING THE STEPS IN THE WRITING PROCESS

Let's use what you have just learned for the following writing assignment.

> Write a short essay explaining the importance of getting a good education.

STEP 1: PREWRITING

> **Your Purpose:** To explain why it is important to get a good education.
> **Outline:** List your main ideas.
>   I. A good education makes us more aware of ourselves and the world.
>   II. A good education will help us to get a job when we get older.
>   III. A good education helps us to become good citizens.
> **Conclusion:** Society's future depends on the education of its young people.

STEP 2: DRAFTING

Let's use the information from your outline to create a first draft, using the "cheeseburger" method.

> In society today it is very important to have a good education.
>
> There are several reasons why this is so.
>
> One of the most important reasons for a good education is that it makes us more aware of ourselves and the world around us. In Social Studies we learn how people lived in the past. In science, we learn how nature and our bodies work.
>
> A good education prepares us for getting a job. We improve our reading skills for future work. Another reason for a good education is to become a good citizen. This prepares us to face the important responsibilities of voting, holding office and sitting on a jury.
>
> Therefore, we can see that it is important to have a good education. The future of our society depends on the quality of the education it provides.

Top Bun (*Topic Sentence*). In the first sentence of your essay, you write the main idea. It should state the assignment's topic. Notice how this topic sentence lets your reader know precisely what you are going to write about.

Cheese Slice (*Connecting Sentence*). The "cheese" sentence connects the main idea to the specific information in your essay. This sentence helps the reader to follow your thoughts by connecting your introduction with the main body of the writing. For example, you might write: *"The following information will explain my opening statement"* or *"There are several reasons why this is so."* Notice how this connecting sentence introduces the next section you are going to write.

Patties of Meat (*Main Sentences*). In the "patties of meat" section, you give specific examples and facts that support your opening statement. It is the main part of your essay. Notice how these sentences give facts that support the main idea or topic sentence.

Ending Sentence (*Bottom Bun*). Your last sentence should be similar to your opening topic sentence, except that it is now expressed as a conclusion. The conclusion is used to remind the reader of what you have just explained in your essay. There are several concluding sentences that you can choose from: *"Therefore, we can see that ......"* or *"Thus, we can see that ......"* Again, notice how this sentence ends the essay by reminding the reader of the purpose of the essay.

STEP 3: REVISING AND PROOFREADING

After you have finished your draft, you should re-read it. You may want to share your essay with other members of your class. Sharing your written work with your classmates allows you to get suggestions about what and how you wrote. Peer editing *(editing by other students)* provides important feedback in helping you improve your essay. Then correct it for errors in grammar, punctuation and spelling. You are now ready for the last reading. Be sure to re-read your essay one last time before you hand it in.

 ## PRE-READING HINTS

You have now learned some practical ways of remembering information, answering test questions and writing down your ideas. In the following units, you will learn a great deal about New York and the United States. To help you through these units, each section will be introduced by an icon. An **icon** is a symbol—something that stands for something else. Think of each icon as your personal guide, telling you what to expect in each section of the activity. The following list identifies each icon used in the book.

 Each activity usually begins with an introduction. Here you will learn what is required of you in order to carry out the activity.

 These sections provide information for doing the activity. For example, you will be given information about New York's geography to create a map of what New York State "looks" like.

 These sections will introduce you to a new word or idea. For example, you will learn the definitions of the words "concept" and "generalization."

 In these sections you will be asked to complete a task. For example, you might be asked to fill in a chart, write a paragraph or locate places on a map of New York State.

 These sections will teach you a new skill. For example, you might learn how to read a map, interpret a line or bar graph, write a business letter or create an outline of a reading selection.

 In these sections you will be asked to carry out research outside of the classroom. For example, you might be asked to read a book from the library, interview an adult or conduct a survey.

 In these sections the activity comes to a close. When this occurs, you will often be asked to think about what you have done and to re-examine the focus question that began the activity.

YOUR SCHOOL YEAR PROJECT

Have you ever looked at a building, a bridge or a video game and thought about all the work that went into making it? Such projects often take many years to complete. Hundreds or even thousands of people have may been involved. In our modern world today, teams of people must often work together for a long time to finish a job. A class project allows you to do the same thing in school.

This school year you will be asked to participate in a major class project. This project is different from a regular homework assignment or a report. Homework is often done in a day or two, while a report can take several weeks. However, this project will be worked on throughout the whole school year. You will be asked to work with a group of your classmates.

THE BENEFITS OF DOING A PROJECT

Working on a year-long project has many benefits.

❖ You will have an opportunity to study in greater detail topics that interest you.

❖ You will learn how to gather and organize information from different sources.

❖ You will learn how to cooperate and work with others as you exchange ideas.

The following description gives only a few examples of what your class may do for its major project. There are many other projects your class may choose to create. If your class should decide to choose another project, try to use some of the suggestions from the project recommended here.

YOUR ASSIGNMENT

Just as the United States is divided into 50 states, each state is divided into separate counties. Each of these counties is further divided into towns and cities. In the project recommended in this book, you and your classmates will have an opportunity to create a project about the **village, town** or **city** where you live. If you live in New York City, you might focus part of your project on your neighborhood or borough, with other parts of the project concerning the whole city.

Your project will have three steps: an investigative step, a planning step and a presentation step. Here is what each step will require:

❖ **Investigative Step.** In this first step, your group will research and gather information necessary to complete the project. To guide you in your research,

❖ CONTINUED

an **Information Sheet** is provided at the end of each unit. This sheet will assign a number of tasks for you to complete.

Your group can use different sources to find information—including encyclopedias, atlases, almanacs, travel guides and other books. A computer source that you may wish to explore is the Internet. The **Internet** is called the "information highway" because it is like a highway in many ways. Highways connect one city to another. The Internet connects distant computers to one another.

❖ **Planning Step.** In this second step, your group will organize its findings and figure out a method for presenting them. The group should use the information it has found to create an exhibit about your town, city or neighborhood. The exhibit can have several parts, each of which may take different forms.

❖ **Presentation Step.** In this last step, your group will present its findings. There are many different ways to do this. The following are a short list of examples your group may decide to use:
- create a **bulletin board** about the geography, history, people and economy of the town or city where you live.
- build a **diorama**—a small three-dimensional model using objects and figures in front of a painted background.
- make a **video** presentation about your town or city showing visitors what is unique and interesting about it.
- write a **song** describing some of the many features about where you live.
- stage a **play** about your town or city. For example, the play might focus on an event from the past or on a famous person who once lived there.

It is still too soon for your group to make a decision about its project and how to present it. As you move through each unit of this book, you will find various suggestions for the project. These suggestions will help you to complete different parts of the project. Each of these suggestions will be like one piece in a big jigsaw puzzle. At the end of the school year, you will then bring all of the pieces of the puzzle together to show off your community as a whole.

Participating with a group of your friends in this year-long project should be fun and interesting. Working on the project will allow you to practice such important skills as conducting research, working with others, drawing conclusions and presenting your ideas to others. Having most of the school year to put the project together will give you an opportunity to produce a polished piece of work that you can take pride in.

UNIT 2
GEOGRAPHY

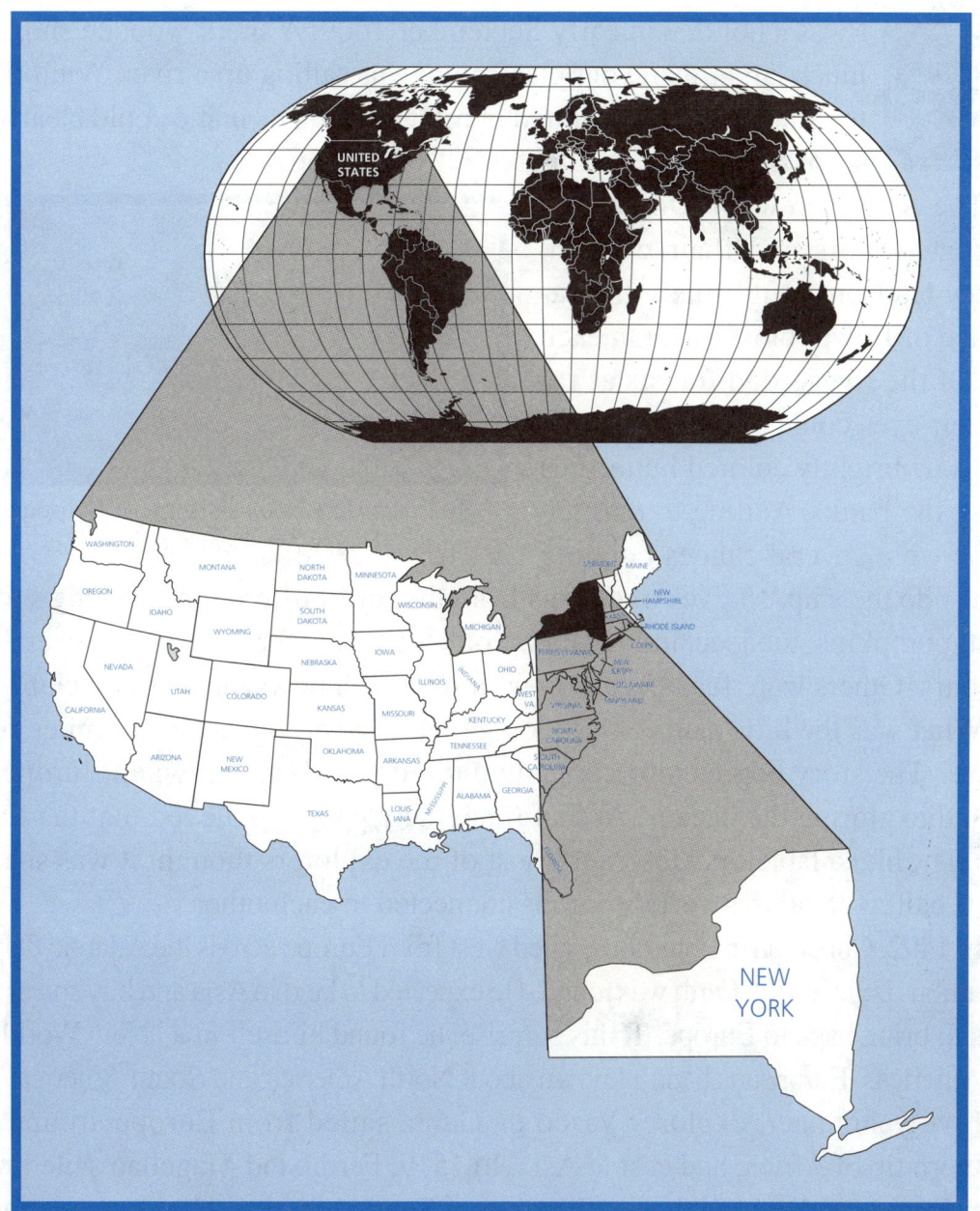

Where we live often determines *how* we live. The study of geography developed from the need to know "where." It tells us where different places are and what they are like. This information is important because we come into contact with people and products from many places.

HENRY HUDSON SEARCHES FOR THE NORTHWEST PASSAGE

It was a hot day in early September 1609. A small wooden ship, not much larger than your classroom, was sailing up a river. Wind filled the ship's six sails. Painted in bright colors, its name could clearly be seen: *Halve Maen*—Dutch for "Half Moon."

The small crew of Dutch and English sailors and their captain, Henry Hudson, could smell the fragrance of flower blossoms. On each side of the river stood forests as far as their eyes could see. Some of the men saw brightly colored butterflies along the banks. Adding to the rich scene were several canoes bobbing

Hudson's *Half Moon* sails up the Hudson as Native Americans look on.

alongside the ship. Native Americans from the forest offered the visiting sailors corn, pumpkins, tobacco and oysters. Some of them were dressed in deerskins and furs. Others wore feathers and were armed with bows, arrows and clubs.

What was the little sailing ship doing on this river, thousands of miles from home? The story begins more than a hundred years earlier, when Europeans started exploring the oceans. At that time many people believed that the Earth was flat, like a tabletop. However, most of the explorers thought it was shaped like a ball, with all the world's oceans connected to each other.

In 1492, Christopher Columbus sailed west from Europe across the Atlantic Ocean. Columbus believed the Earth was round. He expected to land in Asia and buy spices and silks to bring back to Europe. To his surprise, he found himself in a "New World"— the Americas. Europeans hadn't known about North America and South America.

Five years later, explorer Vasco da Gama sailed from Europe around the southern tip of Africa, and east to Asia. In 1519, Ferdinand Magellan sailed west from Europe and around the southern tip of South America. His crew continued across the Pacific Ocean and back to Europe, proving the world was round. At that point, the race was on to discover the best route from Europe to the riches of the "Indies"—as India and East Asia were called at the time.

After studying maps and talking to the wisest geographers of his day, Henry Hudson became convinced that the shortest route to India and East Asia was over the North Pole. Other explorers feared sailing northward through ice and snow, but not Henry Hudson. He had twice tried to sail north of Norway. The wealthy merchants of the Dutch East India Company soon heard of this brave Englishman. In 1609, they invited him to Holland. Soon after, they hired him and supplied him with a ship and small crew. In late March, Hudson and his crew left the Dutch capital of Amsterdam in search of a route northwards.

First, Hudson tried again to sail north of Norway, but was stopped by snow and ice. Then he turned westward, hoping for a passage through the icy waters to the Indies. After crossing the Atlantic to Canada, Hudson turned south, staying near the coast in search of a passage. After sailing past the settlement of Jamestown, Virginia, Hudson turned his ship north again.

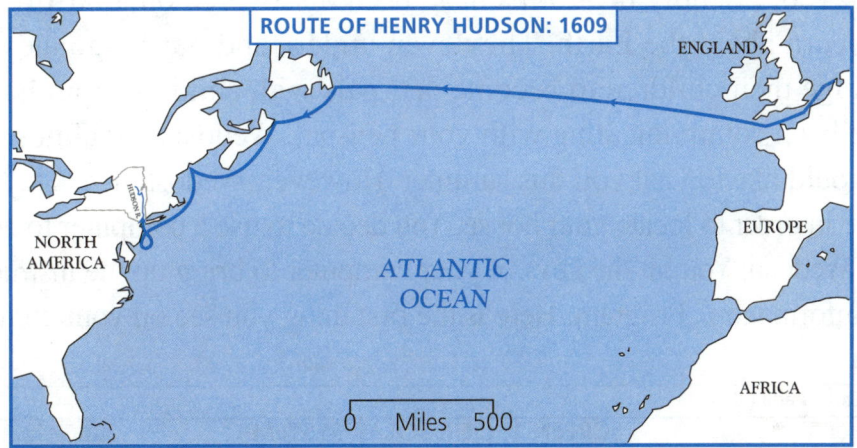

On September 3, Hudson and his men rounded the southern tip of Brooklyn. Many Native Americans came to stare at these unusual men and their ship. Some boarded the *Half Moon* to trade corn and tobacco for beads and knives.

Hudson admired the beauty of the land around him. Its forests could provide plenty of lumber to make ships and houses. The Native Americans had copper pipes for their tobacco. Hudson thought these copper pipes might mean there were copper mines in the area. After going ashore briefly, Hudson returned to the ship. He wrote in his log, "The land is the finest for planting that I have ever in my life set foot upon, and it is rich in trees of every description."

From Staten Island, the ship entered New York Harbor. Hudson began the journey up the river that would later be named after him—the Hudson River. Would this river lead north to the Indies? Would he discover new lands and fame as Columbus had done? What else would he find on his journey?

In this unit you will learn the answers to some of the questions that Hudson and his crew asked themselves as they sailed up the river on that sunny day.

16   NEW YORK: ITS LAND AND ITS PEOPLE

CAN YOU PLEASE GIVE ME SOME DIRECTIONS?

2A

In this activity, you will learn some of the ways that geographers locate places on the Earth. Look for the following important words:

▶ North and South Poles   ▶ Equator   ▶ Region
▶ Continent   ▶ Prime Meridian   ▶ Country

To help you, the ▶ symbol appears in the margin where the **term** is first explained.

It is the year 2100. Friendly life-forms have been discovered on a far-off planet. They are eager to learn about the Earth. They even understand our languages. These life-forms encourage their children to become pen-pals with children from Earth. Imagine that you have been communicating with your pen-pal, Wedosh, for almost a year.

Wedosh would like to visit you this summer. However, Wedosh needs to know exactly where you live in order to locate your house. You decide to use a computer to help you write directions for Wedosh. You hit the keys of your computer to bring up the instructions for the "Geography-Information" Program. Here is the first thing you see on your computer screen:

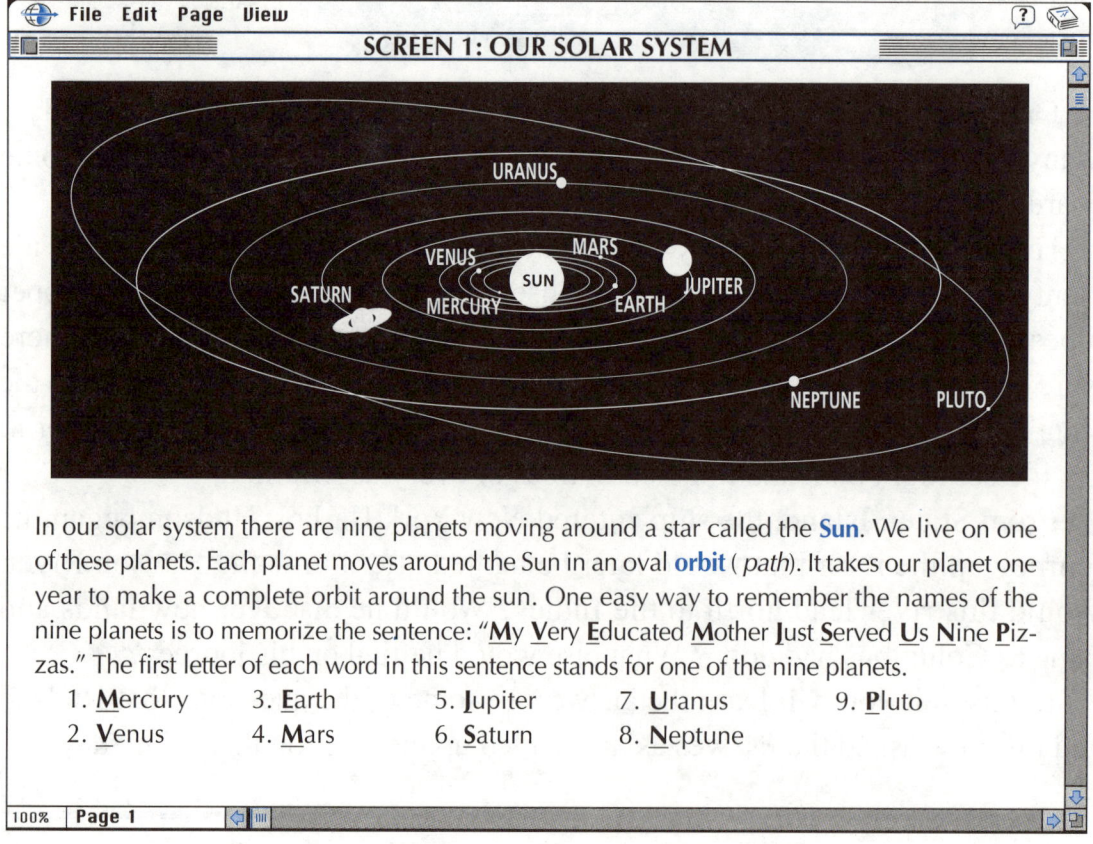

GEOGRAPHY 17

Why don't you take notes after viewing each screen? You can use these notes to help you in writing directions to your pen-pal, Wedosh.

NOTES FOR MY LETTER:
The name of the planet that I live on is called ___?___.

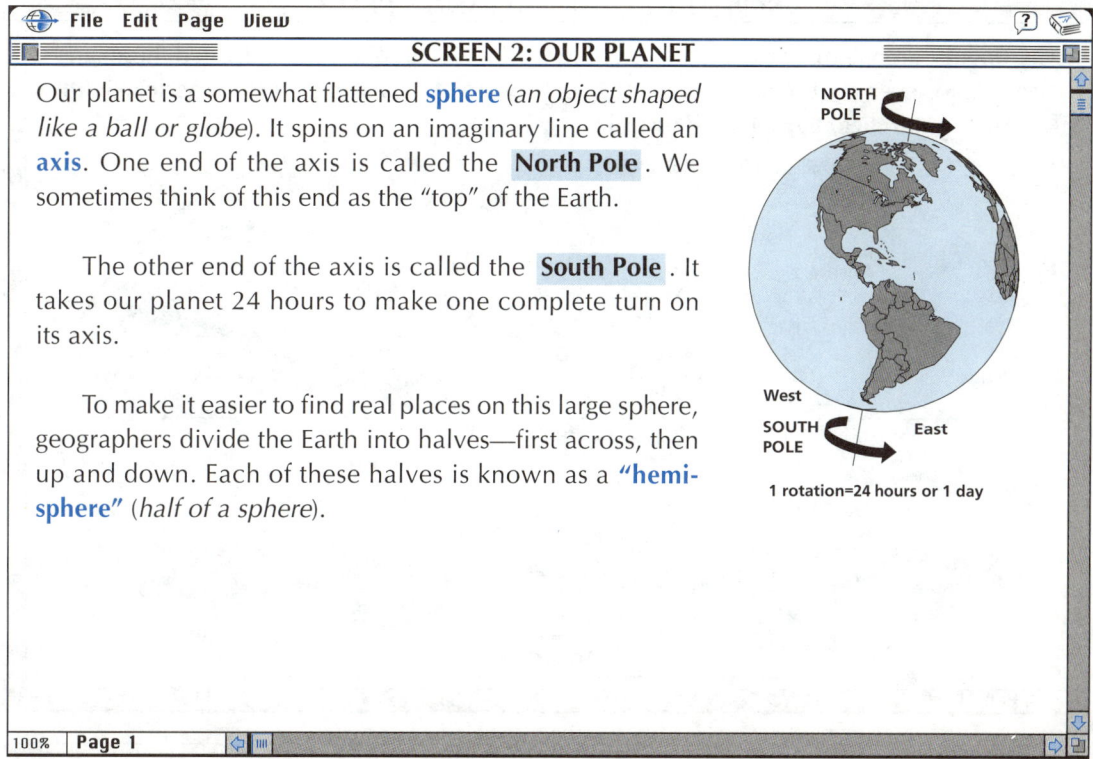

SCREEN 2: OUR PLANET

Our planet is a somewhat flattened **sphere** (*an object shaped like a ball or globe*). It spins on an imaginary line called an **axis**. One end of the axis is called the **North Pole**. We sometimes think of this end as the "top" of the Earth.

The other end of the axis is called the **South Pole**. It takes our planet 24 hours to make one complete turn on its axis.

To make it easier to find real places on this large sphere, geographers divide the Earth into halves—first across, then up and down. Each of these halves is known as a **"hemisphere"** (*half of a sphere*).

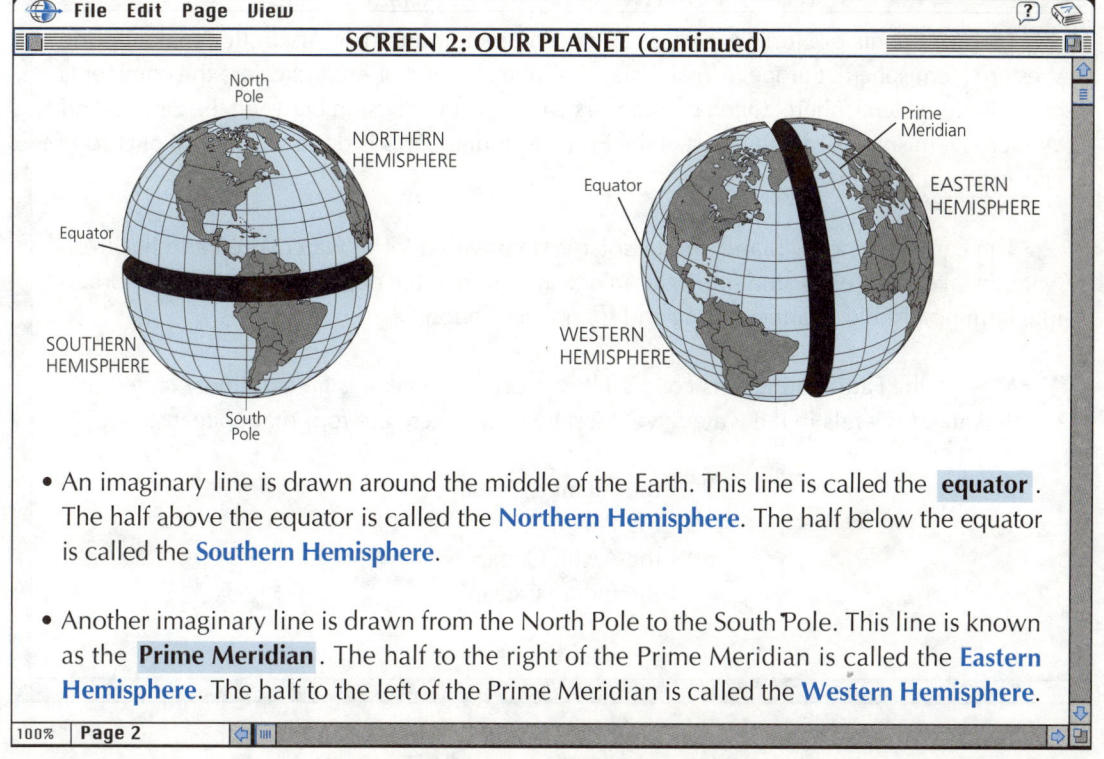

SCREEN 2: OUR PLANET (continued)

- An imaginary line is drawn around the middle of the Earth. This line is called the **equator**. The half above the equator is called the **Northern Hemisphere**. The half below the equator is called the **Southern Hemisphere**.

- Another imaginary line is drawn from the North Pole to the South Pole. This line is known as the **Prime Meridian**. The half to the right of the Prime Meridian is called the **Eastern Hemisphere**. The half to the left of the Prime Meridian is called the **Western Hemisphere**.

18   NEW YORK: ITS LAND AND ITS PEOPLE

> **NOTES FOR MY LETTER:**
> I live in both the ___?___ Hemisphere and the ___?___ Hemisphere.

▶

SCREEN 3: CONTINENTS AND OCEANS

Continents are the major land masses of the world. Geographers have divided these land masses into seven continents. In order of size, they are: **Asia, Africa, North America, South America, Antarctica, Europe** and **Australia.**

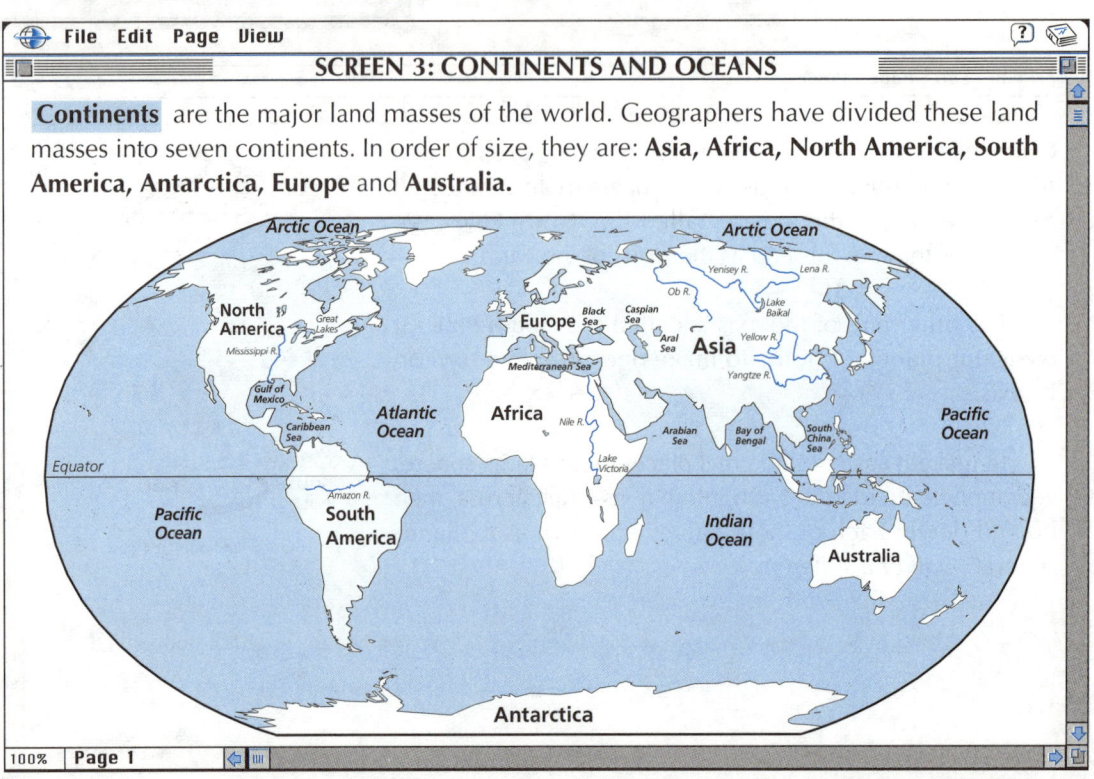

Page 1

SCREEN 3: CONTINENTS AND OCEANS (continued)

The continents of North America, South America and part of Antarctica make up the Western Hemisphere. Europe, Africa, Asia, Australia and part of Antarctica are the continents of the Eastern Hemisphere. Often mapmakers will draw the division between the Eastern and Western Hemispheres slightly west of the Prime Meridian. This is done to show all of Europe and Africa in the same hemisphere.

The Earth is the only planet in our solar system with a lot of water. The Earth has fresh water in lakes and rivers, and salt water in oceans. Human life depends on water—for drinking, farming, fishing, manufacturing and for transportation.

Most of the Earth's surface is covered by oceans. An **ocean** is an extremely large body of salt water. Minerals in the water give it a salty taste. There are four main oceans:

- the Atlantic Ocean
- the Pacific Ocean
- the Arctic Ocean
- the Indian Ocean

Page 2

GEOGRAPHY   19

NOTES FOR MY LETTER:
I live on the continent of ___?___, located between the ___?___ Ocean and the ___?___ Ocean.

✔ CHECKING YOUR UNDERSTANDING ✔

Use the map in screen 3 to answer the following questions:

1. Which continents are located completely in the Southern Hemisphere?
2. Which continents are located completely in the Western Hemisphere?

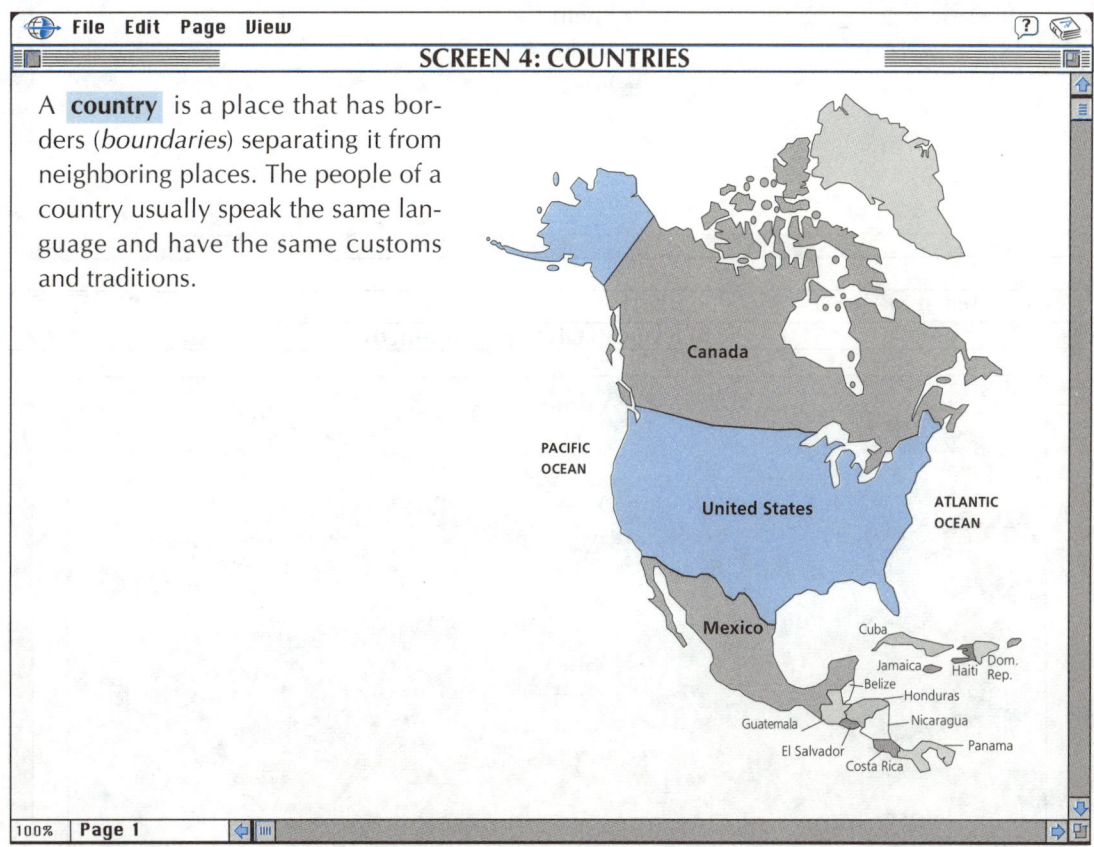

NOTES FOR MY LETTER:
The country in which I live is called ___?___. It is located directly north of a country called ___?___. It is located south of a country called ___?___.

20   NEW YORK: ITS LAND AND ITS PEOPLE

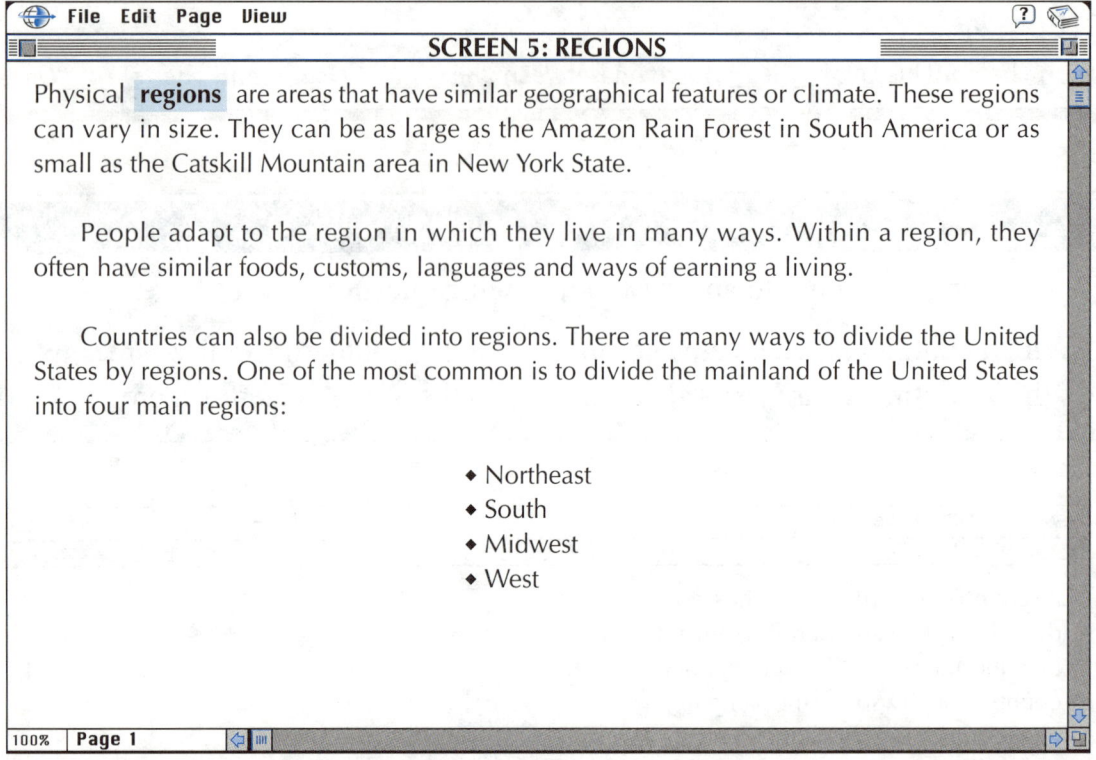

SCREEN 5: REGIONS

Physical **regions** are areas that have similar geographical features or climate. These regions can vary in size. They can be as large as the Amazon Rain Forest in South America or as small as the Catskill Mountain area in New York State.

People adapt to the region in which they live in many ways. Within a region, they often have similar foods, customs, languages and ways of earning a living.

Countries can also be divided into regions. There are many ways to divide the United States by regions. One of the most common is to divide the mainland of the United States into four main regions:

- Northeast
- South
- Midwest
- West

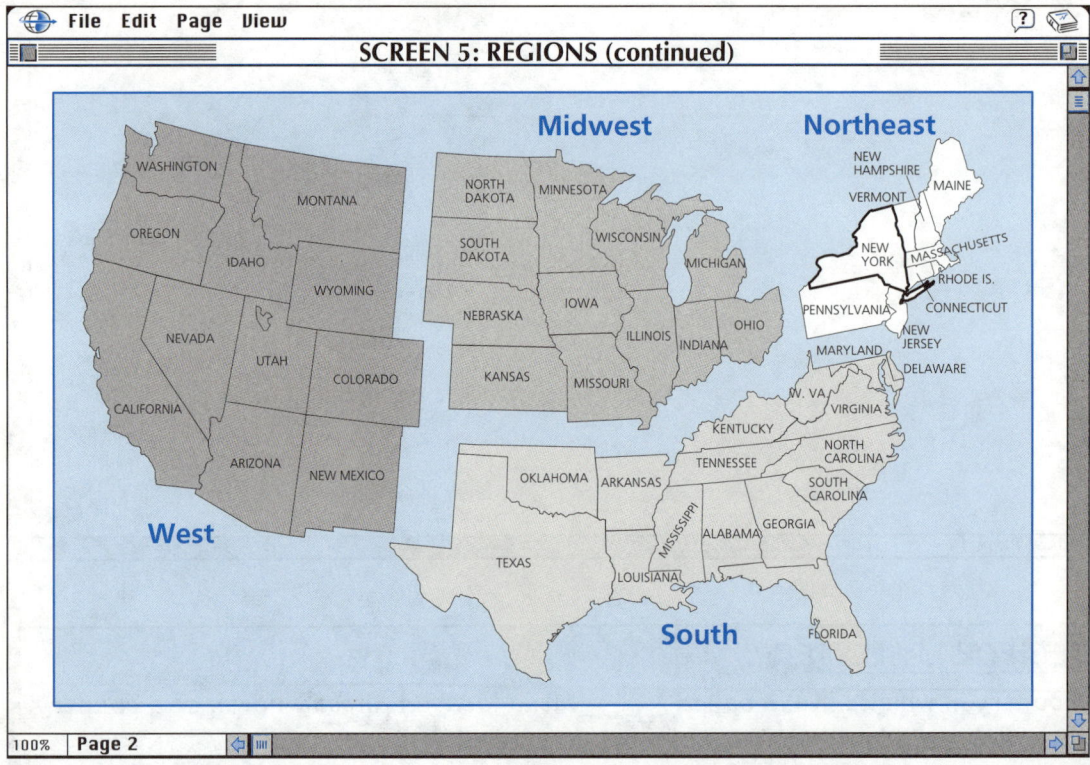

SCREEN 5: REGIONS (continued)

NOTES FOR MY LETTER:
The region I live in is known as the ___?___. The number of states in the region in which I live is ___?___. The names of these states are ___?___.

GEOGRAPHY 21

SCREEN 6: STATES AND COUNTIES

Most countries are divided into smaller political units known as states or provinces. The United States is divided into 50 **states**. Can you locate the state in which you live?

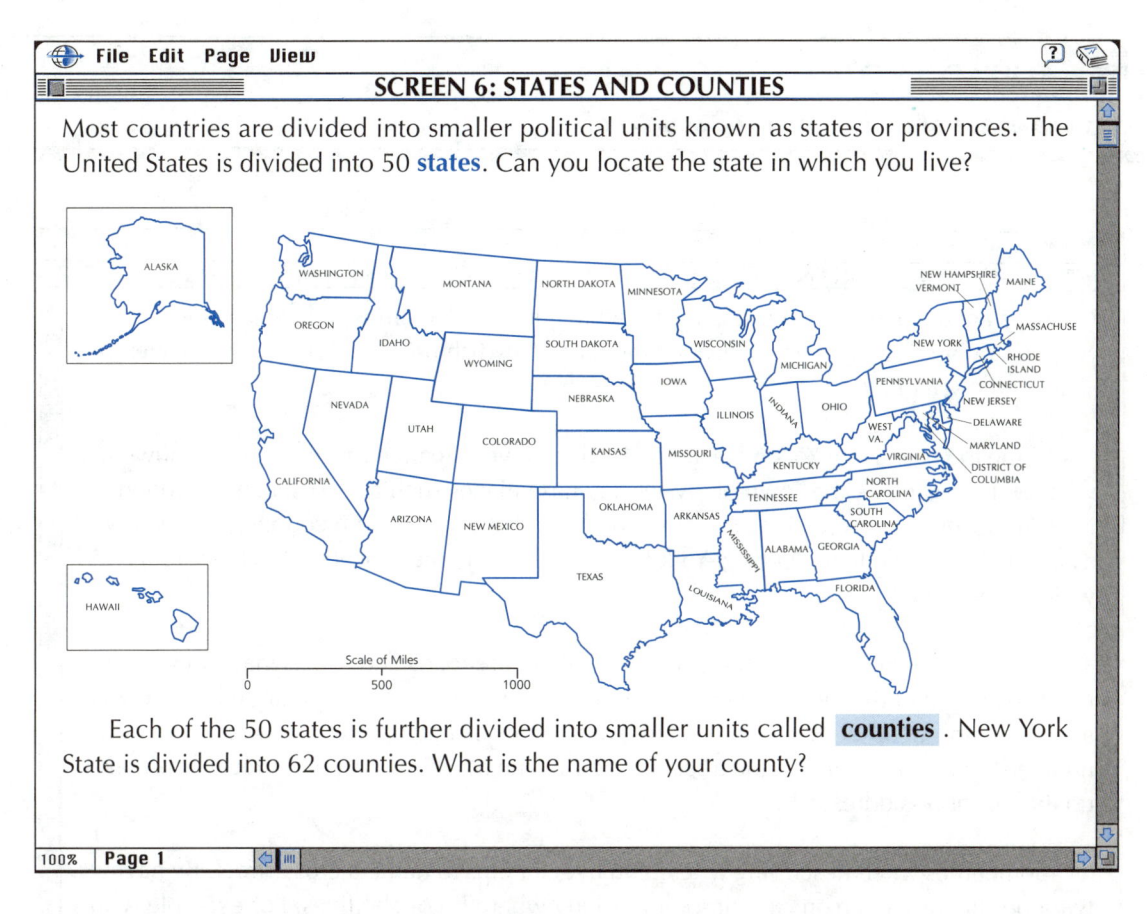

Each of the 50 states is further divided into smaller units called **counties**. New York State is divided into 62 counties. What is the name of your county?

SCREEN 6: STATES AND COUNTIES (continued)

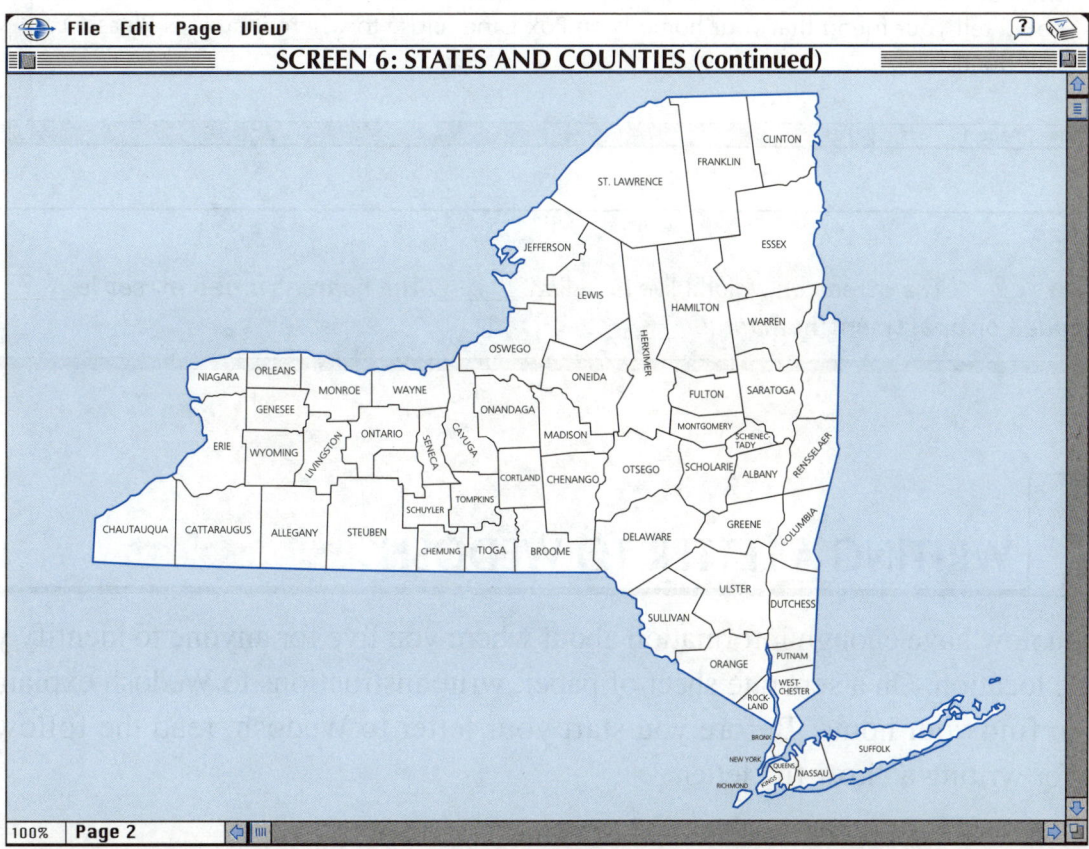

NOTES FOR MY LETTER:
I live in the state of ___?___ and the county of ___?___.

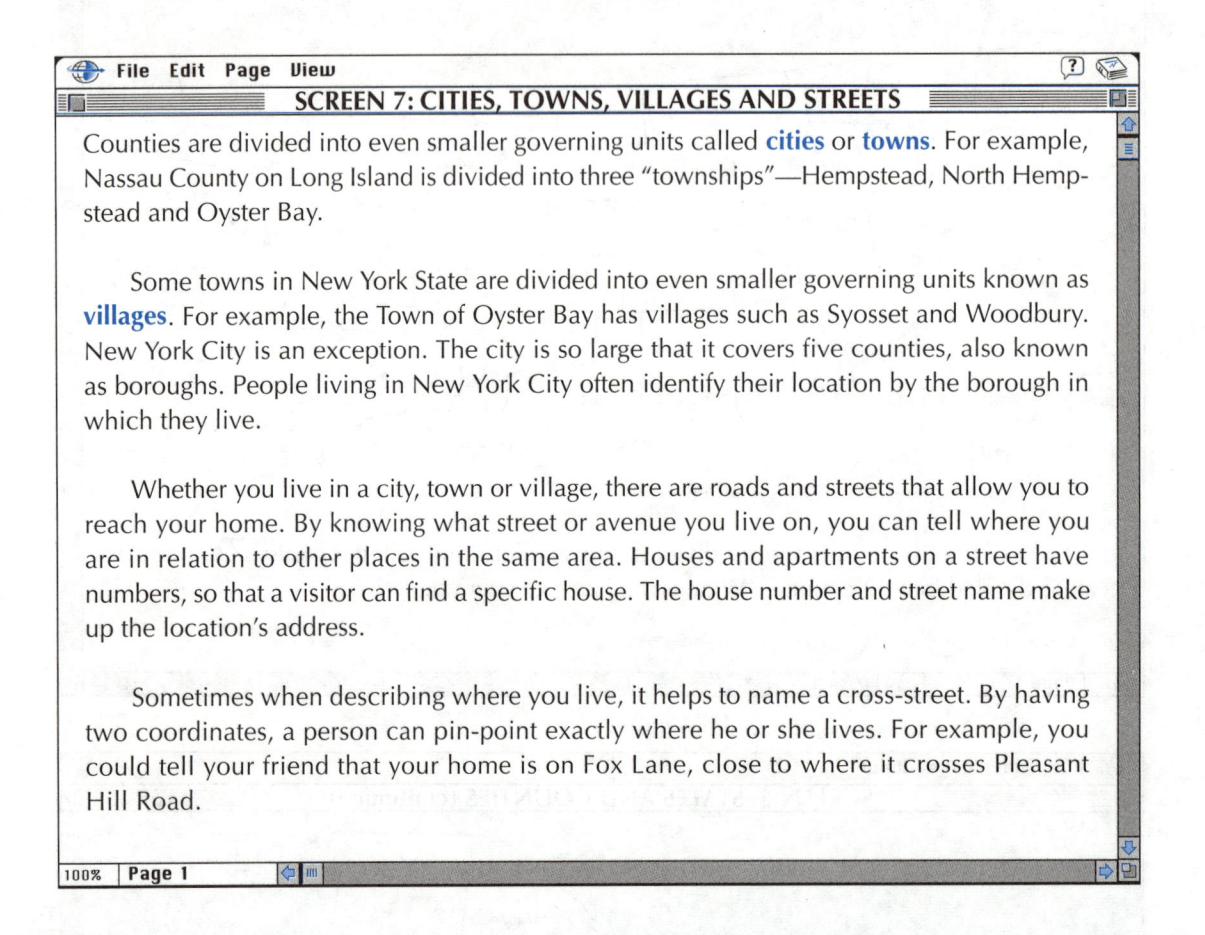

SCREEN 7: CITIES, TOWNS, VILLAGES AND STREETS

Counties are divided into even smaller governing units called **cities** or **towns**. For example, Nassau County on Long Island is divided into three "townships"—Hempstead, North Hempstead and Oyster Bay.

Some towns in New York State are divided into even smaller governing units known as **villages**. For example, the Town of Oyster Bay has villages such as Syosset and Woodbury. New York City is an exception. The city is so large that it covers five counties, also known as boroughs. People living in New York City often identify their location by the borough in which they live.

Whether you live in a city, town or village, there are roads and streets that allow you to reach your home. By knowing what street or avenue you live on, you can tell where you are in relation to other places in the same area. Houses and apartments on a street have numbers, so that a visitor can find a specific house. The house number and street name make up the location's address.

Sometimes when describing where you live, it helps to name a cross-street. By having two coordinates, a person can pin-point exactly where he or she lives. For example, you could tell your friend that your home is on Fox Lane, close to where it crosses Pleasant Hill Road.

NOTES
I live in ___?___. The street on which I live is called ___?___. The nearest cross street is ___?___. My house or apartment number is ___?___.

WRITING A LETTER TO WEDOSH

You now have enough information about where you live for anyone to identify your unique location. On a separate sheet of paper, write instructions to Wedosh explaining how to find your home. Before you start your letter to Wedosh, read the following hints for writing a **"how to"** letter.

THE "HOW TO" FORM OF WRITING

A "how to" writing gives step-by-step directions to the reader about how to do something. "How to" writings can be about almost anything. For example, they can explain how to make a cake, assemble a toy or ride a bicycle. Here are some helpful hints on creating a "how to" writing.

HELPFUL HINTS

1. **Start with a theme statement.** This statement should explain what the reader will be doing. For example:

   Here are the directions for finding my house at 75 Fox Lane.

2. **Use a "bridge" sentence.** Sometimes you will need a connecting sentence to introduce the reader to the details of what you are writing about. For example:

   If you follow my directions carefully, it should take you about an hour to reach my house.

3. **Write a step-by-step list of what to do.** Starting with the first step, explain to the reader how each step should follow another until the task is completed. Some useful words that show the reader you are moving from one step to another are: "first," "next," "then," "later," "afterwards" and "finally." For example:

   First, take Route 680 going east. Then, get off Route 680 at the exit sign reading: Pleasant Hill Road. Next, drive up the hill past two traffic lights. Finally, make a right turn at Fox Lane. Ours is the second house on the right.

4. **Point out what may go wrong.** Tell the reader about any problems that might occur and how to avoid them. For example:

   Sometimes people have trouble seeing the street sign for Fox Lane, since it is partly hidden by a large tree. You can easily recognize Fox Lane by the gas station on the corner.

5. **Write a Conclusion.** Provide a closing sentence. For example:

   If you follow these directions carefully, I'm sure you will have no trouble finding my house. I look forward to seeing you soon.

Now that you better understand the "how to" form of writing, let us put your new skill to use. Review the notes that you made at the end of each computer screen. Use the information in your notes to write a letter to Wedosh, your pen-pal from outer-space.

INTER-GALACTIC COMMUNICATION

Dear Wedosh: [Greeting]

[Theme Statement]: _____

_____

[Bridge Sentence]: _____

_____

_____

B
O
D
Y

[Step-By-Step]: _____

_____

_____

_____

_____

_____

[Conclusion]: _____

_____

Your Pen-Pal, [Closing]

(sign your name)
_____
[Signature]

GEOGRAPHY 25

REVIEWING YOUR UNDERSTANDING

Creating Vocabulary Cards

Equator

What is the equator?

What two hemispheres does it separate?

Prime Meridian

What is the Prime Meridian?

What two hemispheres does it separate?

You will find brief exercises following the Vocabulary Cards in each activity in this book. Completing these exercises will help you sharpen your Social Studies skills.

Locating Places on Maps

Make a copy of the map below. Then label each of the following areas on the map of the world: (1) Northern Hemisphere; (2) Southern Hemisphere; (3) Eastern Hemisphere; (4) Western Hemisphere; (5) North Pole; (6) South Pole; (7) equator; and (8) Prime Meridian.

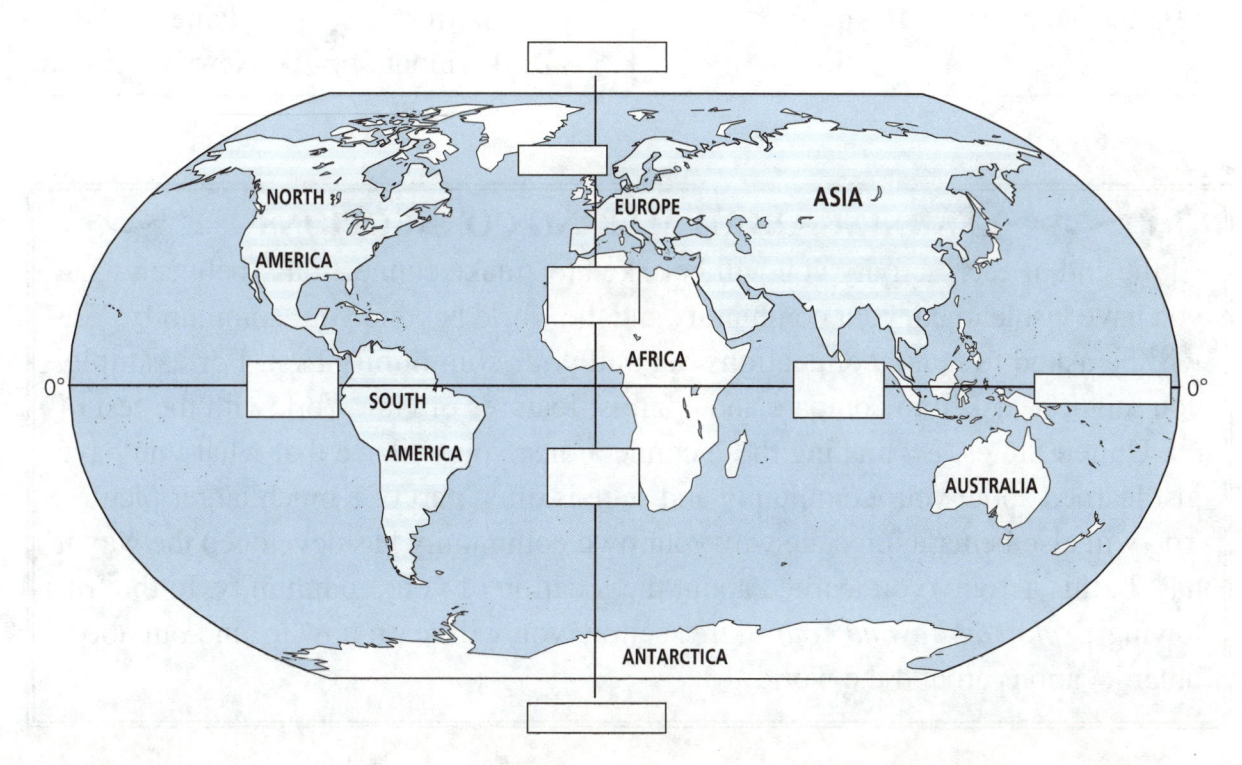

Interpreting a Map of the United States

Use the following map to answer questions 1 and 2:

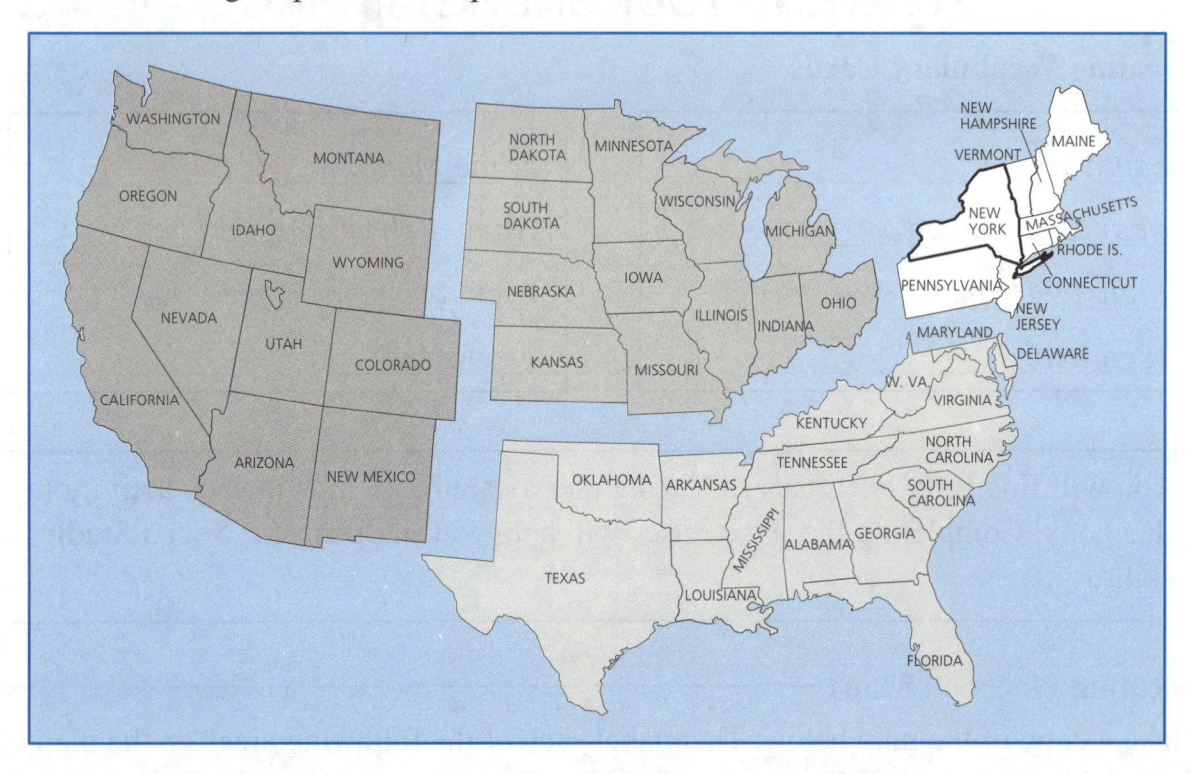

1. **New York is part of which region?**
   A. the Northeast C. the South
   B. the Midwest   D. the West

2. **Which state does NOT border New York**
   A. California   C. Maine
   B. Vermont   D. New Hampshire

LEARNING ABOUT MAKING CONNECTIONS

At the end of each activity you will be asked to "make connections" between what you have just learned, your community and the world beyond your community. You will be asked to make connections beyond your community first. For example, you might be asked to compare and contrast features of New York with the rest of the United States. By making these connections, you will see that what you have just learned about your community and state is often part of a much larger picture. You will also better appreciate why your own community has developed the way it has. In this activity you learned about the location of your community. In the following *Exploring Beyond Your State* section, you will learn how to find out about other locations around the world.

GEOGRAPHY 27

MAKING CONNECTIONS

EXPLORING BEYOND YOUR STATE
LEARNING TO USE AN ATLAS

Where are some of the places mentioned in this activity? This question would be difficult to answer without looking at a map. When people want to find a map or other information about the geography of a place, they often use a special reference book called an atlas.

WHAT IS AN ATLAS?

Skill Builder

An **atlas** is a book that contains many different kinds of maps. A world atlas will probably have maps showing every nation in the world. If the atlas is about the United States, it will have maps of the 50 states. The maps will also show where counties and important cities in each state are located. In addition, an atlas may contain the following types of maps:

❖ **Physical Maps** show land features such as mountains, and may even include the depths of oceans and other bodies of water. The following is a physical map of the United States:

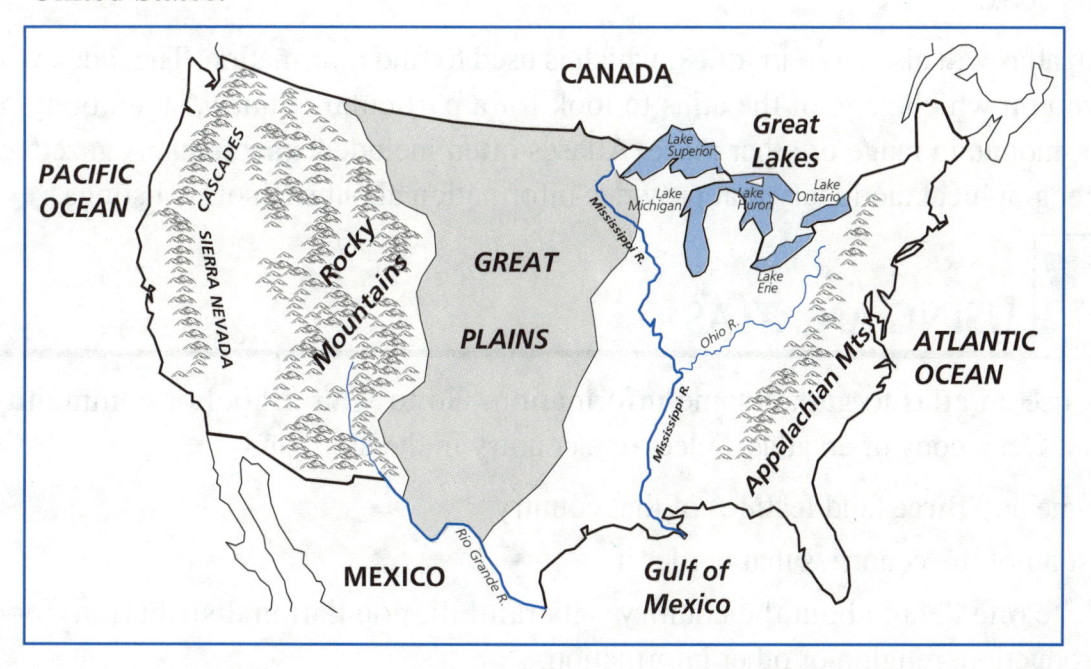

CONTINUED

28   NEW YORK: ITS LAND AND ITS PEOPLE

❖ **Political Maps** show the boundaries of countries or states—where one country or state ends and another begins. The following is a political map:

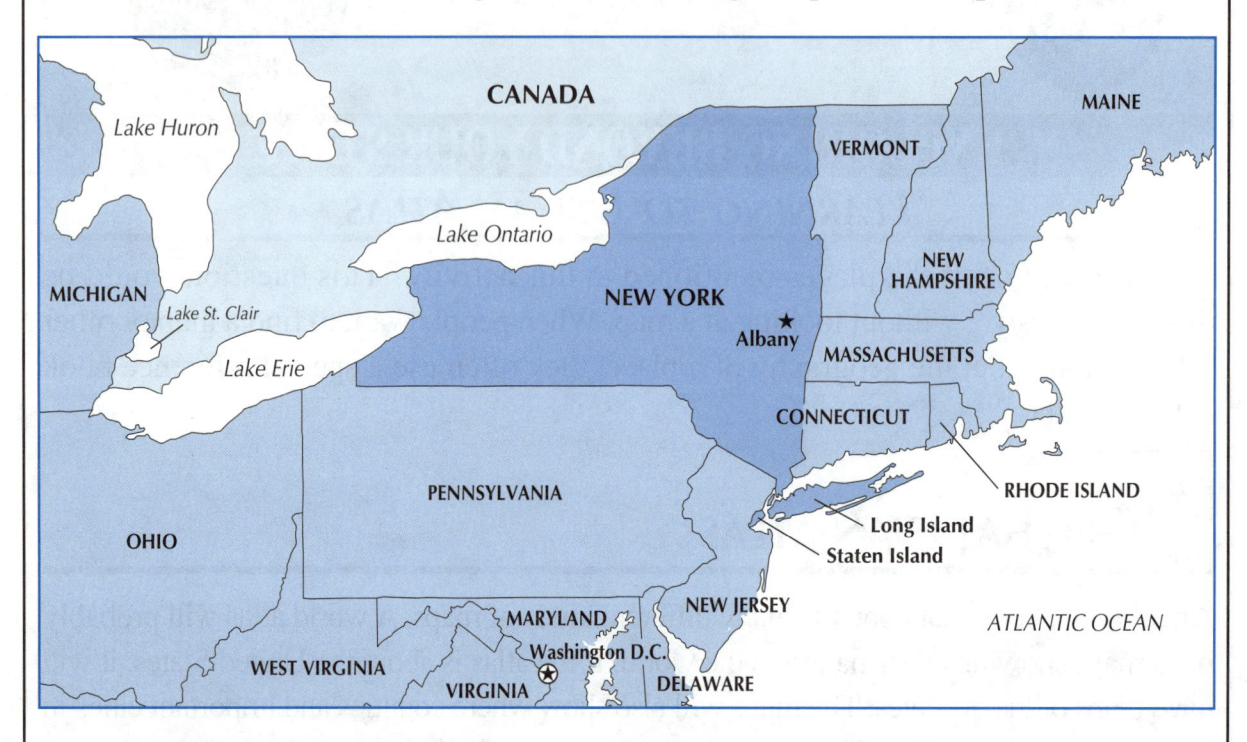

❖ **Theme Maps** usually deal with a single item or topic. They are used to show rainfall, population distribution, food production, highways, natural resources, land use or other special information. You will learn more about theme maps later in this book.

An atlas will also have an *index*, which is used to find information. The index will tell you on which page of the atlas to look for a particular country, state, body of water, mountain range or other place. Atlases often include a *gazetteer*. A gazetteer is a geographical dictionary that provides information about each of its listings.

USING AN ATLAS

Let's use an atlas to gather some information. Go to your school or community library. Get a copy of an atlas. Select **one** country in the atlas, and:

❖ name any **three** land features of that country
❖ list all of the countries that border it
❖ write **one** detail about the country—its rainfall, population distribution, food production, religion or other information.

❖ CONTINUED

LEARNING ABOUT EXPLORING YOUR COMMUNITY

The *Exploring Beyond Your State* sections at the end of each activity help to broaden your outlook. Think of each of these as a kind of telescope that lets you see New York State as part of the larger world.

The following *Exploring Your Community* section takes a different approach. Think of each of these sections as a kind of microscope that lets you see your own community close up and in greater detail. Here you can apply what you have just learned to understanding your community. For example, how has your community been influenced by its location? How did your home address come into being?

EXPLORING YOUR COMMUNITY
THE ROADWAYS OF YOUR COMMUNITY

Ever since colonial times, Americans have recognized the importance of roads. The earliest roads were made of dirt. Eventually, private companies paved many roads with sand and gravel. Others used planks of wood. They collected fees for the use of these roads, which were known as **turnpikes**.

Today, roads continue to be essential to the existence of every community. Think how hard it would be to get to school or to shop if we did not have paved roads. In fact, there are many different kinds of roads in New York State.

An early turnpike in New York State
How does this roadway compare to modern roads in the state?

❖ **Expressways** and **parkways** are roadways with two or more traffic lanes in each direction. They are often used by people traveling to distant places. The New York State (Governor Thomas E. Dewey) Thruway and the Long Island Expressway are both examples of expressways. Usually these types of roads have no traffic lights, so traffic can move quickly. Expressways and parkways are often identified by numbers.

❖ CONTINUED

- ❖ **Interstate highways** are roads that connect one state to another. Interstates usually have a shield with an interstate number to identify them.

- ❖ **Routes** are state roads that connect one part of the state with another. They are also identified by number. Differently shaped signs are used to identify state routes.

- ❖ **Avenues and streets** are local roadways that connect one part of a city or village with other parts. **Avenues** are often wide streets. A **street** is a typical local roadway. A street may not be busy but usually has more traffic on it than a lane, alley or court.

A sign on the New York State Thruway: note the interstate number (*left*) and the state route number (*right*) on the sign.

YOUR TASK: USING A MAP

How many highways, state routes, avenues and streets can you identify in your community? Using a map of your community, answer the following questions:

1. Name an expressway or parkway in or near your community.
2. What other cities, villages or towns are connected to your community by the parkways or expressways named in your answer above?
3. Name a state route in or near your community.
4. Name two avenues in your community.
5. Name three streets in your community.
6. Name one lane or court in your community.

- ❖ Write a "how to" letter telling someone which streets and roads he or she should take to travel from your home to your school.

- ❖ Ask an adult if he or she can remember when some of these roadways were first built.

- ❖ Look at a map of your local area. Then describe what influence the location of parkways and expressways may have had on where people live in your community.

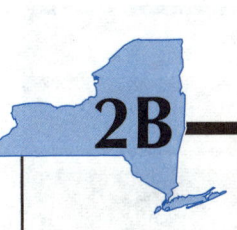

WHAT QUESTIONS MIGHT A GEOGRAPHER ASK ABOUT YOUR SCHOOL?

2B

In this activity, you will be introduced to the five themes of geography. As you read this section, look for the following important words:

- ▶ Geography
- ▶ Location
- ▶ Region
- ▶ Human-Environment Interaction
- ▶ Movement

THE SUBJECT OF GEOGRAPHY

The word "geography" comes from two ancient Greek words—the word for the "Earth" and the word for "writing." In earlier times, **geography** was limited to drawing or writing about the Earth. Today, geography includes not only the study of different places around the world, but also the study of people, where they live and how they are linked to the world around them.

THINK ABOUT IT

List five questions that you think a geographer might ask about your school.
Did you ask the same kinds of questions that a geographer might ask?

Let's check your answers by looking at how geographers view their subject.

THE FIVE THEMES OF GEOGRAPHY

Geographers have identified five themes to help us understand how the world and its peoples are linked. Each theme highlights one part of the study of geography. The **five themes of geography** are *location, place, region, human-environment interaction* and *movement*. Let's see how we can apply these themes to a study of your school.

LOCATION

Location is where something can be found in relation to other things. Each continent, country, state and county has its own unique "location." Even buildings have a location.

- ❖ **Absolute Location** is the exact position of a particular place on the Earth's surface. For example, the absolute location of your school is a unique address. On a map, your school occupies a single place.
- ❖ **Relative Location** is the position of a particular place on the Earth's surface in relation to other locations. Relative location uses such terms as *near, by* or *at the corner of* to identify the location. The relative location of your school tells us more information about your school. It can tell us if it is near a highway, or how far it is from the nearest bus stop.

> ✔ **CHECKING YOUR UNDERSTANDING** ✔
> - What is the absolute location of your school?
> - What is the location of your school relative to the nearest fire station?

A New York City public school
What is the absolute and relative location of your school?

PLACE

What is the place like where you live? Is it hot or cold? Dry or humid? Mountainous or flat? You will learn more about the geographic features that make a place unique later in this unit. Buildings are also "places" with unique features. How would you describe what kind of place your school is?

> ✔ **CHECKING YOUR UNDERSTANDING** ✔
> - Is your school made of brick or wood?
> - How many floors does it have?
> - How many classrooms are there?
> - What are some of your school's unique features?

REGION

▶ **Regions** are areas that are near each other and have similar characteristics or features. People within a region usually have more contact with one another than they do with people outside the region. One region can sometimes be considered to belong to an even larger region. For example, your **community** is part of a larger region called a **county** Your county, in turn, is part of a larger region called a **state**. Your state belongs to an even larger region, (*group of states*) such as the Northeast, Midwest, South or West of the United States. Your state is also part of an even larger region called a **country**.

> ✔ **CHECKING YOUR UNDERSTANDING** ✔
> - In which community is your school located?
> - In which county is your school located?
> - In which state is your school located?
> - In which country is your school located?
> - In which region of the United States is your state located?

HUMAN-ENVIRONMENT INTERACTION

Human-environment interaction means the way in which the physical features of a place affect its people, and how the people affect their environment. For example, people can change their environment by turning forests and hilly grasslands into cities. On the other hand, the environment also shapes what people do. Activities such as skiing and ice skating are popular winter sports in areas that have cold and snowy winters. But they are not found in tropical regions where the climate is warm all year. How might life in a desert be different from life in a large city?

A popular winter sport in New York is skiing. A lift carries skiers up the mountain in Lake Placid.

> ✔ **CHECKING YOUR UNDERSTANDING** ✔
> - How do students in your school dress during the winter months?
> - Is it too hot in the summer to play outdoor sports?

MOVEMENT

People must interact with each other. They trade, travel and communicate to get what they need. The **movement** of goods, ideas and people from place to place is an important theme of geography. For example, it is likely that some of your schoolmates originally came from other places. The knowledge and skills you learn in school are also the products of many different lands and cultures.

> ✔ **CHECKING YOUR UNDERSTANDING** ✔
> - Name a product used in your school that was made in another country.
> - Do you know any people who were not born in New York State? If so, where did they originally come from?

34   NEW YORK: ITS LAND AND ITS PEOPLE

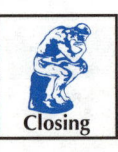

Closing
QUESTIONS ABOUT YOUR SCHOOL

In the beginning of this activity, you were asked to list five questions a geographer might ask about your school. Now that you have learned about the five themes of geography: *location, place, region, human-environment interaction* and *movement*—would you change your questions?

REVIEWING YOUR UNDERSTANDING

Creating Vocabulary Cards

Location
What is the absolute location of your house?
What is its relative location?

Region
What is a region?
Name two regions to which your community belongs:

Learning to Use an Atlas

In the previous activity you learned how to use an atlas. Let's practice your skill by using an atlas to find certain places in New York State. Make a copy of the outline map of New York. Then locate the following cities, rivers and mountains on the map.

Cities:
1. Utica
2. Yonkers
3. Binghamton
4. Watertown
5. Rochester
6. New Rochelle
7. Niagara Falls
8. Troy
9. Buffalo
10. Garden City

Rivers: 1. Hudson River   2. Mohawk River   3. St. Lawrence River

Mountains: 1. Catskill Mountains   2. Adirondack Mountains

MAKING CONNECTIONS

EXPLORING BEYOND YOUR STATE
APPLYING THE FIVE THEMES TO CULTURES AROUND THE WORLD

The five themes of geography tell us about people and their relationship to the places where they live. You have just learned how to apply the five themes of geography to your school. These same five themes can be used to analyze not only your school, but the features of places around the state and the world.

❖ **Location:** The location of a place often influences its culture. For example, Japan is a country of islands in Asia. The seas and oceans surrounding Japan separated it from other nations and protected it from invasion for most of its history. Because Japan was located close to China, it was deeply influenced by Chinese culture. The Japanese form of writing, calendar, silk and use of tea were all borrowed from China.

Japanese women tea farming
Where did the Japanese use of tea come from?

❖ **Place:** The features of a place can also influence the culture of the people who live there. Greece is a country in southern Europe. It is mountainous and has a long coastline on the Mediterranean Sea. The mountains made it difficult for its ancient populations to communicate with one another by land. Instead, they communicated and shipped goods to one another by sea. The Greeks therefore became great sailors and traders. Because the population centers of Greece were cut off from one another by mountains, they developed into independent city-states with their own forms of government. One of these city-states, Athens, became the first place to develop democracy about 2,500 years ago.

❖ **Region:** Another factor that has an impact on a people's culture is the region they belong to. This often tells us whom they associate with and whom they borrow ideas from. The countries of the Middle East, for example, share many common geographical features, such as a warm and dry climate. Many of the Middle Eastern

❖ CONTINUED

people also share a common history, language and religion. Many of them were once part of the Turkish empire, speak Arabic and follow the Islamic religion.

❖ **Human-Environment Interaction:** The northeast section of the United States provides a good example of how humans can sometimes alter their environment. Three hundred years ago, much of this area was forest land. Today, it is heavily populated with cities such as Boston, New York City, Philadelphia, Baltimore and Washington D.C. Concrete roadways, steel bridges and skyscrapers have replaced forest lands. Sometimes the environment can pose limits to human development. In the regions above the Arctic Circle, only a handful of people live there even today. They have adopted a few modern inventions but largely continue to lead traditional life-styles.

Young children in the Middle East attend school to learn to read and write in Arabic. *What features do these children share?*

❖ **Movement:** The movement of ideas, inventions, products and peoples has had a great impact on the development of the world. One invention often spreads from one place to another. For example, corn was probably first grown in Mexico thousands of years ago. From Mexico, the planting of corn spread to the southwestern United States. From there, this knowledge spread east to New York. There was no corn in Europe until the early Spanish explorers brought it from America.

APPLYING THE FIVE THEMES OF GEOGRAPHY

You just read how cultures around the world are often influenced by each of the five themes. Can you think of other examples? Think of **one** example illustrating each theme. Your example can be from the United States or the rest of the world.

Themes of Geography	Example	How the Theme Applies to the Example
Location:		?
Place:		?
Region:		?
Human-environment interaction:		?
Movement:		?

❖ CONTINUED

EXPLORING YOUR COMMUNITY
APPLYING THE FIVE THEMES TO YOUR COMMUNITY

Very often a good way to learn new ideas, such as the five themes of geography, is to illustrate them in a picture or drawing. How good are you at finding items in your community that would illustrate the five themes?

In this section you will create an illustration for each of the five themes of geography. For example, to illustrate "place" you might draw a picture showing the land features of your area. You could draw local mountains, rivers, lakes, hills, grassy fields, the seashore or a skyline of tall buildings. If it often rains or snows in your area, you might show a scene illustrating rain or snow.

Hiking along a road in the Catskill Mountains
How does this picture illustrate human-environmental interaction?

APPLYING THE FIVE THEMES

Copy the five boxes below on to a separate sheet of paper. For each box, draw or find a picture from your community that illustrates the theme. For example, to illustrate location, you might draw or show a picture of a house with a large address sign.

Location:	?
Place:	?
Region:	?
Human-environment interaction:	?
Movement:	?

WHAT ROLE DOES "PLACE" PLAY IN PEOPLE'S LIVES?

2C

In this activity, you will learn about the important role that "place" plays in people's lives. Look for the following important words:

- ▶ Anchorage
- ▶ Manhattan
- ▶ Urban
- ▶ Everglades

The Earth is a place of breath-taking beauty—lush green forests, dazzling white glaciers and brilliant desert sunsets. It has climates and land features where life for human beings can be comfortable and easy, or quite harsh.

FEATURES THAT MAKE A PLACE UNIQUE

Each location on Earth has special features that make it different from other places. Geographers often study a location to determine what kind of place it is. The special features of a place include the following:

❖ how hot or cold the place is generally, and how much rainfall it receives.

❖ whether the place is in the mountains, in a flat valley or on a plain.

❖ what plants and animals live there.

❖ whether the place has valuable resources.

❖ whether the place is near or far from a body of water.

The falls of the Genesee River at Rochester, N.Y. How does this feature make Rochester unique?

THINK ABOUT IT

Which features do you think have the greatest effects on how people live?

A LOOK AT THREE PLACES IN THE UNITED STATES

The kind of place we live in often determines **how** we live. This can be seen by looking at three very different places—Anchorage, Manhattan and the Everglades.

ANCHORAGE, ALASKA

If you live in the city of **Anchorage**, Alaska, you would find the weather to be very cold in winter and for much of the fall and spring. Snow is on the ground for most of the year. Even parts of the ocean freeze over. During these months, the mountains surrounding the city of Anchorage look like massive snow drifts. Daylight is short: only five hours in December. Despite the bitter cold, one can still spot moose, eagles and sheep just outside the city. In late spring, the snows melt. Summers are warm, with long days. The sun does not set until after midnight, and after a few hours it rises again.

Anchorage is an important city because of Alaska's valuable natural resources—especially oil and gas. Many oil companies have their headquarters in Anchorage. They employ thousands of workers. The cold climate affects people's activities as well as their work. Most food has to be shipped or flown up to parts of Alaska from warmer areas. In winter, people wear heavy coats, boots, hats and gloves. Many Alaskans enjoy such winter sports as skiing and bobsledding. In the summer months, they go hiking and fishing.

> **THINK ABOUT IT**
>
> What is daily life like in Anchorage, Alaska?

MANHATTAN, NEW YORK

A second place is **Manhattan**, the oldest section of New York City. It is an island located in the southeastern corner of the state. The island is relatively flat with some rocky areas. The rocks are exposed because thousands of years ago glaciers scraped and leveled the surface of Manhattan.

Manhattan has moderately cold winters. Heavy snowfalls usually occur a few times each winter, but melt quickly. Many people find the months of July and August uncomfortable because the air is hot and humid. Large numbers of New Yorkers go on vacation during this period or keep their air conditioners running day and night.

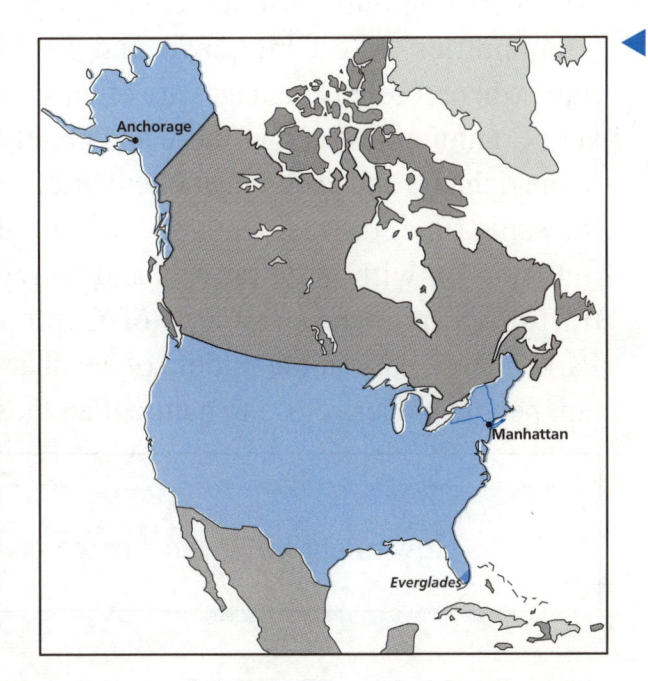

Manhattan is the nation's center for international business, finance, art, music, publishing and fashion. Many of the world's tallest buildings are found there. The Empire State Building and the World Trade Center, made of glass and steel, are just two of the hundreds of "skyscrapers" in Manhattan.

40   NEW YORK: ITS LAND AND ITS PEOPLE

Manhattan is also a world-class cultural center. Tourists like to see the dinosaur skeletons at the American Museum of Natural History, the modern art works at the Guggenheim Museum and the paintings and sculpture at the Metropolitan Museum of Art. Manhattan is also home to Lincoln Center for the Performing Arts, including the Metropolitan Opera. Radio City Music Hall, several television stations and the theaters of Broadway are found there. So are many world famous universities as well as the United Nations. There are also thousands of restaurants and stores in Manhattan.

▶ Manhattan is a large **urban** (*city*) area. Many people live busy, hurried lives. They travel from nearby areas to work in Manhattan. They rush between work and home. Other people go to Manhattan to take advantage of its many cultural opportunities.

Dinosaur skeletons at the American Museum of Natural History
Have you ever visited a natural history museum?

Most Manhattan residents live in apartment houses, large and small. Manhattanites mix with a great number of people from diverse backgrounds. Some live in special communities, like Chinatown and Little Italy, where foreign languages are often spoken. Communities such as these add greatly to the richness and excitement of city life. At the same time, the residents of Manhattan must put up with large crowds and heavy traffic. Despite the existence of Central Park, a large park in the middle of Manhattan, people are less close to nature than those who live in a city such as Anchorage.

A view of lower Manhattan
How might living in Manhattan be different from life in Anchorage, Alaska?

THINK ABOUT IT

How might life in Anchorage be different than life in Manhattan?

THE FLORIDA EVERGLADES

▶ A third, quite different place in the United States is the **Everglades**. The Everglades is a large, swamp land located in the southern part of the State of Florida. The Everglades is a very rainy area, and fresh water flows through the swamp on its way to the

Gulf of Mexico and the Atlantic Ocean. The climate in the Everglades is very warm and humid all year.

Very few people live in the Everglades. Trees and high blades of saw grass cover the marsh. Wildlife flourishes—including alligators, crocodiles, snakes, panthers and many types of exotic (*unusual*) and often beautiful birds. The northern Everglades have been converted by man-made canals and ditches into farmland where sugar cane and vegetables are grown. The southern part of the Everglades is now a national park.

Taking a ride on an air-boat in the swampy Everglades
Is life in the Everglades different from living in Manhattan?

> **THINK ABOUT IT**
>
> How might life in Manhattan be different from life in the Everglades?

As you can see, the place where people live—its climate, topography, resources, population and nearness to water—can greatly affect how they live. For example, in Anchorage people might use a 4-wheel drive vehicle to get to work. In the Everglades, people might use a boat to get around. In Manhattan, people often travel by taxi, bus or subway.

THE MAGIC OF READING A BOOK

Have you ever listened to a grandparent explain what it was like growing up in a far off land? Or maybe heard a parent tell stories about visiting a unique and exciting country? Wouldn't it be nice if you could visit some of the places you have heard about?

You may not have the time or money to journey to far-off lands. But there is a way to visit these unique places without ever leaving home. Reading books is one of the best ways to "travel" to other places around the globe. Books let you visit a place without having to pack anything more than your imagination.

Let's take a look at some of the books available to you. On the next few pages are several books about places to visit. Choose **one** book from the list, or one that your teacher or school librarian recommends. After reading the book, complete a copy of the following **Book Evaluation Form**.

Book Evaluation Form

Title of the book: _____

Author's name: _____

Place described in the book: _____

Write down any words from the story that are unfamiliar to you. Create a card with the meaning of each word.

✦✦✦✦✦✦✦✦✦✦✦✦✦✦✦✦✦✦✦✦✦✦✦✦✦✦✦✦✦

Choose a short section of the book (*up to one page*) that you particularly enjoyed reading. Read the section to someone else—a friend or a parent.

- Ask the listener for his or her impression.
- Was the listener's impression of this section the same as yours?
- Describe any similarities or differences.

List at least two features of the place: _____

How did the characteristics of the "place" affect the lives of its people?

✦✦✦✦✦✦✦✦✦✦✦✦✦✦✦✦✦✦✦✦✦✦✦✦✦✦✦✦✦

Would you recommend this book to others? Explain your reasons.

Here are some suggested books you may wish to choose from:

AROUND THE WORLD IN EIGHTY DAYS
J. Burningham
(*Jarrold*)

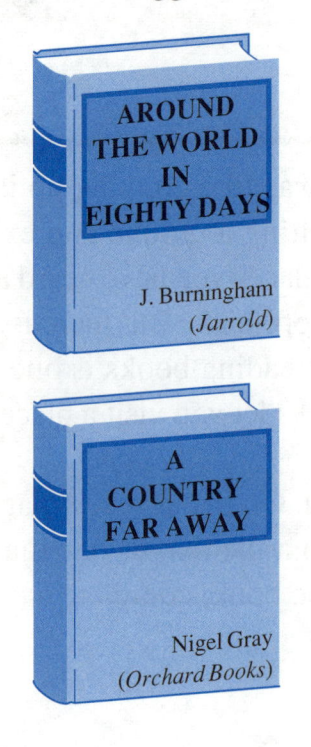

This book tells the classic story of Phileas Fogg and his famous trip "around the world in eighty days." The author gives his impressions as he travels through 24 countries along his 44,000 mile journey.

A COUNTRY FAR AWAY
Nigel Gray
(*Orchard Books*)

This is a story of two young boys—one black and one white—who live on opposite sides of the globe. The book describes their daily lives. Although the boys are from different societies and places, their lives actually turn out to be quite similar.

GEOGRAPHY   43

THE CHALK DOLL

Charlotte Pomerantz
(*Lippincott Books*)

In this story, Rose's mother recalls growing up on the island of Jamaica. She is too poor to buy a doll for Rose. She tells Rose of her own happiness as a child playing with things she made. The book describes life in Jamaica.

WITH LOVE FROM GRAN

Dick Gackenbach
(*Clarion*)

This is the story of a boy and his grandmother. She goes on a trip around the world and sends him back presents from each place she visits.

MY TWO WORLDS

Ginger Gordon
(*Clarion*)

This book is about an eight-year old girl who lives in New York City. For Christmas, she goes to the Dominican Republic, where her family came from. The story is about her life in these two worlds—New York and the Dominican Republic.

RUSSIAN GIRL: LIFE IN AN OLD RUSSIAN TOWN

Russ Kendall
(*Scholastic*)

This is the story of contemporary life in Russia seen through the eyes of nine-year old Olga. It describes the people she meets and the many customs she experiences.

GOING HOME

Nicholas Mohr
(*Bantam Skylark*)

Felita is a twelve-year old girl in New York who returns to Puerto Rico for a visit. She is surprised to find both admiration and jealousy from the people she meets there. By summer's end she learns a great deal about her Hispanic heritage.

THE ROLE OF PLACE IN PEOPLE'S LIVES

Some of the things we learn about in books are so interesting that we enjoy sharing them with others. The following are some suggestions on how you might share what you have read with your classmates:

- show your classmates the location of the place on a map of the world.
- join in a class discussion to decide which place would be the most interesting to visit.
- make a drawing of the place that you read about.
- suggest any available movies or documentaries about the place that you read about.

REVIEWING YOUR UNDERSTANDING

Creating Vocabulary Cards

Urban
Define the word "urban."
Name an urban area in New York State:

Everglades
Define the word "Everglades."
Why do so few people live in the Everglades?

Visiting Your Dream Place

You may have once heard someone you know talk about taking a trip to a tropical paradise like Hawaii. Or perhaps a relative has mentioned going on a safari in Africa. Almost all of us have dreamed about an interesting or unique place we would like to visit. Choose a place you have heard about and thought of visiting one day. Write an imaginary postcard to a friend describing the place. Be sure to mention some of the area's interesting and unique geographic features.

MAKING CONNECTIONS

EXPLORING BEYOND YOUR STATE

Geography and Its Effect on Where and How People Live

It would be wonderful if every place where people settled had a good water supply, a comfortable climate, lots of natural resources, fertile soil and level land to build on. However, many places do not. Yet people have learned to adapt to just about every climate and landform on Earth. How many people can live in an area, and the kind of lives they lead, are often affected by geographical factors.

WATER

Human life depends on water for drinking, farming, fishing, cooking, manufacturing and transportation. Therefore, people often settle where water supplies are plentiful—near oceans, rivers and lakes. For example, in Egypt the largest number of people live along the Nile River or Mediterranean coast.

Rice being harvested in Indonesia
Why do you think Indonesians planted crops on the hillside in the background?

CLIMATE

The world has an astonishing variety of climates, from hot areas along the equator to very cold places near the North and South Poles. People who live in hot, humid areas wear lightweight clothing, while people in cold climates often wear several layers of heavy clothing. How do you think a typical Hawaiian's clothing compares with the clothing of Inuits living near the North Pole?

NATURAL RESOURCES

Natural resources include plants, animals and minerals. These resources are used to grow food, supply energy, make clothing, provide housing and serve as raw materials. Oil, for example, is an extremely important natural resource. Today, oil provides fuel to power our automobiles and machinery. This gives countries with large oil deposits a great advantage. There are only about two million people living in Kuwait. Yet it is one of the richest nations in the world because of its large supply of oil.

❖ CONTINUED

FERTILE SOIL AND LEVEL LAND

People look for land that is fertile and flat to settle on. Such land is easier to farm and can produce a rich harvest of food crops. However, a country's location on level plains can also have disadvantages. For example, Poland is located on a flat plain in northern Europe. It has few natural borders to prevent invasions. As a result, Poland has frequently been invaded by other countries.

ANSWERING A QUESTION

It has often been said that geography has an important effect on where people live and how they live. Based on what you have just read, would you agree? Give **two** examples to support your opinion.

EXPLORING YOUR COMMUNITY
DESCRIBING THE PHYSICAL FEATURES OF YOUR COMMUNITY

In this activity you read about several places far from your community. Let's now turn our attention back to where you live. This is a special place, too, with some unique features.

DESCRIBING YOUR COMMUNITY'S FEATURES

Describe each of the following features of your community:

* its climate
* its topography (*land features*)
* its plants and animals
* its minerals
* its rivers, lakes or other bodies of water
* the features of areas surrounding your community

Create a bulletin board showing these features. Your bulletin board should include one drawing or photograph of each feature.

Sylvan Beach, New York
How does living near a beach make this community a special place?

HOW WOULD YOU MAP YOUR COMMUNITY?

2D

In this activity, you will learn how maps help us to locate places. Look for the following important words:

- ▶ Map
- ▶ Symbol
- ▶ Legend (Key)
- ▶ Scale
- ▶ Latitude
- ▶ Longitude

Your friend in California has sent you a map of an imaginary community that he made as a school project. You look at his map, and say to yourself: "This seems like an interesting project for me to do. I'm going to make a map too."

WHAT ARE MAPS?

You ask your teacher for advice on how to begin. Your teacher explains that **maps** are the language of geography. Each map is really a small picture, diagram or model of a larger place. It shows where things are located. Your teacher says the easiest way to understand maps is by mapping things in a small area. She suggests you start by making a map of your desktop.

You draw a picture of a box representing your desktop. Your teacher then puts three objects in different locations on the top of your desk. She says, "Now pretend you are a bird, flying over the desk. Can you describe *exactly* where the objects on your desk are located?"

You find this hard to do. Your teacher agrees that it is not easy. Your teacher tells you that **cartographers** (*people who make maps*) have the same problem. To help them locate places on a map, cartographers make a grid like the one on the "desk map" to the right. A **grid** uses straight lines that cross each other. The crossing lines create boxes. The rows along the top and side are given letters and numbers.

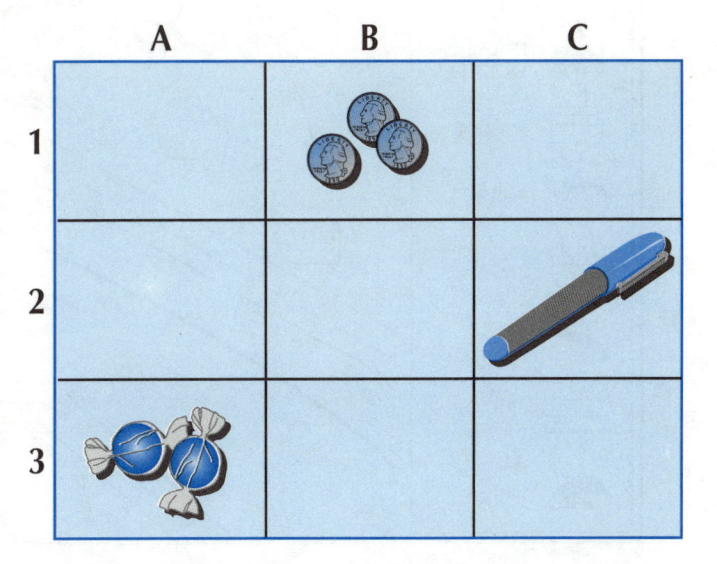

48 NEW YORK: ITS LAND AND ITS PEOPLE

> ✔ **CHECKING YOUR UNDERSTANDING** ✔
>
> Write down the number and the letter of the grid box that contains:
> - the candy
> - the coins
> - the pen

LEARNING TO INTERPRET A MAP

Maps are drawings, models or diagrams of a part of the Earth. They come in different sizes and shapes. Some maps show countries, states or cities. These maps will indicate political boundaries. Other maps show geographic features such as mountains, oceans and rivers. Still others show airports, parks and schools. A **globe** is a special kind of map. It is a three-dimensional sphere that represents the entire Earth.

THE TITLE

To understand a map, first look at its title. The title tells you what information is found on the map.

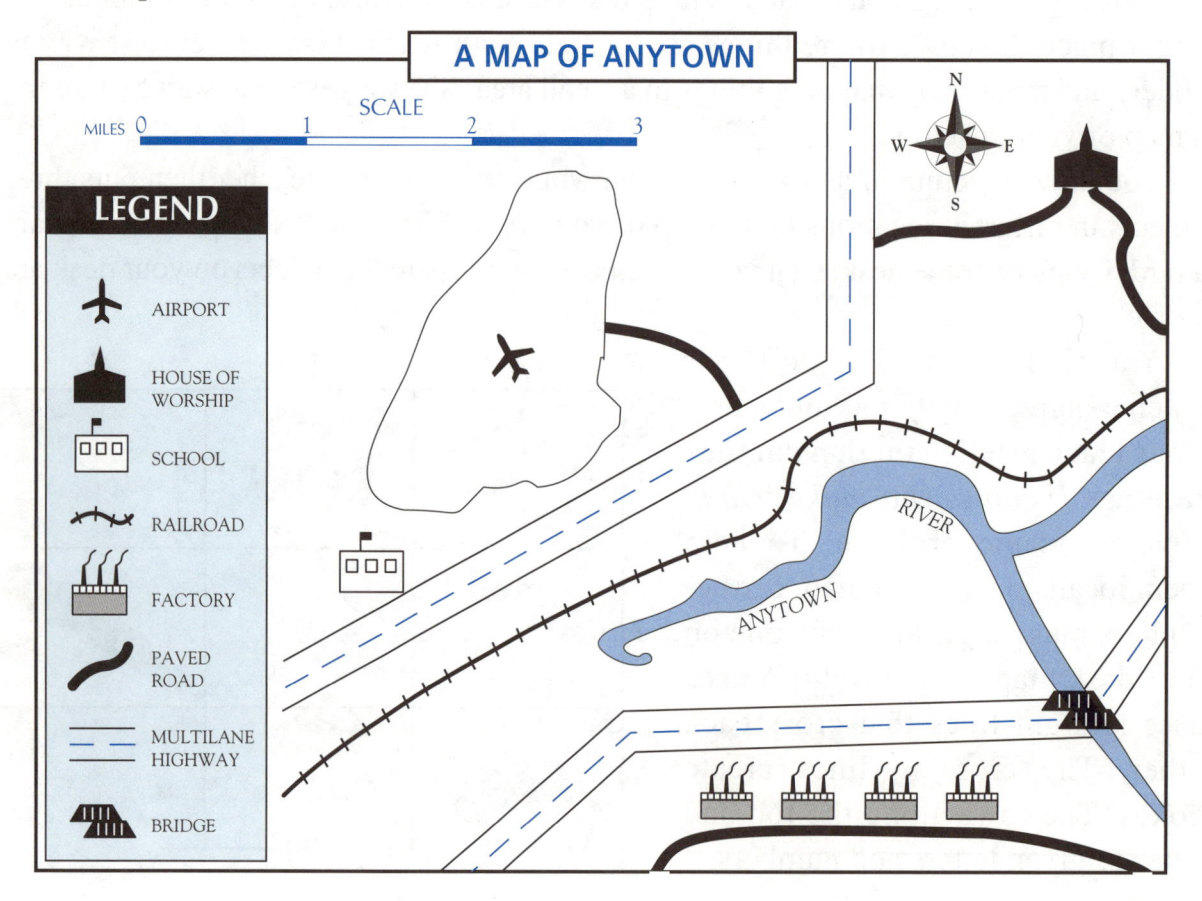

A MAP OF ANYTOWN

LEGEND
- AIRPORT
- HOUSE OF WORSHIP
- SCHOOL
- RAILROAD
- FACTORY
- PAVED ROAD
- MULTILANE HIGHWAY
- BRIDGE

THE LEGEND

The secret to using any map is to understand its symbols. Instead of writing the word "highway," "railroad," "airport" or "school" each time it appears on the map, mapmakers use symbols to represent these things. A map **symbol** is a drawing that stands for an actual place or a real thing.

Mapmakers provide a **legend** to explain each symbol in words. The legend unlocks the meaning of the symbols used on the map. The legend is sometimes called the "key." Symbols may appear as shapes, lines, dots, dashes or drawings. Each map will have its own unique set of symbols. For example, the symbol for an airport on one map may be entirely different on another map. Each symbol is explained in the legend, so you can tell what it means.

✔ Checking Your Understanding ✔

There are 8 symbols on the map of Anytown. On a separate sheet of paper, draw the symbol used for:

- a factory
- a school
- a church
- an airport

DIRECTION INDICATOR

To make it easier to find directions on a map, mapmakers provide a **direction indicator**. It is often called a **compass rose**. The compass rose shows the four **cardinal** (*basic*) directions:

- **north** (N)
- **south** (S)
- **east** (E)
- **west** (W)

A compass rose can also show other directions. Sometimes we need to find places that fall in between the four basic directions. A compass rose shows the intermediate (*in-between*) directions:

- **northeast** (NE)
- **northwest** (NW)
- **southeast** (SE)
- **southwest** (SW)

Let's see how well you understand what you have just read. On the Anytown map, in which direction would you travel to go from the bridge to the school? Here are the steps to figure out the answer. Most maps show north at the top and south at the bottom. Look at the compass rose in the upper right hand corner of the Anytown map. If you traveled from the bridge (*in the eastern part of Anytown*) to the school (*in the western part*) you would be traveling west.

50   NEW YORK: ITS LAND AND ITS PEOPLE

> ✔ **CHECKING YOUR UNDERSTANDING** ✔
>
> In which direction would you be traveling if you went from:
>
> - the house of worship to the bridge?
> - the airport to the bridge?
> - the factories to the river?
> - the school to the airport?

SCALE

Just as a model airplane is a small version of a large, real airplane, a map is a small diagram of a large, real place. If a map were the same size as the area it shows, it would be too big to use. Imagine a map the actual size of your school!

The larger the area represented, the less detail the map can have. For example, a map of the United States can only show outlines of the states and some cities. A map of your school can show much more detail, such as each classroom.

▶ Mapmakers use a device called a **scale** to show what distances the measurements on a map stand for in real life. The scale can be used to figure out the distance between any two places on a map. Scales tell us the real distance, usually in miles or kilometers. Map scales are usually shown as a line marked: "Scale of Miles." Mapmakers may use one inch to represent (*stand for*) one real mile. On a map of a large area, one inch may represent 100 miles or more.

Let's see how we can go about finding the approximate distance from Rochester to Syracuse. First, look at the map to the right. Put a ruler under the scale on the map. You will see that one inch on the scale of miles represents a real distance of 100 miles.

On the map, line up the edge of a piece of paper with Rochester. Then move the paper to the left until it touches Syracuse. Mark both spots with a pencil or pen. Now use a ruler to measure this distance. It measures about three-fourths of an inch. Therefore, the distance from Rochester to Syracuse is about 75 miles ($\frac{3}{4}$ths of 100 = 75).

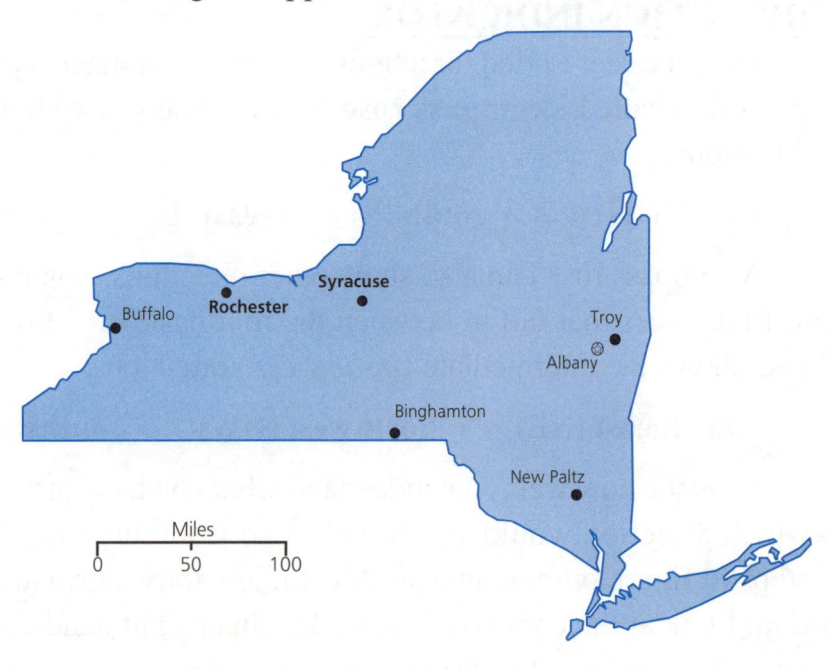

✔ CHECKING YOUR UNDERSTANDING ✔

Let's practice your new skill. What would be the distance from:

- Albany to Syracuse?
- Buffalo to Albany?
- Troy to Binghamton?
- New Paltz to Albany?

DRAWING AN IMAGINARY MAP

Now you have enough information to draw a map as good as the one your friend from California has drawn. You decide to map an imaginary town named after you. For example, if your name is Brian, you'll call the town Brianville. If your name is Maria, the town will be called Mariaville. To help you, use the following steps to create your map:

1. Decide how many different features you wish to show on your map.
2. Think of where on the map you will place each feature.
3. Place each feature on your map.
4. Create symbols for a legend or "key" to explain the features on your map.
5. Add a direction indicator (*compass rose*) showing north, south, east and west.
6. Include a scale of miles.
7. Finally, put a title at the top of your map: MY MAP OF __?__ VILLE

REVIEWING YOUR UNDERSTANDING

Creating Vocabulary Cards

Maps

What is a map?

Name four items used on a map to help locate places:

Legend

What is a legend?

What is a legend used for?

Traveling Around Your Neighborhood

Examine the following map of an imaginary neighborhood. Then answer the questions that follow:

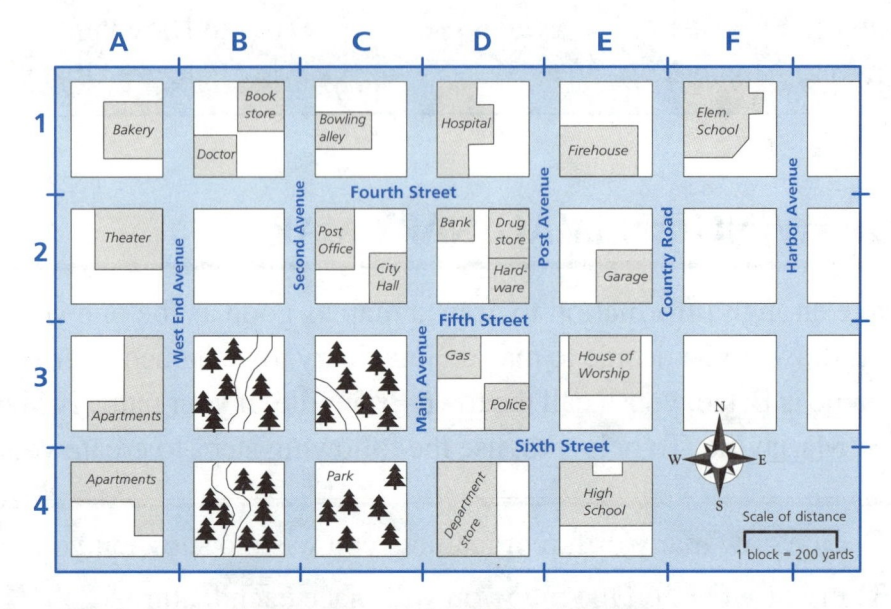

1. Which street is located directly north of Sixth Street?
2. In which grid box is the hospital located?
3. How many avenues do you cross in going from the firehouse to the doctor?
4. Which stores are located along Post Avenue?
5. The hospital is three blocks from the department store. How many yards apart are they?

Finding Direction and Distance

Follow the line to find the direction you are traveling. Use the compass rose and scale to help you answer the following questions.

1. In which direction would you travel to get from **A** to **B**?
2. In which direction would you travel to get from **B** to **C**?
3. In which direction would you travel to get from **F** to **G**?
4. How many miles would you travel to get from **A** to **B**?
5. What is the total distance you would travel from **E** to **G**?

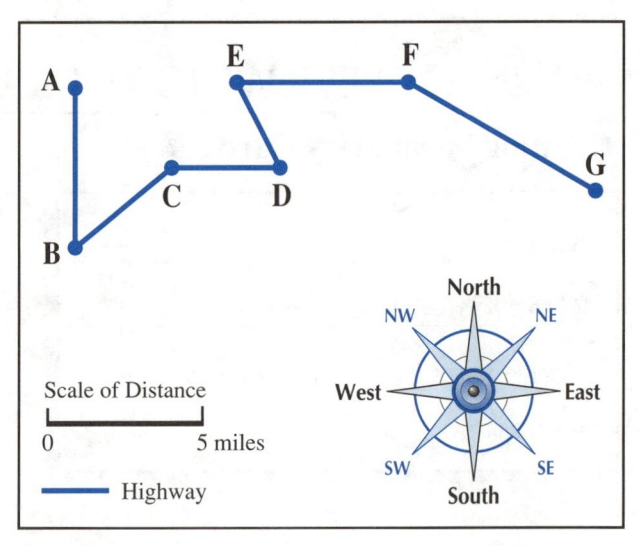

GEOGRAPHY 53

MAKING CONNECTIONS

EXPLORING BEYOND YOUR STATE
LEARNING ABOUT LATITUDE AND LONGITUDE

In order to help find the exact location of any place on a map or globe, geographers have created two sets of imaginary lines—called "latitude" and "longitude" lines.

LINES OF LATITUDE

Latitude is the name given to imaginary horizontal lines that run *across* the Earth. A mnemonic device to help us recall which way latitude lines run is to think of them as steps of a **lad**der because lines of latitude run horizontally. They are sometimes called **parallels** because latitude lines run parallel to each other. Like parallel lines, they never meet. Latitude lines are used to show how far north or south of the equator a location is.

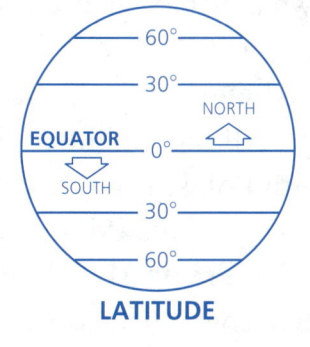

Since a map or globe would be too crowded and confusing if *every* line of latitude were shown, mapmakers usually draw only some latitude lines. The **equator** is the most important latitude line. It stretches all around the middle of the Earth. It is the same distance from the North Pole as it is from the South Pole.

All other latitude lines are identified by how far north or south of the equator they are. Lines of north latitude are found in areas north of the equator. Lines of south latitude are found in areas south of the equator.

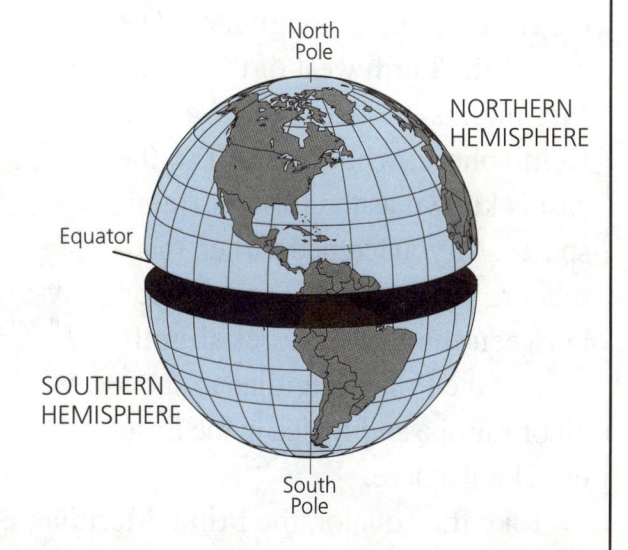

Each latitude line is assigned a number in degrees to show its distance from the equator. The symbol for **degrees** is °. Going in either direction from the equator, we mark latitude lines from 1° to 90°. An "N" or "S" is added after the number of degrees to show if the line is north or south of the equator. For example, a latitude line

❖ CONTINUED

87 degrees north of the equator would be written as 87° N. Lines south of the equator have an "S" after the number of degrees.

At the equator, 0° degrees latitude, the weather is generally hot. The sphere of the Earth curves away from the Sun as you go towards the North and South Poles. As a result, the higher the latitude number, generally the colder the climate will be. The angle of the Earth's tilt as it revolves around the Sun makes the seasons change. When it is winter north of the equator, it is summer south of the equator. At the equator, there are no seasonal changes.

LINES OF LONGITUDE

▶ **Longitudes** are a set of imaginary lines that run up and down a map or globe. They are drawn as lines connecting the North Pole to the South Pole. They are sometimes called **meridians**. Unlike latitude lines, they are not parallel. All the longitude lines meet at both the North and South Poles. Longitudes are used to show location east and west of the Prime Meridian.

The **Prime Meridian** is the most important longitude line. Geographers use it to divide the Earth into two hemispheres (*east and west*) and to mark the starting line of longitudes. The half of the Earth west of the Prime Meridian is known as the Western Hemisphere, while the half to the east is known as the Eastern Hemisphere. As you learned earlier, mapmakers often draw the division between the hemispheres slightly west of the Prime Meridian to show all of Europe and Africa in the Eastern Hemisphere.

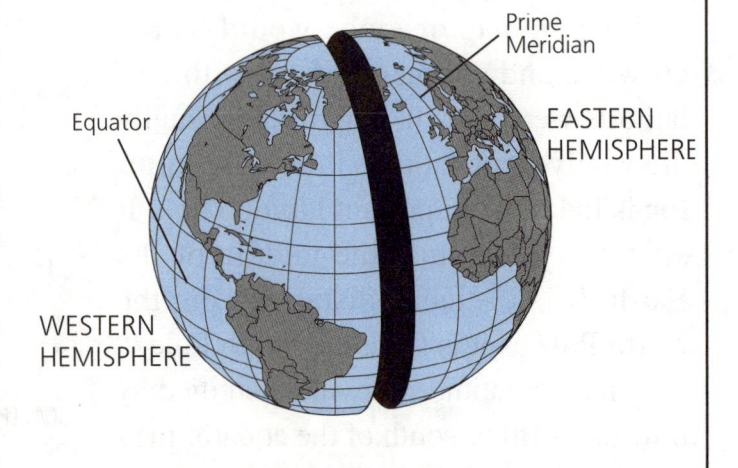

Like the equator, the Prime Meridian is identified as zero degrees (0°). Going in either direction from the Prime Meridian, we mark longitude lines from 1° to 180°, adding "**E**" or "**W**" to indicate if the line is east or west of the Prime Meridian.

Because longitude lines are not parallel, they are not always the same distance from one another. At the equator, each degree of longitude is about 69 miles apart.

❖ CONTINUED

However, as one moves closer to the North or South Pole, each degree of longitude measures fewer and fewer miles. Finally, all longitude lines meet at both the North and South Poles.

When latitude and longitude lines both appear on a map or globe, they form a grid pattern. By knowing the points at which latitude and longitude lines intersect (*meet*), you can locate any place on the surface of the Earth.

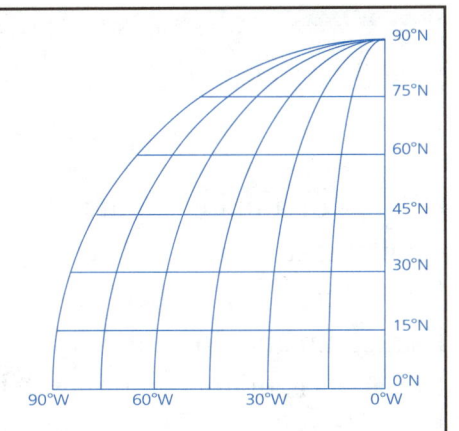

USING LATITUDE AND LONGITUDE

Look at the map to the right. What is the approximate latitude and longitude of Elmira? To find out, put your finger on the small dot representing Elmira. Move your finger down until it touches the 42° N latitude—this line is 42° **north** of the equator. Next, move your finger from Elmira slightly to the left, until it touches 77° W longitude. This line is 77° **west** of the Prime Meridian. Elmira's approximate latitude and longitude are where these two lines cross—at 42° N latitude and 77° W longitude. Because latitudes are always "N" or "S" and longitudes are always "E" or "W," we can simply write 42° N, 77° W.

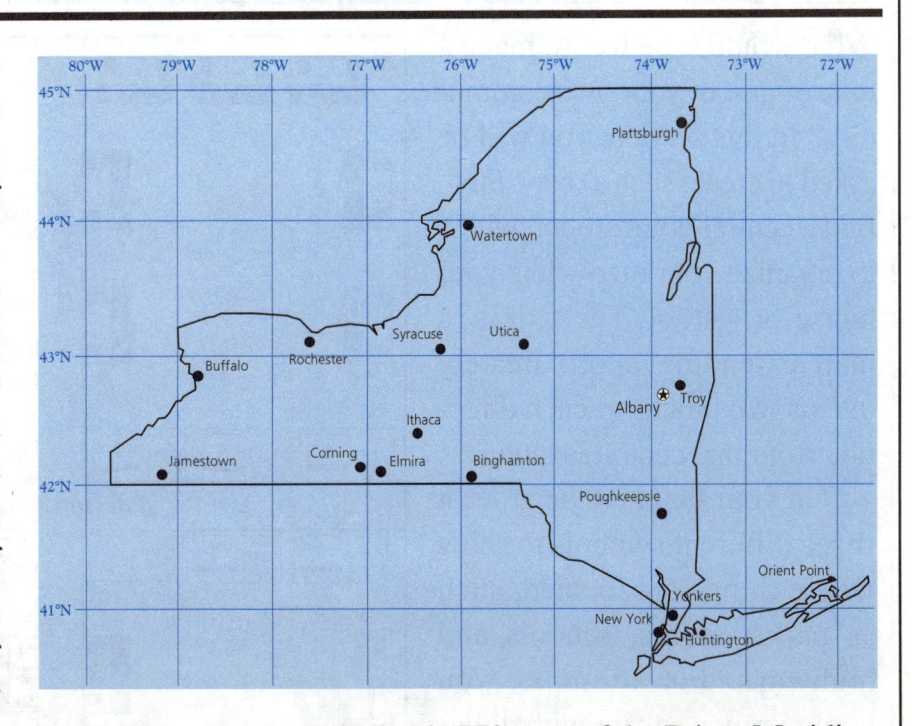

✔ CHECKING YOUR UNDERSTANDING ✔

Figure out the approximate latitudes and longitudes of:

1. Syracuse
2. Watertown
3. Orient Point
4. Poughkeepsie
5. Buffalo
6. Albany
7. Jamestown
8. Yonkers
9. Rochester

◆ CONTINUED

EXPLORING YOUR COMMUNITY

CREATING A MAP OF YOUR COMMUNITY

Think of a map as a picture, taken from high in the air. In the past, people could only make maps by observing carefully what they saw while sailing along a coast or traveling on horseback and on foot. For example, Henry Hudson drew maps as he sailed up and down the Atlantic coast. Today, many maps are based on photographs of areas actually taken by satellites in outer space.

CREATING A MAP

What would it be like to make a map of part of your own community? In this section, you will be asked to create such a map. First, find a central point around which to organize your map—like your house or school. Then, draw a map extending approximately one or two blocks in each direction from that central location.

On your map, create at least **three** different symbols to show where things are located, such as parks, stores, schools and highways. For example, you might draw a square with dollar signs $$$ inside it to symbolize a bank.

Then compare and contrast the symbols that you have created with those of your classmates. See if the class can arrive at some symbols that most students think are best.

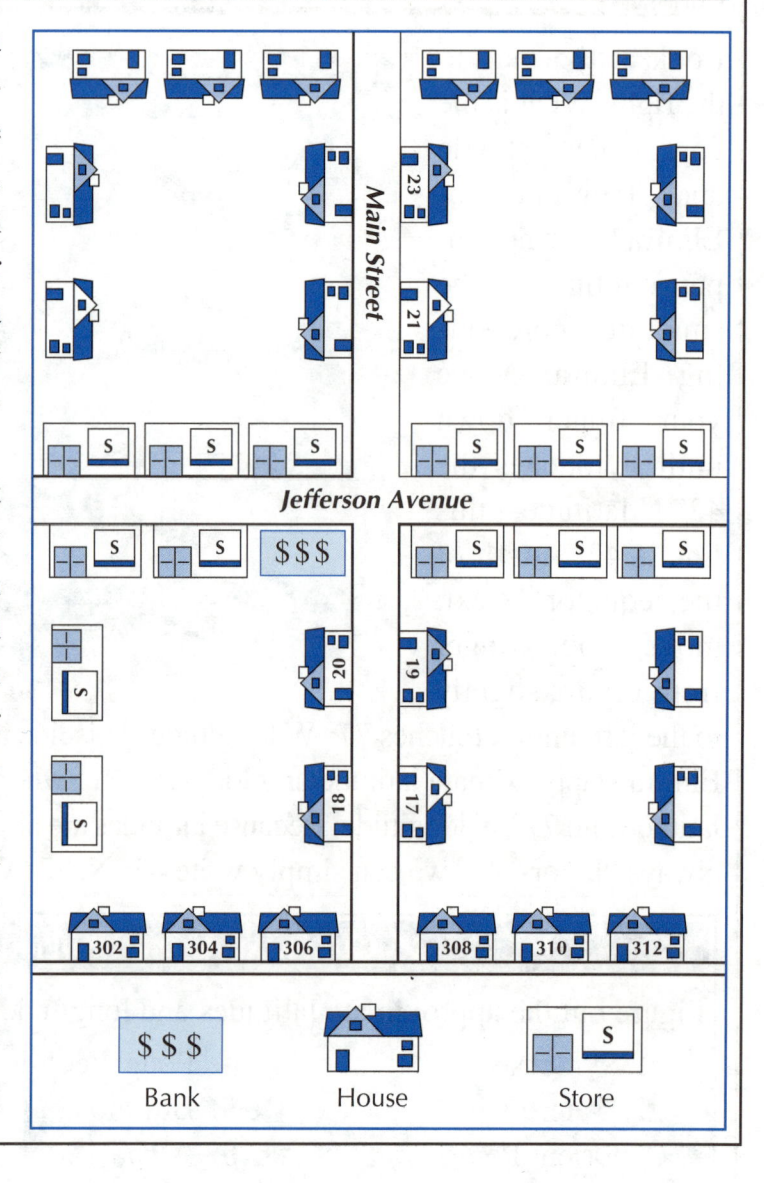

GEOGRAPHY 57

WHAT DOES NEW YORK STATE "LOOK" LIKE?

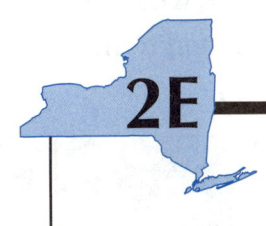

2E

In this activity, you will learn about some of the important physical features of New York State. Look for the following important words:

- ▶ Mohawk River
- ▶ Hudson River
- ▶ Great Lakes
- ▶ Finger Lakes
- ▶ Weather
- ▶ Climate

One day you get a letter from your friend in California. She writes that she will be visiting you this summer. Before arriving, she would like to learn about the physical features of New York State. New York State is so large that you don't know what to write.

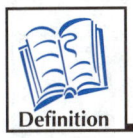

TWO WAYS TO DESCRIBE NEW YORK

You decide to ask your teacher what to write. Your teacher says, "Please try this first. Draw what an apple looks like. Then, write a description of what an apple looks like." That seems simple enough, you think to yourself.

MY APPLE DRAWING	MY APPLE DESCRIPTION
?	?

After you have completed the task, your teacher asks:

❖ Which was easier—drawing an apple or describing it?
❖ Which provides more information, the drawing or the description?
❖ Did they both provide the same kind of information? Explain your answer.

Ah! Now you understand what your teacher meant. To give someone accurate information about a place, it is sometimes best to provide both a picture **and** a description. You decide to send your friend a written description and a "picture" of New York State.

You start by getting a book about New York from the library. However, there is a problem. The book has no pictures, only written descriptions of New York State. You again ask your teacher for help. She says that written descriptions give you an opportunity to play the role of an "amateur cartographer."

58   NEW YORK: ITS LAND AND ITS PEOPLE

"A cartographer? What's that?" She tells you that **cartographers** are people who make maps. Modern cartographers often begin with a photo of the region they intend to map, taken from an airplane or satellite. Then they review other maps and conduct research about the region to fill in the details. Your teacher hands you an outline map of New York. She says this map should help you to "picture" New York. With the descriptions in your book, you can fill in the details on your outline map.

When you turn to your library book on New York, here is what you find:

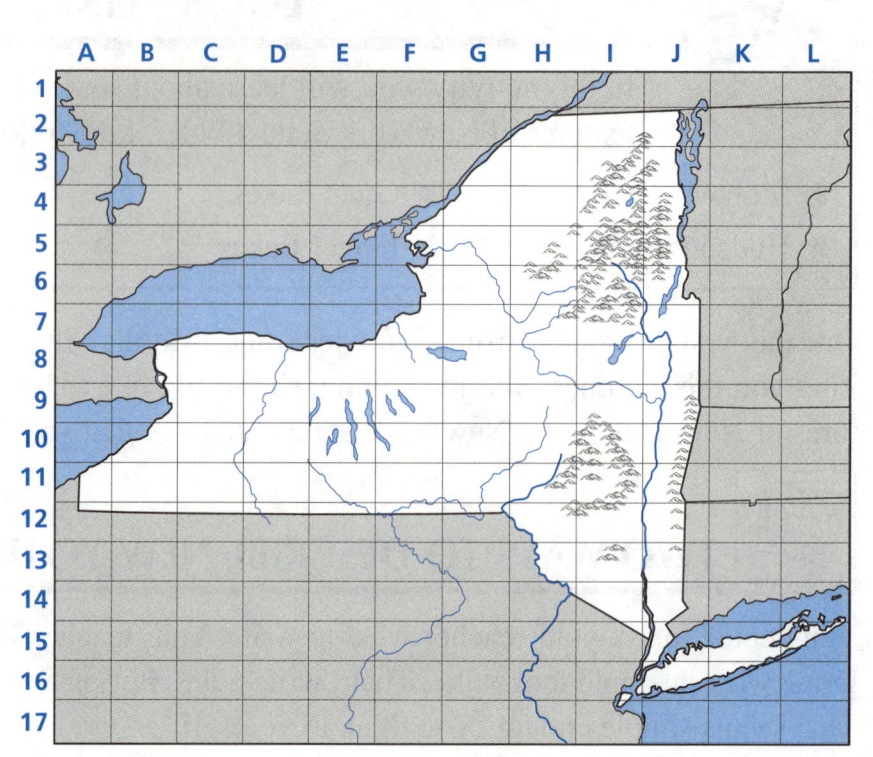

THE GEOGRAPHY OF NEW YORK: THE EMPIRE STATE

SIZE
New York State is shaped something like a giant triangle. It has a total area of over 54,000 square miles, including its bodies of water. In size, it ranks 27th out of the 50 states in the United States.

THE BOUNDARIES (BORDERS) OF NEW YORK
New York has always been considered one of the most important states in the United States. Its location helps to explain why: a large portion of New York's borders consists of bodies of water. In fact, New York is the only state that touches both the Atlantic Ocean and the Great Lakes.

In the far north, New York State shares a land boundary with **Canada**. (*To help you find places on the map above, grid letters and numbers are supplied for the general location. For example, the location of Canada is generally around* E3). To the northwest, **Lake Erie** (around A10), **Lake Ontario** (around D6), the **Niagara River** (around B8) and the **St. Lawrence River** (around G3) make up the rest of the border with Canada.

Along its eastern side, New York shares a border with three New England states: **Vermont** (K4), **Massachusetts** (K10) and **Connecticut** (K13). To the south, New York borders **New Jersey** (I16) and **Pennsylvania** (D14). The southeastern end of the state—New York City and Long Island (K15)—touches the **Atlantic Ocean** (K17). There are hundreds of miles of Atlantic Ocean shoreline on Long Island. This provides New York with some of the best beaches in the nation.

> **THE AMATEUR CARTOGRAPHER**
> On your map, label the states that border New York State.

RIVERS AND LAKES

Rivers are long, narrow bodies of fresh water that flow into other rivers or the ocean. There are 70,000 miles of rivers and streams in New York State. In addition, there are thousands of lakes and ponds. These bodies of water make up one of New York's most important resources. Among New York's major rivers are the **Hudson**, **Mohawk**, **St. Lawrence**, **Genesee**, **Niagara**, **Oswego**, **Delaware**, **Susquehanna**, **Allegheny** and **Chenango**.

The two largest rivers entirely within the state are the Hudson and Mohawk. Beginning in the center of the state, the **Mohawk River** (H8) winds for 148 miles before joining the Hudson River just north of Troy. The **Hudson River** (I6) starts high in the Adirondack Mountains and flows south to empty into the Atlantic Ocean.

The St. Lawrence River as seen from the Canadian side
What other major rivers are there in New York State?

Together, these two rivers form one of the nation's greatest waterways. Barges can travel from New York City north on the Hudson River. They can connect, through the Mohawk River and a system of canals, to the **Great Lakes** : Lake Huron, Lake Ontario, Lake Michigan, Lake Erie and Lake Superior. A mnemonic device to help you remember the names of the Great Lakes is **H.O.M.E.S**.

Lakes are bodies of water surrounded by land. There are 8,000 lakes in New York—some small and others quite large. The two largest are **Lake Erie** (A10) and **Lake Ontario** (D6), both part of the Great Lakes. Lake Erie lies along the southwestern corner of New York State. Lake Ontario, to the northeast of Lake Erie, is the smallest of the Great Lakes.

Northeast of Syracuse is **Oneida Lake** (G8), the largest lake found entirely within New York State. **Lake Champlain** (J3) is a long, narrow lake that separates New York and Vermont. In western New York are the six **Finger Lakes** (E10), named by Native

Americans for their long narrow shape, resembling fingers.

In addition to its many rivers and lakes, New York has one of the world's most spectacular waterfalls—**Niagara Falls** (B9). Located near Buffalo, Niagara Falls is made up of two waterfalls, separated by a small island. The "American Falls" is in New York while the "Horseshoe Falls" is in Canada. Other New York waterfalls include Taughannock Falls near Cayuga Lake (*northwest of Ithaca*) and the 18 waterfalls in Watkins Glen State Park.

Niagara Falls, also the site of the city of Niagara Falls

> **THE AMATEUR CARTOGRAPHER**
> On your map, draw the major rivers and lakes of New York State. Also show the location of Niagara Falls.

TOPOGRAPHY

Cartographers also study the land forms or **topography** of the Earth. These land forms were created by different processes that occurred throughout the history of our planet. New York's mountain areas were created by pressures on the Earth's crust, causing it to rise up and fold. Less than two million years ago, the **Ice Age** began. The Earth's climate grew colder. Continuous snow created huge sheets of ice known as **glaciers**. These glaciers extended outward from the North and South Poles. They eventually covered most of New York State. As the glaciers moved, they cut into mountains and created valleys. When they finally melted, they created rivers and lakes.

As a result of these forces, we can think of New York State today as a large triangle with three highland areas. The southwest part of New York contains a high plateau known as the **Appalachian Plateau**, with its highest part in the Catskill Mountains. Along the eastern side of the Hudson River, from Poughkeepsie to Albany, are the **Taconic Mountains**. To the north is a third highland area called the **Adirondack Mountains** (I5).

On each side of the highland areas, and running through the middle of them, are New York's lowlands. The lowland area in the southeast is part of the **Atlantic Coastal Plain**. Long Island and Staten Island are located here. A second lowland area begins north of the Adirondacks, and follows along the northwest border with Canada. The St. Lawrence River, Lake Ontario and Lake Erie are located in this lowland area, known as the **St. Lawrence Lowlands**.

The other lowland areas are actually two corridors (*narrow passageways*) carved through the highlands. One corridor runs from the Great Lakes Plain east to the Hudson River, and is known as the **Mohawk Valley**. A **valley** is an area of lowlands between mountains and hills. The second corridor is a long valley running along the eastern side of New York State. It begins with the coastal plain in the southeastern part of the state and runs northward through the **Hudson Valley** into Lake Champlain. This narrow valley was formed in part by the movement of glaciers. The Mohawk Valley connects with the Hudson-Champlain Valley near Albany, forming the shape of a giant "T" resting on its side. [—|]

The Hudson River
What is New York State's other major river?

THE AMATEUR CARTOGRAPHER

On your map, label:

- Appalachian Plateau
- Catskill Mountains
- Taconic Mountains
- Adirondack Mountains
- Atlantic Coastal Plain
- Great Lakes Plain
- St. Lawrence Lowlands
- Mohawk Valley
- Hudson Valley

CLIMATE

We often hear people talk about the weather. **Weather** is a description of an area's day-to-day temperature, wind and amount of sunshine. A key factor that plays a role in an area's weather is its temperatures—how hot or cold it is. Weather also involves the amount of **precipitation**—the moisture that falls to Earth as rain, snow, hail and sleet. New York averages 32 to 54 inches of precipitation each year.

Climate is different from weather. **Climate** is the average of all of these weather conditions over a long period of years. Climate is affected by location, landforms and nearness to bodies of water.

New York State is located midway between the North Pole and the equator. Its climate varies from region to region. In general, most upstate areas have cold winters. Cities located in the "snowbelt"—Buffalo, Rochester and Syracuse—often receive heavy amounts of snowfall.

A sailboat gently floats along in the Erie Basin Marina with Buffalo City Hall in the background. *How might this Buffalo summer scene be different in winter?*

With an average of 108 inches of snow a year, Syracuse receives more snow than any other city in the state.

During the summer, temperatures are pleasant in the Catskills and Adirondack Mountains. On the other hand, summers in New York City and Long Island sometimes become unpleasantly hot and people travel to the beaches. Moisture from the ocean makes the air humid (*wet*) as well as warm. In winter, the same warm ocean currents usually prevent New York City from having heavy snow and extreme cold.

Temperatures vary in the state from north to south. In the north, at Lake Placid, the average winter temperature is about 15°F (–9°C). In summer it is 65°F (18°C). In the Albany area, in the central part of the state, the average winter temperature is about 23°F (–5°C), with an average summer temperature of about 72°F (22°C). In Setauket, on Long Island, the average winter temperature is 33°F (0.5° C). In summer, the average temperature is about 74°F (23°C).

THE AMATEUR CARTOGRAPHER

On your map, locate the cities in the snow belt. In addition, label the winter and summer temperatures for Lake Placid, Albany and Setauket.

HOW GOOD A CARTOGRAPHER ARE YOU?

How well did you do as an amateur cartographer? Compare your map with the one found on page 427. Then:

❖ Describe any similarities or differences you find.

❖ Write a brief description of each item on your map. Include these descriptions when you send your map to the friend who asked you about New York's geography.

REVIEWING YOUR UNDERSTANDING

Creating Vocabulary Cards

Weather

What does weather mean?

Give an example of weather:

Climate

What does climate mean?

What is the climate of your area?

GEOGRAPHY

Describing the Weather

In this activity, you learned about the difference between weather and climate.

- ❖ Describe today's weather.
- ❖ Using a thermometer, record today's temperature in Fahrenheit and Celsius.
- ❖ Record the temperatures in your area for at least 5 days. Then, create a graph showing those temperatures.

MAKING CONNECTIONS

EXPLORING BEYOND YOUR STATE
TAKING A FLIGHT ACROSS THE UNITED STATES

The United States is the fourth largest country in land area in the world. It stretches over 3,000 miles from the Atlantic Ocean to the Pacific Ocean. Besides the forty-eight states on the mainland, the United States includes Alaska, Hawaii, Puerto Rico and several smaller territories around the world. The United States has almost every imaginable climate and geographic feature—mighty mountains, thick forests, dry deserts, rolling plains, grassy prairies and icy Arctic glaciers. What would it be like to take an imaginary plane ride across the United States—flying west from New York City to San Francisco? Let's find out.

STARTING YOUR TRIP

You take off from New York City's Kennedy International Airport. As your plane leaves, you can see the windows of Manhattan's skyscrapers sparkling in the sunlight.

ATLANTIC COASTAL PLAIN, APPALACHIAN MOUNTAINS AND THE GREAT LAKES

As you fly west, you pass over the Atlantic Coastal Plain, with its suburbs, towns, farms and forests. As you continue west, you reach the hilly Piedmont and then the

The TWA Building at Kennedy International Airport in New York City

❖ CONTINUED

Appalachian Mountains. You fly along the southern edge of the Great Lakes which look like flat patches of blue. Soon you pass over the nation's third largest city, Chicago, on the shore of Lake Michigan.

PRAIRIES

Your plane turns southwest, and you pass over the prairies. These flat, grassy plains are some of the most productive farm lands in the world. It is here that vast quantities of wheat, corn, hay and livestock are raised. Next, you pass over the Mississippi River, one of the world's largest rivers. The Mississippi flows southwards over a 1,000 miles, emptying into the Gulf of Mexico at New Orleans.

THE GREAT PLAINS

Your plane turns westward again, and the land gradually becomes more hilly and much drier. Greens give way to yellows and browns. This is the area known as the Great Plains. Far fewer people live here. Towns are smaller and further apart. From your airplane window, roads look like thin threads, and there are few signs of traffic.

THE ROCKY MOUNTAINS

Eventually you see the Rocky Mountains, their peaks rising to 12,000 feet above sea level. They seem to reach up to you from the ground below. These mountains continue for many miles, till you reach a dry plateau known as the **Great Basin**. The ground looks dry and dusty—almost desert-like—with strange rock formations. Soon you pass over another mountain chain called the **Sierra Nevada**.

REACHING THE PACIFIC

Now you reach a large, green central valley with farms. Then there is another range of low, brownish hills. Finally, you see a narrow strip of coastal plain along the deep blue of the Pacific Ocean. The climate is sunny and warm. Below, a long, red bridge known as the Golden Gate Bridge arches over San Francisco Bay. Soon the plane lands in San Francisco, a hilly town famous for its cable cars, restaurants and many fine universities.

Today, you can fly across the mainland of the United States on a jet in only five hours. In 1869, a similar trip took about 2 weeks by

The Golden Gate Bridge, San Francisco

CONTINUED

train. Just 200 years ago, it is probable that no Native American living in what is today the United States ever saw both the Atlantic and Pacific Oceans in his or her lifetime. Even further back in time, it took Native American tribes hundreds of years to migrate to different parts of the United States.

COMPLETING A MAP

We hope that you have enjoyed your flight. Now that you have landed:

1. Complete a map of your trip across the United States. On your map, locate and mark each of the places mentioned on your imaginary trip.
2. What similarities do you see between New York State and the United States? What differences?

EXPLORING YOUR COMMUNITY
TAKING A HELICOPTER RIDE OVER YOUR COMMUNITY

Have you ever taken a ride in a helicopter? If not, here is your chance. Let's take an imaginary flight over the community where you live. Try to imagine what such a flight would be like once your helicopter lifted off the ground.

DESCRIBING A FLIGHT

❖ Describe where your imaginary helicopter ride would begin and where it might end.
❖ On your flight, describe each of the features of your community that you might see as the helicopter flies over it.
❖ We hope that you will enjoy your imaginary flight. Enjoy the ride, and don't forget to put your seatbelt on!

A helicopter view of Manhattan with Brooklyn in the distance
What sights could you spot from a helicopter in your community?

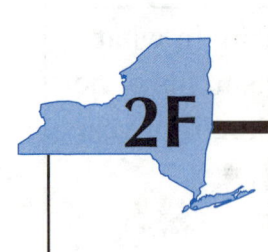

WHAT DO NEW YORK'S REGIONS "LOOK" LIKE?

2F

In this activity, you will learn to identify the seven major regions of New York State. Look for the following important words:

▶ Upstate/Downstate ▶ Plateau

Your friend was very happy with the map and written description you sent her to describe New York State. But she still wants more information. What are the main regions of the state? Where are the state's most important cities?

GEOGRAPHIC REGIONS OF NEW YORK STATE

Introduction

In this activity, you will read about the different regions in New York State—including their landforms and major cities. You will then be asked to use these descriptions to make a map of the region. To help you keep track of differences among the regions, make a copy of the following chart:

Geographic Region	Describe Its Approximate Location	Describe Its Main Physical Features	Identify Its Major Cities
St. Lawrence Lowlands	?	?	?
Adirondack Mountains	?	?	?
Great Lakes Plain	?	?	?
Hudson and Mohawk Valleys	?	?	?
Appalachian Plateau	?	?	?
New England Upland	?	?	?
Atlantic Coastal Plain	?	?	?

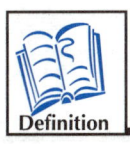

WHAT ARE REGIONS?

You already know from Activity 2B that a **region** is an area with similar geographic features. Places within a region are more like one another than they are like areas outside the region. New York is so large that it has several regions. Geographers sometimes disagree, however, about the best way to divide the state into regions.

The simplest way to divide New York State is into two regions—"upstate" and "downstate." But what do these terms mean? There is no single answer. Some people draw an imaginary line from Binghamton to Albany. They consider everything south and east of this line as **downstate**; land north and west is considered **upstate**.

Other people mark the dividing line at the northern border of Westchester County. They think of land north of this line as "upstate," while land south of it is "downstate." Throughout this book we will use this second definition of upstate/downstate.

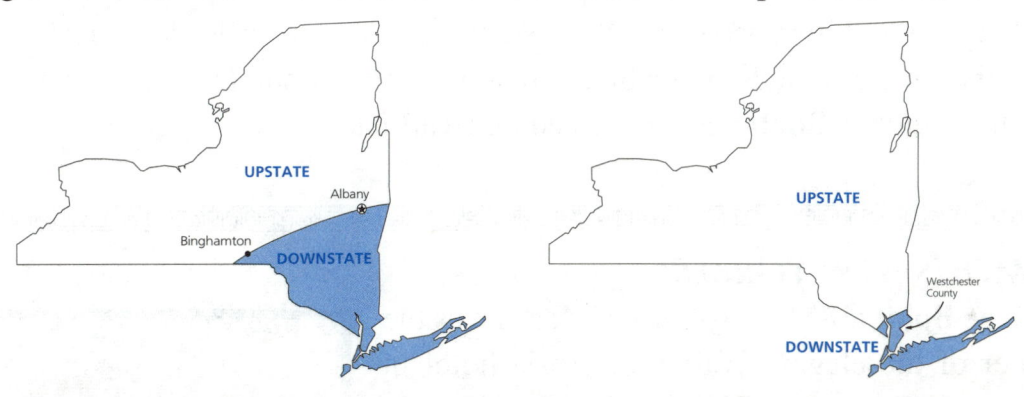

Most professional geographers divide New York State into more than two regions. Once again, there is no single list of regions that all geographers accept. In this book, you will learn about the major land regions of New York that most geographers agree to.

Think of New York as having seven major land regions. Moving from north to south and from west to east, the regions are: the St. Lawrence Lowlands, the Adirondack Mountain Region, the Great Lakes Plain, the Hudson and Mohawk Valleys, the Appalachian Plateau, the New England Upland and the Atlantic Coastal Plain.

THE AMATEUR CARTOGRAPHER

In the next few pages, you will read about the seven regions of New York. You will find a blank outline map for each region. Photocopy or trace the outline to make your own map. You will be asked to label cities, land forms and major bodies of water in each region. At the end of this activity, you will be asked to put all of these regional maps together to form a larger map of New York State.

ST. LAWRENCE LOWLANDS

The St. Lawrence Lowlands consist of the St. Lawrence River, Lake Champlain and the narrow plains extending from these bodies of water. The area is separated from the Adirondack Mountains by a hilly region known as the Tughill Plateau. Most of the St. Lawrence Lowlands is flat, rising no more than 300 feet above sea level. It is also narrow, less than 20 miles wide. The region is known for its dairy farms and fruit orchards.

Many dairy farms and fruit orchards are located throughout the St. Lawrence Lowlands.

The Thousand Islands are a group of more than 1,000 islands that stretch for 50 miles along the St. Lawrence River. Wellesley Island, twenty miles long, is the largest. Some of the smaller islands are no bigger than your classroom. One of the main attractions in the region is Boldt Castle, located on Heart Island.

FAMOUS NEW YORKERS

George Boldt (1851–1916) made a fortune as the owner of the elegant Waldorf-Astoria hotel in New York City and the Bellevue-Stratford hotel in Philadelphia. Soon after marrying, he decided to build a castle as a gift for his wife Louise. He selected Heart Island—one of the Thousand Islands. To show how much he loved his wife, he had the island reshaped in the form of a heart. In 1900, construction began on the $2.5 million, 120-room castle. Sadly, his wife died suddenly in 1904. A grieving George Boldt ordered all construction to stop immediately—even though only one more year was needed to complete the project. Soon the castle fell into disrepair. In 1977, the Thousand Islands Bridge Authority bought the property and began to restore the castle.

Boldt Castle, Thousand Islands
For whom was Boldt Castle originally built?

The largest city in the region is **Plattsburgh** (G3), located on Lake Champlain. The city is named after the owner of a large tract of land—Zephaniah Platt of Dutchess County. One of the major attractions in the city is the State University of New York at Plattsburgh.

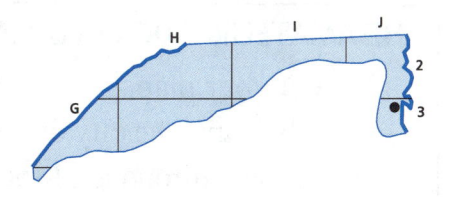

> **THE AMATEUR CARTOGRAPHER**
>
> On your map, give a title to the region and its major rivers. Also label the city of Plattsburgh and the Thousand Islands area.

ADIRONDACK MOUNTAIN REGION

Just south of the St. Lawrence Lowlands are the Adirondack Mountains. The Adirondack region covers almost 5,000 square miles and is circular in shape. Its landscape includes mountain peaks, forests, lakes, rushing streams and waterfalls. The region is favored by tourists who enjoy hiking or canoeing on many of its 2,000 lakes. Because of its cold winters, few people live in the Adirondacks all year round. **Mount Marcy** in the Adirondacks, rising 5,344 feet, is New York's highest mountain.

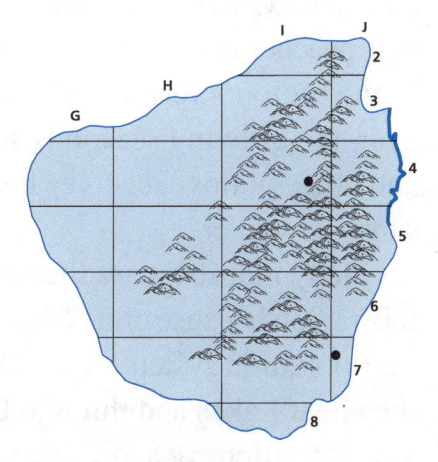

Poor soil makes the Adirondacks unsuitable for farming. The many forests in the region have led to the growth of a local lumber industry. Lead, iron and zinc mining are other industries in the area. Since 1892, development has been limited because most of the Adirondacks has been preserved as one of the nation's largest parks.

Lake Placid (I4) is one of the Adirondack's most beautiful lakes. It was the site of the 1932 and 1980 Winter Olympic Games. **Lake George** (J7) is a popular summer destination for tourists. **Fort Ticonderoga**, also in the area, was built by the French in 1755 to control the area where Lake George drains into Lake Champlain. Today, the fort is a major tourist attraction. Another popular tourist site is **Ausable Chasm**, a gorge (*narrow canyon*) carved out by the Ausable River.

Lake Placid is one of the Adirondacks' most popular tourist attractions.

THE AMATEUR CARTOGRAPHER

On your map, give a title to the region and label its major rivers and lakes. Also label the city of Lake Placid. Use your own symbol to mark the location of the Adirondack Mountains. See if you can find and label Mount Marcy.

GREAT LAKES PLAIN

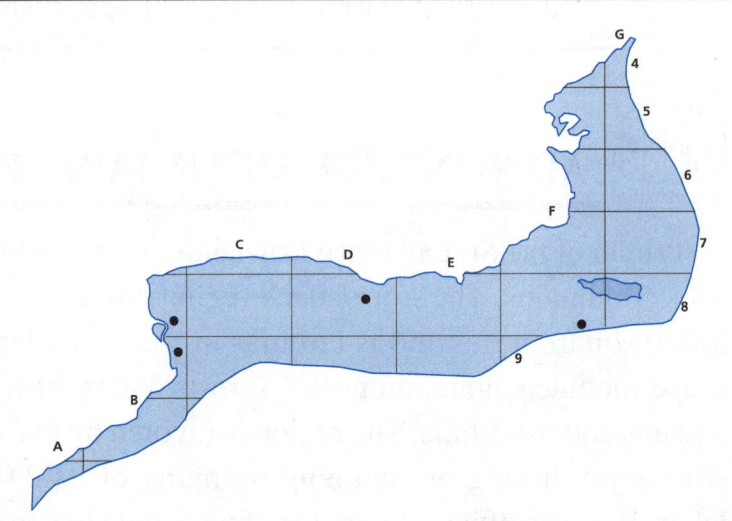

The **Great Lakes Plain** is a lowland area located in the northwestern part of the state. This region runs along the shores of Lake Erie and Lake Ontario. Apples, cherries, peaches and grapes grow well in the region's fertile soil. However, the growing season is short and the plains receive heavy snows in winter.

Many industries are located in this region because of its excellent transportation system. After 1825, farmers from the Midwest could ship their goods on the Great Lakes and through Buffalo to the Erie Canal. In addition, Niagara Falls provides electricity at a low price. Three of New York State's largest urban areas are located on the Great Lakes Plain—Buffalo, Rochester and Syracuse.

Buffalo (B9), located on the eastern shore of Lake Erie, is the state's second largest city. The city has become an important center for professional sports. Visitors can also enjoy nearby **Niagara Falls** (B8). The Albright-Knox Gallery, Buffalo Zoological Gardens, Beaver Island State Park and the Peace Bridge are some of its other attractions.

Rochester (D8), the state's third largest city, is located south of Lake Ontario. Many people link the city with it biggest company, Eastman Kodak. This company makes cameras, film and other photographic equipment. The city's cultural institutions include the University of Rochester, the Rochester Institute of Technology, the Eastman School of Music and the Museum of Arts and Sciences.

The Rochester skyline
Rochester has many important businesses. Can you name one?

Just at the southern border of this region is **Syracuse** (F10), located near a salt spring. Syracuse first became an important city after the building of the Erie Canal. Today, Syracuse is the fifth largest city in New York State. It boasts the Everson Museum of Art, the Salt Museum and Syracuse University.

> ### THE AMATEUR CARTOGRAPHER
> On your map, give a title to the region and label the cities of Buffalo, Niagara Falls, Rochester and Syracuse.

APPALACHIAN PLATEAU

The Appalachian (or Allegheny) Plateau region occupies most of southwestern New York. Sometimes it is called the "Southern Tier." It is located south of the Great Lakes Plain and southwest of the Hudson and Mohawk Valleys. Of all of New York's geographic regions, this is the largest.

A **plateau** is an area of land that is higher than the regions around it. In fact, the Appalachian Plateau has many different land features, including the **Catskill Mountains** (H10) and the **Finger Lakes**. (E 9+10). The Catskills are located in the eastern part of the region. They are part of the Appalachian Mountain chain. Some of the Catskill Mountains reach heights of 4,000 feet. The Finger Lakes are located northwest of the Catskills. West of the Finger Lakes are rolling hills.

Farming is important in the Appalachian Plateau. The best farm land in the region is in the Finger Lakes area. Because of its fertile soil, this area is known for its vineyards (*where grapes are grown*) and nurseries.

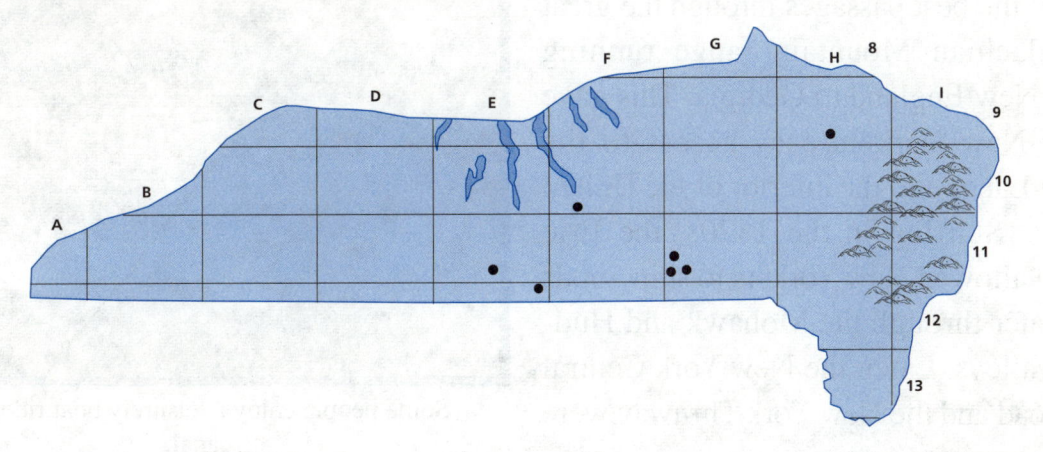

Located in the Appalachian Plateau is the tri-city region of **Binghamton** (G11), **Endicott** and **Johnson City**. These cities have the Roberson Memorial Center, Chenango Valley State Park and one of the nation's oldest zoos, Ross Park Zoo. The State

72 NEW YORK: ITS LAND AND ITS PEOPLE

University of New York at Binghamton is also located in this area. **Corning** (E11) has given its name to one of the world's most famous brands of glassware. Today, Corning has a museum highlighting the long history of glass-making in the world. Visitors can watch glass-blowers and glass-cutters at work in the Corning glass factory.

Ithaca (F10) is on the southern shore of Lake Cayuga, in the scenic area of the Finger Lakes. Cornell University and the Rensselaer Art Gallery are located near Ithaca. One of America's greatest writers, Mark Twain, is buried at the Woodlawn Cemetery in **Elmira** (E12). Twain wrote the well-known adventure tale *Tom Sawyer* while living in Elmira. On the eastern end of the Appalachian plateau lies **Cooperstown** (H9), one of the state's most popular tourist attractions. The town is home to the Farmer's Museum and the Baseball Hall of Fame.

The Corning Glass Works Museum helped put Corning on the map. Tourists visit the museum to see its many glass objects.

THE AMATEUR CARTOGRAPHER

On your map, give a title to the region and label the Finger Lakes and the Catskill Mountains. Also label the cities of Binghamton, Endicott, Johnson City, Corning, Ithaca, Elmira and Cooperstown.

THE HUDSON AND MOHAWK VALLEYS

The Hudson and Mohawk Valleys provide one of the best passages through the great Appalachian Mountain range running from New England to Georgia. This gave early New Yorkers easy access to the Great Lakes and the interior of the United States. Starting in the 1820s, the Erie Canal allowed New Yorkers to ship goods by water through the Mohawk and Hudson Valleys. Later, the New York Central Railroad and the New York Thruway were built along the same route.

Some people enjoy a leisurely boat ride on a canal.

The fertile soil on the banks of the Mohawk and Hudson Rivers makes these areas ideal for fruit orchards, dairy farms and other farms. Some of America's best apples and grapes come from this region. Waterfalls on the Mohawk and Hudson rivers provide a source of energy. These falls once powered early factory machines. Today, they provide power for making electricity.

THE HUDSON VALLEY

The Hudson River was named after the Dutch explorer Henry Hudson. The valley along the banks of the Hudson is only about 30 miles wide. It cuts through ridges sometimes over a thousand feet high. Many important cities developed in the valley, including Albany, Schenectady, Kingston and Poughkeepsie. In the south, the Hudson River meets the Atlantic Ocean at New York City.

Schenectady along the Mohawk River in 1830
What other major cities in New York are located along the Mohawk River?

Albany (J9) is one of the oldest cities in the United States and the state's sixth most populated city. In 1789, Albany became the capital of New York State. This means it is where the state's government is located. Albany's neighbor to the northwest is **Schenectady** (I9). The city is home to the General Electric Company. The Schenectady Museum, Jackson Botanical Garden and Union College are also located in Schenectady.

Another important city in the Hudson River valley is **Kingston** (I12). Kingston can be thought of as a city of firsts. It was the first capital of New York State. The first meeting of the New York State Senate also took place in Kingston. **Poughkeepsie** (J13) has many beautiful areas made up of lakes and small villages. It is the location of Vassar College, one of the best-known women's colleges in the nation. **Hyde Park** (J12) near Poughkeepsie, was once home to President Franklin D. Roosevelt. Today, it is a public park where visitors can see mementoes of Roosevelt's life and times.

The 11 marble and glass buildings of the Empire State Plaza dominate the Albany skyline.

THE MOHAWK VALLEY

The Mohawk River is an important **tributary** (*river branch*) flowing into the Hudson River. The river was named after an Iroquois tribe that lived in the area. Starting in upstate New York, the Mohawk Valley runs eastward. Because of its geographical location between the Appalachian and Adirondack Mountains, early pioneers used this valley as a route through to the interior of the American continent. In addition, the Mohawk Valley was an ideal location in which to build a canal that would connect the

74   NEW YORK: ITS LAND AND ITS PEOPLE

Great Lakes to the Hudson River. New York's first factories opened along the banks of the Mohawk in the early 1800s. Many factories once made carpets and fabric for clothes here. During the 1970s and 1980s, many industries in this region closed down. Despite this, the Mohawk Valley continues to be a major center of population in New York State.

Utica (H8) is located in the Mohawk Valley, at a spot where several Native American trails once met. The city was built on the site of Fort Schuyler. Many industries around Utica contribute to the economic health of the city. The Children's Museum, with its many "hands-on" displays, and the Italian Cultural Center are some of the city's attractions.

The city of Saratoga Springs (J8) was the scene of a famous battle during the American Revolution. Today, it is famous as a health spa and for its horse racing. Saratoga became a gathering place for wealthy New Yorkers in the early 1800s. They went to improve their health by bathing in Saratoga's spring waters. In 1863, the racetrack was built to entertain those who came to use the springs.

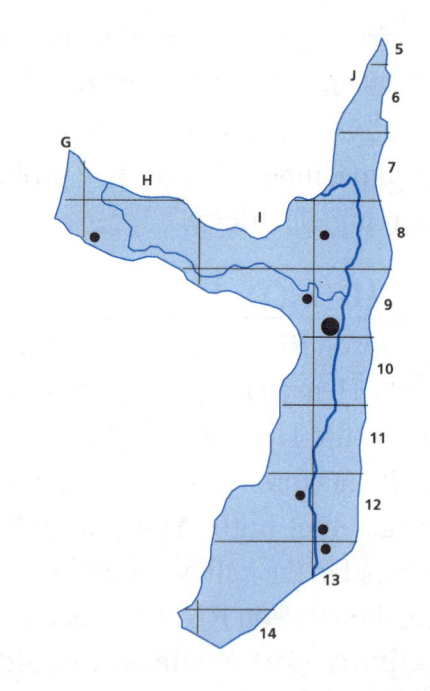

The racetrack attracts thousands of visitors to Saratoga each summer.

THE AMATEUR CARTOGRAPHER

On your map, give a title to the region and its major rivers. Also label the cities of Utica, Saratoga Springs, Albany, Schenectady, Kingston, Poughkeepsie and Hyde Park.

NEW ENGLAND UPLAND

This is an area of low mountains and rolling hills, found along New York's eastern border. It runs from the northern border of New York City to about halfway up the state. The New England Upland includes the Taconic Mountains and the southern part of the Hudson River Valley. Some of New York City's northern suburbs, such as Westchester, are considered to be a part of this region.

Close to where the Hudson River meets the New England Upland lies **West Point** (I14). West Point is the home of the United States Military Academy, where many U.S. Army officers have received their training.

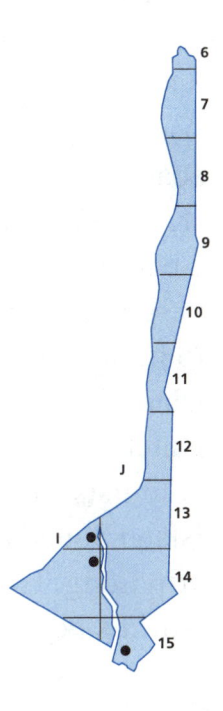

Yonkers (J15) is the fourth largest city in New York. It lies just north of New York City. One of its most noted attractions is the Hudson River Museum of Westchester. This museum focuses on the area's natural, social and cultural history. During part of the American Revolution, **Newburgh** (I13) was the site of George Washington's headquarters. Now a museum, the building that served as his headquarters was the very first historic house ever bought by a state.

Generals Grant, Lee, Pershing, MacArthur and Eisenhower all graduated from West Point.

THE AMATEUR CARTOGRAPHER

On your map, give a title to the region and label the Hudson River. Also label West Point and the cities of Yonkers and Newburgh.

ATLANTIC COASTAL PLAIN

This region is part of a wide, flat plain that runs along the eastern coast of the United States from Massachusetts to the southern tip of Florida. In New York State, the Atlantic Coastal Plain includes Long Island and Staten Island (*a part of New York City*). Some geographers place Manhattan and the Bronx in the New England Upland. However, in this book, all of New York City will be considered part of the Atlantic Coastal Plain.

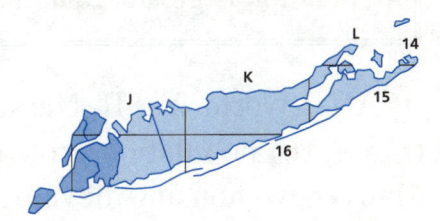

LONG ISLAND

Islands are pieces of land surrounded by water on all sides. Long Island is located at the southern end of New York State. It extends 120 miles out into the Atlantic Ocean. Some people think the island is shaped like a giant fish. The fish's head is near New York City and its two fins are at its eastern end.

76   NEW YORK: ITS LAND AND ITS PEOPLE

There are also special types of islands. One type is known as a **barrier island**. It is an island created by waves pushing sand up to form pieces of land that rise above the ocean surface. Barrier islands protect coastlines from erosion by ocean waves. **Fire Island**, (K16) off the coast of Long Island, is an example of a barrier island.

Long Island was one of the first parts of the state to be settled by Europeans. The western end of the island (*now part of New York City*) was settled by the Dutch in the early 1600s. Soon afterwards, English colonists from Connecticut rowed across Long Island Sound and established the first towns on eastern Long Island. Long Island has some of the world's best beaches, making it a favorite summer vacation spot. Fishing and farming have been important ways of earning a living on the island since the 1600s.

Montauk Lighthouse on Long Island marks the easternmost point of New York State. Commissioned by President George Washington in 1795, it was completed the following year.

A NOTE ABOUT LONG ISLAND

Although Brooklyn and Queens are geographically part of Long Island, these two areas joined Staten Island, the Bronx and Manhattan to form New York City. Ever since, when people speak of "Long Island" they are usually referring to only the two eastern counties—Nassau and Suffolk. These two counties are **not** part of New York City. With over two and a half million people living in Nassau and Suffolk, their population is greater than that of 16 states.

After World War II, **Nassau County's** (J15 + 16) population grew a great deal. Many new housing developments were built and people moved from New York City to the county's many towns and villages. There are many popular vacation and recreation spots in Nassau County. **Jones Beach** is one of the area's most beautiful beaches. Nassau's scenery, landmarks and museums attract millions of visitors each year. Some attractions that visitors particu-

President Theodore Roosevelt delivers a speech at his home at Sagamore Hill on Long Island.

larly enjoy are Sagamore Hill, which was once President Theodore Roosevelt's home in Oyster Bay, and Old Westbury Gardens.

Suffolk County (K15 + L15) gets more sunshine than any other county in the state. Many New England farmers and fishermen first settled in Suffolk in the mid-1600s. Towns such as Huntington and Montauk still have homes dating back to this period. The pirate Captain Kidd came to Suffolk in 1690. Some believe that Kidd buried his treasure somewhere on Long Island, but the treasure has never been found. The Hamptons, on the eastern end of Long Island, attract many tourists during the summer. Suffolk County grows more food, in dollar amounts, than any other county in the state.

NEW YORK CITY

New York City is the nation's largest city. Many consider it to be the greatest city in the world. New York City is an entertainment, financial and cultural center. People from all over the world go to visit and live there. The city itself is made up of five "boroughs" (*areas*): the Bronx, Brooklyn, Manhattan, Queens and Staten Island.

The **Bronx** (J15) is New York City's most northern borough. Fordham University and Lehman College are located here. It contains the Bronx Zoo, home to more than 3,600 different kinds of animals. The New York Yankees are also based in the Bronx, playing at Yankee Stadium.

Brooklyn (J16) is the westernmost point of Long Island. It is the most heavily populated of the boroughs. Many of its neighborhoods are closely identified with particular ethnic groups. Visitors to Brooklyn enjoy seeing the Brooklyn Bridge, Brooklyn Museum, Prospect Park and the Brooklyn Botanical Gardens. At the southern tip of Brooklyn is Coney Island, known for its beaches, amusement rides and boardwalk.

The llama ride at the Bronx Zoo
What zoos have you visited?

The Brooklyn Bridge connected Brooklyn with Manhattan. The drawing on the left shows the bridge when it opened. The photo on the right was taken 100 years later.
What differences do you notice between these pictures?

Manhattan (I16) is the oldest part of New York City and still the center of city life. Manhattan contains the city's major businesses and places of entertainment. Millions of people visit Manhattan to see Radio City Music Hall, the New York Stock Exchange, the Empire State Building, Madison Square Garden and the United Nations. Central Park is located in Manhattan, as well as world-class museums like the Metropolitan Museum of Art and the American Museum of Natural History.

Radio City Music Hall

New York Stock Exchange

Queens (J16) is the largest borough in terms of area. It is the home of many different ethnic groups. Among its more recent arrivals are Dominicans, Koreans, Colombians, Jamaicans and Chinese. A visitor to Queens today can see New York's two great airports, La Guardia and Kennedy International. Shea Stadium, where the New York Mets play baseball, was built in Queens for the 1964 World's Fair.

In many ways **Staten Island** (I16) is different from the other four boroughs. It has fewer people than any other borough. Many people think of Staten Island as a group of small towns rather than as part of a large city. Before the Verrazano-Narrows Bridge was built in 1964, the only direct way to get from Staten Island to any of the other boroughs was by ferry.

THE AMATEUR CARTOGRAPHER

On your map, give a title to the region and label its major rivers. Also label the two counties of Long Island and the five boroughs of New York City.

YOUR FINAL TASK

When you read about each region in New York, you completed a map for that region. Now cut out and combine all seven maps. Fit your seven regions together to form a single map of New York State. Compare your map to the map of New York State that appears on page 427. Are these two maps similar? If not, make corrections on your map.

GEOGRAPHY

REVIEWING YOUR UNDERSTANDING

Creating Vocabulary Cards

Plateau
Define the term:
The Appalachian Plateau occupies most of which portion of New York State?

Upstate/Downstate
Describe the area most often referred to as "upstate" New York:
Describe the area often referred to as "downstate" New York:

Finding Out More About New York State

There are many interesting places in New York State besides those listed in this activity. Look up the following places in a travel guide, encyclopedia or atlas. Then add them to your map. Provide a brief description on a separate sheet of paper.

- Fort Ticonderoga
- Oyster Bay
- New Paltz
- Monticello
- Cold Spring Harbor
- Stony Brook
- Lake George
- Howe Caverns
- Seneca Falls
- James Town

People wait to take a boat ride in Howe Caverns, a geological wonder 160–200 feet below ground.

Looking at Your Town or City

The town that you live in is part of one of the regions that you just read about. Let's learn more about your town or city:

- Name a region that your town or city is a part of.
- On a map, highlight this region.
- On that map, mark the location of your town or city.
- Name some of the other cities, towns or communities located in your county.

MAKING CONNECTIONS

EXPLORING BEYOND YOUR STATE
CULTURAL REGIONS OF THE WORLD

In this activity you looked at New York State's different physical regions. However, areas can also be divided into regions based on cultural differences. **Culture** refers to a way of life shared by a group of people. You might think of culture as the ABCs of human society: **a**ttitudes, **b**usiness, **c**ustoms, **d**ress, **e**xpressions, **f**ood, **g**overnment, **h**ousing, **i**ndustry, (how many more can you add?).

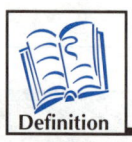

WHAT ARE CULTURAL REGIONS?

Cultural regions are areas in which people share common cultural characteristics, such as language, history, or religious beliefs. A cultural region can be small—like the Shaker religious community near Albany. It can also be large—like **Latin America** (*Mexico, the Caribbean area, and the countries of Central and South America*). Several features make Latin America a cultural region. The majority of its people follow the Catholic religion. The major languages spoken are Spanish and Portuguese. Finally, the peoples of Latin America communicate more with one another than they do with peoples from countries outside this region.

Cultural regions can be identified by various characteristics. The map shows one way that many geographers have divided the world into its major cultural regions.

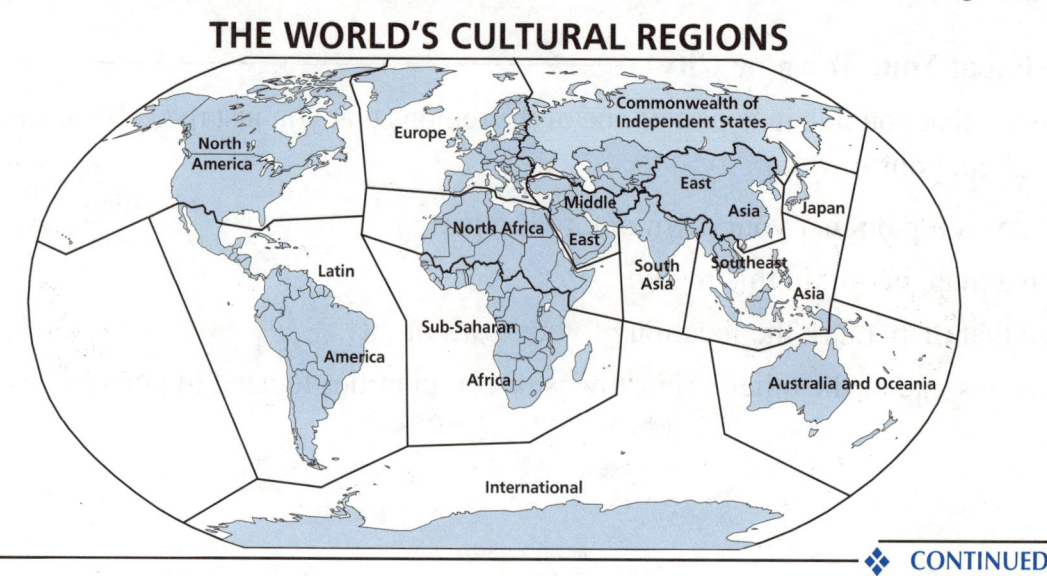

THE WORLD'S CULTURAL REGIONS

◆ CONTINUED

LISTING CULTURAL FEATURES

In a cultural region people share some common cultural characteristics. Your own community can be thought of as a cultural region. What cultural characteristics do people in your neighborhood share?

EXPLORING YOUR COMMUNITY
DRAWING OR WRITING ABOUT WHERE YOU LIVE

A group of New York artists began to settle in the Hudson Valley in the 1820s. These artists were united by their love for painting scenes of nature. Their canvasses reflected outdoor landscapes, mountain-top thunderstorms and powerful waterfalls. These talented artists used their paint brushes to draw the area where they were living. They painted so many pictures of the area that they became known as the **Hudson River School**.

This painting by A.B. Durand is typical of the Hudson River School of painting.

Painting is not the only way to describe where you live. Another method is to use words to "paint" a picture. Maybe that is what Henry Hudson had in mind when he wrote, "nowhere have I ever beheld such a rich and pleasant land" to describe the Hudson Valley.

MAKING A PICTURE

What is your community like? Explore the area where you live. Then either draw, photograph or paint a scene that shows a beautiful or interesting sight in your community. Finally, write a description of this sight.

2G WHERE WOULD YOU LOCATE YOUR BASKETBALL TEAM?

In this activity, you will apply your knowledge of geography to a specific purpose: choosing the best city for a new women's basketball team. Look for the following important words:

- ▶ Population Density
- ▶ Per Capita Income
- ▶ Almanac
- ▶ Table

Wow! It is hard to believe your good fortune over the last two weeks. First, you won over $100 million in the New York State Lotto. Then you successfully bid on buying a new women's basketball team. All your life you have been a basketball fan, and at last your dream has come true. You are now the proud owner of a team. There is just one problem. You must find a city in New York State in which to locate your new team.

THINK ABOUT IT

1. In which city would you locate your basketball team?
2. Why would you want to locate the team in that city?

CHOOSING A CITY FOR A BASKETBALL TEAM

You decide to hire a panel of experts to help you with this important decision. They tell you that the location of your basketball team requires a lot of thought and investigation. The final decision depends on many factors. For one thing, you cannot choose New York City or Albany, since they have already been selected by someone else. Your experts have narrowed the list of cities in New York State that you can choose from to the following:

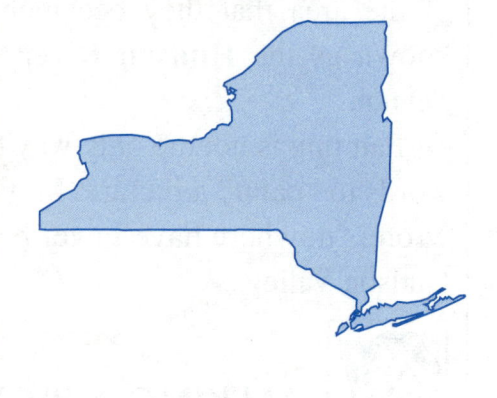

- ❖ Buffalo
- ❖ Rochester
- ❖ Yonkers

Make a copy of the map above. Then, using an atlas, mark the location of each of these cities. This will allow you to see where each city is located and help in your decison.

LOOKING AT SOME DEMOGRAPHIC FACTORS

As the owner of a women's basketball team, you will need fans to attend games to help make a profit. Your experts now tell you there are **demographic** (*having to do with population*), economic and cultural factors to think about. These include:

- **Population.** The city should have a population large enough to support a team.
- **Population Density** is the average number of people living in an area. To find the population density of a city, divide the number of people living in it by the size of the city's land area. For example, assume a city has a population of 6,000 people. The area of the city is 30 square miles. To find the city's population density use a calculator to divide the population by the number of square miles:

$$\frac{6,000}{30} = 200 \quad \left\{ \begin{array}{l} \text{The city has a population density} \\ \text{of about 200 people per square mile.} \end{array} \right.$$

- **Unemployment.** The city should have a low unemployment rate. This means that most people are working and can afford to attend some games or to buy products from advertisers who sponsor the games.
- **Per Capita Income** is the average amount of money each person earns. The city should have many people who earn a reasonable income to spend on advertisers' products or on activities like attending a basketball game.
- **Tourist Attractions.** The city should have interesting tourist attractions. This will encourage people in surrounding areas to visit the city. While they are visiting, they may want to attend a basketball game.

You ask your experts, "Where can I find that kind of information about each city?" They tell you that this information is available in most almanacs. An **almanac** is an important reference book.

Eastman House is a popular tourist attraction in Rochester. The founder of Eastman Kodak once lived here. Today, it is a museum.

84   NEW YORK: ITS LAND AND ITS PEOPLE

ALMANAC

An almanac is a book of facts. A new edition is published every year, so it is always up-to-date. An almanac covers a wide range of subjects—such as art, astronomy, business, countries of the world, education, entertainment, farming, geography, history and religion. Almanacs also contain lists of movie stars, explorers, musicians, writers, Nobel prize winners and athletes.

A variety of information can be found in an almanac. For example, you can find out which team won the football Super Bowl last year, or which city in New York State has the largest population. Although there are many different almanacs, two of the best known are:

- *The World Almanac and Book of Facts*
- *The Information Please Almanac*

Skill Builder
HOW TO FIND INFORMATION IN AN ALMANAC

Almanacs are easy to use. The key is knowing how to use the almanac and where to look. To locate the information you need, use the following steps:

❖ Get a copy of *The World Almanac and Book of Facts*.

❖ Open to the **index** in the almanac. The index of a book is a way for a reader to find specific information. While a table of contents gives a reader a general idea of what is in the book, an index helps a reader to find specific things, by giving the page number where the information is located.

Cities, U.S.	**686–95**
Area codes, telephone	396–426
Buildings, tall	696–702
Climatological data	180–84, 185
Consumer price indexes	113
Farthest east, north, south, west	540
Housing prices	727
Unemployment benefits	142

❖ Look for the listing "Cities, U.S." by turning to the page shown in your almanac.

❖ CONTINUED

Much of the information found in almanacs is presented in table form. If you are unsure about how to read or use a table, the following will help you.

INTERPRETING INFORMATION IN A TABLE

A **table** is an arrangement of words or numbers in columns. It is used for organizing large amounts of information so facts can be easily located and compared. The table shows different categories of information. These categories are named in the headings found across the top of the chart. The table below shows the population of New York State compared to the U.S. population from 1850 to 1990. The dates are listed down the left-hand side. You can find a year's population by looking down the column and then across the row.

New York's Population in Comparison to the U.S. Population

Years	N.Y. Population	U.S. Population	NY's Population*
1850	3,097,394	23,191,876	13%
1870	4,382,759	39,818,449	11%
1890	6,003,194	62,947,714	9.5%
1910	9,113,614	91,972,266	10%
1930	12,588,066	122,775,045	10%
1950	14,830,192	150,697,361	10%
1970	18,241,391	203,302,031	9%
1990	17,990,455	248,709,873	7%

*As a percentage of the U.S. Population

✔ Checking Your Understanding ✔

- In what year did New York first show a population of more than 10,000,000?
- In what year did the U.S. population reach 200 million?
- In which 20-year period did New York's population increase the most?

There are other sources of information besides almanacs. Some of the information you need may also be found by looking in:

- an encyclopedia. Look under New York State.
- *I Love New York Travel Guide*. The New York State Department of Economic Development, Bureau of Media Services, provides this free travel guide. The guides are available at tourist information centers and libraries or by calling 1-800-CALL NYS (225-5697)
- the tourism agencies of many cities in New York State. You can find their addresses and telephone numbers by looking in your local phone book.

86   NEW YORK: ITS LAND AND ITS PEOPLE

USING AN ALMANAC

While gathering your information, you should fill in the following table to keep track of the data you find.

	BUFFALO	ROCHESTER	YONKERS
Population	?	?	?
Population Density	?	?	?
Rate of Unemployment	?	?	?
Per Capita Income	?	?	?
Major Tourist Attractions	?	?	?

MAKING A DECISION

YOUR DECISION

After you have done your research and completed the table, you should **compare and contrast** the information you have recorded. To do this, you need to weigh one piece of information against another. There is no single correct answer. Each city will have its own advantages and disadvantages. After you have considered all the information:

❖ In which city would you locate your women's basketball team?
❖ Explain some of the factors that helped you reach your decision.
❖ Is this city different from the city you chose at the start of this activity? If so, what factors made you change your mind?

❖ In addition to a name, each team needs its own **logo**—a team symbol that will appear on its members' shirts. For example, Buffalo's football team uses a charging buffalo as its team's symbol. Make a copy of the basketball shirt to the right. On your copy, design your team's new logo. Explain why you chose your particular design. In addition, what two colors would you choose to be your team colors?

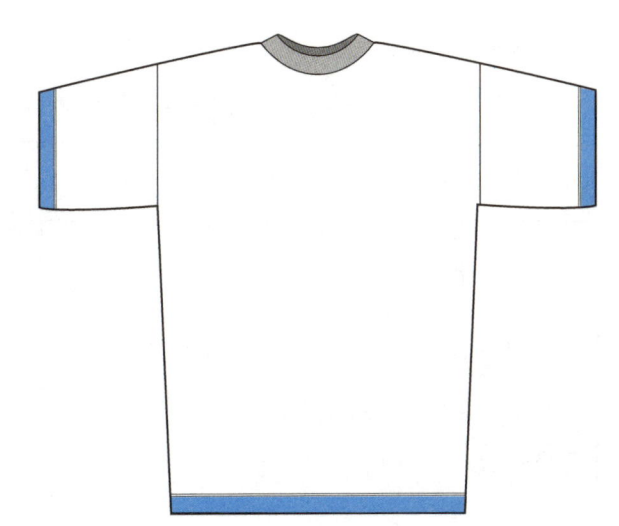

CLASS DECISION

After you have made your decision, compare it to the choices of your classmates. Students who have chosen the same city should organize themselves into a group. Then students in that group should make an oral presentation to the class. The presentation should focus on their reasons for selecting that city. Each group should have an opportunity to defend its choice. Finally, the class should vote which city it thinks is best for locating the basketball team.

FAMOUS NEW YORKERS

Jackie Robinson (1919–1972) was the first African American to play major league baseball. Before Robinson, there was an unwritten rule that excluded African Americans from playing in the major leagues. Robinson's success with the Brooklyn Dodgers from 1947 to 1956 encouraged the end of color barriers in baseball and other sports. In his early years, Robinson faced much abuse—beanballs aimed at his head, jeers, insults, hate mail and even death threats. Despite this, he kept calm and refused to fight back. His courage soon won admiration from other players, sportswriters and fans around the nation. At his funeral, the Reverend Jesse Jackson's comments summed up the feelings of many Americans: "When Jackie took the field, something reminded us of our birthright to be free."

Jackie Robinson
Why did his playing baseball for the Brooklyn Dodgers make news?

REVIEWING YOUR UNDERSTANDING

Creating Vocabulary Cards

Population Density

Define population density:

Why might a city's population density be important to a business?

Per Capita Income

Define per capita income:

Why might a city's per capita income be important to a business?

Separating Relevant from Irrelevant Information

An important Social Studies skill is the ability to tell the difference between relevant and irrelevant information.

❖ **Relevant information** is information connected to your topic. Relevant information is useful and appropriate and has some connection with what you are looking for.

❖ **Irrelevant information** is information not related or connected to your topic. It is either not useful for solving the problem you are working on, or it has no connection with what you want to know.

How well do you understand the difference between relevant and irrelevant information? Imagine you wanted to identify the name of a state from the following information. You will need to decide which clues would be relevant and which would be irrelevant.

A. **This state borders New York State.** This information is relevant. It narrows your search from 50 states to the five states that border New York—(1) Vermont, (2) Massachusetts, (3) Connecticut, (4) New Jersey and (5) Pennsylvania.

B. **This state has a governor.** This information is true, but irrelevant. Since every U.S. state has a governor, the information is not helpful.

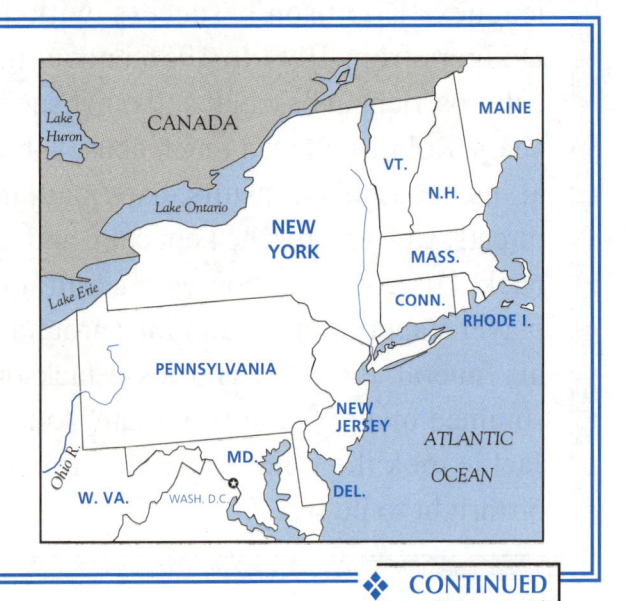

❖ CONTINUED

C. **This state has a major league baseball team.** This information is relevant. Only two of the five states bordering New York State have major league baseball teams—the Pittsburgh Pirates and the Philadelphia Phillies in Pennsylvania and the Boston Red Sox in Massachusetts. This piece of information further narrows your search to Pennsylvania and Massachusetts.

D. **This state has a state flag.** This information is also true, but irrelevant. Every state has its own flag. This clue does not help you identify the state in question.

E. **This state borders Lake Erie.** This final clue is relevant. It eliminates Massachusetts, which does not border Lake Erie. Pennsylvania, however, does border Lake Erie. Therefore, the answer is Pennsylvania.

Now that you understand the difference between relevant and irrelevant information, let's put your knowledge to the test. Use the information in the following box to identify the mystery city referred to by the clues.

IDENTIFY THE MYSTERY CITY:
1. This city is located in New York State.
2. This city is located in the Hudson and Mohawk Valleys.
3. This city is part of upstate New York
4. This city is home to a well-known university.
5. People in this city often celebrate weddings with large parties.
6. The Erie Canal once passed through this city.
7. The area's salt deposits first made this city economically successful.

✔ CHECKING YOUR UNDERSTANDING ✔
1. Was clue #1 relevant? If so, why?
2. Was clue #2 relevant? If so, why?
3. Was clue #3 relevant? If so, why?
4. Was clue #4 relevant? If so, why?
5. Was clue #5 relevant? If so, why?
6. Was clue #6 relevant? If so, why?
7. Was clue #7 relevant? If so, why?
8. What is the name of the mystery city?

MAKING CONNECTIONS

EXPLORING BEYOND YOUR STATE
THE IMPORTANCE OF LIVING NEAR WATER

In this activity you tried to select the best location for a women's basketball team. Your decision was made, in part, by finding a place that would be attractive to both team members and their fans.

WHY PEOPLE SETTLE NEAR WATER

One thing that Buffalo, Rochester and Yonkers have in common is that they are all located near important lakes or rivers. The same is true for many major cities in the United States. If you look at a map of the United States you will see that cities such as New Orleans, Boston and Los Angeles are near major bodies of water. People enjoy living close to water. Rivers and lakes provide water for drinking and fish to eat. Water is also important as a means of transportation and for irrigating crops.

Skyline of Syracuse
Is Syracuse located near a body of water?

USING A MAP

Do New Yorkers also like to live near water? To find out, let's examine where most New Yorkers live. Below is a list of the state's 10 most populated cities.

(1) New York City   (5) Syracuse   (8) New Rochelle
(2) Buffalo   (6) Albany   (9) Mount Vernon
(3) Rochester   (7) Utica   (10) Schenectady
(4) Yonkers

❖ CONTINUED

Make a copy of the outline map to the right. Then use an atlas to help you mark and label the location on the map of each of the 10 most populated cities in New York State. Draw a line connecting the cities.

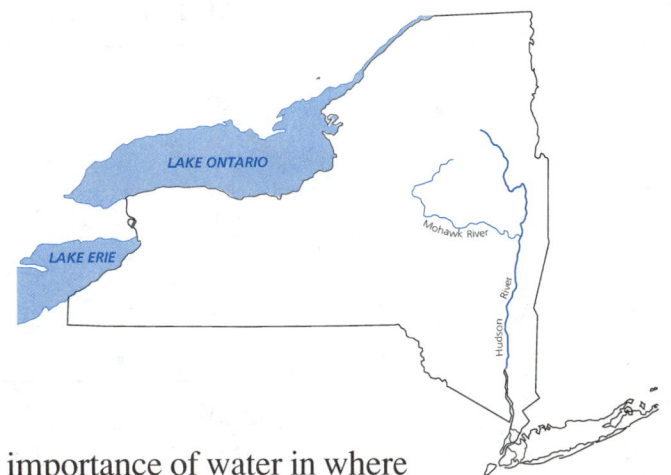

1. What geographical factors do you think influenced people to live along this line?
2. Does this show the continuing importance of water in where people live? Explain your answer.

FAMOUS NEW YORKERS

George W. Goethals (1888–928). Water is important in determining where people live and how they travel. George Goethals was to make an important contribution to water travel. In the 1800s, the United States needed a canal to eliminate the need for ships to sail around South America. In 1907, President Theodore Roosevelt named Brooklyn born Colonel Goethals of the Army Engineers to construct the Panama Canal. From 1904 to 1914, some 30,000 workers drilled, blasted, dug and dredged in building the Panama Canal. The canal opened in 1916. Goethals was made first governor of the Canal Zone.

George Goethals

EXPLORING YOUR COMMUNITY
READING MILEAGE CHARTS

Charts can be used to show a variety of interesting and useful information.

Skill Builder

INTERPRETING A MILEAGE CHART

The mileage chart on page 92 shows the average distances from one city to another when traveling on commonly used roadways.

❖ CONTINUED

MILEAGE CHART

	Albany	Binghamton	Boston, MA.	Buffalo	Montreal, Canada	New York City	Philadelphia, PA.	Rochester	Syracuse
Albany	•	128	160	281	235	156	230	217	135
Binghamton	128	•	300	216	332	175	182	152	70
Boston, MA.	160	300	•	456	318	207	310	391	312
Buffalo	281	216	456	•	390	418	385	70	144
Montreal, Canada	235	332	318	390	•	380	458	313	256
New York City	156	175	207	418	380	•	110	354	272
Philadelphia, PA.	230	182	310	385	458	110	•	347	257
Rochester	217	152	391	70	313	354	347	•	82
Syracuse	135	70	312	144	256	272	257	82	•

To find the distance from Binghamton to New York City you will need to use the information on the chart. Find New York City on the left-hand column. Using your left hand, hold a finger on the name New York City. Then using your right hand, put a finger on Binghamton, in the top row. Now move your right finger straight down and slide your left finger straight across. Your fingers will meet at "175." Thus, it is 175 miles from New York City to Binghamton.

READING A MILEAGE CHART

Let's practice the skill of reading a mileage chart. What is the distance from:

1. Syracuse to Rochester?
2. Philadelphia, PA. to Buffalo?
3. Montreal, Canada to New York City?
4. Boston, MA. to Albany?
5. Which two cities in the chart are farthest apart?

How far is your local community from each of the cities on the mileage chart? Using an atlas, find your community on a New York State map. Then measure the distance from your community to each city in the chart. Make a copy of the chart and add the name of your community to the bottom of the column on the left and along the top. If your community already appears on the map, select a nearby community instead.

SUMMARIZING YOUR UNDERSTANDING

Directions: Make a copy of the following organizer. Then complete the blanks.

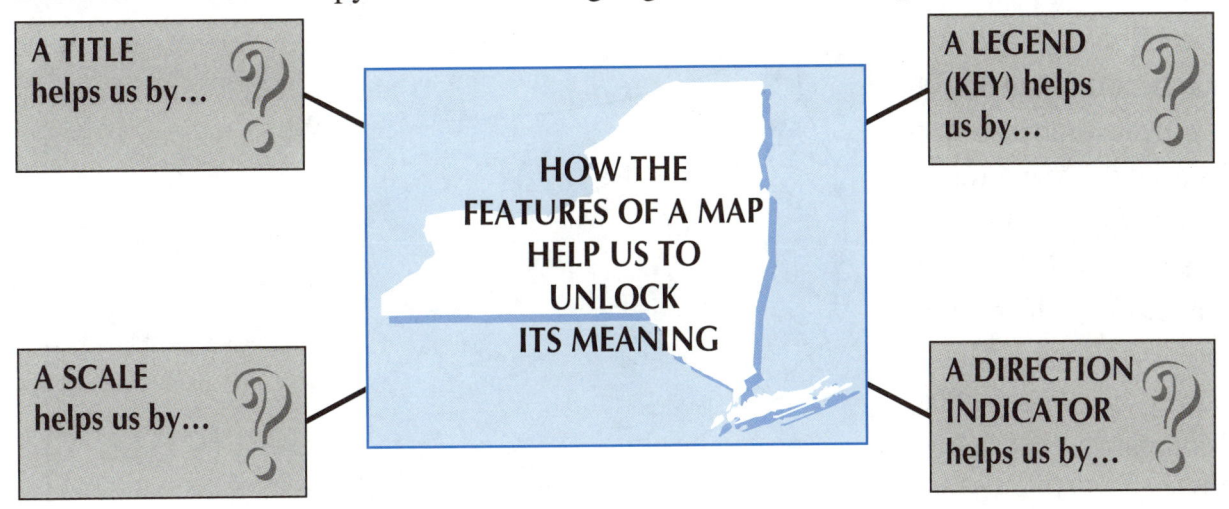

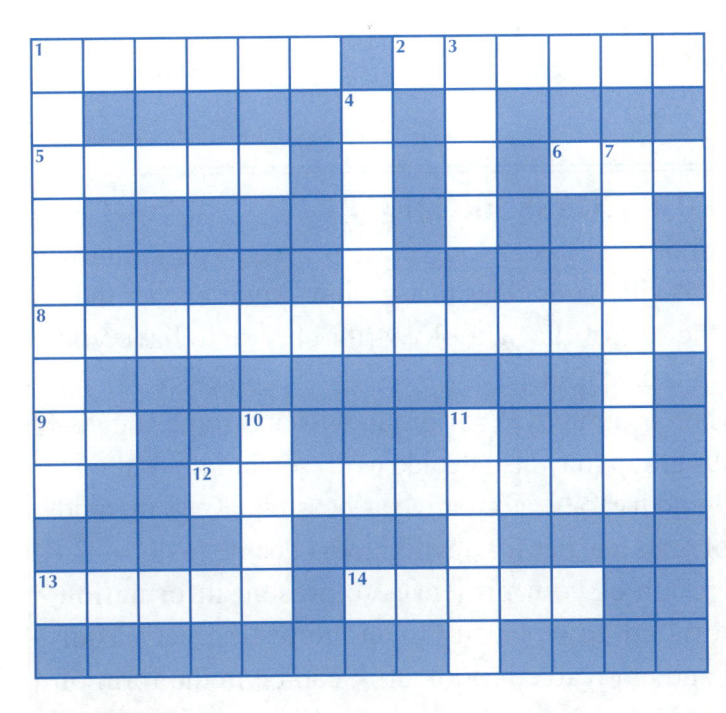

- A TITLE helps us by…
- A LEGEND (KEY) helps us by…
- A SCALE helps us by…
- A DIRECTION INDICATOR helps us by…

HOW THE FEATURES OF A MAP HELP US TO UNLOCK ITS MEANING

DOWN

1. The southernmost point on the Earth (2 words).
3. The largest of the seven continents.
4. A device on a map used to measure the distance between two places.
7. A line of latitude that divides the Earth into the Northern and Southern Hemispheres.
10. Diagrams of places used to show where things are located.
11. A book of many different maps.

ACROSS

1. A drawing on a map that stands for an actual place or thing.
2. States make up a larger region called a _____.
5. Another name for city.
6. Another name for the legend on a map.
8. A line of longitude identified as zero degrees (2 words).
9. Two letters that identify the island located at the southeastern end of New York State.
12. A dictionary which provides information on geographic listings.
13. Bodies of fresh water surrounded by land.
14. One of the five themes of geography.

IDENTIFYING GEOGRAPHIC FEATURES OF THE UNITED STATES

Directions: Place the number of each of the following items in its correct location on the map of the United States: (1) Great Lakes; (2) Mississippi River; (3) Gulf of Mexico; (4) Rocky Mountains; (5) Appalachian Mountains; (6) Great Plains; (7) Atlantic Ocean; (8) Pacific Ocean.

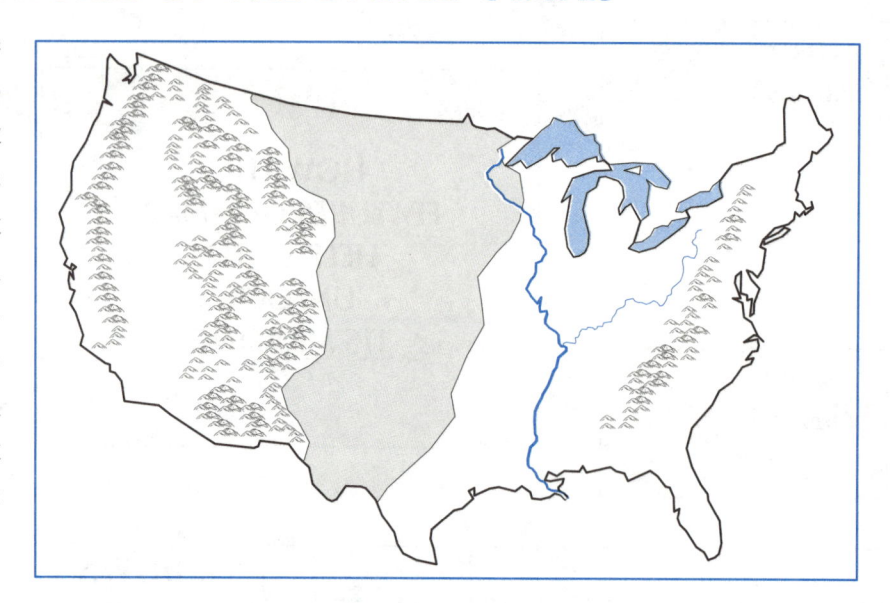

STARTING YOUR CLASS PROJECT

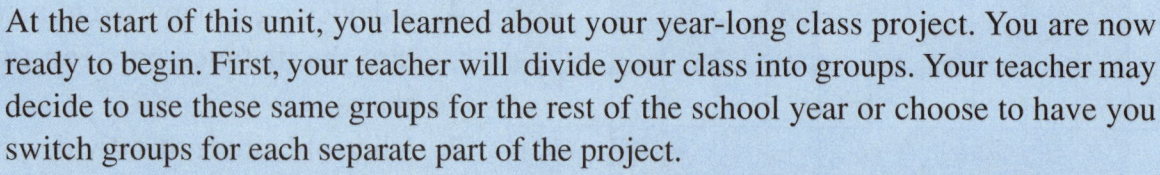

At the start of this unit, you learned about your year-long class project. You are now ready to begin. First, your teacher will divide your class into groups. Your teacher may decide to use these same groups for the rest of the school year or choose to have you switch groups for each separate part of the project.

The first part of the project focuses on geography. Your group will find some suggestions for this part on the next page. Your group may also decide to do something different from what is suggested. Each group should try to be as creative as possible. Keep in mind that you must also have the approval of your teacher for anything you decide to do.

The purpose of the geography section of your project is to present information about the geography of your neighborhood, town or city in an interesting way. Your project should be easy to understand and enjoyable to look at. It can be in the form of a large chart, a bulletin board or a booklet. You might even want to prepare a short skit, make a video or design some other kind of activity to explain the geography of your community. The choice is yours—with your teacher's approval.

Remember that each part of your project should fit together with the other parts, like pieces in a giant jigsaw puzzle. Your teacher may have you display each part of the project when you complete it at the end of each chapter. At the end of the school year, you will bring all of the pieces of the project together to show it as a whole. At that time, your class may invite other classes, parents and the public to come and learn more about their community.

INFORMATION SHEET #1: GEOGRAPHY

MY NEIGHBORHOOD, VILLAGE, TOWN OR CITY IS: _____

CREATING ITEMS FOR YOUR EXHIBIT

Following is a list of suggestions for your project. Feel free to add others that you think would describe and explain the geography of your village, town or city.

DRAWING A MAP
Draw a map of your village, town or city, showing its (1) bordering counties; (2) major physical features and (3) major highways, parkways and roadways.

CREATING AN ACROSTIC
An **acrostic** is a series of written lines in which the first letter of each written line forms a word or phrase when you read it downwards. Begin by writing the name of your town or city vertically. Then make each letter the first letter of a phrase that provides information about your town or city. For example, here is an acrostic using the Town of Colonie, located near Albany:

Come and study at Siena College located within the Town of Colonie
  Olympic-size swimming pool in the 150-acre town park
    Located in eastern New York State along the Hudson and Mohawk Rivers
      Only 150 miles from New York City
        Neighborhood pocket parks are plentiful in Colonie: there are 15 in all
          Its Watervliet Meeting House was the first Shaker settlement in the nation
            Excellent schools in North and South Colonie Central School Districts

MAKING A WALL CHART OR BULLETIN BOARD
Another way to display information about the geography of your community is to make a wall chart or bulletin board display. Focus on the main geographical features of your community and show how they have influenced life-styles where you live.

- Land Forms
- Occupations
- Climate
- Clothing Styles
- Natural Resources
- Houses
- Bodies of Water
- Recreational Activities

❖ CONTINUED

You could also use postcards or photographs to illustrate this information. For example, someone from your group might take a photograph of a local factory or houses to show the types of occupations and styles of homes people have in your area.

PLANNING A NATURE WALK

People often enjoy nature walks. A nature walk helps clear the mind and sharpens the senses. Almost every village, town or city has a place where people can take a walk to enjoy nature and fresh air, whether woodland trails or sandy beaches. Write a description of a place in your town or city where nature lovers can take a walk to enjoy its beauty and natural wonders. Be sure to:

- give clear and accurate directions for locating each nature walk
- provide a map that shows the recommended walking route
- add notes about land formations, flowers, trees and wildlife
- describe what a person should wear and what equipment, if any, a person might need
- provide interesting historical stories or anecdotes about the walk
- if the walk is in a park, provide information about the park's hours and admission charges.

CREATING A FLORA AND FAUNA SCRAPBOOK

What do deer, mice, rabbits, chipmunks, rabbits, foxes, squirrels, porcupines, skunks, raccoons, beavers, otters, mink and woodchucks have in common? They are all animals found in New York State. One of the natural wonders of any town or city is its fauna and flora. **Fauna** refers to the animals found in an area, while **flora** refers to an area's plants. What kinds of animals and flowers are commonly found in your neighborhood, town or city? Create a scrap book of the flora and fauna in your community.

- Collect leaves and flowers from some plants and trees that grow in your area.
- Dry them thoroughly.
- Glue them into the pages of your flora and fauna scrapbook.
- Add pictures of some of the birds and other wild animals in your community.
- Write a short description of each plant and animal.

UNIT 3
AMERICAN HERITAGE

View of Buffalo in 1825

Immigrant children selling bread on the streets of New York City

Construction of locks on the Erie Canal

The term "American Heritage" refers to what we have gained from the past—our ideas, laws, type of government and customs. We enjoy the life-styles we lead today because of the struggles and accomplishments of those who lived before us. In this unit, you will learn about the history of your community, state and nation.

NEW YORK CELEBRATES THE ERIE CANAL

On October 26, 1825, New Yorkers celebrated the completion of the Erie Canal. Governor DeWitt Clinton, the main sponsor of the canal, began the celebration by leading a parade through the streets of Buffalo to a group of waiting barges. Stretching for hundreds of miles along the length of the canal, cannons stood ready to sound their thunder. At exactly 10:00 a.m., the cannons in Buffalo began firing. As soon as the blast was heard in the next town, those cannons fired also. The roar of cannons echoed the entire length of the canal and down the Hudson River all the way to New York City. The chain of cannon fire took an hour and half to travel the route, after which it reversed itself, and the cannons fired all the way back from New York City to Buffalo. When the cannons had silenced, Clinton and other officials got onto the barges.

ERIE, OSWEGO and CHAMPLAIN CANALS

During the next week, the barges moved slowly along the canal from town to town. They carried goods from the West—barrels of flour, apples, butter, whitefish, special woods and newly-made brooms and pails. At Lockport, the barges had to be lowered through a system of five locks. At Waterford, the barges passed through another 16 locks. These locks were spaces that could be closed off. They acted like giant bathtubs in which boats could be raised or lowered with the water, in order to pass over the mountains and come down gradually to the level of the Hudson River.

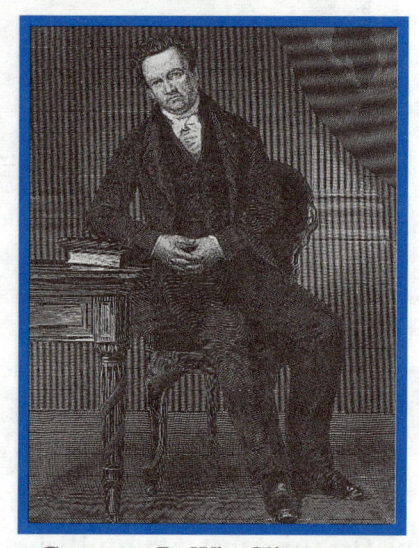

Governor DeWitt Clinton was the main sponsor of the Canal.

As the barges reached each new location, the townspeople greeted Governor Clinton and the other officials with cheers, church bells, music and fireworks. At Albany, it seemed as if the whole city had come out to greet them. From Albany the barges turned south, down the Hudson River.

They entered New York harbor on November 4, to be greeted with ships from all nations, spread out as far as the eye could see. Governor Clinton poured a barrel of water from Lake Erie into the Hudson. Then he went on land to meet President John Q. Adams and four former Presidents—John Adams, Thomas Jefferson, James Madison and James Monroe.

New Yorkers had been inspired by the success of canals in Great Britain and nearby Massachusetts. The Erie Canal was the most ambitious canal ever constructed up to that time. In 1817, Clinton had convinced the New York legislature to build it. A path 50 feet wide was to be cut through forests, swamps and hillsides. Then a ditch 40 feet wide and 4 feet deep had to be dug, with a towpath on one side for mules to pull barges along the canal.

Without the equipment we have today, thousands of workers were needed to cut trees, pull out tree stumps and blast through rock. One out of every 4 workers was Irish. Other workers included local farmhands, African Americans and immigrants from England and Germany. In summer, workers fought off mosquitoes and disease. In winter, they suffered from the freezing temperatures—all to earn a dollar a day.

A lock along the Erie Canal

The first sections of the canal opened in 1819. Six years later the entire canal was completed. Completion of the canal was cause enough for a gala celebration. But many New Yorkers wondered whether the canal was worth all the expense and hardship it had cost to build. What effect would the canal have on the future of New York and the nation?

In this unit you will learn the answers to these and other important questions about New York's past.

3A HOW WOULD YOU EDIT THIS ARTICLE?

In this activity, you will learn about the Native American groups that once lived in New York. Look for the following important words:

- ▶ Fact
- ▶ Opinion
- ▶ Native American
- ▶ Algonquian
- ▶ Iroquois
- ▶ Wigwams
- ▶ Longhouses
- ▶ Sachem
- ▶ Iroquois Constitution

To help you, the ▶ symbol appears in the margin where the **term** is first explained.

Imagine that your school will soon print its annual student magazine. This year's edition will focus on the Native Americans who once lived in New York. You have been given your first assignment by the Editor-in-Chief—the person who puts the magazine together. "Here is an article to read," the editor says. "It was written by one of your classmates. I need you to make sure it contains only facts. I don't want any opinions in this article. Read it and report back to me when you have finished. However, before you begin, you should read this comparison of facts and opinions."

Skill Builder
THE DIFFERENCE BETWEEN FACT AND OPINION

A statement of **fact** (*factual statement*) is something that can be checked for accuracy. You check something for **accuracy** by looking at other sources to see if they agree that the statement is correct.

Correct	*Incorrect*
Albany is the capital of New York.	Syracuse is the capital of New York.

An **opinion** is a statement of personal beliefs. It is not a statement that is true or false. An opinion *cannot* be checked for accuracy. There are two main types of opinion statements:

Opinions of personal taste express a person's feelings. For example, "New York is the best state to live in."

Opinions about the future make a prediction. For example, "When I grow up, I will go to college."

"Telling the difference between fact and opinion is only one part of your assignment," the editor continues. "I also need you to check facts and to look for errors in punctuation, spelling and grammar. Lastly, I would like to know what you thought was the most interesting thing about the Native Americans of New York." Here is the article you are asked to read.

THE FIRST NEW YORKERS: THE NATIVE AMERICANS

EDITOR'S INSTRUCTIONS: Read the following paragraphs and identify all opinion statements. In addition, identify one factual statement.

A NOTE OF NAMES

The first settlers in the Western Hemisphere (*North and South America*) have been identified by various names. When Christopher Columbus landed, he called them "Indians" because he thought he had landed in the Indies. In the 1960s, the term **Native American** began to be used, to show that these were the first people to live in the Americas. More recently, some people have called them **Indigenous Peoples**. Indigenous means native to a particular area.

(1) Hundreds of thousands of years ago the land that is now New York was covered by thick forests. **(2)** At least 20,000 years ago, people from Asia crossed the narrow plain that once connected Siberia to Alaska. **(3)** The new arrivals were hunters, moving from place to place in search of food. **(4)** From Alaska, these people spread southwards throughout North and South America.

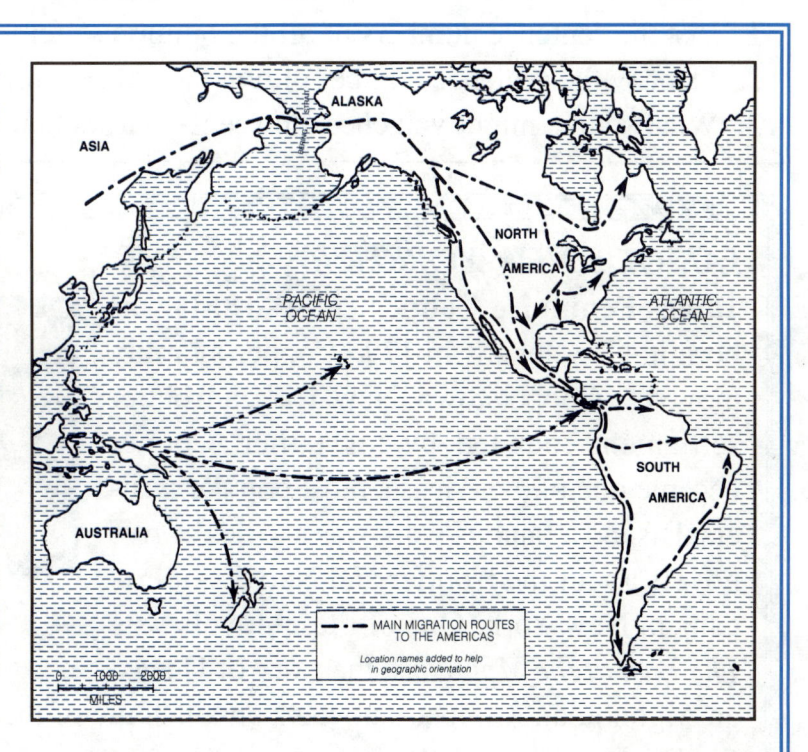

MAIN MIGRATION ROUTES TO THE AMERICAS
Location names added to help in geographic orientation

◆ CONTINUED

THE ALGONQUIANS AND IROQUOIS ENTER NEW YORK

(5) About five thousand years ago, the first Native Americans entered New York. (6) The first group belonged to the **Algonquian** (al-gong-kwee-en) family. (7) A second group of Native Americans arrived in New York as recently as 1,000 years ago. (8) They occupied the northwest of New York. (9) They became known as the **Iroquois** (ir-e-kwoi).

(10) Both the Algonquian and Iroquois were made up of several tribes of people who shared similar customs and beliefs. (11) These tribes were divided into smaller groups known as **clans**—groups of related families. (12) To many Native Americans, their clan was more important than their tribe.

THE ALGONQUIANS AND IROQUOIS INFLUENCE NEW YORK

(13) The Native Americans were the most important people ever to live in New York. (14) Although small in number, their influence survives in the words we use, the foods we eat and the stories we tell. (15) For example, many Algonquian words have entered the English language, such as *moose, squash, moccasin* and *tomahawk*. (16) It is important for us to learn more about these peoples.

✏️ YOUR NOTES ✏️

1. List the sentence numbers of **all** the opinion statements.
2. Identify the sentence number of **one** factual statement.
3. What source might you check to see if your factual statement is accurate?

FAMOUS NEW YORKERS

James Fenimore Cooper (1789–1851) was born in New Jersey. In 1790 Cooper's family moved to Cooperstown, New York, a frontier settlement founded by his father. Cooper became one of America's most popular writers. His most famous work was a series of five novels about the frontier and Native Americans in New York. One of these novels was *The Last of the Mohicans*, the story of Uncas, an Algonquian. Cooper's novels contain some of the first descriptions of frontier life read by many Americans.

An illustration from one of Cooper's novels

ALGONQUIAN AND IROQUOIS HOMES

EDITOR'S INSTRUCTIONS: Continue to identify all opinion statements and find one factual statement. Also, find answers to certain questions.

(1) The Native Americans of New York lived in villages. **(2)** The Algonquian peoples made round houses, or **wigwams**. **(3)** The men took branches that could be easily bent and drove them into the ground in a circle. **(4)** Then they tied the branches together at the top with vines, roots or strips of bark. **(5)** Women covered the frame with tree bark or mats of grass. **(6)** An animal skin was used for a door. **(7)** The family slept on animal skins. **(8)** A fire stood at the center of the wigwam for cooking and heating. **(9)** A hole at the top of the wigwam let the smoke from the fire escape.

(10) The Iroquois made their houses in a different shape. **(11)** From five to ten families shared a **longhouse**, which was 50 to 100 feet long, and about 20 feet wide. **(12)** Like a wigwam, it was made of branches covered with bark. **(13)** Holes in the roof allowed smoke to escape. **(14)** Benches along the sides of the longhouse were used by families for sitting, eating and sleeping. **(15)** Life in the longhouse was smoky, crowded and noisy, especially in winter when people spent most of their time inside. **(16)** We are much better off today in the kinds of houses we live in.

Interior of an Iroquois longhouse

(17) Some Algonquian tribes built longhouses for tribal meetings or religious ceremonies. **(18)** Each village had a leader, known as a **sachem**. **(19)** Both Iroquois and Algonquians often surrounded their villages with high walls. **(20)** Logs were pushed into the ground next to each other. The tops of the logs were sharpened to a point. **(21)** The wall of logs protected villagers from wild animals or enemy tribes. **(22)** Life was a great deal safer a thousand years ago than it is today.

YOUR NOTES

1. List the sentence numbers of **all** opinion statements, and **one** factual statement.
2. How was life in the wigwam similar to life in the longhouse?
3. Why did the Iroquois and Algonquians surround their villages with walls?

104 NEW YORK: ITS LAND AND ITS PEOPLE

> **EDITOR'S INSTRUCTIONS:** Continue to identify all opinion statements and one factual statement. You will also need to check some punctuation, especially the use of periods and question marks.
> - Periods (.) are used when you wish to end a sentence.
> - Question marks (?) are used at the end of a question.
>
> In addition, continue finding answers to certain questions.

ALGONQUIAN AND IROQUOIS LIFESTYLES

GATHERING FOOD

(1) Generally, Algonquian and Iroquois men hunted and fished. **(2)** They used stone, wood and bone to make tools, weapons and other objects. **(3)** Spears, hooks and nets of plant fibers were used for fishing. **(4)** Bows and arrows, spears and clubs were used to kill deer, rabbits, moose, squirrels, beavers, ducks and turkeys. **(5)** Some meat and fish were preserved by drying and then stored for use in winter. **(6)** If a village did not store enough food for winter, its members could starve [./?]

An Iroquois out hunting
What kinds of animals did they usually hunt for?

(7) Algonquian and Iroquois men built canoes for fishing and trading with other villages. **(8)** The Algonquians sewed pieces of bark together to cover the frame. **(9)** Then they used sticky tree sap to cover where the bark was sewn together to make the canoe waterproof. **(10)** Algonquian canoes were similar but lighter than Iroquois canoes and could easily be carried from one stream to another. **(11)** Algonquian canoes were probably much better than Iroquois ones.

A Native American fishing from a canoe
What were canoes made out of?

◆ CONTINUED

PLANTING CROPS

(12) How were these tribes able to produce enough food to live on [./?] **(13)** Women gathered berries, nuts and other wild plants to eat. **(14)** They were also in charge of growing corn, squash and beans. **(15)** To plant crops, men cleared the land by burning the trees. **(16)** The ashes were then mixed with the soil. **(17)** Women used sticks to loosen the soil and plant seeds. **(18)** After 15 to 20 years, the village moved to a new place and cleared the lands for new fields [./?]

APPEARANCE

(19) The first residents of New York made skirts, moccasins, leggings and clothes from the skins of deer and other animals. **(20)** They used sharp porcupine needles to scratch designs in the leather. **(21)** They sometimes tattooed their faces and decorated themselves with paint, feathers and shells. **(22)** Most men wore their hair long, but some shaved the sides of their heads and left a short strip of hair on top. **(23)** I think that the Native Americans had a better sense of fashion than most of us do today [./?]

A village of longhouses
What activities took place in the longhouse?

THE ROLE OF WOMEN

(24) What was the role of women in Native American societies [./?] **(25)** Women had a special role in both Algonquian and Iroquois societies. **(26)** They grew and prepared the food, while men were often away hunting or trading. **(27)** Women were widely respected and helped to make many community decisions, such as choosing the sachems. **(28)** In Iroquois society, one's

A Native American village
What role did Native American women play?

name and residence depended on the woman's side of the family. **(29)** For example, when an Iroquois man married, he left his family's home and lived in the longhouse of his wife's family. **(30)** Iroquois children took their names from their mother's family, not their father's.

❖ CONTINUED

106   NEW YORK: ITS LAND AND ITS PEOPLE

RELIGIOUS BELIEFS

(31) The Algonquian and Iroquois tribes had similar religious beliefs. **(32)** They worshipped a "Great Spirit," believed to exist in all things. **(33)** Tribal medicine men or women helped communicate with the spirit world. **(34)** Animals identified with each clan were also considered special spirits **[./?]** **(35)** To please the Great Spirit, the tribes celebrated several special holidays of thanksgiving.

✎ YOUR NOTES ✎

1. List the sentence numbers of **all** the opinion statements.
2. Identify the sentence number of **one** factual statement.
3. Which is the correct punctuation for sentence:
   ▶ 6: (period / question mark)   ▶ 23: (period / question mark)
   ▶ 12: (period / question mark)   ▶ 24: (period / question mark)
   ▶ 18: (period / question mark)   ▶ 34: (period / question mark)
4. What types of foods did the Algonquian and Iroquois eat?
5. What role did religion play in Algonquian and Iroquois society?

THE ALGONQUIAN TRIBES OF NEW YORK

EDITOR'S INSTRUCTIONS:
List all opinion statements and one factual statement. Editors also need to check a writer's spelling. In this section, use a dictionary to find the correct spelling for the words highlighted in blue print.

The main Algonquian tribes in upstate New York were the Mohican, Wappinger and Delaware (*or Lenape*). A large number of Algonquian-speaking tribes lived on Long Island, including the Montauk, Shinnecock and Massapequa. Members of the Algonquian tribes were the first people to live on Long Island.

A trading post in upstate New York where Native Americans traded furs for beads and silver ornaments

◆ CONTINUED

THE ALGONQUIAN TRIBES OF UPSTATE NEW YORK

Members of the Delaware tribe were located in New Jersey, [Pennsylvania/Pensylvannia] and Delaware, as well as New York. The tribes of the **Wappinger Confederacy** (*alliance or league*) lived along the Hudson between Manhattan and Poughkeepsie. Their traditional enemies were the Mohawk (*an Iroquois tribe*). The Mohicans lived in the northern Hudson Valley. Their largest village, Schodac, was near present-day Albany. Like the Wappinger, their traditional [enemies/enemeis] were the Mohawk.

NATIVE AMERICAN PEOPLES OF NEW YORK

THE ALGONQUIAN TRIBES OF LONG ISLAND

Long Island was home to a number of Algonquian tribes. Many places on Long Island today are named after these tribes, such as Canarsie, Rockaway, Jamaica and Montauk. The Algonquians of Long Island were famous for their **wampum**. These were beads made from shells and strung together. Wampum was used in ceremonies or for money or gifts. Tribes also had ceremonial pipes of clay or stone. These were used to smoke tobacco leaves on special [occasions/ocassions], and were greatly prized.

In central Long Island, Tackapausha, the sachem of the Massapequa tribe, signed treaties giving lands to English settlers. In eastern Long Island, the Montauk became

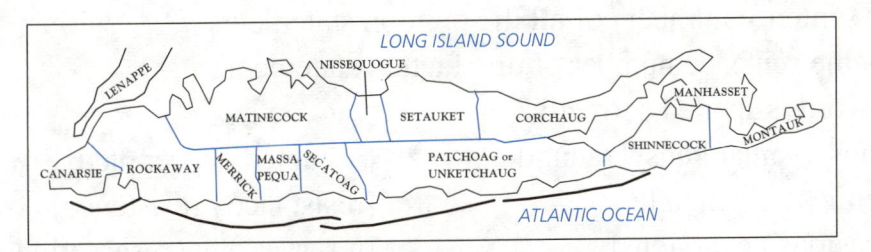

CONTINUED

the most powerful tribe. They hunted whales and fished in the ocean in large canoes made from logs. They must have been very brave to risk these ocean adventures!

The wisest sachem in all Long Island history was **Wyandanch** of the Montauk. In 1637, Wyandanch crossed Long Island Sound to meet the commander of the local English fort, **Lion Gardiner**. As a present, Wyandanch gave the commander an island on the eastern end of Long Island, now known as Gardiner's Island. This event made Gardiner the first English landowner in New York.

In 1653, hostile Connecticut tribes raided the main Montauk village and kidnapped Wyandanch's daughter. Wyadanch went to Gardiner and received help from the English in getting his daughter back. As a reward, Wyandanch gave Gardiner a large area of land near present-day Smithtown. The English made Wyandanch the "Great Sachem" of all Long Island, in charge of all the other tribes. However, the other sachems never [accepted/acceppted] his title.

The introduction of guns by the Europeans made conflicts with other tribes bloodier. As the number of settlers in colonial New York increased, the Algonquians were pushed out of their traditional homelands. The Iroquois destroyed many of the Algonquian villages in the Hudson Valley. Large numbers also died from exposure to European diseases like smallpox. The Native Americans had no [resistance/resistence] to these illnesses.

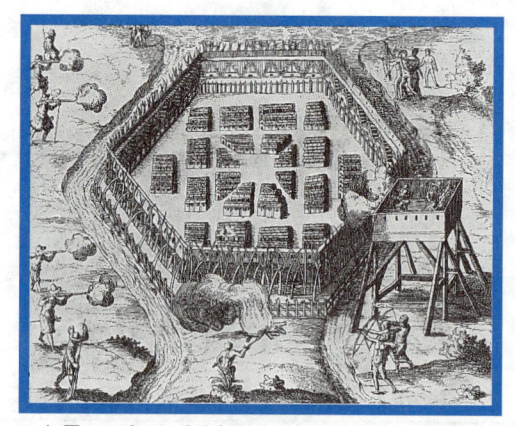

A French and Alongquian force attacks an Iroquois village

Today, only a few thousand Algonquians remain on [reservations/resarvations] in New York. For example, the Shinnecocks have a reservation in Southampton, on Long Island. Most of the surviving Algonquians, however, intermarried with other peoples. They are found throughout the country today.

✎ Your Notes ✎

1. List the sentence numbers of **all** the opinion statements.
2. Identify the sentence number of **one** factual statement.
3. Which word is spelled correctly?
    ▶ [Pennsylvania/ Pensylvannia]
    ▶ [accepted / acceppted]
    ▶ [enemies / enemeis]
    ▶ [resistance / resistence]
    ▶ [occasions / ocassions]
    ▶ [reservations / resarvations]

> **EDITOR'S INSTRUCTIONS:** Identify all opinion statements. Editors also check a writer's grammar. One frequent error is using the wrong verb forms: "He (singular) do (should be <u>does</u>) what he wants." A similar mistake is to use a plural noun with a singular verb: "They (plural) eats (should be <u>eat</u>) their dinner early." In this section look for problems in the use of nouns with verbs and answer certain questions.

THE IROQUOIS CONFEDERACY

Five Iroquois tribes occupied most of western New York. The **Seneca** (sen-i-ka) lived near the Genesee River. The **Cayuga** (ka-yu-ga) lived east of the Seneca in the Finger Lakes area. The **Mohawk** occupied the Mohawk River Valley, while the **Onondaga** (on-an-da-ga) lived in the valley south of Lake Ontario. The **Oneida** (o-nye-da) settled in the lands between the Mohawk and the Onondaga.

The Iroquois thought of their territory as one giant longhouse, stretching from Lake Ontario almost to the Hudson River. The Mohawks [were/was] called the keepers of the "Eastern Door," while the Seneca were the keepers of the "Western Door." Trails connected the tribes. The most important trail ran from Lake Erie to the Hudson River. This later proved to be the best route for roads and canals.

THE LEAGUE OF FIVE NATIONS

Around 1570, these five tribes formed the Iroquois Confederacy or **League of Five Nations.** According to legend, the Great Spirit visited Deganawida, the "peacemaker," in a dream. To end the constant fighting between the tribes, Deganawida was told to unite them. He persuaded **Hiawatha,** a Mohawk, to preach peace and unity throughout the lands of the five tribes. The tribes promised not to fight each other again.

The capital of the Confederacy was located in the village of Onondaga, where the Great Council met once a year. At the Great Council, the leading sachems of the Iroquois met to deal with important matters facing the whole Confederacy—such as whether to go to war. Such decisions required the approval of all five tribes before the Confederacy could act.

The Iroquois' method of government was one of the most advanced among all the Native Americans. Thomas Jefferson and the other founders of our country [was/were] influenced by the **Iroquois Constitution** in designing the government of the United States.

▸ CONTINUED

110   NEW YORK: ITS LAND AND ITS PEOPLE

Historic Documents: *The Iroquois Constitution*

The Iroquois Constitution

The Onondaga lords shall open each council by expressing their gratitude to their cousin lords, and greeting them, and they shall offer thanks to the Earth where men dwell, to the streams of water, the pool, the springs, the lakes, to the corn and the fruits, to the medicinal herbs and the trees, to the forest trees for their usefulness, to the animals that serve as food and who offer their furs as clothing, to the great winds and the lesser winds, to the Thunderers, and the Sun, the mighty warrior, to the moon, to the messengers of the Great Spirit who dwells in the skies above, who gives all things useful to men, who is the source and the ruler of health and life. Then shall the Onondaga lords declare the council open.

Not all Iroquoian-speaking people joined the League. The Susquehanna to the south, the Erie and Neutral to the west, and the Huron to the north were all Iroquoian peoples who never became members. One Iroquoian tribe several hundred miles away, however, [joins/joined] the League in about 1715. This was the **Tuscarora** (tus-ka-ror-uh) tribe. They were officially admitted into the Confederacy, making it the League of Six Nations.

THE IMPACT OF THE EUROPEANS

The Iroquois were greatly respected for their bravery in battle. They were great warriors. Young boys were trained to be warriors from an early age. By the time they were teenagers, they began raiding other tribes or European settlements. When they captured prisoners, they either [kills/killed] them through torture or adopted them as members of their tribe.

Hendrick, Great Sachem or Chief of the Mohawks, a member tribe of the Six Nations

Most people would agree that the arrival of Europeans doomed the Iroquois. In the 1700s, the Iroquois became deeply involved in the struggle between the English and the French for control of North America. The Iroquois generally helped the English and fought against the French. When the American Revolution broke out, most of the Iroquois nations sided with the British. The Oneida and Tuscarora, however, took the side of the colonists. This destroyed the unity of the Confederacy. The council fire, symbol of Iroquois unity, was allowed to burn out.

❖ CONTINUED

Led by **Joseph Brant,** Mohawk warriors raided a settlement near Albany in 1778. More than 30 Americans were killed. General George Washington sent 4,000 soldiers into Iroquois territory in 1779 to burn their villages and crops. The Iroquois tribes never fully recovered from these blows. After the Revolution, Brant led the Mohawk to Canada. The Oneida sold most of their lands and moved west. The Seneca recognized the new country as the United States, and obtained some reserved lands. The Cayuga [went/goes] with the Mohawk to Canada. The Onondaga moved to western New York.

Today, the Iroquois [is/are] found on seven reservations in Canada and five in New York. Most Iroquois have mixed with other peoples and live in big cities like Buffalo, New York City or Toronto. Every year at Labor Day, members of the Six Nations meet for the Six Nations Festival at Cobbleskill, New York.

Joseph Brant, also known as Joseph Thayendanegea, was a Mohawk Chief.

From our studies of the Algonquians and Iroquois, we can see how people once used nature to their benefit. We can also see how they were affected by war and exposure to new cultures. We can learn a great deal from their experiences.

YOUR NOTES

1. List the sentence numbers of **all** the opinion statements.
2. Which is the correct word to be used?
   - ▶ [were/was]
   - ▶ [was/were]
   - ▶ [joins/joined]
   - ▶ [kills/killed]
   - ▶ [went/goes]
   - ▶ [is/are]
3. What was the Iroquois Confederation?
4. What famous United States document borrowed ideas from the Iroquois?

REVIEWING AND CHECKING THE ARTICLE

Now that you have finished reviewing the article, it's time to write to your Editor-in-Chief. You must tell her whether the article was completely factual or contained opinions. You should also discuss any errors that the article contained.

112 NEW YORK: ITS LAND AND ITS PEOPLE

> Dear Editor-in-Chief,
> I have reviewed the article. I found that the article contained (some/many) opinions. I found (some/many) sentences with errors. In addition, the most interesting thing that I learned about the Native Americans living in New York was ...
>
> Sincerely,
>
> _____
> (sign your name)

Two days later you meet the editor again. She thanks you and asks you to do one more thing—to check the **accuracy** of the article. Remember, a factual statement is accurate if you can show that it is true and error-free. Since it would take too long to check every fact in the article, she suggests you choose **any two** factual statements. You can refer to either a textbook, encyclopedia or almanac to check the accuracy of these two factual statements.

Statements You Selected to Check	Source Used	The Statement is:
(1) ?	?	☐ Accurate ☐ Not Accurate
(2) ?	?	☐ Accurate ☐ Not Accurate

FAMOUS NEW YORKERS

Eli S. Parker (1825–1898) was a chief of the Seneca tribe. During the Civil War, he served as an officer in the Northern Army. It was there that he became a close friend of General Ulysses S. Grant. When Grant was elected President in 1868, he remembered his friend from the Civil War and named him Commissioner of Indian Affairs. Parker served as Commissioner from 1869 to 1872. During his time as Commissioner, Parker dedicated himself to improving conditions for his fellow Native Americans.

Eli Parker

REVIEWING YOUR UNDERSTANDING

Creating Vocabulary Cards

Factual Statement

What is a "factual statement"?

Give an example of a factual statement:

Opinion Statement

What is an "opinion statement"?

Give an example of an opinion statement:

Learning to Use an Encyclopedia

One place to find information about Native Americans is in a **reference book**. One very useful reference book is an **encyclopedia**. The term comes from the ancient Greek for a "general education." Encyclopedias give their readers access to current knowledge on a wide variety of subjects.

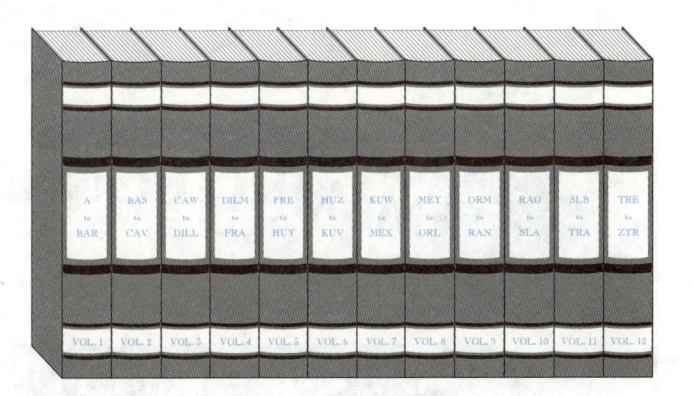

ENCYCLOPEDIA

Encyclopedias contain articles with information on many topics. You can find facts about history, science, music and current events. Encyclopedias also have articles about countries, states and famous people. Subjects are arranged in alphabetical order. Encyclopedias often consist of many volumes. The first volume starts with the letter "A" and the last volume ends with the letter "Z." Each volume has guide words or letters on the spine to help you find particular subjects more easily.

USING A VENN DIAGRAM

A **Venn diagram** uses circles to compare two or more items and show how they are related. Each item is represented by a circle. The area where the circles overlap shows how the items are similar. The outer part of each circle shows how the items are different.

114   NEW YORK: ITS LAND AND ITS PEOPLE

Let's use your knowledge of Native Americans to compare and contrast the Algonquians with the Iroquois. The Venn diagram below has been started for you. Make a copy of the diagram and then add **two** other points in each part of the diagram to compare and contrast these two Native American groups.

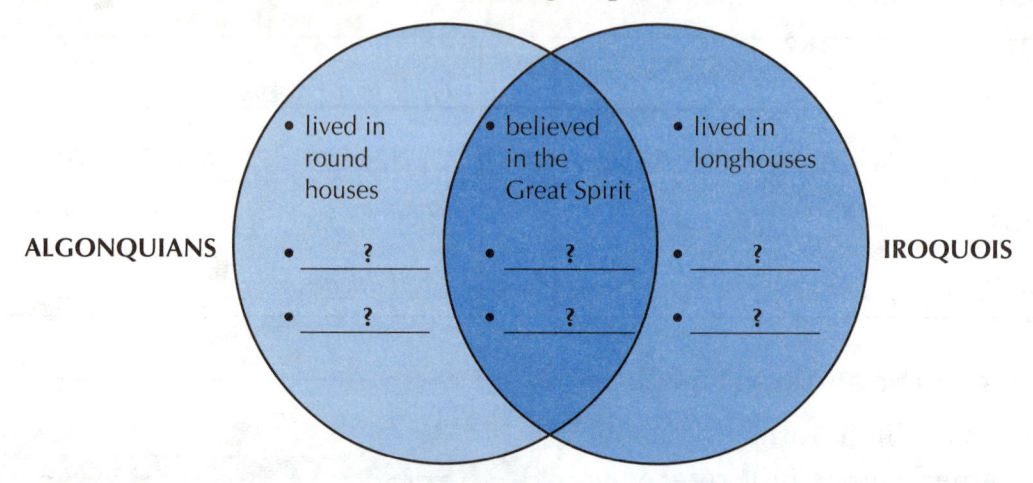

ALGONQUIANS
- lived in round houses
- ____?____
- ____?____

- believed in the Great Spirit
- ____?____
- ____?____

IROQUOIS
- lived in longhouses
- ____?____
- ____?____

MAKING CONNECTIONS

EXPLORING BEYOND YOUR STATE

THE NATIVE AMERICANS OF THE UNITED STATES

In this activity, you learned about New York's Native American tribes. There existed a great variety of cultures among Native Americans living in other parts of what would later become the United States.

SOME MAJOR NATIVE AMERICAN TRIBES

Five hundred years ago, there were as many as $2\frac{1}{2}$ million Native Americans living in the Americas north of Mexico. They were spread throughout the following areas:

SOUTHEASTERN WOODLANDS

This area is between the Atlantic Ocean and the Mississippi River. Here, Native American peoples planted corn, beans, tobacco and other crops. They lived in villages and often formed "confederacies," run by elected councils. Among the main tribes in this area were the Creek, Choctaw and Cherokee.

❖ CONTINUED

THE GREAT PLAINS

This area is between the Mississippi River and the Rocky Mountains in the west. It stretches from Canada in the north to Texas in the south. Although the Great Plains are large in size, very few people lived on them until the Europeans brought horses to the Americas. Horses helped Native Americans hunt buffalo. After 1600, Plains tribes lived off the large herds of wild buffalo, eating buffalo meat and using the skins to make clothes, shoes and tents. The main tribes in this area were the Sioux, Cheyenne, Comanche, Blackfeet and Kiowa.

Native Americans participating in a buffalo hunt
What were buffaloes used for by Native Americans?

THE SOUTHWEST

This area is made up of present-day Arizona and New Mexico. The Southwest is very hot and dry. The Native Americans living here learned to build adobe buildings, made from sun-dried bricks, on the sides of cliffs. These homes became known as **pueblos**—from the Spanish word "pueblo," for village. Pueblo peoples irrigated the land and grew corn, beans and squash. Navajo and Apache tribes later moved into this region. The Navajo lived in huts known as **hogans**, made of mud and branches.

PACIFIC NORTHWEST

The Pacific Northwest area is a narrow strip of land stretching from southern Alaska into California. These lands are rich in natural resources. Native Americans lived in this area, mainly by fishing salmon, hunting whales and sea lions, and gathering nuts and berries. They carved ceremonial masks and totem poles. A **totem pole** is a carved and painted log, usually showing symbolic animals and spirits. A totem pole was often placed near the entrance to a home to show which clan the family belonged to. The tribes of this region included the Chinook, Kwakiutil, Nootka, Haida and the Tlingit.

Portrait of an unidentified Native American from the Pacific Northwest

❖ CONTINUED

Your Task: COMPLETING A MAP

Make a copy of the outline map of the United States. Use it to mark the location of the Native American tribes mentioned in this section. Shade in on your map the approximate area each group occupied. Then add the names of the groups that inhabited that area.

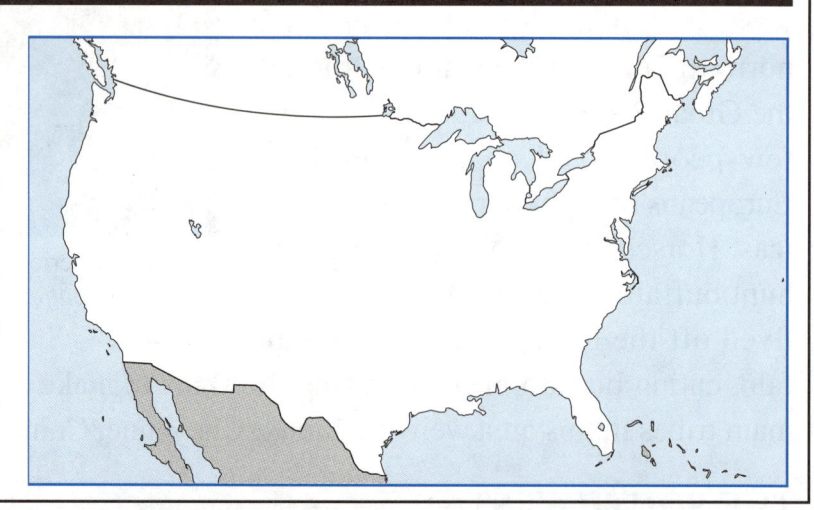

EXPLORING YOUR COMMUNITY
STEPPING INTO YOUR COMMUNITY'S PAST

What do you know about the Native American tribes who once lived in your local area?

Research: VISITING A TOWN OR COUNTY MUSEUM

Most communities in New York have a museum dedicated to their early history. In your local museum, you are sure to find a section devoted to the Native Americans that lived in your area. Look for the following information:

- **Name.** Name the Native American groups that lived in your area.
- **Daily Life.** Briefly describe what their daily life might have been like.
- **Clothing.** Describe how these Native Americans dressed and how they made their clothing.
- **Buildings.** Describe or draw what their homes may have looked like.

Your Task: WRITING IN A DIARY

Imagine that you are a young member of a local Native American group several hundred years ago. Write a diary entry for **one** day in your life. Your diary entry should summarize what life was probably like as a member of this group.

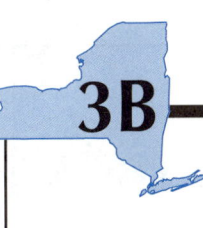

ARE YOU A GOOD HISTORIAN OF COLONIAL TIMES?

3B

In this activity, you will read about some exciting events in the days when New York was a colony. Look for the following words:

- New Netherland
- Patrons
- American Revolution
- Declaration of Independence

Historians are people who study the past. They often try to understand what it was like to live in another time. As you read the following pages, you will be asked to play the role of an amateur historian. Try to imagine what it would have been like to live in the past.

THE EUROPEANS COME TO NEW YORK

Five hundred years ago, trade between Europe and East Asia was very profitable. Most European traders used land routes that were long and dangerous. They wanted to find an easier and safer way. European nations sent out explorers to find an all-water route to the "Indies"—the islands of East Asia.

A Note on the Countries of Western Europe

Portugal, Spain, France, Great Britain and Holland were all active in early overseas exploration. Spain and France were kingdoms in Western Europe. Great Britain, an island west of Europe, was made up of three kingdoms: England, Scotland and Wales. After 1603, the King of England ruled over all three kingdoms. People from Great Britain are often referred to as British, but can also be called English, Scottish or Welsh (depending on where they come from). Holland, sometimes referred to as the Netherlands, became independent in the 1580s. The people of Holland are known as the Dutch.

THE EUROPEANS EXPLORE NEW YORK

As you read, look for answers to the following questions:
1. Who were some of the early explorers of New York?
2. What was Henry Hudson trying to find?

In 1492, **Christopher Columbus** sailed west across the Atlantic Ocean to find a shorter route to the Indies. Instead, he found a new continent, the "Americas." When he returned to Europe, he spoke of great riches in what became known as the "New World." Later, explorers from other European countries sailed in search of gold and other riches. In 1524, **Giovanni Da Verrazano**, an Italian explorer sailing for France, became the first European to enter New York harbor.

Giovanni da Verrazano

It was another 85 years before Europeans again entered the waterways of New York. **Henry Hudson**, an English sea captain, was hired by Dutch merchants who were also looking for a faster route to Asia. In September 1609, Hudson reached New York harbor and began sailing up the river that bears his name today. Hudson and his crew sailed as far north as present-day Albany. By that time he decided that the Hudson River was not the Northwest Passage to Asia that he was seeking, and turned around. In the same year, another explorer, **Samuel de Champlain**, journeyed through the lakes and forests of upstate New York for the King of France. Lake Champlain in the northeastern part of the state is named after him.

French explorer Samuel Champlain explored Canada and upstate New York.

THE DUTCH COLONY OF NEW NETHERLAND

As you read, look for answers to the following questions:
1. Where did the early settlers of New York establish a colony?
2. What kinds of goods did the Native Americans and Dutch trade?

Based on Hudson's explorations, the Dutch set up a successful fur trade with the native peoples of the Hudson River Valley. They were the first Europeans to settle in New York. The Dutch called their colony New Netherland . The Dutch government gave ◄ control of the colony to the Dutch West India Company.

In 1624, thirty families came to settle **Fort Orange**, known today as Albany. More settlers arrived the next year and established a second fort at the tip of Manhattan island. The Dutch governor, **Peter Minuit**, gave beads and other trinkets to the Algonquians of Manhattan to buy the island. The settlement was called **New Amsterdam**, after the Dutch city of Amsterdam.

The New Netherland colony was a trading post for furs. Beaver skins and other furs were highly valued in Europe at this time. The city of New Amsterdam, with its fine natural harbor, soon became a leading center for trade. In order to provide protection against attacks from Native Americans or other European countries, the settlers built a long wall along the north side of New Amsterdam. Later, this wall became Wall Street.

Peter Minuit is said to have "purchased" Manhattan Island for $24 in beads and trinkets from the Algonquians.

At first, the Dutch got along quite well with most of the Native Americans. Their friendship was important to the Dutch, because the Native Americans showed them how to fish, hunt and grow new crops. In return, the Native Americans received goods such as guns, sugar, metal tools and woven cloth. Unfortunately, relations between the Dutch and Native Americans soon became less friendly. War broke out in the 1640s and almost led to the destruction of the colony of New Netherland.

Dutch settlers sign a treaty with Native Americans at Fort Amsterdam

THE DUTCH COLONY GROWS LARGER

> *As you read, look for answers to the following questions:*
> 1. What was a patroon?
> 2. How did New Netherland become a British colony?
> 3. Why were the English interested in gaining control of New Netherland?

In the following years, Dutch colonists set up new farming communities at Haarlem (*Harlem*), the Broncks (*Bronx*), Schenectady, Breukelen (*Brooklyn*), Wiltwyck (*Kingston*) and Rensselaerwyck (*Rensselaer*). Growth of the colony of New Netherland was slow. Few Dutch people wanted to leave the comfort and safety of the Netherlands for the dangers of the "New World."

To encourage more people to settle in New Netherland, the Dutch West India Company came up with a plan. Sixteen square miles of land were given to wealthy landowners called **patroons**. In exchange for the land, each patroon agreed to bring in 50 new settlers. The patroon offered settlers land, seed and animals in exchange for payments of rent. However, most of the patroons were unsuccessful.

The earliest known view of New Amsterdam (1651) In what ways has New York City changed in the last 350 years?

Despite the failure of the patroon system, the number of settlers in New Netherland slowly began to grow. The Dutch welcomed people from other countries in Europe. Walking around New Amsterdam in 1660, a visitor might see Irish, British, German, French, Native American and African people in the streets. Most Africans in New Netherland were brought as enslaved peoples.

One thing that made the Dutch colony unusual was its acceptance of diverse religions. Many religious groups, including Quakers and Jews, were allowed to practice their religion in New Netherland. The Dutch governor, **Peter Stuyvesant**, sometimes complained about this religious freedom. He thought all the settlers should belong to the Dutch Reformed Church. But the merchants in Holland who owned the colony told Stuyvesant that religious freedom should be protected.

Peter Stuyvesant became Governor in 1647. Many of those living in New Netherland complained about his arrogance and bad temper.

As the years went by, more and more English people settled in New Netherland. English colonists from Connecticut crossed the waters of Long Island Sound to start their own towns on Long Island. In 1650, the Dutch agreed to give the Connecticut Valley and western Long Island to England.

The government in England, however, had its eyes on the whole Dutch colony. New Netherland was viewed as a valuable trading center, with an excellent port and an important river leading into the interior. Most important of all, the Dutch settlement physically separated the English colonies along the Atlantic coast. When England and Holland went to war for control of world trade in 1664, four English ships sailed into the harbor of New Amsterdam. Governor Stuyvesant wanted to fight, but the townspeople refused. Without soldiers to fight, Peter Stuyvesant had no choice but to surrender.

THE AMATEUR HISTORIAN: RECREATING THE PAST

1. **Creating Models.** What did Fort Orange or the walled city of New Amsterdam look like? Build a small model of Fort Orange or New Amsterdam out of cardboard, clay, paper maché or other materials. Label as many buildings as you can and tell the role each building played in the life of the settlement.
2. **Locating Historical Places.** On a map of New York State, locate some of the original Dutch settlements: Fort Orange (*Albany*), Haarlem (*Harlem*), the Broncks (*Bronx*), Schenectady, Breukelen (*Brooklyn*), Wiltwyck (*Kingston*) and Rensselaerwyck (*Rensselaer*).

THE ENGLISH TAKE OVER THE NEW YORK COLONY

NEW NETHERLAND BECOMES NEW YORK

The colony of New Netherland lasted less than 60 years. The King of England, Charles II, gave the conquered colony to his brother James, the Duke of York. In the Duke's honor, New Netherland was renamed **New York**. New Amsterdam became **New York City**. Fort Orange was renamed **Albany**.

The English agreed to let the Dutch settlers keep their lands and businesses. The Dutch influence on New York left an important mark. Many of the names of cities were originally Dutch words. Many of the earliest churches and other buildings in New York date back to the days of Dutch rule.

Under English rule, New York continued to prosper. New York City became an important port. Other parts of the colony developed rapidly. **Fort Stanwix** (*now Rome*), and Oswego became centers for the fur trade. On Long Island, coastal ports like Cold Spring Harbor and farm villages like Smithtown developed.

LIFE IN COLONIAL NEW YORK

As you read, look for answers to the following questions:

1. How did the jobs of men and women on farms differ in colonial New York?
2. Explain why churches were an important part of life in colonial New York.

Outside New York City, most colonists were farmers, living in the valleys of the Hudson or Mohawk Rivers or on Long Island. Many of them owned their own small farms and grew food to meet their own needs. Others rented land from wealthy landowners. A large number of these farmers sold lumber and wheat to the merchants of New York City.

Life in colonial New York was hard. One of the toughest jobs for settlers was clearing the land to be able to plant crops.

Families in these days were often large, with five or more children. Everyone on the farm had a special job. The men cleared land, farmed, fished, hunted and built houses and farm buildings. The women cooked, cleaned, sewed, and helped with the farmwork. During leisure time, people would sing, dance and enjoy a meal with their friends and families.

New York City was dominated by a small group of wealthy merchants, landowners and lawyers. They financed overseas trade or owned large pieces of land in the Hudson Valley. The city also had a large middle class made up of shopkeepers and craftsmen. The craftsmen made the ships, sails, bricks, furniture and other things needed by colonial society. Finally, there were many workers, servants and slaves. They owned no property. They did many of the hardest jobs and often lived in the worst conditions.

New York under British rule continued the Dutch policy of religious freedom. The church was the center of life and the main meeting place in many New York towns. It was a place of learning and a place to go with family to meet friends. New homes were often constructed near the church. In many places, the minister was the most important person in the community.

NEW YORKERS ENJOY BASIC RIGHTS

As you read, look for answers to the following questions:

1. Describe the government of the New York colony.
2. Describe the charter that the Governor gave to the citizens of New York.

At first, New Yorkers had little say in their government. The English king appointed a **Governor** to lead the colony. The Governor chose his own group of advisers, known as the **Council**. In 1665, the towns of Long Island won some powers of local self-government. Then in 1682 the Governor of New York gave all citizens a charter. This charter guaranteed freedom of religion and trial by jury. It also created a law-making body called the **Assembly**. The members of the Assembly were elected to represent the colonists. Membership in the Assembly was limited. Women, enslaved peoples, Native Americans and workers without land were not allowed to vote.

By the late 1700s, it seemed to many New Yorkers that Great Britain was controlling more and more of what they could do. Disagreements arose between the Assembly representing the colonists and the Parliament (*law-making body*) in Great Britain. The colonists felt that many of the laws passed by Parliament benefited the people living in Great Britain more than the colonists. Many people in other American colonies felt the same. Eventually, these feelings would lead to the **American Revolution**.

George III was the King of England at the time of the American Revolution.

THE AMATEUR HISTORIAN: RECREATING THE PAST

1. **Writing Letters.** Pretend you are a person living in the colony of New York in the early 1700s. Write a letter to your friends in Europe. In your letter describe what life was like in colonial New York in those days.

2. **Writing An Editorial.** An editorial is an article written in a newspaper. It provides opinions about important issues. Pretend it is the 1700s. Write a five-sentence editorial giving your opinion about whether women, slaves, Native Americans and workers without land should be allowed to vote for members to the Assembly.

NEW YORK'S ROLE IN THE AMERICAN REVOLUTION

Between 1754 and 1763, Great Britain and France fought a war for control of Canada and the lands west of the Appalachian Mountains. The Iroquois sided with the British, while other Native American tribes helped the French. The war became known as the **French and Indian War**. By 1763, Great Britain had conquered Canada and won the war.

THE ROAD TO THE AMERICAN REVOLUTION

> *As you read, look for answers to the following questions:*
> 1. How did the British need for money after the French and Indian War lead to disagreements with the American colonists?
> 2. Who were the patriots and the loyalists?

Great Britain wanted the Americans to help pay some of the costs of fighting the war. The British placed many new taxes on the colonists, without first discussing this with them. The cry of "no taxation without representation" quickly spread throughout the British colonies. Many colonists began to feel they would be better off without Great Britain as a Mother Country. Finally, fighting broke out between colonists and British soldiers in 1775. This was the start of the American Revolution. A **revolution** is a change of government by force.

Some colonists, to protest English taxes on tea, disguised themselves as Native Americans and dumped tea into Boston Harbor.

The idea of breaking away from Great Britain divided the American colonists. Many colonists believed that they should become independent from England. They called themselves **patriots**. Among the patriots were farmers and settlers who had come to New York from countries other than England. A large number of African Americans, both free and enslaved, also supported the patriots. Those who were enslaved hoped to gain their freedom if the colonists became independent. Two of the six Iroquois nations also supported the patriots.

Other colonists opposed the idea of independence from Great Britain. They were known as **loyalists** or **Tories**. New York had more active loyalists than any other colony. While these people opposed many of the new taxes, they still believed New York was better off under British rule. Among the loyalists were wealthy business people, rich farmers and large landowners. The British offered freedom to any slaves who fought on their side. This convinced many enslaved blacks to fight on the side of the British. In addition, four of the six Iroquois nations supported the British.

THE IDEA OF INDEPENDENCE GROWS

Protests turned to warfare when shots were fired between British soldiers and colonists at Concord, Massachusetts in 1775. Fighting quickly spread to the other colonies. Leaders from all 13 colonies called a meeting of the **Continental Congress** in Philadelphia. They discussed the possibility of independence. After much debate, they decided to declare their independence from Great Britain.

Fighting broke out between American colonists and English soldiers in Massachussetts in 1775.

A committee was chosen to write a **Declaration of Independence**. **Thomas Jefferson** was the main author. This document explained to the world why the colonists sought independence from Great Britain.

Historic Documents: *The Declaration of Independence*

The Declaration of Independence laid the foundation for the United States to become the first democratic nation in modern times. It also served as an inspiration to later generations. The first paragraph of the Declaration, issued on **July 4, 1776**, stated:

> ### The Declaration of Independence
> We hold these truths to be self-evident [obvious], that all men are created equal, that they are endowed [given] by their Creator [God] with certain unalienable [cannot be taken away] rights, that among these are life, liberty and the pursuit of happiness. That to secure [protect] these rights, governments are instituted [created] among Men, deriving [getting] their just powers from the consent of the governed, that whenever any form of government becomes destructive [harmful] of these ends, it is the right of the people to alter [change] or abolish [end] it, and to institute [create] new government ...

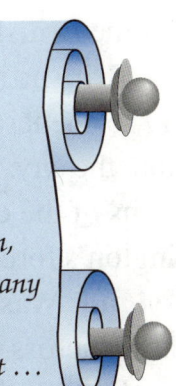

Sometimes, words written over 200 years ago are hard to understand. Let's see how well you understand this document by answering the following questions:

1. What do you think the writers meant by the following words or phrases?
   - ❖ "All men are created equal"
   - ❖ "Unalienable rights"
   - ❖ "Liberty"
   - ❖ "Life"
   - ❖ "Pursuit of happiness"

2. The second sentence of the Declaration explains why governments are created.
   - ❖ Can you explain the writers' position in your own words? Do you agree?

NEW YORK'S ROLE IN THE AMERICAN REVOLUTION

As you read, look for answers to the following questions:

1. Why did the British and the colonists believe that New York was an important place to control at the time of the American Revolution?
2. Why has the Battle of Saratoga been called the "turning point" of the American Revolution?

Some of the earliest battles of the Revolution were fought in upstate New York. The colonists hoped to attack British Canada from New York. **Fort Ticonderoga**, located at the southern end of Lake Champlain, controlled travel between Quebec and the American colonies. In May 1775, a group of colonists from Vermont, known as the Green Mountain Boys, entered northern New York. Led by **Ethan Allan**, they captured the fort. Later, the fort was recaptured by the British and held by them until 1777.

The capture of Fort Ticonderoga

British troops left New York City in 1775. In April 1776, General **George Washington** led the colonial army into the city. Washington built fortifications in various sections of the city. In August, British troops attacked Washington's forces at Brooklyn Heights in the **Battle of Long Island**. Washington soon had to retreat. He moved his army across the East River from Brooklyn to Manhattan.

During the next two months, Washington faced the British again at Harlem Heights and White Plains. Washington lost these battles and was forced to retreat up the Hudson and southward into New Jersey. The British took over New York City, which became their American headquarters for the rest of the Revolution.

George Washington commanded the colonial army against the British.

The location of New York, between New England and the Southern Colonies, made it important to control. The British thought they could divide the colonies in two if they could capture the rest of New York. They drew up a plan to send three armies through different parts of New York. The three armies were to meet near Albany.

THE BRITISH PLAN FOR TAKING NEW YORK

THE BRITISH PLAN	WHAT HAPPENED
One army was to be sent from Canada to Lake Ontario, under the command of **Colonel Barry Saint Leger**. His army was to march east along the Mohawk River to Albany.	At the **Battle of Oriskany**, American troops under the leadership of **General Nicholas Herkimer** fought the British to a draw. Finally, additional American soldiers arrived and drove the British away.
A second army, under the command of **General William Howe**, was to march north along the Hudson River from New York City to Albany.	Instead of moving up the Hudson, General Howe decided to turn south to attack Philadelphia. Later, British troops began marching up the Hudson, but it was too late.
The largest army, commanded by **General John Burgoyne**, was to march south from Canada along Lake Champlain. Its mission was to capture first Fort Ticonderoga and then Albany.	At the **Battle of Saratoga**, American soldiers under the command of **General Horatio Gates** defeated the British. They captured five thousand British soldiers.

2. **Mapping Battles.** Make a map showing the sites where major battles of the American Revolution were fought throughout New York State. You can draw pictures of soldiers from both sides fighting at various places. Use different colors for each side. Be sure to include the dates of the battles. Find out if any battles were fought near where you live, and be sure to include these battles on your map.

3. **Considering Other Points of View.** Imagine you are a British soldier sent to colonial New York during the American Revolution. Write a letter to a local colonial newspaper explaining the British viewpoint of the war.

REVIEWING YOUR UNDERSTANDING

Creating Vocabulary Cards

American Revolution
What was the "American Revolution"?
Why did it begin?

Declaration of Independence
What is the "Declaration of Independence"?
Why was it issued?

Making a History Collage

A **collage** is an artwork of several different pictures on the same topic brought together. In this activity, you learned about New York's history during colonial times. Make a collage of some of the events that you learned about. You can draw pictures or photocopy illustrations from history books or encyclopedias. For example, you might want to illustrate daily life in colonial America. For this, use pictures of different people and how they lived.

Creating a Historical Cape

You have probably watched television and seen Superman or Batman wearing a cape. Some people make "fashion statements" with capes. Select an event from this activity. Create different ways of showing the event. For example, use a picture of a person closely related to the event, or a date cut from paper to show when it took place. Create several items that tell a story about the event. Cut an old bed sheet into the shape of a cape. Spread out the fabric and decide how you will cover it with your items. Arrange the items on the fabric, then paste or glue these items onto the cape. To wear the historical cape, simply tie the top two corners around your neck.

MAKING CONNECTIONS

EXPLORING BEYOND YOUR STATE
COLONIAL AMERICA

Many important events occurred in New York during the colonial period. These years were just as eventful for the other English Colonies.

THE ENGLISH COLONIES

Spain and Portugal were the first European countries to claim control of the "New World," based on the voyages of Columbus. The English came to believe that they had to establish their own colonies to avoid being overpowered by other European nations.

The first English colonies, Virginia and Massachusetts, soon extended up and down the Atlantic Coast. Dutch New York stood right in the middle of these two areas of English settlement. New York's location explains why it was so important for the English to take the colony from the Dutch in 1664.

Settlers came to the English colonies for many reasons. Some were searching for religious freedom. Others wanted land and a better life. Enslaved peoples were brought in large numbers from Africa to the Southern colonies of Virginia, the Carolinas and Georgia to work the land. Some were also brought to New York.

The population of the English colonies grew rapidly. By 1730, the thirteen colonies had spread along the entire Atlantic coast from the border of Florida to the edge of Canada. Different patterns of life developed in three separate regions:

❖ **New England.** The colonies of New England—Massachusetts, New Hampshire, Connecticut and Rhode Island—had less fertile land and were colder than the other colonies. Most of the early settlers were hard working Puritans. New Englanders had small farms where they grew crops for their own use. Many people from this area became sailors, merchants or fishermen. After the American Revolution, many New Englanders moved to western New York.

New England Puritans on their way to church

❖ CONTINUED

❖ **The Middle Colonies.** New York, New Jersey, Delaware and Pennsylvania occupied the coastline between New England and the Southern colonies. Winters were not as harsh as in New England and summers were longer. Uncleared forests and fertile soils attracted many settlers to this area. Good farmland in the Hudson and Delaware River Valleys allowed settlers to prosper. People were also attracted to these colonies by the atmosphere of religious freedom. The Middle Colonies became the "bread basket" of colonial America, since they supplied most of the grains and other basic foods eaten by the colonists. Philadelphia and New York City became major seaports.

❖ **The Southern Colonies.** The climate of the Southern Colonies—Virginia, Maryland, North and South Carolina and Georgia—was warmer than in the other colonies. The soil was well-suited to agriculture. Some Southerners developed large plantations, which grew tobacco, cotton, rice and indigo (*a plant making blue dye*). These crops were shipped to England in exchange for manufactured goods. Most of the larger plantations used enslaved African Americans as their main work force.

COMPLETING A MAP

Seeing the location of the colonies helps us to understand how their different lifestyles developed. Make a copy of the following map. Then, using an atlas:

❖ label each of the 13 colonies.
❖ draw a border around each of the three regions:
  • New England
  • the Middle Colonies
  • the Southern Colonies
❖ label the colonial ports of:
  • Boston
  • New York City
  • Philadelphia
  • Charleston

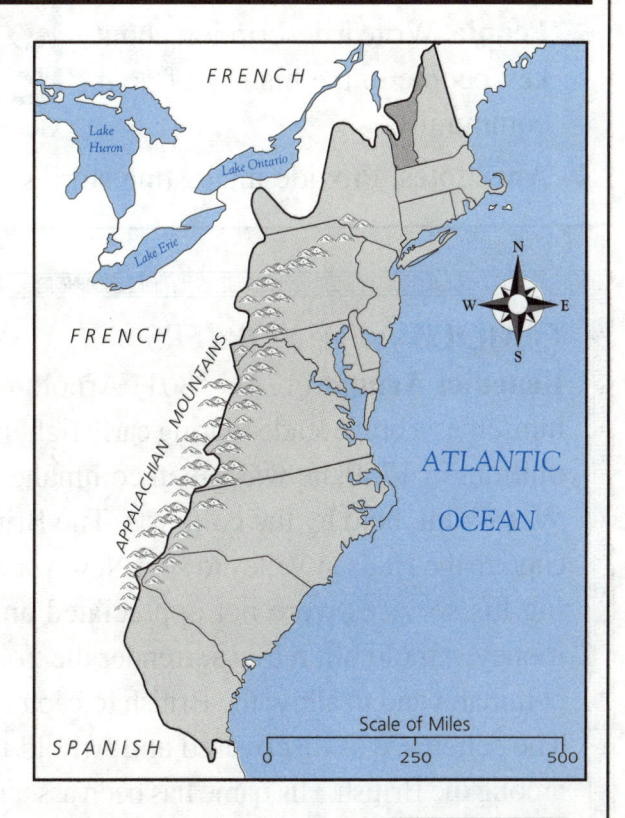

❖ **CONTINUED**

EXPLORING YOUR COMMUNITY
Writing About Your Community's History

What do you know about your community's early history? When was it settled? Who lived there? Imagine that you have been hired to be on the visitor's information staff of your community.

WRITING A STORY

You and the committee have the task of writing a story about the beginnings of your community. In writing your story, be sure to include each of the following:

❖ **Map.** Draw a simple map that shows the original boundaries of your community.

❖ **Illustrations.** Locate illustrations or photographs of your community's early history in your local library or museum.

❖ **People.** Write a description about key people in the history of your community.

Governor Peter Stuyvesant's home, "Whitehall," in 1658

❖ **Anecdotes.** Provide interesting stories about your community's history.

FAMOUS NEW YORKERS

Benedict Arnold (1741–1801) Arnold distinguished himself as a brave leader during early fighting in the Revolution. In 1780, he was given command of the fort at West Point, held by the colonists. The British hoped to capture the Hudson Valley to split New York in two. Feeling his services were not appreciated and in need of money, Arnold offered to surrender the troops under his command and to allow the British to capture West Point. The scheme was discovered and Arnold fled to safety among the British. His name has been associated ever since with betrayal and treason.

Benedict Arnold

ARE YOU A GOOD HISTORIAN OF EARLY NEW YORK STATE?

In this activity, you will read about New York State from the time of independence (1776) to just before the Civil War (1860). Look for the following words:

- Articles of Confederation
- Age of Homespun
- War of 1812
- Erie Canal

In the previous activity, you learned how historians often try to understand what it was like to live in the past. In this activity, you will read about New York's early years as a state while you continue to play the role of an amateur historian.

A NEW STATE AND NATION ARE BORN

At the end of the American Revolution, many New Yorkers celebrated their victory over the British. However, becoming a new state in an independent country soon led to unexpected problems.

ADOPTING A NEW CONSTITUTION

As you read, look for answers to the following questions:
1. List two problems Americans faced in setting up a new government.
2. Why did Americans create a weak central government after the Revolution?

After the Declaration of Independence, each of the former colonies became a separate, independent state. New York and the other new states each wrote its own state **constitution**—a written plan explaining how the government would work. New Yorkers adopted their first state constitution at Kingston in 1777. **John Jay** was the major author. That same year, **George Clinton** was elected as the state's first Governor.

The thirteen states also created a weak national government under an agreement called the **Articles of Confederation**. The new nation was called the **United States of America**. After their experiences with Great Britain, the former colonists did not want the central government to be too strong. Therefore, the states kept the most important powers for themselves—such as coining money, collecting taxes and raising an army.

Unfortunately, the new nation had so many problems in its first few years that Americans began to demand a change. In 1787, a convention met in Philadelphia and wrote a new constitution. This constitution proposed a stronger national government. There was to be a President, a Congress and a Supreme Court. In addition, the new national government would have the power to collect taxes, issue money and raise its own army.

In New York, there were heated debates about whether to approve the new Constitution. Some people feared the new national government would impose harsh new taxes and would not respect people's rights. Other New Yorkers, like **John Jay** and **Alexander Hamilton**, argued that the United States would not last very long unless the new Constitution was adopted.

Eventually, New York and the other states all agreed to accept the new Constitution. **George Washington** was elected as the nation's first President. For a short time, New York City served as the nation's capital. Washington was sworn in as President at Federal Hall in New York City on April 30, 1789. John Jay became the first Chief Justice of the U.S. Supreme Court. Alexander Hamilton, became the first Secretary of the Treasury.

Washington and his advisors: [left to right] Secretary of War Knox, Secretary of State Jefferson, Attorney General Randolph, Secretary of the Treasury Hamilton, and President Washington

THE AGE OF HOMESPUN

As you read, look for answers to the following questions:
1. What is meant by the Age of Homespun?
2. What caused the War of 1812 between the British and the Americans?

In the first years after independence, New York State grew rapidly. Many of the soldiers who had fought in the Revolution were paid with farmland in upstate and western New York. Many people from New England also moved to New York. Soon new townships sprang up with names like Rome, Ithaca, Syracuse, Buffalo, Rochester and Utica. By 1820, New York was the state with the largest population (*most people*). Almost one and a half million people called themselves New Yorkers.

▶ These years (1800–1850) are sometimes called the **Age of Homespun**. Pioneer farmers in western New York made most of the things they needed for survival by hand. They cleared forests, built their own homes and obtained their food by hunting and farming.

In the early 1800s, New York City benefited from a new war between Britain and France. Both countries bought goods and supplies shipped out of New York. However, as the war went on, the British began stopping American ships. This violated America's right to freedom of the seas. In 1812, war broke out between the British and the Americans. The conflict became known as the **War of 1812** because it started in that year.

Much of the fighting during the War of 1812 took place in upstate New York. In 1813, British troops from Canada burned the settlement at Buffalo. Other major battles took place at Fort Niagara, Sacket's Harbor and Plattsburgh. New Yorkers rejoiced when the war ended in 1815. American independence had been preserved.

THE AMATEUR HISTORIAN: RECREATING THE PAST

1. **Drawing A Poster.** Imagine that you are a supporter of the new U.S. Constitution. Draw a poster that you think would convince others to support it.
2. **Illustrating Yesterday's Fashions.** During the Age of Homespun, New York's farmers and workers dressed in a strong, loosely woven cloth of wool or linen. These fabrics came to symbolize their simple way of life. Using history books from your school or public library, find illustrations that show the way New Yorkers dressed in the Age of Homespun. Then make your own illustrations of these styles or your own article of clothing.

THE TRANSPORTATION REVOLUTION IN NEW YORK STATE

In the early 1800s, goods were moved in carts and wagons, and in sleighs in winter. The Appalachian Mountains were a major barrier to trade between the east coast and inland America. It became very important to have a good water route between the Atlantic Ocean and the Great Lakes, because it was much cheaper to ship goods by water. Building a canal to connect the Great Lakes with the Mohawk and Hudson Rivers was expected to greatly increase trade between both areas.

THE ERIE CANAL

As you read, look for answers to the following questions:
1. Why did some people believe it was important to build a canal connecting the Hudson River and Lake Erie?
2. In what ways did the canal help to develop New York and the United States?

In 1816, Governor **DeWitt Clinton** of New York proposed that a canal be built between the Hudson River and Lake Erie. Farmers could then ship goods from the Great Lakes to New York City entirely by water. Some New Yorkers thought that the canal would be a waste of money. After long debate, New York State lawmakers voted to build the canal.

Work began in 1817 and continued for seven years. Thousands of workers, many of them
▶ Irish immigrants, used hand tools to build the canal. The first section of the **Erie Canal** opened in 1819. Eventually, the canal was 363 miles long, stretching from Buffalo to Albany.

The canal made huge profits from the tolls it collected. Farmers in the Midwest were able to ship their goods to Eastern markets. The cost of shipping a ton of wheat fell from more than $100 to less than $5. Cities along the route, like Buffalo, Rochester, Syracuse, Rome, Utica and Albany prospered as a result of the canal. The Erie Canal became so successful that lawmakers voted to widen it in 1835. Meanwhile, construction was begun on many smaller canals across New York to connect to the Erie Canal.

TURNPIKES, STEAMBOATS AND RAILROADS

As you read, look for answers to the following questions:
1. Describe some of the improvements in transportation that took place during the "Transportation Revolution."
2. How did these improvements help the development of New York State?

The completion of the Erie Canal led many people to move to the western part of the state. Besides canals and rivers, people used roads. In the early 1800s, many private companies built special roads in New York called **turnpikes**. Carts, wagons, stagecoaches and riders on horseback paid a special toll to use these roads.

～ A NOTE ON TURNPIKES ～
Where does the name "turnpike" come from? Originally, owners of a section of a road used sharp pointed sticks, called pikes, to stop traffic. This allowed the owner of the road to collect a toll for horses and carriages that traveled along the road. Once the toll was paid, the owner would *turn* the set of *pikes* aside to allow traffic to pass.

PATH OF THE FIRST NEW YORK STATE TURNPIKE: 1815

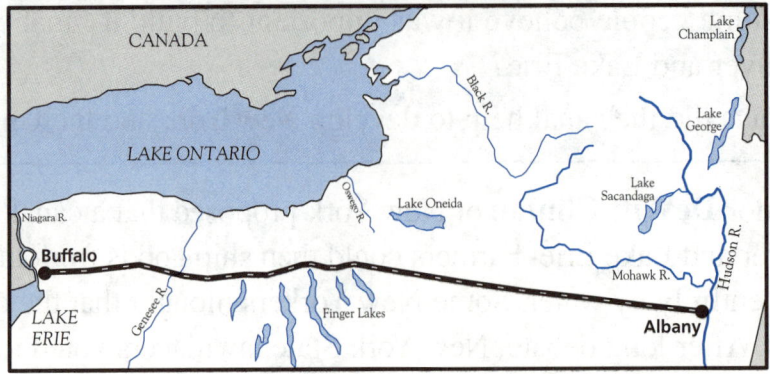

Another important improvement in transportation in these years was the invention of the steamboat. For more than a thousand years, people had used wind to propel their ships or animal power to pull them. In 1807, inventor **Robert Fulton** used the power of steam to move a boat. His steamboat, called the *Clermont*, connected a steam engine to a large wheel with paddles that turned in the water.

Steamboats could be used to go up rivers against the current. Fulton began a service up and down the Hudson River from Albany to New York City. It took about 32 hours to make the trip from Albany to New York City. Soon other inventors improved on Fulton's design. By 1830, steamboat travel was the leading method of water travel throughout the country.

Robert Fulton

Perhaps even more important than the steamboat was the invention of the railroad. Here, a steam engine was used to power "wagons" on fixed tracks. As early as 1828, the first American railroad started running in Baltimore, Maryland. Three years later, the Mohawk and Hudson Railroad began service in New York State. This line connected Albany and Schenectady. By the 1840s, railroads criss-crossed the state. The New York Central ran through western New York, parallel to the Erie Canal.

The Mohawk and Hudson Railroad in 1831

PATH OF THE ERIE RAILROAD: 1850

New Yorkers soon had many different ways to travel around their state. Cities along the routes of canals and railroads, like Utica, Syracuse, Rochester and Buffalo, continued to grow. Manufacturers in New York were able to ship their goods by canal and railroad to other parts of the nation.

138   NEW YORK: ITS LAND AND ITS PEOPLE

THE AMATEUR HISTORIAN: RECREATING THE PAST

1. **Pretending to be Governor Clinton.** Look up the Erie Canal in an encyclopedia or history book. Find some of the arguments used by Governor Clinton for building the Erie Canal. Then, write a brief speech that would convince New York State lawmakers to provide money to build the canal.
2. **Completing A Railroad Map.** Copy the map on page 137 above showing the route of the Erie Railroad. Using an atlas, write the names of as many cities as you can that are located along its route.

REVIEWING YOUR UNDERSTANDING

Creating Vocabulary Cards

Age of Homespun

What was the "Age of Homespun"?

When was it?

Erie Canal

What is the "Erie Canal"?

Why was it built?

Creating a Visual Biography of Alexander Hamilton

Alexander Hamilton was one of New York's most famous people. He was a leader in the move for American independence and helped convince New Yorkers to approve the new U.S. Constitution.

- Leader in the move for American independence
- ?
- ?
- ?

Alexander Hamilton

What other achievements of Hamilton can you add? Let's create a "visual biography" of his life. For each oval, describe and give the date of one of Hamilton's achievements or of an important event in his life.

MAKING CONNECTIONS

EXPLORING BEYOND YOUR STATE
THE INFLUENCE OF OUR CONSTITUTION

The national government created by the **Articles of Confederation** in 1781 was weak. It could not collect taxes, settle disputes among the states or raise its own troops. Most of these powers were held by the 13 independent states.

THE NEED FOR A NEW CONSTITUTION

When a small uprising of farmers broke out in Massachusetts in 1786, there was no national army to put it down. Fortunately, order was restored by the Massachusetts militia. But many people throughout the country, especially merchants and landowners, began demanding a stronger national government.

In 1787, representatives from the different states met in Philadelphia to strengthen the national government. They included such leaders as George Washington, Alexander Hamilton and Benjamin Franklin. The representatives decided to replace the Articles of Confederation with a new constitution. The idea of having a written constitution was unique since no other country had a written constitution at that time.

The main issue facing the members of the Constitutional Convention was the structure of the new national government. How could they create a national government strong enough to protect the people without also threatening their liberties?

They decided to give the government many important powers, but to divide these powers up. First, powers were divided between the national government and the 13 state governments. Then the power of the national government itself was divided among three separate branches: the legislative, executive and judicial. This would ensure that no one branch of the national government would become too strong.

One of the delegates to the Constitutional Convention was 81-year old Benjamin Franklin. He was elected President of the Convention.

❖ CONTINUED

GETTING THE CONSTITUTION APPROVED

Even with this design, the proposed Constitution had many opponents. At least 9 of the 13 states had to approve the new Constitution before it went into effect. Each state called a special convention to decide whether or not to approve it.

Approval by New York was important because of the state's size and location. Alexander Hamilton and John Jay were important supporters of the new plan. With James Madison, a Virginian, they wrote a series of essays that appeared in local newspapers. Their essays were meant to persuade members of the New York Convention to adopt the new Constitution.

Eventually, the Constitution was **ratified** (*approved*). Americans, especially New Yorkers, can be justly proud of this achievement. Our Constitutional system of government has contributed to the growth of democracy around the world.

WRITING A "WHAT IF" STORY

In a "what if" story you try to imagine "what" might have happened "if" something had turned out differently. What if the U.S. Constitution had not been approved by the 13 states? Write a "what if" story where you imagine that each state decided to go its own way and become an independent country. How might your life be different today? Start your essay with the following question:

What if the U.S. Constitution had not been approved by the 13 states?

EXPLORING YOUR COMMUNITY
RESEARCHING YOUR COMMUNITY'S PAST

In this activity, you read about lifestyles and transportation in New York in the early 1800s. What can you find out about your community during these same years?

WRITING A REPORT ABOUT YOUR COMMUNITY'S PAST

In a brief report, describe what life was like during this period in your neighborhood, village, town or city. There are many community organizations that can help you to find this information. Here are some resources to help you:

◆ CONTINUED

- ❖ **Local libraries.** The best place to begin any research project is your local library. Local libraries have large collections of books and old newspapers about your community. In addition, libraries often have collections of old photographs. These photographs are fun to look at and show a great deal about life in the past.
- ❖ **History Museums.** Most local history museums have displays that feature different time periods and objects from your community's past.

> The **Curtiss Museum of Local History** is located in Hammondsport. Glenn Curtiss was an early pioneer in aviation. He converted his motorcycle business into building engines that powered airplanes. His accomplishments are on display in the museum. His "flying boat" made the first crossing by air over the Atlantic Ocean. The museum has many of his aircraft on display.

- ❖ **Art Museums.** Local art museums usually display works of art, furniture and other memorabilia. They also often have slides, movies and videotaped presentations about their community's past.

> Visitors to the **Albany Institute of History and Art** can enjoy paintings dating back to 1791. In addition, they can view furniture, household items and folk art from the Albany and Upper Hudson River Valley area.

- ❖ **Historical Societies.** Many communities in New York have a local historical society dedicated to preserving their community's past. They will often have documents, artifacts and maps from the earliest periods of their community.

> The **Buffalo and Erie County Historical Society Museum** shows just about everything made in Buffalo from the 1840s to the 1980s. You can look at boxes of Cheerios and Wheaties made by a Buffalo branch of General Mills, or see one of George Pierce's old cars, a 1901 Pierce-Arrow.

- ❖ **Historic Homes and Villages.** Many towns and cities have homes that have been preserved. They were often the homes of famous people. In them you can see how people used to live, their furniture and leisure activities. Sometimes a community will have an entire group of restored homes.

> **Old Bethpage Village** is a restored village of Long Island buildings. You can walk among homes that bring to life the world of 19th century farmers. The Powell Farm house is the only building located on its original site. The other buildings in the village have been brought from other sites on Long Island.

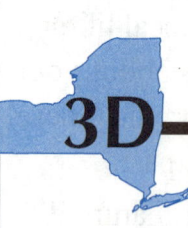

3D HOW WOULD YOU "DIAGRAM" WHAT YOU READ?

In this activity, you will learn about New York at the time of the Civil War. Look for the following important words:

- Main Idea
- Supporting Details
- Reform
- Seneca Falls Convention
- Abolitionists
- Underground Railroad

Although you have been reading for three or four years, have you ever thought about what a complicated process reading is? Let's look at this process.

Describe what you do when you read something to find its main idea.

WHAT DOES IT MEAN TO READ SOMETHING?

When you read, you try to understand the meaning of a group of words. This takes time and practice. To do it easily, you need to develop special skills. This activity will help you improve these skills.

A "reading passage" is usually a series of paragraphs that deal with a common theme. Each paragraph will contain a **main idea**. The other sentences usually give specific details, supporting or describing the main idea more fully. The following paragraph is an example:

New York has been a leader in educating its people for almost 200 years. During the state's early years, most children were taught at home. Where schools did exist, education was expensive. Children who could afford to go to church-run schools were often taught by untrained teachers. In 1812, the state legislature passed a law providing money for education and encouraging towns to establish local school systems. By the 1860s, the state was a leader in the number and quality of its schools. At the same time, working class parents pressured the state into providing free elementary education statewide.

Erasmus Hall Academy in Brooklyn was one of New York State's earliest public schools.

◆ CONTINUED

Notice that the main idea of this paragraph, that New York State has been a leader in educating its people, helps us to understand what the rest of the paragraph is about. The other sentences are supporting details —*specific facts or examples* that explain or illustrate the main idea.

Many people find that a diagram helps them to better understand a reading. Let's see what this reading might look like if it were put into the form of a diagram.

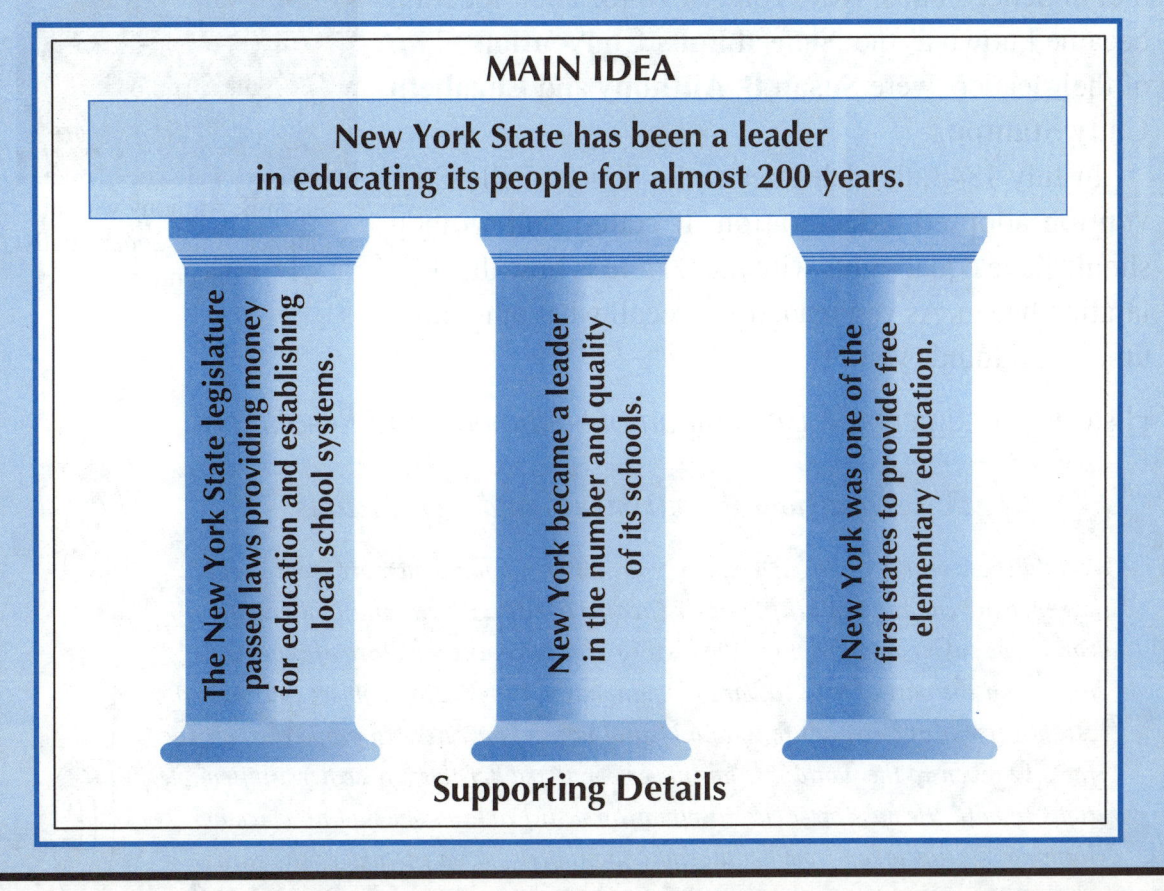

MAIN IDEA

New York State has been a leader in educating its people for almost 200 years.

- The New York State legislature passed laws providing money for education and establishing local school systems.
- New York became a leader in the number and quality of its schools.
- New York was one of the first states to provide free elementary education.

Supporting Details

Now it is your turn. Read the following passage about New York's struggle for reform. After reading the passage, you will create a diagram showing the main idea and three supporting details for a paragraph in the reading.

THE REFORM MOVEMENT IN NEW YORK

In the early 1800s, several reform movements arose in America. To **reform** something is to change it to make it better. During this period, New York reformers focused on giving more rights to women, improving prison conditions and bettering the treatment of the insane.

◆ CONTINUED

Rights For Women. In the early 1800s, women in New York and other states were treated as second-class citizens. They could not vote, attend college or enter many professions, such as medicine and the law. To protest these conditions, a group of women reformers met in Seneca Falls, New York, in 1848. Their meeting became known as the **Seneca Falls Convention**. Two of their leaders were **Susan B. Anthony** and **Elizabeth Cady Stanton**.

In July 1848, the delegates at the Seneca Falls Convention adopted a declaration. It stated that women should have equal rights with men. Here is how the declaration began. As you read, try to recall what other document it reminds you of.

Susan B. Anthony was an organizer of the Seneca Falls Convention.

Historic Documents: *A Declaration of Sentiments and Resolutions*

A Declaration of Sentiments and Resolutions

We hold these truths to be self-evident: that all men and women are created equal; that they are endowed [given] by their Creator [God] with certain unalienable [cannot be taken away] rights. The history of mankind is a history of repeated injuries on the part of man toward woman, having as its direct object [purpose] the establishment of an absolute tyranny [total power] over her. To prove this, let the facts be given to the world: He has never permitted her to exercise her unalienable right to vote. He has forced her to submit [give in] to laws she had no voice in forming. He has taken from her all right to property, even the wages she earns.

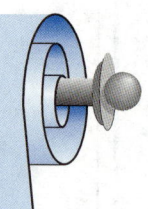

Prison Reform. Conditions in most of the nation's prisons were horrible. Prisons did nothing to help reform prisoners. Most city and county jails punished criminals by placing drunks, thieves and murderers together in one large room. Prisons were often dirty and unhealthy. Some prisons required their inmates to keep a strict silence. Guards often beat the prisoners. Food was of poor quality.

In the 1830s, New York led the world in the effort to reform prisons. **Eliza Farnham** was the warden in charge of a women's prison in New York State. She believed in treating prisoners fairly. She allowed prisoners to talk, ending the rule of strict silence. She opened a prison library and even established a school inside the prison to teach the inmates to read and write.

❖ CONTINUED

Improved Treatment For Mental Illness. In the 1800s, most people lacked the knowledge they needed to care for those with mental illnesses properly. Many mentally ill patients were locked in unheated rooms, chained to their beds and beaten into obedience. Sometimes, mentally ill people were even sent to jail.

Dorothea Dix led the fight for better treatment of the mentally ill. New York became a leader in improving the treatment of these patients. In 1821, a center opened in Manhattan to care for insane patients who were poor. In Utica, mentally ill patients were permitted to work outdoors and to enjoy limited recreation. Some New York counties established separate buildings to care for those with mental illness. However, they offered little in the way of special treatment. Major improvements in the treatment of mental illness were not to come for another century.

COMPLETING A "MAIN IDEA" DIAGRAM

Let's look at the paragraph dealing with prison reform and convert it into a "main-idea" diagram. Make a copy of the diagram below, and fill in each part that needs to be completed.

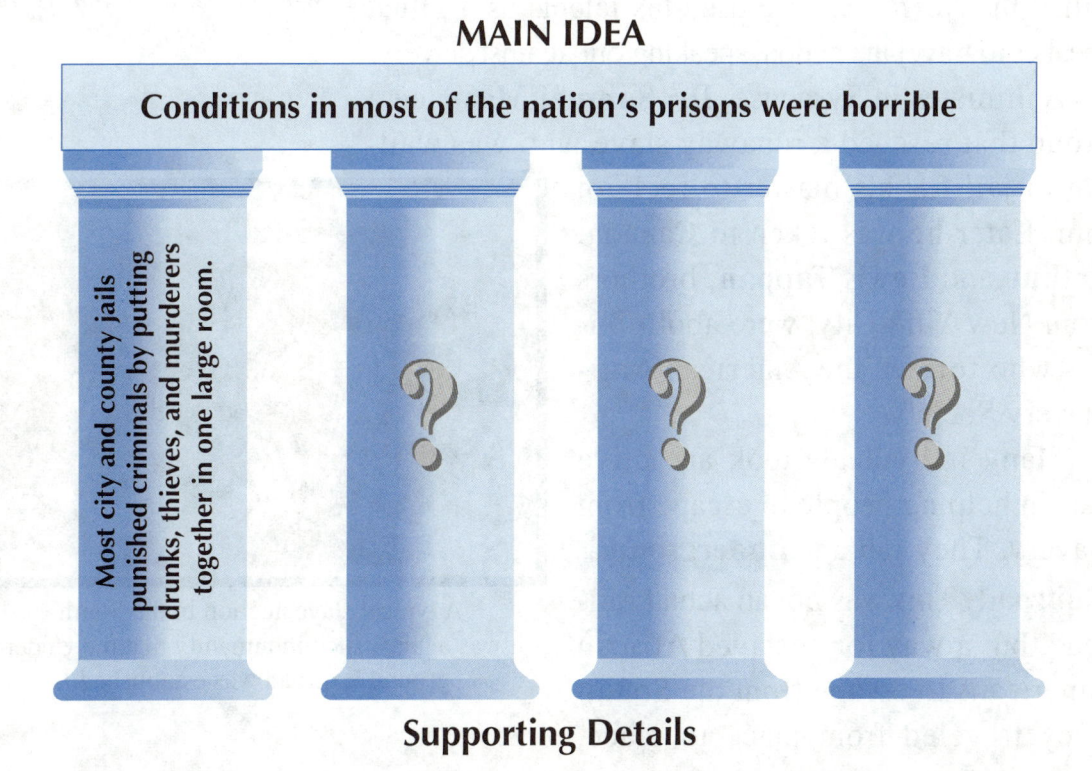

MAIN IDEA

Conditions in most of the nation's prisons were horrible

Most city and county jails punished criminals by putting drunks, thieves, and murderers together in one large room.

? ? ?

Supporting Details

Sometimes you may want to diagram an entire reading passage, not just one paragraph. In this case, you can create a "reading map." A **reading map** divides the main topic of the reading into smaller and smaller parts. It puts the main idea in the middle and surrounds it with supporting details. Other details are then added to explain these points. Let's see how this is done by reading about New Yorkers and the struggle to end slavery.

NEW YORKERS STRUGGLE AGAINST SLAVERY

▶ People who opposed slavery were known as **abolitionists**. Although slavery ended in New York in 1828, it still continued in the South. Many New Yorkers believed no person had the right to own another and that slavery was wrong. These New Yorkers fought against slavery in many ways.

One way New Yorkers fought against slavery was to try to persuade others to end it. **Frederick Douglass**, who had escaped from slavery himself, was New York's most famous abolitionist. In 1847, Douglass settled in Rochester. He soon started an abolitionist newspaper called the *North Star*. He used his talents as a gifted speaker to travel the nation, speaking out against slavery.

A minister in Syracuse, **Dr. Samuel May**, led a group that rescued a runaway slave who was waiting in jail for his master to reclaim him. Later he was taken to Canada. **Arthur** and **Lewis Tappan**, brothers from New York City, were abolitionists who formed the American Anti-Slavery Society.

▶ Many individuals took an active part in helping people to escape from slavery. They ran an **Underground Railroad**. This was not an actual railroad, but a way for enslaved African Americans to escape from the South. They traveled from place to place,

Frederick Douglass
Which other abolitionists can you name?

A typical slave auction in the South
It was against such inhumanity that the Underground Railroad was established.

◆ CONTINUED

AMERICAN HERITAGE 147

hiding in homes along the way, until they reached a place where slavery was illegal. Many slaves escaped to Canada, so that they could not be returned to the South.

During these years many New Yorkers acted as "conductors" of the Underground Railroad. They operated "stations" along the way where "passengers" could hide, be fed and receive fresh clothes. One such station was operated by **Gerritt Smith**, a wealthy New Yorker. One of the best known "conductors" in the Underground Railroad was **Harriet Tubman**. She escaped from slavery and settled in Auburn, New York. Tubman helped so many people escape through New York State on their way to Canada that she was called the "Moses of her People."

COMPLETING A DIAGRAM

Let's see how this reading might look when put into a reading "map." Make a copy of the map. Then fill in each uncompleted part.

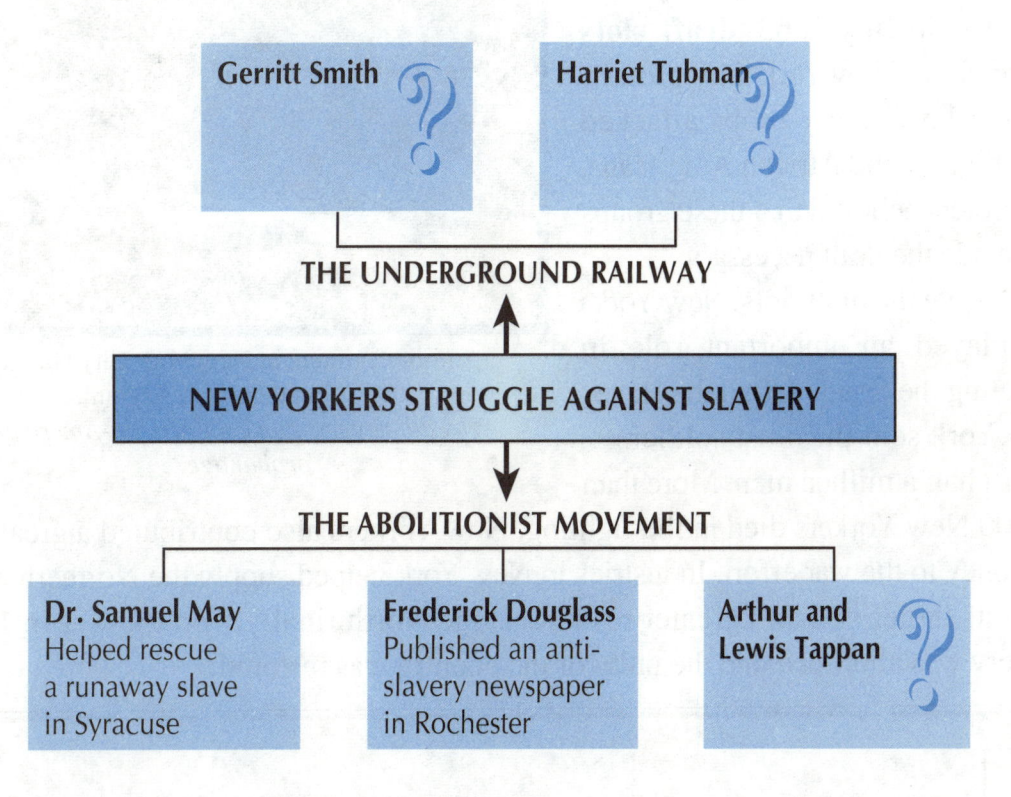

```
   ┌──────────────┐    ┌──────────────┐
   │ Gerritt Smith│    │Harriet Tubman│
   │      ?       │    │      ?       │
   └──────┬───────┘    └──────┬───────┘
          └──────────┬────────┘
            THE UNDERGROUND RAILWAY
                     ▲
                     │
   ┌─────────────────────────────────────┐
   │  NEW YORKERS STRUGGLE AGAINST SLAVERY│
   └─────────────────────────────────────┘
                     │
                     ▼
              THE ABOLITIONIST MOVEMENT
     ┌───────────────┼───────────────┐
┌─────────────┐ ┌─────────────┐ ┌─────────────┐
│Dr. Samuel May│ │Frederick    │ │Arthur and   │
│Helped rescue │ │Douglass     │ │Lewis Tappan │
│a runaway slave│ │Published an │ │     ?       │
│in Syracuse   │ │anti-slavery │ │             │
│              │ │newspaper in │ │             │
│              │ │Rochester    │ │             │
└─────────────┘ └─────────────┘ └─────────────┘
```

Now let's practice the technique of "mapping" on the final reading in this activity. Read the following passage and create a "reading map" to show how its main ideas are connected to supporting details.

NEW YORK IN THE CIVIL WAR

One of the most difficult periods in New York's history was the Civil War. A **civil war** is a war among people in the same country. The American Civil War began a few months after Abraham Lincoln was elected President. Many Southerners feared that he would abolish slavery. Southern states broke away from the United States and formed their own country, the **Confederate States of America**. Lincoln refused to allow the nation to be divided in two. Fighting began in 1861.

Although many New Yorkers signed up to fight for the North, more men were needed. In 1863, the U.S. government passed a "draft" law requiring all men between the ages of 20 and 45 to serve in the army. The law permitted a man to avoid serving if he could find someone to take his place, or if he paid a fee of $300. The draft law and the system of substitutes was unpopular with many New Yorkers. In July 1863, **draft riots** broke out in New York City protesting the law. Angry mobs attacked abolitionists and African Americans. The rioters believed that these groups had made the draft necessary.

Despite the draft riots, New Yorkers played an important role in defeating the South. Of all the states, New York sent the most soldiers—almost half a million men. More than 50,000 New Yorkers died in the fighting. New Yorkers also contributed a great deal of money to the war effort. Industries in New York helped supply the Northern army. With its larger size and greater resources, the North finally won the war in 1865. Slavery was abolished and the unity of the country was restored.

Anti-draft rioters in New York City burned the Colored Orphan Asylum.
Why did rioters attack an African-American orphanage?

CREATING YOUR "READING MAP"

Now that you have finished reading this passage, create your own "reading map" to show how its main idea and supporting details are connected to each other.

REVIEWING YOUR UNDERSTANDING

Creating Vocabulary Cards

Seneca Falls Convention

What was the Seneca Falls Convention?

Name two leaders at the Convention:

Abolitionists

What was an "abolitionist"?

Name two abolitionists from New York State:

Pretending to be Someone Else

One way to learn about a historical figure is to "be" that person—dress, act and speak as that person would. Select **one** person that you read about in this or a previous activity. Find out more about that person. Then design and make clothing similar to what that person might have worn. Come to class dressed as that person and be prepared to answer questions from other students about that person's life.

MAKING CONNECTIONS

EXPLORING BEYOND YOUR STATE
THE AMERICAN CIVIL WAR

The Civil War was the most destructive struggle in American history. More Americans were killed during the Civil War than in any other war. It would take Americans another century to heal the divisions caused by the war.

CAUSES OF THE CIVIL WAR

The Civil War began in 1861. Great events such as the Civil War often have several causes:

❖ CONTINUED

SECTIONALISM

One of the most important causes of the Civil War was sectionalism. During the early 1800s, the Northeast, South and Northwest sections (*regions*) of the United States each developed differently. Many Americans felt greater loyalty to their own section of the country than they did to the United States. This was called sectionalism.

NORTHEAST	SOUTH	NORTHWEST
The Northeast became a center of manufacturing, shipping, fishing and small farms. This section also experienced the first growth of the new class of factory workers. Factories and cities began to drastically change people's lifestyles.	A key institution in the South was slavery. Although most Southerners did not own slaves, much of the South's economy was based on profits made through the use of slave labor on large plantations, growing crops such as cotton.	The Northwest—now Wisconsin, Illinois, Indiana, Michigan, and Ohio—became the "bread basket" of the nation. Its grain was shipped by rivers and canals to the Northeast and South. Most people in the Northwest worked on small farms.

STATES' RIGHTS

Many Americans believed that the states had created the national government by approving the Constitution. Therefore, each state had a right to reject national laws or even to leave the United States if it wished. These views led the Southern States to **secede** (*withdraw*) from the United States when Lincoln was elected President.

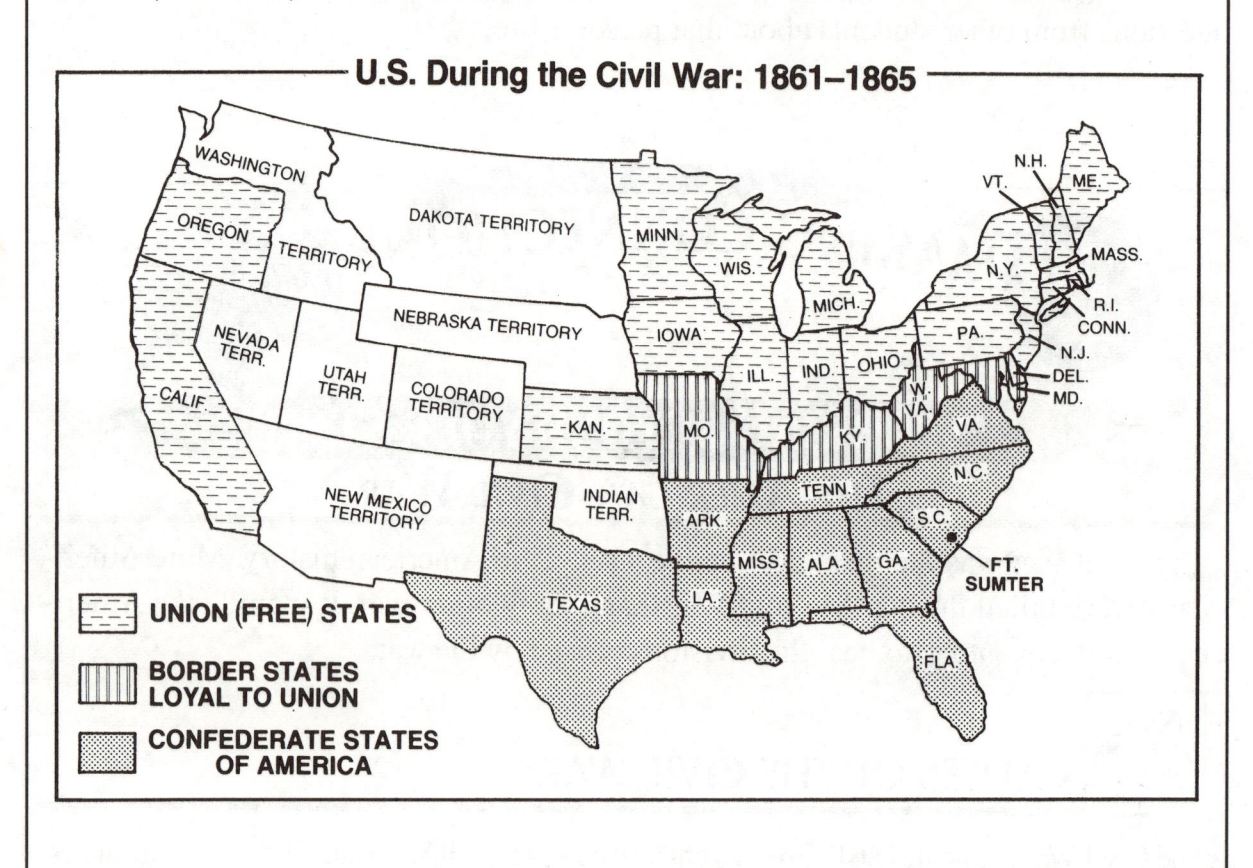

U.S. During the Civil War: 1861–1865

- UNION (FREE) STATES
- BORDER STATES LOYAL TO UNION
- CONFEDERATE STATES OF AMERICA

❖ CONTINUED

THE ISSUE OF SLAVERY

Many historians believe the most important cause of the Civil War was the issue of slavery. Slave owners did not see themselves as evil. They pointed to the existence of slavery in the Bible. Most slave owners also resented Northerners telling them what to do. They felt they treated their enslaved workers better than factory owners treated workers in the North. Although Lincoln began the war to keep the country united, it soon became a war over slavery. Lincoln issued the **Emancipation Proclamation** in 1862. It stated that enslaved people in the rebelling states would be freed on January 1, 1863. In 1865, Congress passed the 13th Amendment, abolishing slavery in the United States.

MAKING A READING MAP

In this activity you learned how to make a "reading map." Make a "reading map" about the causes of the Civil War.

EXPLORING YOUR COMMUNITY

TAKING A FIELD TRIP TO A LOCAL CEMETERY

You might be surprised to learn that one of the most interesting places in which to explore your community's history is a local cemetery. The earliest settlers, especially those traveling through the wilderness, often marked a grave with a pile of stones or wooden marker. As Americans began to set down roots in a particular community, churches and synagogues began marking graves with gravestones. The gravestone was meant to be a permanent symbol to mark a person's final resting place.

Often, people would write their **epitaph** (*a group of words written on a gravestone*) while they were still living. The inscription was carved or chiseled into the stone. The message was an attempt to leave behind a lesson to loved ones.

THE ART OF GRAVESTONE RUBBING

One of the most interesting things you can do when exploring an old cemetery is to make a "rubbing" of a gravestone. **Gravestone rubbing** allows you to learn a great deal about the history of a place and can be a lot of fun. However, be sure to have your teacher get permission from the people who run the cemetery before you begin.

❖ CONTINUED

Your Task: GRAVESTONE RUBBING

Gravestone rubbing is very simple to do. First, get a large piece of paper such as wrapping paper or shelf paper. The thinner the paper, the better the rubbing will come out. You will also need a dark crayon, a piece of charcoal or a thick pencil to use for the rubbing.

- **Condition.** Select a gravestone that is in good condition. The gravestone should have sharp, clear letters.
- **Selection.** Pick a gravestone that you find particularly interesting. You might be interested in a gravestone that is very old, has a different style engraving, a unique inscription, an unusual decoration or an interesting symbol carved into it.
- **What To Do.** Cut your wrapping or shelf paper to the size of the gravestone. Tape it over the face of the stone. Lightly rub your crayon, charcoal or thick pencil over the paper. You will see the impression from the gravestone start to create an image on the paper.
- **Focus on the Person.** Once you have completed your gravestone rubbing, you should focus on the person.

  - What was the person's name?
  - What were the dates of his or her birth and death?
  - How old was the person when he or she died?
  - Was the person married?
  - Are any of the person's relatives buried nearby?

Some old gravestones at a cemetery on Long Island.

HOW GOOD ARE YOU AT RECOGNIZING DIFFERENT TYPES OF READINGS?

3E

In this activity, you will learn about the Industrial Revolution and its effects on New York. You will also learn new ways to improve your reading skills. Look for the following important words:

- Industrial Revolution
- Urbanization
- Subway
- Tenements

It would be hard to recognize other people if we didn't know the general pattern of the human face. Knowing this general pattern helps us to detect slight differences in the features that make a person's face unique—the eyes, facial shape, hair color, nose and mouth. It is the same with reading. Although there are many types of readings, we can better understand specific types of reading selections if we recognize their general patterns.

THREE TYPES OF READINGS: PROBLEM-SOLUTION, SEQUENTIAL AND DESCRIPTIVE

There are three major forms of reading passages: the problem-solution reading, the sequential reading and the descriptive reading. A fourth type, the cause-and-effect reading, will be covered in the next activity.

TYPES OF READING		
Problem-Solution	**Sequential**	**Descriptive**
This type of reading identifies problems and describes some solutions. Key words in this type include *problem, recommendation, solution* and *result*.	This type of reading presents events in chronological order. Chronological order is the order in which events occurred in time. Key words in this type of reading include *later, before, after, next, following, then* and *preceding*.	This type of reading *describes* a person, place or event. The main idea sentence often states what is being described. The rest of the selection provides the characteristics of what is being described. Key words will usually focus on the *who, what, when* and *where* of what is being described.

In this activity, you will be presented with three reading passages. For each passage, you will need to identify what kind of reading it is and explain the reason for your choice. As you previously learned, it may help to **first** create a diagram of the reading.

THE INDUSTRIAL REVOLUTION COMES TO NEW YORK STATE

READING SELECTION #1

The Industrial Revolution began in England in the late 1760s. It was called a "revolution" because it changed the way people made goods. Instead of working at home, people began to make goods in workshops and factories. New machines helped people to produce goods more quickly and cheaply.

The Industrial Revolution spread from England to the United States in the early 1800s. The first cotton factory in New York opened in the Mohawk Valley in 1809. In the 1830s and 1840s, the Erie Canal and new railroad lines brought cheap coal from Pennsylvania to New York. This coal provided fuel to run factories throughout New York State. The same railroads and canals also allowed New York manufacturers to sell their goods to consumers throughout the nation.

In the 1860s, the Civil War created a great demand for clothing, uniforms and other supplies from New York. Following the Civil War, New York City became the nation's center for making clothes. Its workshops made coats, dresses, shirts, hats, furs, boots and shoes.

By the late 1880s, New York had emerged as the nation's leading industrial state. There were many reasons for this. The state's rivers, canals and railroads provided excellent transportation links with other parts of the nation. New York had an excellent harbor for shipping goods to Europe. Large numbers of skilled and unskilled workers lived in New York. So did many inventors and businessmen with new ideas. Lastly, New York banks had large amounts of money to lend to growing businesses.

New York City's excellent harbor helped New York State become a center of industry.
What other factors helped New York to become a leading industrial state?

AMERICAN HERITAGE 155

COMPLETING A DIAGRAM

Your Task

Make a copy of the diagram below. Then complete each part called for in the diagram.

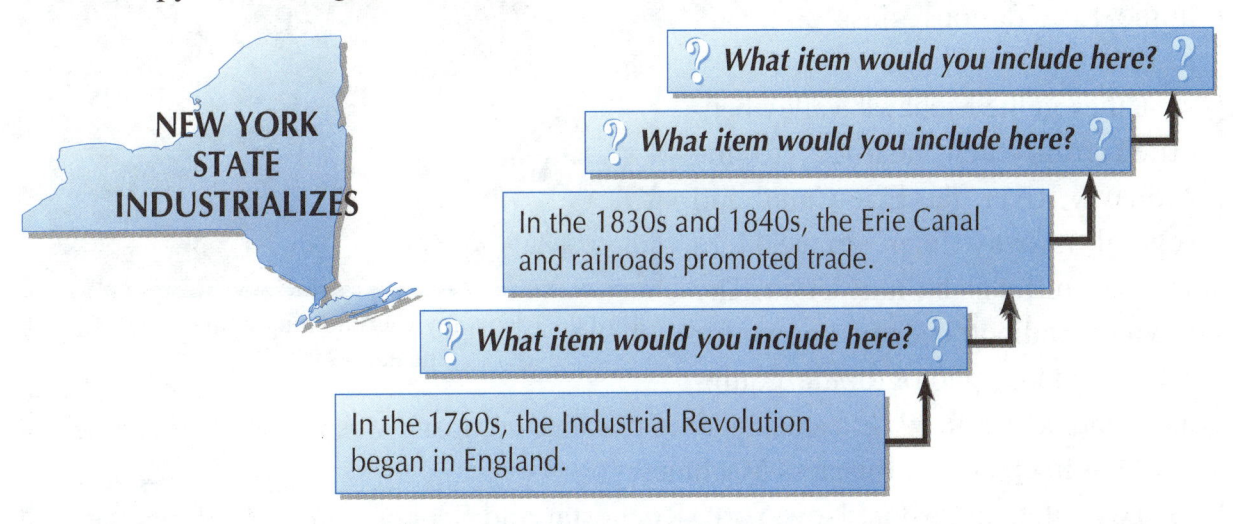

NEW YORK STATE INDUSTRIALIZES

- What item would you include here?
- What item would you include here?
- In the 1830s and 1840s, the Erie Canal and railroads promoted trade.
- What item would you include here?
- In the 1760s, the Industrial Revolution began in England.

Identify the type of reading: ___?___ *Explain your answer.*

THE INDUSTRIAL GROWTH OF UPSTATE NEW YORK

Information

READING SELECTION #2

By 1900, the cities and towns of upstate New York were experiencing great industrial growth. To the north, towns along the St. Lawrence River specialized in making lumber and paper. On the Great Lakes Plain, Buffalo became known for its iron products. After the completion of the Erie Canal and the railroads, the people of Syracuse began manufacturing machinery, farm tools and foods such as candy.

The Burden Iron Works factory in Troy

In the southwestern part of New York, Jamestown became a leading furniture center. Nearby, a successful oil well was drilled at Wellsville in 1879. Binghamton

❖ CONTINUED

was linked by train to New York City in 1848. It became known for its iron products and leather goods. The town of Corning, near Elmira, became home to a famous glass company in 1868.

Cities in the Mohawk Valley benefited from their nearness to the Mohawk River, the Erie Canal and several railway lines. In 1847, a woolen mill was built at Utica. The town of Endicott became known for rubber goods, photographic equipment and books. In 1911, a small adding machine company was formed there named I.B.M.—International Business Machines.

Buffalo's economy was booming in the late 1800s and early 1900s.

Two cities in upstate New York, Rochester and Schenectady, developed very special industries. Rochester, like New York City, was an early center for clothing manufacture. In the 1850s, **John Bausch** and **Henry Lomb** began producing optical goods there such as lenses for eyeglasses and other uses.

In the 1880s, a Rochester bank clerk named **George Eastman** began a photography company. In 1888, he developed the Kodak Camera. To take a picture all customers had to do with the Kodak camera was to click its shutter. The customer then returned the camera to Eastman's factory, where the film was taken out and developed. The Kodak camera became an instant success. Eastman became one of the richest men in America, while Rochester became a national center for photography.

In 1889, **Thomas Edison** formed the Edison General Electricity Company with its headquarters in Schenectady. Edison developed the electric light bulb and many other inventions using electricity. In 1892, Edison's company became General Electric (G.E.), a leading manufacturer of electrical equipment. Today, G.E. is still one of the state's major employers.

George Eastman

COMPLETING A DIAGRAM

Your Task

Now let's see how this reading could be presented in the form of a diagram.

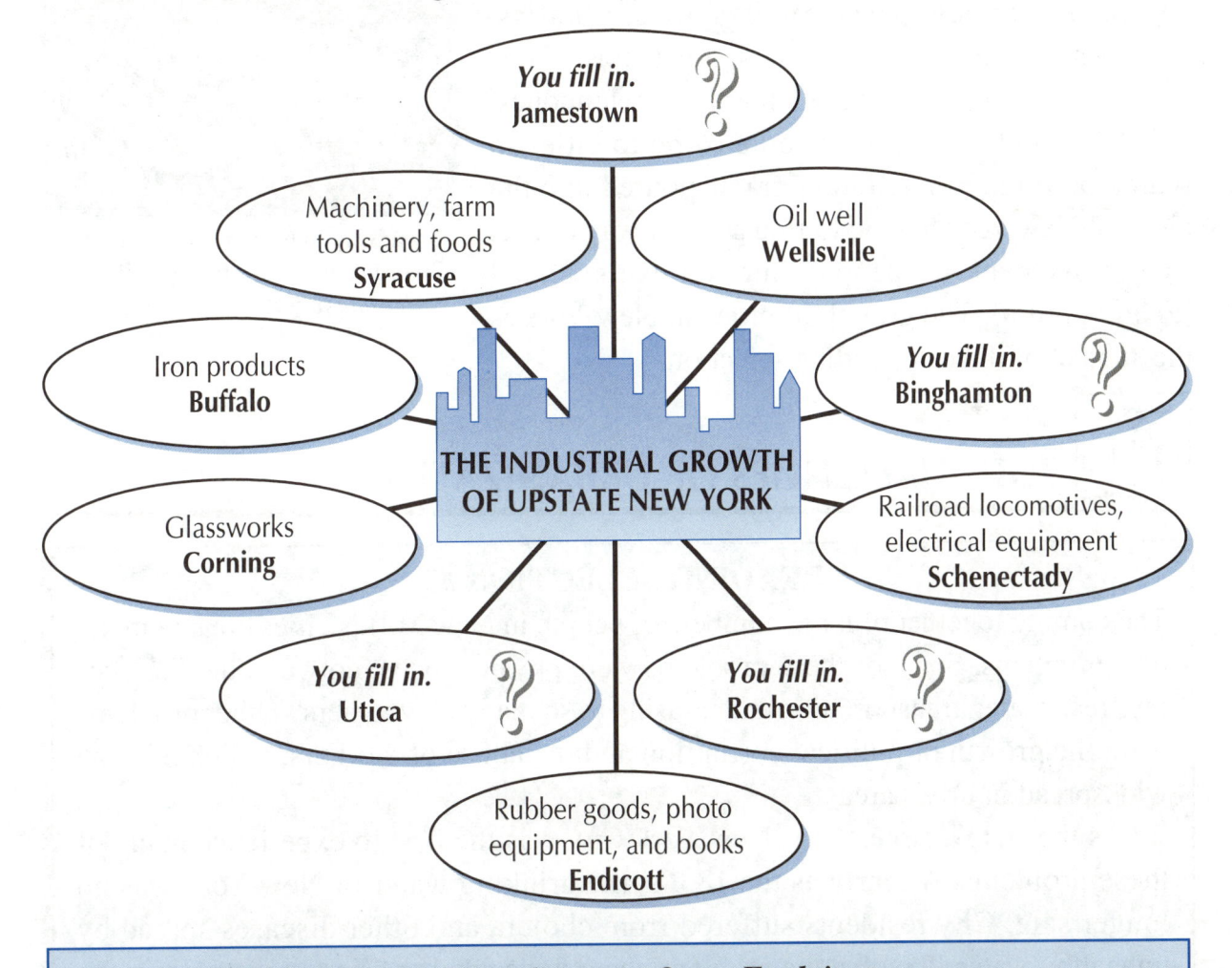

THE INDUSTRIAL GROWTH OF UPSTATE NEW YORK

- *You fill in.* **Jamestown**
- Machinery, farm tools and foods — **Syracuse**
- Oil well — **Wellsville**
- Iron products — **Buffalo**
- *You fill in.* **Binghamton**
- Glassworks — **Corning**
- Railroad locomotives, electrical equipment — **Schenectady**
- *You fill in.* **Utica**
- *You fill in.* **Rochester**
- Rubber goods, photo equipment, and books — **Endicott**

> **Identify the type of reading: ___?___ Explain your answer.**

You have just read how industrialization led to many important changes both around New York City and in upstate New York. New Yorkers were able to enjoy a greater variety of goods and services than ever before. More people began living in cities instead of in the countryside. People could travel by train, buy their clothes in stores, enjoy electric lights at night and speak with friends on the telephone.

These changes also brought problems. Industrialization created harsh working conditions for many laborers. They worked long hours and were barely paid enough to live on. The workshops and factories in which they worked were often uncomfortable and unsafe. Meanwhile, a few rich industrialists lived in great luxury and splendor.

These contrasts were felt most strongly in cities, where the very rich lived alongside the very poor.

Cities offered New Yorkers many new and exciting opportunities for culture and entertainment. They had their own newspapers, universities, libraries, churches, theaters, hospitals and sports teams. Cities were the first places to have telegraphs, telephones, streetcars and electricity. People came to cities in search of work. Foreign immigrants poured into the cities of New York hoping to find a better way of life. The movement of people into cities is called ▶ **urbanization**. The growth of cities in New York is the subject of the next reading selection.

Broadway in New York City (1886)
What problems did industrialization create for New York's cities?

THE CHALLENGES OF URBANIZATION

READING SELECTION #3

The coming together of large numbers of people in New York's cities created many new problems. Some of these problems were physical ones: how could cities supply fresh water, transportation and housing to so many newcomers? Other problems were the growth of political corruption and the abuse of workers, which became widespread in urban areas.

As the state's largest city, New York City was the first to experience many of these problems. As early as the 1830s, the drinking water of New York was no longer safe. City residents suffered from cholera and other diseases spread by unhealthy water. To solve the problem, the city decided to bring in water from the Croton River to Manhattan. Even this proved insufficient, and the city began building a second aqueduct (*large water pipe*) in 1885. Later, more water had to be carried an even greater distance from the Catskill Mountains. Other cities faced similar difficulties. Rochester taxpayers, for example, had to be persuaded to construct city waterworks. The project was only begun following the Civil War.

A second problem faced by New York and other cities was the need to transport large numbers of workers each day. In the early 1800s, workers had to live close to factories or workshops so that they could walk to work. In 1830, the first coaches on rails were introduced. These coaches were pulled by horses. The horse-car soon became the main method for taking people to work. In the 1880s, **trolleys** (*electric streetcars*) replaced horsecars.

◆ CONTINUED

In New York City, the streets were so crowded that the city began looking at other ways for people to travel. The city constructed elevated railway lines, known as the "el." However, the overhead tracks, station noise and smoke created problems of their own. In 1900, an underground **subway** was begun in Manhattan. By 1930, New York City had the world's largest subway system.

In the late 1800s a third problem facing city residents in New York State was the need for more housing. Builders designed special apartment buildings that could squeeze as many families as possible into a tight living space. These five-story brick apartment houses were known as **tenements**. Many of them lacked daylight, fresh air and adequate plumbing.

A typical New York City tenement

In 1890, the writer **Jacob Riis** exposed the miseries of life in the tenements. In his book, *How The Other Half Lives*, Riis discussed what life was like during the hot summer months:

Historic Documents: *From "How the Other Half Lives" by Jacob Riis*

> With the first hot nights in June police dispatches record the deaths of men and women who roll off roofs and window-sills while asleep. The time of greatest suffering among the poor is at hand. It is the hot weather, when life indoors is nearly unbearable with cooking, sleeping, and working, all crowded into small rooms in the tenement. In the hot July nights, when the big buildings are like hot furnaces, their very walls giving out heat, men and women lie panting for air and sleep. Then every truck on the street, every crowded fire-escape, becomes a bedroom, preferred to any in the house. Life in the tenements spells death to an army of little ones. Sleepless mothers fan the brow of their sick babies. There is no sadder sight than this.

The growth of cities also gave rise to political corruption. Political "bosses" did favors for city residents to win votes. Then they used their control of city government to make money. In the 1880s, Governor **Grover Cleveland** introduced a civil service law to prevent dishonesty. Under the new law, people had to pass a test to

❖ CONTINUED

160 NEW YORK: ITS LAND AND ITS PEOPLE

work in state government. Cleveland also gave city mayors throughout the state greater power to appoint their own officials.

A final problem that affected cities was the poor treatment of workers. People worked long hours in dangerous conditions for low pay. Many workers were immigrants unable to defend their rights. Other workers were children. To prevent these abuses, the New York State Legislature passed a law in 1886 creating the position of state factory inspector. The state also outlawed some forms of child labor. In these same years, workers started to organize into labor unions.

Your Task: COMPLETING A DIAGRAM

The following diagram maps this reading.

NEW YORK'S GROWING CITIES

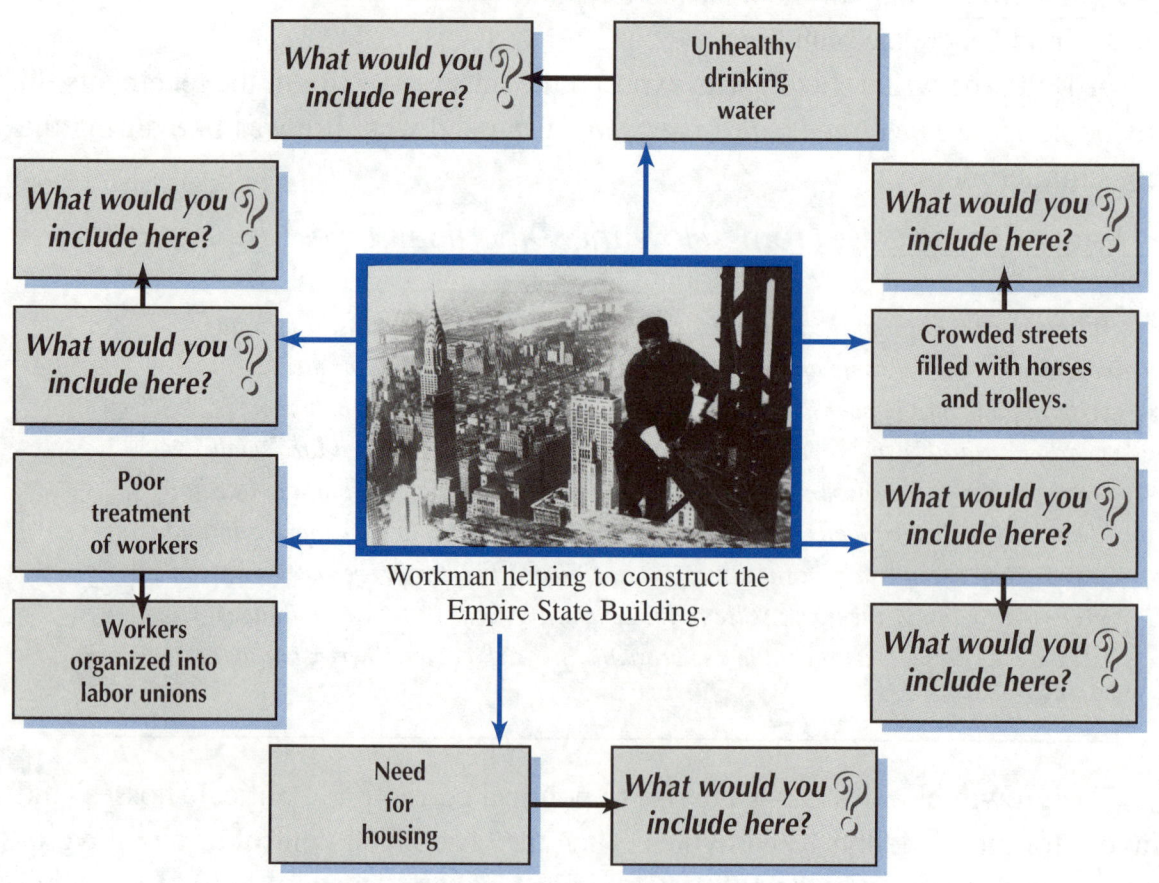

- Unhealthy drinking water → *What would you include here?*
- *What would you include here?*
- *What would you include here?*
- Crowded streets filled with horses and trolleys. → *What would you include here?*
- *What would you include here?*
- Poor treatment of workers → Workers organized into labor unions
- Need for housing → *What would you include here?*

Workman helping to construct the Empire State Building.

Identify the type of reading: ___?___ Explain your answer.

REVIEWING YOUR UNDERSTANDING

Creating Vocabulary Cards

Industrial Revolution

What was the "Industrial Revolution"?

How did it change the way goods were made?

Urbanization

What is "urbanization"?

Name two problems that came about as a result of urbanization:

Writing A Letter

Pretend you are Thomas Edison or George Eastman. Write a letter to a member of your family explaining one of your inventions. In your letter be sure to describe what your invention looks like and how it works. Also discuss how you expect this invention to change the lives of people living in America.

Completing A Chart

The following chart shows some cities in New York State where large numbers of people live. Complete a copy of the chart by recording their present populations.

POPULATION OF SELECTED CITIES IN NEW YORK STATE

City	1865	1900	1920	1940	1960	Present Year
N.Y.C.	1,123,682	3,347,202	5,620,048	7,454,995	7,781,984	???
Albany	62,613	94,151	113,344	130,577	129,726	???
Buffalo	94,210	352,387	506,775	575,901	532,759	???
Rochester	50,940	162,608	295,750	324,975	318,611	???
Elmira	13,130	35,672	45,393	45,106	46,517	???
Syracuse	31,784	108,374	171,717	209,326	216,038	???

A. Find and identify each city on a map of New York State.
B. Which city grew the most in population from 1960 to today?
C. What factors do you think caused some cities to grow more rapidly than others?

MAKING CONNECTIONS

EXPLORING BEYOND YOUR STATE
THE RISE OF INDUSTRIAL AMERICA

The years following the end of the Civil War were a period of great change in the United States. Let's examine some of these changes.

CHANGES IN THE UNITED STATES

THE GROWTH OF AMERICA'S CITIES

Industrialization affected cities like Chicago, Philadelphia, New Orleans, and Cleveland as well as the cities of New York. The growth of railroads helped connect these cities and made it possible for manufacturers in one part of the country to sell goods in another.

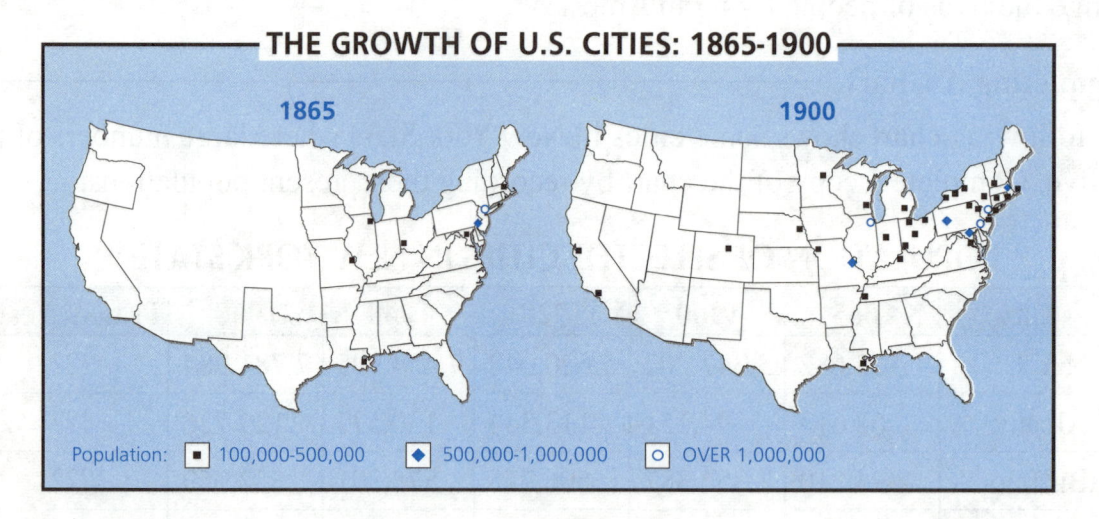

THE GROWTH OF U.S. CITIES: 1865-1900

1865 | 1900

Population: ■ 100,000-500,000   ◆ 500,000-1,000,000   ○ OVER 1,000,000

A GROWING POPULATION

The growth of population, especially in the North, provided new markets for manufactured goods. It also provided additional workers for industry. Population growth was further increased by a steady stream of immigrants from Europe.

THE RISE OF WEALTHY INDUSTRIALISTS

A few individuals organized new industries. **Cornelius Vanderbilt**, from New York, organized a steamship service from New York City to Europe. Later, he invested in

◆ CONTINUED

railroads across New York. In Pennsylvania, **Andrew Carnegie** took control of the steel industry. From Ohio, **John D. Rockefeller** achieved almost total control over the American oil business.

IMPROVED WORKING CONDITIONS

In 1903, a fire killed 148 workers at the **Triangle Shirtwaist Factory** in New York City. Most of the workers were women—many of them immigrants. An investigation showed that the workers could not escape because the factory owners had locked the doors. As a result, people across the nation demanded that the government take steps to help protect workers.

What was the impact of the Triangle Shirtwaist Factory fire on city workers?

THE OPENING OF THE GREAT PLAINS AND FAR WEST

In 1869, the first railroad was completed connecting one side of the nation to the other. The discovery of gold and silver drew miners and other settlers to California, Nevada and Colorado. New laws gave cheap lands to settlers, while the U.S. Army forced Native Americans from the Great Plains to **reservations** (*lands set aside by the government*). As settlers moved west, the Great Plains were divided into ranches for raising cattle and farms for growing wheat.

The link up of the first transcontinental railroad at Promontory Point, Utah—May 10, 1869

RESEARCHING A TOPIC

Here are two tasks to choose from. The information called for in each task is available in your school or local library. Select **one** of these tasks:

❖ On a map of the United States, trace the route across the country of one of the major railroad lines. Identify which railroad you are tracing.

❖ Select a city in New York and give its population for the following years:
- 1850
- 1900
- 1950
- Present

❖ CONTINUED

EXPLORING YOUR COMMUNITY
INTERPRETING HISTORIC PHOTOGRAPHS

Historians look at many sources to determine what happened in the past. One important tool that helps historians understand the past are old photographs. They tell us how people looked and dressed, and what they did.

DESCRIBING A PHOTOGRAPH

Carefully examine each of the following photographs. You are trying to learn about life in New York in the late 1800s and early 1900s. Determine what is happening in each case. For example, what does the scene in the first photograph tell us about the education of young people? Also look at how people dressed. What does that tell us?

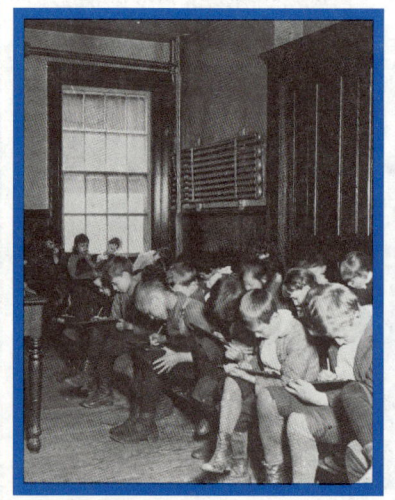

1. Children in a New York school copying their lesson

2. New York family working in their apartment making cigars

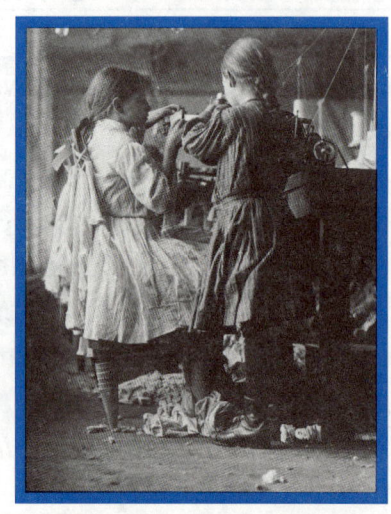

3. Two young girls working in a New York clothing factory

LIFE IN YOUR COMMUNITY

Was life in your community similar to what these photographs show? Choose **one** of the following time periods. Then find some family or library photographs that illustrate what life was like at that time. For each photograph, write a paragraph explaining what the photograph shows about life in your community in that period:

- ❖ The Industrialization of My Community: 1865–1920
- ❖ Life in My Community: 1870–1920
- ❖ My Community Grows: 1880–1920

WHAT EFFECT HAVE KEY EVENTS HAD ON NEW YORK STATE?

3F

In this activity, you will read about the causes and effects of several key events in the history of New York State from the 1880s to the 1930s. Look for the following important words:

- Cause
- Effect
- Ellis Island
- World War I
- Depression
- New Deal

Have you ever seen the movie *Back To The Future?* In this film, the main character travels back in time. In doing so, he meets his mother while she was still a teenager. His sudden appearance in his mother's teenage life threatens to change events so that he will never be born. Such time travel into the past is unrealistic, but part of the excitement of the film is that it reveals an important truth. If we could change even a single past event, we might change the entire course of history. Why is this so?

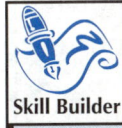

UNDERSTANDING CAUSE-AND-EFFECT RELATIONSHIPS

Skill Builder

Every event has some effects. Sometimes these effects can influence the entire future of a society. For example, a leader may decide that his or her nation should go to war. This decision can change the country's entire development. Historians often study the events of the past to better understand its cause-and-effect relationships.

❖ The **cause** of something is *what made it happen*. For example, turning on a light switch makes electricity flow to the bulb and lights it up. The cause of the light's going on was that someone turned on the switch.

❖ An **effect** is what happens *because* of a situation, action or event. For example, the light's going on was the *effect* of turning on the switch. Sometimes a single cause can start a whole chain of many effects.

CAUSE
Someone turned on the switch.

EFFECT
The light went on.

In this activity, you will read about three events in New York's history. You will learn how each of them had both **causes** and **effects**.

IMMIGRATION

Between 1861 and 1914, almost 30 million people came from Europe to the United States. About 7 out of every 10 of these immigrants first arrived in New York City and passed through a government inspection station at **Ellis Island**.

This sudden wave of immigration had several causes. Many people were escaping from religious persecution or terrible poverty. Jewish people in Russia, for example, came here to escape attacks on their villages by Russian soldiers and citizens. Italians came because there was not enough good farmland or jobs in parts of Italy.

Immigrants being examined at Ellis Island
What do you think the officials were looking for?

This increase in immigration to the United States had many effects. Until 1880, most immigrants were from Ireland and Germany. After this period, most immigrants came from Southern and Eastern European countries such as Italy, Poland and Russia. These immigrants were often Catholic and Jewish, and most did not speak English. They had little money and different customs.

To overcome these difficulties, the new immigrants often sought the friendship and protection of friends and relatives from the "Old Country"—the country from which they had immigrated. They moved into neighborhoods with names like "Little Italy," "Chinatown" and "Germantown." They went to churches and synagogues where they worshipped with people who came from the same country. Because they were in a new land they felt comfortable surrounded by those who practiced the same customs and held the same beliefs.

Immigrants often lived with people whom they felt comfortable with.

❖ CONTINUED

Life was difficult for most immigrants. They usually took the hardest jobs at the lowest pay. Because they worked in factories and sweatshops, they crowded into cities to be close to work. The flood of immigrants into cities created a greater demand for city services.

Another effect of immigration was to add to the richness and diversity of American life. Immigrants brought new foods, music forms, arts, literature and ideas to the United States. Some of the immigrants were famous inventors, artists or performers. Others had special skills or a deep knowledge of their own culture.

A final effect of the great wave of immigrants was that it created new prejudices. Many Americans felt hostile to the immigrants. They believed that their own culture and background were superior. The immigrants often faced unfair treatment and discrimination. To stop the flow of immigrants, Congress passed laws in 1921, 1924 and 1929 establishing a **quota system**. This system set quotas or limits on the number of people who could come to America.

COMPLETING A DIAGRAM

If we put the information in this reading passage into a graphic organizer, this cause-and-effect reading would look something like this:

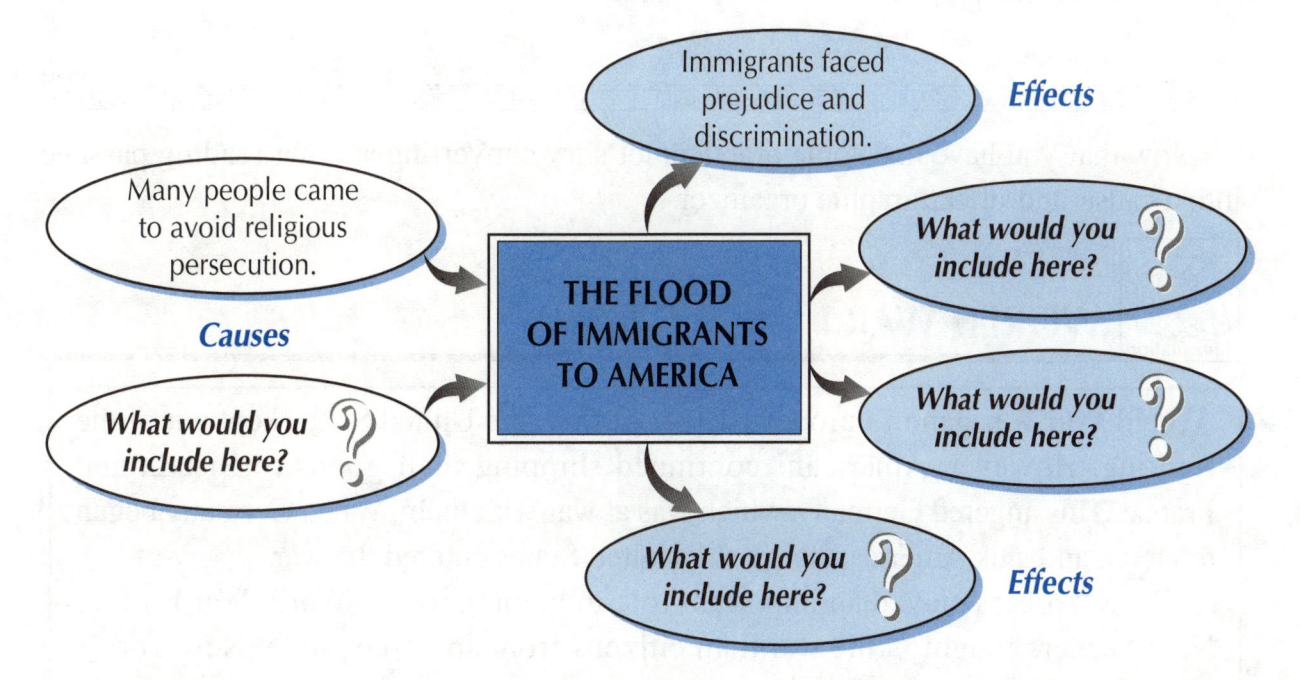

Causes
- Many people came to avoid religious persecution.
- What would you include here?

THE FLOOD OF IMMIGRANTS TO AMERICA

Effects
- Immigrants faced prejudice and discrimination.
- What would you include here?
- What would you include here?
- What would you include here?

FAMOUS NEW YORKERS

Emma Lazarus (1849–1887) was born in New York City. As a Jew, she felt a close bond with the thousands of Jewish immigrants who fled Russia for the safety of the United States. She worked hard to provide immigrants with food, housing, job training and schools. In 1886, France gave the United States a statue to honor 100 years of American independence. Lazarus was asked to write a poem that could be sold to raise money to build a base for the statue. In 1902, her poem, "The New Colossus" was placed on a plaque at the base of the Statue of Liberty. The statue has stood in New York harbor for over a hundred years as a symbol of freedom and hope. Her poem was addressed to the world, and ended with these words:

> *Give me your tired, your poor,*
> *Your huddled masses yearning to breathe free,*
> *The wretched refuse of your teeming shore.*
> *Send these, the homeless, tempest-tossed to me:*
> *I lift my lamp beside the golden door ...*

The Statue of Liberty

Now that you have had some practice, let's try converting another reading passage into a cause-and-effect graphic organizer.

WORLD WAR I

World War I began in Europe in 1914. At first, the United States kept out of the fighting. However, Americans continued shipping their goods to Britain and France. This angered Germany, which was at war with them. When Germany began to attack and sink American ships, the United States entered the war.

New Yorkers played an important role in helping to win World War I. More New Yorkers fought in the war than citizens from any other state. New York's

❖ CONTINUED

factories made goods for the army and navy. People cut down their use of fuel, despite cold winters. Many African Americans moved from the South to New York seeking to fill the large number of wartime jobs. About 14,000 New Yorkers were killed in the war. The war ended the great wave of European immigration to the United States.

Women demonstrating in front of the White House for the right to vote

The war brought other changes. In New York, voters approved a new law giving women in the state the right to vote. After the war ended in 1918, New Yorkers and other Americans turned away from trying to help foreign nations. In the 1920s, most New Yorkers enjoyed a period of good times known as the "Roaring Twenties." Industries in New York continued to grow. This growth produced new wealth and provided people with leisure time to enjoy music, sports and the movies.

COMPLETING A DIAGRAM

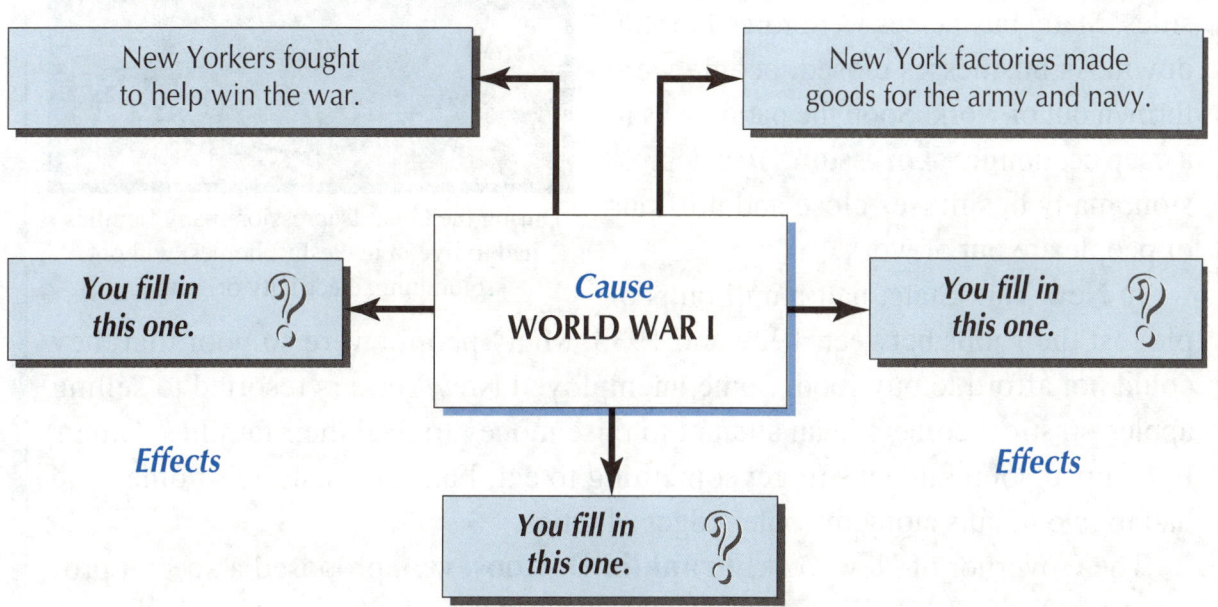

Your Task

- New Yorkers fought to help win the war.
- New York factories made goods for the army and navy.
- You fill in this one.
- You fill in this one.
- You fill in this one.

Cause
WORLD WAR I

Effects

Do you know the saying, "practice makes perfect"? Let's try converting one last cause-and-effect reading into a graphic organizer to be sure we fully understand it.

170   NEW YORK: ITS LAND AND ITS PEOPLE

THE NEW YORK STOCK MARKET CRASH

In the **New York Stock Exchange,** located in New York City, people buy and sell shares (*stocks*) of most of the nation's large corporations. On October 29, 1929, the price of stocks began to fall as many people started to sell their stocks. Soon, people began to panic, afraid that their stocks would lose all their value. By the end of the day, stock prices had dropped tremendously. The decline was so great that people said the stock market had "crashed." Hundreds of thousands of Americans had lost all of their savings.

Huge crowds gathered outside the New York Stock Exchange as word of falling stock prices spread throughout the nation.

The stock market crash had many effects. Companies could no longer sell stocks to raise money for expansion. People stopped spending except to buy necessities. Many businesses were forced to shut down. As businesses closed, people were thrown out of work. Soon the nation was in a deep economic **depression**. In a depression, many businesses close and millions of people are out of work.

During the Great Depression many families had to live in makeshift homes, without plumbing, electricity or water.

In New York State, half a million people lost their jobs between 1929 and 1933. Many people were so poor that they could not afford to buy food. Some unemployed New Yorkers resorted to selling apples on street corners in an attempt to raise money to feed their families. Others lined up at soup kitchens to get something to eat. Families lost their homes and had to live in huts along the outer edges of cities.

The Governor of New York, **Franklin D. Roosevelt**, proposed a special program of relief in 1931. His program gave food, shelter, clothing and medical aid to needy people. It also put unemployed people to work on various public projects. They were hired to build schools, roads and bridges. Within one year, the program had helped a million and a half New Yorkers.

◆ CONTINUED

This program was so popular that Governor Roosevelt was encouraged to run for President. In 1933, he became President of the United States. He adopted many of the ideas he had tried out in New York. Roosevelt called his program the **New Deal**. Many new government agencies were created under this program. They provided work for needy New Yorkers and other Americans.

President Franklin Roosevelt (seated) signs a New Deal program into law.

Under the New Deal, young people were paid to work in parks and forests. Adults worked on roads, dams and other projects. Between 1932 and 1937, over a billion dollars were spent on various programs in New York State. By 1938, most people were back at work. The worst of the Great Depression was over. The New Deal had served to restore self-respect to many Americans. It also helped people feel more confident about the future. Finally, the New Deal increased the size and power of the national government and made it responsible for managing the nation's economy.

COMPLETING A DIAGRAM

Complete the following cause-and-effect diagram based on the reading:

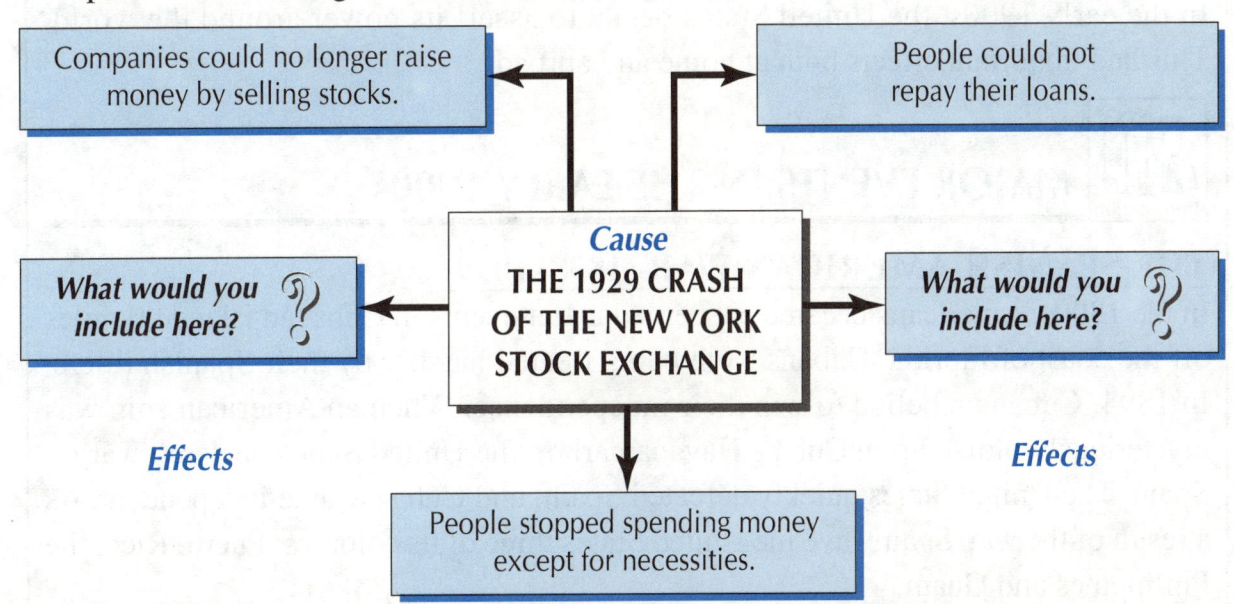

- Companies could no longer raise money by selling stocks.
- People could not repay their loans.

Cause
THE 1929 CRASH OF THE NEW YORK STOCK EXCHANGE

- What would you include here?
- What would you include here?

Effects

- People stopped spending money except for necessities.

REVIEWING YOUR UNDERSTANDING

Creating Vocabulary Cards

Cause
What is a "cause"?
Give an example of a cause:

Effect
What is an "effect"?
Give an example of an effect:

Finding Cause And Effect In Your Newspaper

The events reported in our daily newspapers also have their own causes and effects. Choose any event described in a recent newspaper article. Create your own cause-and-effect chart showing the event and its causes and effects.

MAKING CONNECTIONS

EXPLORING BEYOND YOUR STATE
AMERICA'S EXPANDED ROLE IN THE WORLD

In the early 1900s, the United States began to assert its power around the world. This had important effects both at home and abroad.

MAJOR EVENTS IN THE EARLY 1900s

THE SPANISH-AMERICAN WAR (1898–1899)

In the 1890s, Americans became concerned about events in Cuba, an island 90 miles off the coast of Florida. Cubans were being treated harshly by their Spanish rulers. In 1894, Cubans rebelled to win their independence. When an American ship was mysteriously blown up in Cuba's Havana harbor, the United States declared war on Spain. The United States quickly defeated Spain, and Cuba became independent. As a result of the war, Spain gave the United States three of its colonies: Puerto Rico, the Philippines and Guam.

❖ CONTINUED

AMERICA ACQUIRES COLONIES IN THE PACIFIC

Some Americans believed that it was wrong for a democratic nation to have colonies. Others believed that America should keep Puerto Rico, Guam and the Philippines. They felt that these colonies would help supply raw materials to America's growing industries. They also thought that they would be able to help the people on these islands by teaching them the American way of life. Hawaii, Samoa and Midway were also added as American colonies at this time.

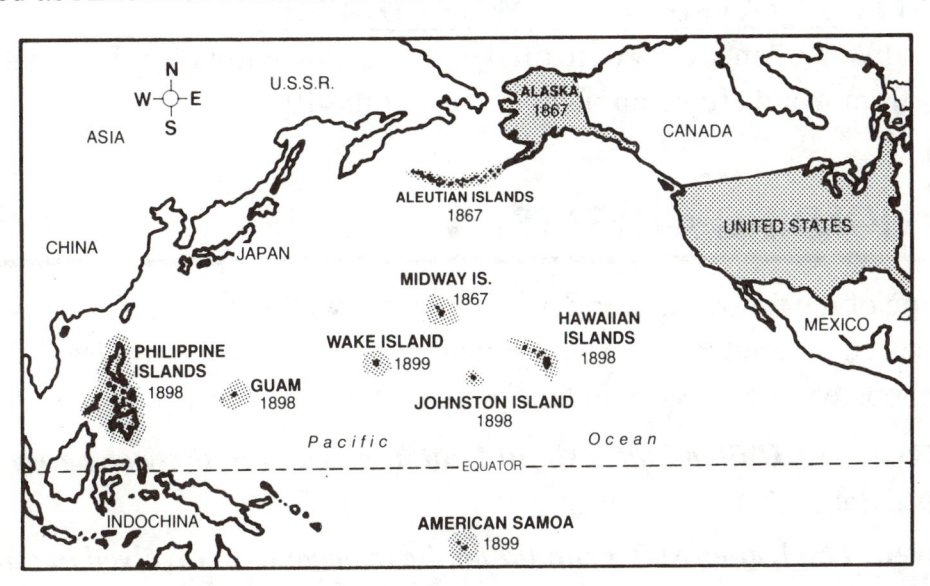

U.S. INFLUENCE IN THE CARIBBEAN AND LATIN AMERICA

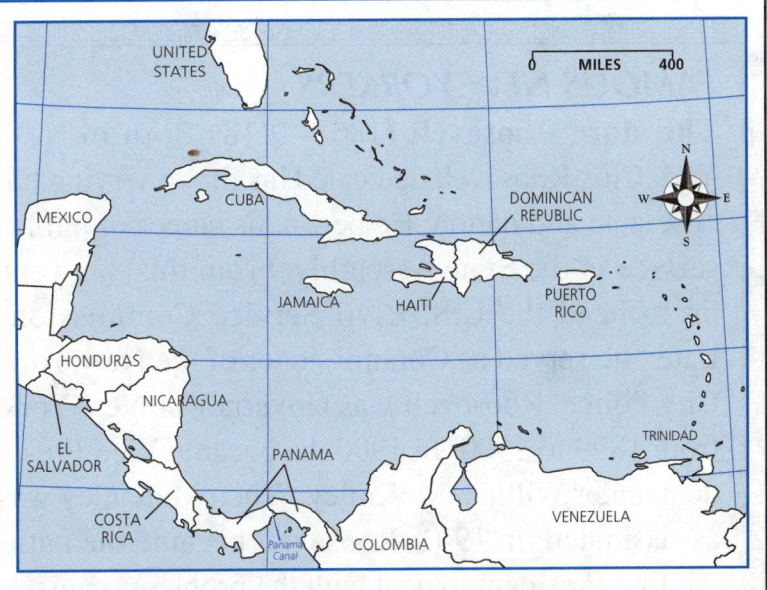

In 1903, the United States built a canal across Panama to connect the Atlantic and Pacific Oceans. The **Panama Canal** made it possible for the United States to send its navy quickly between its east and west coasts. To protect American influence, the U.S. government often sent troops to countries around the Caribbean Sea: Haiti, Dominican Republic, Nicaragua and Venezuela. President Theodore Roosevelt, a New Yorker, felt that the United States should act as the "world's policeman" in Latin America, rather than see Britain or Germany interfere in this region.

▼ CONTINUED

THE UNITED STATES IN ASIA

In 1899, the United States began a policy to prevent foreign nations from controlling China. The U.S. policy kept China open to trade with all nations. Americans further opposed efforts by European countries to tear China apart into several separate colonies. Americans also opened up Japan to foreign trade. For centuries, the Japanese had opposed contacts with Western countries.

THE UNITED STATES AFTER WORLD WAR I

After World War I, Americans were tired of international troubles. The United States withdrew from world affairs throughout most of the 1920s.

HOLDING A DEBATE

Choose **one** of the following resolutions to debate with your classmates. After making your selection, conduct some background research in the library. Then choose one side and prepare a short speech in favor of your point of view:

❖ **Resolved:** *The United States should not have entered the war between Spain and its colony, Cuba.*

❖ **Resolved:** *The United States should not have become so involved in other areas around the world.*

FAMOUS NEW YORKERS

Theodore Roosevelt (1858–1918) Born in New York City, Roosevelt dedicated his life to serving his city, state and nation. He began his career of public service in the State Assembly. From this, he went on to head the U.S. Civil Service Commission. Later, he served as Commissioner of the New York City Police. Roosevelt was Governor of New York from 1899 to 1900. In 1900, he became Vice-President under William McKinley. When McKinley was assassinated in 1901, Roosevelt became the nation's 26th President. He was the first President to deal with the problems caused by the Industrial Revolution in the United States. The power of the national government also grew greatly under his Presidency. In foreign affairs, Roosevelt willingly took on the responsibility of turning the United States into a world power.

Theodore Roosevelt

EXPLORING YOUR COMMUNITY
WHOM HAS YOUR COMMUNITY HONORED WITH A MONUMENT?

Communities across the nation often honor people who are important to them. Sometimes they put up a **statue** or other **monument** to honor someone who lived in the community or who came from there. A monument can consist of a simple stone block. It can also be as elaborate as an entire building. Either way, a monument reflects community pride.

IDENTIFYING MONUMENTS

How familiar are you with the contributions of some of the important people in your community who have been honored with a monument? You may often pass a statue or other monument without taking notice of the person it honors. Your task is to locate **two** monuments constructed in or near your community. For each one:

❖ **Who.** Identify the person the monument was built to honor.

❖ **Where.** Describe where the monument is located. Is it in a park or near the entrance to a building?

❖ **What.** Explain what the person accomplished in his or her lifetime to deserve having a monument constructed in his or her honor.

❖ **Why.** Explain the reasons why the community decided to build the monument.

❖ **Photo.** Provide a picture or photograph showing the monument.

A statue of Major General Philip Schuyler in the center of Albany
Why did Albany construct a statue to honor Philip Schuyler?

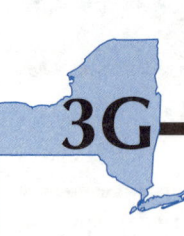

WHAT WAS IT LIKE LIVING THROUGH WORLD WAR II?

3G

In this activity, you will learn about New York State's role in World War II. Look for the following important words:

- ▶ Primary Source
- ▶ Secondary Source
- ▶ World War II
- ▶ Pearl Harbor
- ▶ D-Day
- ▶ Narrative Essay

A good historian is like a detective. A detective arrives after a crime has taken place. The detective then tries to figure out who committed the crime by looking for clues. He or she may interview witnesses, examine evidence and check facts. From these clues, the detective tries to put together the story of what really happened.

DISTINGUISHING BETWEEN PRIMARY AND SECONDARY SOURCES

Historians are not involved in solving crimes, but they do try to figure out what took place in the past. Both detectives and historians look through many sources for clues to tell them what really happened. In this section, you will be challenged to act as a historian by looking at several sources. Historians rely on sources of two types:

PRIMARY SOURCES

▶ **Primary sources** are the original records of an event. They include eyewitness reports, records written at the time of the event, letters sent by people involved in the event, speeches, diaries, photographs or audio and video tapes. Most of the facts we know about past events come from primary sources.

> ✔ **CHECKING YOUR UNDERSTANDING** ✔
> Can you think of some other examples of a primary source?

SECONDARY SOURCES

▶ **Secondary sources** are the writings and viewpoints of an event presented by historians and other authors who did not experience the event. The author of a secondary source usually does not have firsthand experience of the event. Secondary sources, such as textbooks and magazine articles, provide summaries of the information found in primary sources. Historians often read these writings to learn about other historians' ideas.

AMERICAN HERITAGE 177

> ✔ **CHECKING YOUR UNDERSTANDING** ✔
>
> Can you think of some other examples of a secondary source?

A TIME CAPSULE IS DISCOVERED

Imagine you and your classmates have been called to the principal's office. She says that La Guardia Elementary School is being torn down to make way for a larger building. Some workers have found a time capsule among the rubble. The principal explains that a **time capsule** is a collection of items buried in a container, to be opened by people living sometime in the future.

The principal knows that your class has been reading about World War II. She suggests that you look at the items in the time capsule. She hopes they will help the class to understand that time period. She proposes that once you finish examining the items you write a **narrative** (*a story relating an event*) about World War II. The principal reaches into the time capsule and pulls out the first item.

A LETTER

It is a note from a group of fourth graders, written over 50 years ago. Here is what it says:

December 20, 1944

Dear Citizens:

We are living at a time of terrible war. We are very concerned about the future. The trouble began when Germany, Italy and Japan came under the control of dictators. Japan attacked China and several other Asian countries. Italy invaded parts of Africa. **Adolf Hitler**, the Nazi dictator of Germany, arrested and murdered Jewish people and other German citizens.

Five years ago, in 1939, **World War II** started in Europe when Hitler and his armies invaded Poland. Soon, Nazi Germany controlled much of Europe. At first, we Americans kept out of the war. However, in 1941, Japanese planes attacked our ships at **Pearl Harbor** in Hawaii. This surprise attack brought us into the war. American troops are now fighting in Europe, Asia and the Pacific. The fighting is fierce, but Germany and Japan are slowly pulling back from their earlier victories.

New York's **Franklin D. Roosevelt** is our President. Over 900,000 New Yorkers have fought in this war. Our factories lead all other states in producing tanks, airplanes and other goods for use in the war. Women have been doing factory work and other jobs once held by men. The supply of gasoline, sugar, coffee, shoes and other goods is limited by the U.S. government. These controls ensure there are enough supplies for the army and navy.

This is a very hard period in our lives. We hope that when you read this, the world will again be at peace. As you examine each item in this time capsule, we hope that it will help you to learn what life was like for us growing up during this war.

Sincerely,

4th Grade Students of La Guardia Elementary School

178 NEW YORK: ITS LAND AND ITS PEOPLE

✔ CHECKING YOUR UNDERSTANDING ✔

1. Is this letter a primary or a secondary source? How can you tell?

A DIARY

Inside the time capsule is a diary. A **diary** is a daily record of a person's experiences and feelings. This diary contains many interesting entries:

> *September 14, 1941.* Two days ago a German submarine attacked the U.S. destroyer Greer off the coast of Ireland. In a speech to the American people, President Roosevelt compared Hitler to a rattlesnake. He has now ordered U.S. naval ships to escort all merchant ships across the Atlantic Ocean, and ordered U.S. ships to "shoot on sight" any German submarines they find. I fear our nation is moving closer to war with Germany.

> *December 8, 1941.* Japan attacked Pearl Harbor yesterday with hundreds of planes. In less than two hours, 10 warships were sunk or disabled and thousands of U.S. servicemen were killed. President Roosevelt has called a special meeting of the U.S. Congress. It appears he is going to ask Congress to declare war on Japan. This will surely bring the United States into war with Germany too, since Germany and Japan are allies (friends).

> *May 9, 1942.* President Roosevelt has ordered 112,000 Japanese Americans living on the West Coast to move to "internment camps." They must sell their homes, land and all belongings and immediately move to isolated sections in the interior of the United States where these camps are located. The government fears they will try to help Japan win the war. Some Americans believe people of Japanese ancestry are less loyal than other Americans. However, there is no real evidence to show this. In fact, over 71,000 of them were born in the United States like myself.

January 13, 1943. There are stories in the newspapers that Hitler is attempting to murder the entire Jewish population of Europe. The stories tell about concentration camps in German-controlled Europe. It is said that in these camps innocent people are killed with poison gas and their bodies are burned in huge ovens. The article said witnesses are reporting that there are millions of Jews, Gypsies, Poles and others being killed. More and more newspaper stories are calling this attempt to murder an entire group of people a Holocaust.

June 10, 1944. General Dwight Eisenhower, who commands all American troops in Europe, launched an invasion against Hitler several days ago. June 6 is being called D-Day. The radio has said that a fleet of 4,000 warships and almost 3 million soldiers are invading northern France. They plan to attack German positions. I pray that this attempt at liberating (freeing) Europe will be successful and put an end to Hitler's plans to take over all of Europe.

November 4, 1944. President Roosevelt's bid for re-election has been successful. His opponent was Thomas Dewey, the Governor of New York. Election results show that President Roosevelt has been elected to a fourth term as President of the United States. He is the first President to be elected four times.

✔ Checking Your Understanding ✔

1. Is the diary a primary or secondary source? Explain.
2. What does the diary tell you about life during World War II?
3. What does the diary tell you about the writer's concerns and feelings?

PHOTOGRAPHS

Inside the time capsule are three photographs. Each photograph appeared in local newspapers in 1944 and was placed by the students in the time capsule to show something about World War II.

180   NEW YORK: ITS LAND AND ITS PEOPLE

Photo #1

The Mochida family awaits evacuation to a detention camp in the center of the nation.

Photo #2

Women are at work in an aircraft factory. Factory lights are reflected on the noses of the fighter planes.

Photo #3

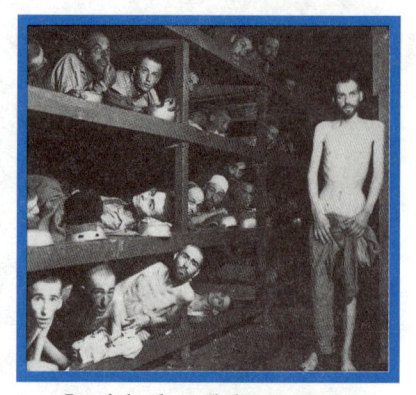

Jewish slave laborers at a German concentration camp somewhere in Europe.

> ✔ **CHECKING YOUR UNDERSTANDING** ✔
>
> 1. Are these photographs primary or secondary sources? Explain.
> 2. What do these photographs tell you about life during World War II?

SONGS

Also included in the time capsule is a list of songs that were popular in the 1940s. Each song illustrates a different side of life during World War II.

(In the library, find the words to one of these songs.)

- ❖ Boogie-Woogie Bugle Boy of Company B
- ❖ There's a Star-Spangled Banner Waving Somewhere
- ❖ We Did It Before and We Can Do It Again
- ❖ Rosie the Riveter
- ❖ Cleaning My Rifle (And Dreaming of You)
- ❖ God Bless America
- ❖ He Wears A Pair of Silver Wings
- ❖ Praise The Lord and Pass The Ammunition
- ❖ The Sun Will Soon Be Setting On The Land of the Rising Sun
- ❖ Comin' In On A Wing and A Prayer

> ✔ **CHECKING YOUR UNDERSTANDING** ✔
>
> 1. Are the songs primary or secondary sources? Explain.
> 2. What does the song you looked up in the library tell you about life during World War II?

POSTERS

Americans not fighting in the war seldom had a chance to forget the battles going on overseas. No matter where they went, Americans saw posters to remind them. Each poster focused on some message that the government wanted to get across to its citizens. Two of these posters are found in the time capsule:

Poster #1

This poster encourages Americans to use less fuel, rubber, etc.

Poster #2

Americans should watch what they say, spies could be anywhere.

✔ Checking Your Understanding ✔

1. Are these posters primary or secondary sources? Explain.
2. What do the posters tell you about life during the war?

A CHART

Included in the capsule was a chart listing casualties in World War II up to May 1944.

	Soldiers Killed	Soldiers Wounded	Civilians Killed
Great Britian	398,000	475,000	65,000
France	211,000	400,000	108,000
Soviet Union	7,500,000	14,102,000	15,000,000
United States	292,131	670,846	very few
Totals	**8,401,131**	**15,647,846**	**15,173,000**
Germany	2,850,000	7,250,000	5,000,000
Italy	77,500	120,000	100,000
Japan	1,576,000	500,000	300,000
Totals	**4,503,500**	**7,870,000**	**5,400,000**

182 NEW YORK: ITS LAND AND ITS PEOPLE

> ✔ CHECKING YOUR UNDERSTANDING ✔
>
> 1. Is the chart a primary or secondary source? Explain.
> 2. What does the chart tell you about World War II?

A MAP

One of the best ways to understand what happened during the war is to look at maps. Maps can show, for instance, the location of the various countries fighting the war and where the most important battles took place. They can also provide information about what was happening on the "home front." Included in the capsule was the following map:

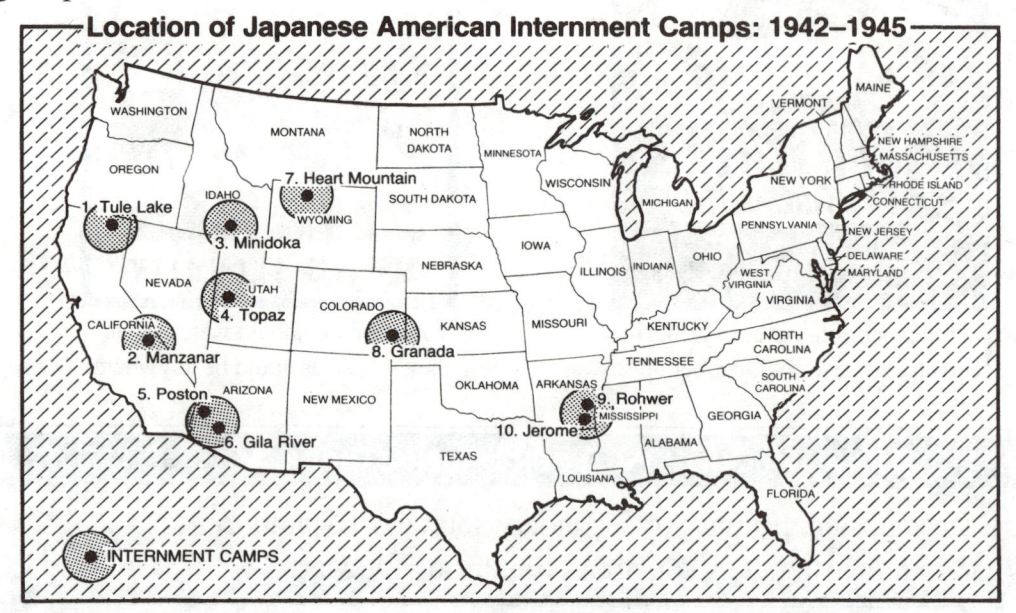

Location of Japanese American Internment Camps: 1942–1945

1. Tule Lake
2. Manzanar
3. Minidoka
4. Topaz
5. Poston
6. Gila River
7. Heart Mountain
8. Granada
9. Rohwer
10. Jerome

INTERNMENT CAMPS

> ✔ CHECKING YOUR UNDERSTANDING ✔
>
> 1. Is the map a primary or secondary source? Explain.
> 2. What does the map tell you about life on the home front during the war?

Closing: WRITING A NARRATIVE ESSAY ABOUT WORLD WAR II

You and your classmates have finished reviewing the items found in the time capsule. It is now time to write a narrative essay about what life might have been like in the United States during World War II. Before you begin your narrative, you might want to read the Skill Builder on the following page.

HOW TO WRITE A NARRATIVE ESSAY

What is a "narrative"? Narrative writing is used to *narrate*, or *tell*, about an event or a series of related events. In a narrative, the writer describes each event or detail as it happened in time.

When is narrative writing used? Narrative writing is used to tell a story as events unfold. For example, you might use the narrative form to tell about a historical event like World War II or an interesting day at your school.

Helpful hints. Start at the beginning and move step-by-step through the story. Stay on the point of the story and try to be specific. You don't need to write every detail that happened. Instead, focus on things that contribute to your theme.

REVIEWING YOUR UNDERSTANDING

Creating Vocabulary Cards

Primary Source

What is a "primary source"?

Give an example of a primary source:

Secondary Source

What is a "secondary source"?

Give an example of a secondary source:

Primary and Secondary Sources

Listed below are some sources that a historian might use to write a history of New York. Next to each number write if the item listed is a primary or secondary source:

1. A painting on the wall of a cave, done 6,000 years ago.
2. A diary written by Henry Hudson about his journey to the "New World."
3. A letter written by Governor DeWitt Clinton to his wife about the Erie Canal.
4. A recent copy of an artist's drawing of the steamboat, *Clermont*.
5. A newspaper from 1800, describing events in that year.
6. An oil painting of the Battle of Saratoga, done in 1986.
7. A book about the construction of the Erie Canal, written in 1960.
8. A recent atlas of major battles that took place in New York State, from 1776 to 1783.

Writing a "What If" Story

The United States, Great Britain and the Soviet Union defeated Germany, Italy and Japan and won World War II. Can you imagine what would have happened if the United States and its allies had lost the war instead? Write a short story using the title, "How my life would be different today if the United States had lost World War II."

MAKING CONNECTIONS

EXPLORING BEYOND YOUR STATE
WORLD WAR II AND ITS AFTERMATH

After Germany was defeated, the United States prepared to invade Japan. When they learned that the invasion might result in a million U.S. dead or wounded, American leaders decided to use a new weapon against Japan—the **atomic bomb**. The cities of **Hiroshima** and **Nagasaki** were selected as targets. When the bomb was dropped on Hiroshima, nearly 100,000 people were killed. An additional 36,000 died at Nagasaki. A few days later Japan surrendered, ending the war.

A Shinto shrine was one of the few things that remained standing after the atomic bomb was dropped on Hiroshima.

World War II was a disaster for most of the world. More than 50 million people lost their lives. Much of Europe, North Africa and Asia lay in ruins. World War II also brought about important changes in the United States. America became the greatest economic superpower in the world.

THE CREATION OF THE UNITED NATIONS

In 1945, most world leaders recognized the need for an international peace-keeping organization. This led to the creation of the **United Nations**. Its goals were to keep world peace, promote international cooperation, end hunger and disease and improve

❖ CONTINUED

education around the world. Since the creation of the United Nations, its membership has grown to include almost every nation in the world today.

At first the United Nations did not have a permanent home. It met in different locations. After some discussion, the United Nations decided to make its headquarters in New York City. The Rockefeller family donated 18 acres of land on the east side of Manhattan for the project. The buildings that house the United Nations were designed by some of the world's leading architects. The interiors of the buildings were furnished by donations from member nations around the world.

One of the buildings of the United Nations in New York City

WRITING ABOUT CURRENT EVENTS

Find an article in a newspaper that deals with the United Nations. Summarize the article and describe the role of the United Nations discussed in the article.

FAMOUS NEW YORKERS

Colin Powell is the son of Jamaican immigrants to the United States. He grew up in the Bronx and attended City College in Manhattan. After graduating, Powell entered the army. Powell served as President Reagan's National Security Advisor. His performance in that post was noticed by George Bush. In 1989, President Bush nominated Powell, then a four-star general, to be Chairman of the Joint Chiefs of Staff—making him the highest ranking military officer in the nation. During the Persian Gulf War of 1991, Powell received national attention from the news media because of his distinguished service. Afterwards, Powell retired from the U.S. Army. He has been sought after by both major political parties as a possible future candidate for President of the United States.

Colin Powell

EXPLORING YOUR COMMUNITY
COMMUNITY VETERANS' ORGANIZATIONS

In this activity, you learned about life in the United States during World War II. Throughout its history, America has been involved in a number of major wars. These include the American Revolution, the Civil War, World Wars I and II, the Korean War, the Vietnam War and the Persian Gulf War. Communities across the nation have sent their young men to fight in these wars, and more recently, their young women.

Soldiers raise the American flag in Iwo Jima during World War II. Following the war, many soldiers who fought together formed veterans' organizations.

People who once served in the armed forces of their country are known as **veterans**. The nation honors these patriots in November on **Veteran's Day**. Veterans also play an important role in celebrating other public holidays, such as July 4th and Memorial Day in late May.

Often, veterans have formed organizations to share their experiences and to express pride in their accomplishments. Some of these organizations are the American Legion, the Veterans of Foreign Wars and the Vietnam Veterans. Frequently, these organizations conduct charity work and perform community services like sponsoring scholarships or sports teams. They also provide help to fellow veterans.

CONDUCTING RESEARCH

Let's find out about **one** veterans' organization in your community. Call your local Chamber of Commerce or look in the "Government Pages" of your telephone book to find the names of local veterans' organizations. Then call one organization to find out:

❖ What is its general purpose?
❖ When was the local branch started?
❖ What services does it provide to its members?
❖ What services does it provide to the community?

Finally, you might want to invite representatives from that organization to your class to speak about their experiences as veterans of the armed forces. They may want to speak about the work of their organization in performing community services.

HOW WOULD YOU OUTLINE THIS READING?

3H

In this activity, you will learn about some of the key developments that occurred in New York State in the past 50 years. In addition, you will learn the skill of outlining. Look for the following important words and people:

- Outline
- Roman Numerals
- Suburbs
- Oral History

An **outline** is a brief plan in which a topic is divided up into different parts. The purpose of an outline is to show how a topic and its parts are related. An outline can also serve as a blueprint to help guide you through a reading.

HOW OUTLINES ARE ORGANIZED

Outlines begin with general topics and then provide details. The major topics are numbered with **Roman Numerals** (I, II, III). If the topic listed by a Roman numeral needs to be further divided, its sub-topics are identified by **capital letters** (A, B, C). If these sub-topics need to be further divided, each smaller topic is given an **Arabic Numeral** (1, 2, 3).

Let's look at how this process of outlining works. Assume you want to create an outline about your own life. Here is what it might look like:

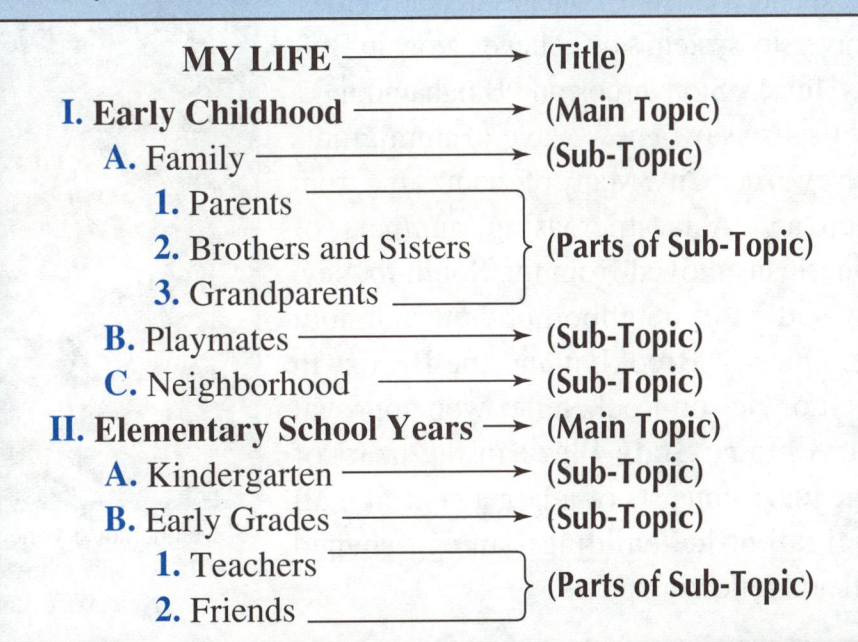

```
        MY LIFE  ─────→ (Title)
  I. Early Childhood ─→ (Main Topic)
     A. Family ───────→ (Sub-Topic)
        1. Parents
        2. Brothers and Sisters  } (Parts of Sub-Topic)
        3. Grandparents
     B. Playmates ────→ (Sub-Topic)
     C. Neighborhood ─→ (Sub-Topic)
  II. Elementary School Years → (Main Topic)
     A. Kindergarten ─→ (Sub-Topic)
     B. Early Grades ─→ (Sub-Topic)
        1. Teachers   } (Parts of Sub-Topic)
        2. Friends
```

188   NEW YORK: ITS LAND AND ITS PEOPLE

Notice that in this example, each smaller part helps us to understand a larger idea. For example, "Teachers" and "Friends" help us to understand the sub-topic "Early Grades." "Kindergarten" and "Early Grades" help us to understand the larger topic "Elementary School Years." This larger topic is one of the two main parts that make up the general theme of "My Life." Now let's look at a reading about the recent history of New York State. After reading the passage, complete the outline that follows.

NEW YORK IN THE LAST FIFTY YEARS

New York has undergone many changes since the end of World War II. Each decade (*10 years*) has seen new and important developments. During the 1950s, many New Yorkers moved out of cities and into suburbs. A suburb is a community outside of a city where many people who work in the city live. One of the first of these suburbs was **Levittown** on Long Island. After World War II, families could purchase a house there at a very affordable price—less than $10,000. This helped Long Island's Nassau County become the fastest growing county in the nation.

In the 1950s, New Yorkers became accustomed to new and better ways to travel. New highways were built linking cities around the state. The most important of these highways was the **New York Thruway**. The St. Lawrence River was widened to allow ocean-going ships to travel inland. Airlines introduced jet planes that could fly from New York to Europe in just a few short hours. New York's large airports became some of the busiest in the world. The **State University of New York**, begun in the late 1940s, expanded existing colleges in many cities. The new university system saw colleges grow in Buffalo, Albany, Ithaca, Stonybrook and Binghamton.

The 1950s also saw a new wave of immigrants arriving in New York City. Many of them came from Puerto Rico and Asia. Increasing numbers of African Americans moved from the South to New York. They settled in neighborhoods throughout Manhattan, Queens, Brooklyn and the Bronx. In 1959, Governor Nelson Rockefeller won approval to build the **Empire State Plaza** in the heart of Albany. The plaza consists of a large, central mall with several tall office buildings, an egg-shaped concert hall and reflecting pools.

Manhattan skyline at night
The 1950s saw many changes in New York State.

❖ CONTINUED

The early 1960s were a time of great prosperity for New York. New skyscrapers lined Fifth Avenue in New York City. During 1964 and 1965, New Yorkers celebrated their success by hosting the World's Fair. People visited pavilions representing many countries. The atmosphere changed in the late 1960s, when America became involved in a war in Vietnam. Many New Yorkers, especially young people, opposed the war. One of the nation's largest rock and roll concerts was held in 1969 at Woodstock. Almost 500,000 young people attended this festival.

The 1970s were a time of economic difficulties for New York. Oil prices rose sharply. Unemployment began to increase. Many taxpayers moved out of the cities to the suburbs or to other states. State and local governments cut services, even though an increasing number of New Yorkers needed public assistance for food, clothing, medical services and housing. For the first time ever, New York State began losing both population and jobs. Buffalo saw more than twenty percent of its population move elsewhere. In 1977, New York launched its "I love New York" campaign to prevent the loss of more jobs and to restore tourism and a feeling of pride in the state. New York City began promoting itself as the "Big Apple." These campaigns were very successful. Tourism increased, becoming the state's second largest industry.

The "I Love New York" logo appeared throughout the nation.

Nevertheless, the decline in the state's population continued throughout the 1980s. New Yorkers faced other problems as well. The state's forests were threatened by pollution and acid rain. In many large cities, people faced unemployment and inadequate housing. However, some things got better. Lake Placid, one of the two thousand lakes in the Adirondacks, became the site of the 1980 Winter Olympics. Race relations improved so much that Peekskill, once the scene of race riots, elected an African-American mayor in 1987.

In the 1990s, many rebuilding projects were started around the state. Rochester, for example, began reconstructing its downtown area to attract more businesses. Buffalo accomplished a major modernization of its transportation system. The city is now a center for medical, nuclear and aerospace research. Utica built a new business complex of offices and manufacturing plants just outside the city.

❖ CONTINUED

New Yorkers continue to enjoy many advantages that will help them into the next century. New York remains a world leader in finance, commerce, technology and the arts. Important companies like IBM, Kodak and General Electric continue to have their headquarters in New York. The state is rich in many natural resources. Its most valuable resource remains its people. The great diversity of talent that has marked the state since its early beginnings will enable New Yorkers to overcome their present problems and to provide for a better future.

COMPLETING AN OUTLINE

Below is what this reading would look like in outline form. Notice that some items have been omitted. Make a copy of the outline. Then fill in the items that have been omitted.

NEW YORK IN THE LAST FIFTY YEARS

I. **New York in the 1950s**
   A. Many New Yorkers moved out of cities and into suburbs.
   B. New highways were built around the state.
   C. The St. Lawrence River was widened for use by ocean-going ships.
   D. *What do you think goes here?*
   E. *What do you think goes here?*

II. **New York in the 1960s**
   A. The early 1960s were a time of prosperity.
   B. *What do you think goes here?*
   C. *What do you think goes here?*
   D. *What do you think goes here?*

III. **New York in the 1970s**
   A. Oil prices rose.
   B. *What do you think goes here?*
   C. *What do you think goes here?*
   D. *What do you think goes here?*
   E. *What do you think goes here?*
   F. *What do you think goes here?*

IV. *What do you think goes here?*
   A. New York's population began to decline.
   B. *What do you think goes here?*
   C. *What do you think goes here?*

V. What do you think goes here?
   A. *What do you think goes here?*
   B. *What do you think goes here?*
   C. *What do you think goes here?*
   D. *What do you think goes here?*

REVIEWING YOUR UNDERSTANDING

Creating Vocabulary Cards

Outline
What is an "outline"?
What is an outline used for?

Suburbs
What are "suburbs"?
Where did they first develop in New York?

Creating an Outline About Some of New York's Recent Governors

Let's practice your newly learned skill of outlining. Look over the following reading passage. Then organize it into outline form.

THREE NEW YORK GOVERNORS

The executive branch of the government of New York State is headed by the Governor. Since 1777, more than fifty people have held this office—four of them even went on to become Presidents of the United States. Three of New York's most noted Governors during the last 50 years have been Thomas E. Dewey, Nelson Rockefeller and Mario Cuomo.

Thomas E. Dewey was Governor from 1943 to 1954. He led the state through the final years of World War II. He began the state university system (*known as SUNY*). Dewey helped to end racial discrimination and expanded state health services. He also began construction of the New York State Thruway and opened what is now Kennedy International Airport. Dewey ran twice for President of the United States, but lost the election both times.

Thomas Dewey

◆ CONTINUED

Nelson Rockefeller was the grandson of John D. Rockefeller, founder of the Standard Oil Company. He served as Governor from 1959 to 1973. Rockefeller carried out far-reaching programs to increase public services and expand state facilities. Many of his programs led to greater spending by the state govenment and eventually higher taxes. He turned the state capital into a showcase by building the Empire State Plaza to house state government buildings and the state museum. In 1973, Rockefeller left to become Vice President under President Gerald Ford.

Nelson Rockefeller

Mario Cuomo was Governor from 1983 to 1995. As Governor, Cuomo provided a high level of social services, increased aid for education and expanded environmental protection. Responding to fears that evacuation from Long Island would be impossible during a nuclear accident, Cuomo ordered the closing of a nuclear plant at Shoreham. Despite the demand of many voters to bring back the death penalty, Cuomo continued to oppose it. As New Yorkers struggled with high taxes and other problems, his popularity declined. In 1995, he lost his campaign for re-election to George Pataki.

Mario Cuomo

The outline has been started for you. Copy it into your notebook, and then complete it.

THREE NEW YORK GOVERNORS

I. **Governor Thomas Dewey (1943–1954)**
   A. He led the state through the final years of World War II.
   B. *What do you think goes here?*
   C. *What do you think goes here?*
   D. *What do you think goes here?*
   E. *What do you think goes here?*

II. *What do you think goes here?*
   A. *What do you think goes here?*
   B. *What do you think goes here?*
   C. *What do you think goes here?*
   D. *What do you think goes here?*

III. *What do you think goes here?*
    A. *What do you think goes here?*
    B. *What do you think goes here?*
    C. *What do you think goes here?*
    D. *What do you think goes here?*
    E. *What do you think goes here?*

MAKING CONNECTIONS

EXPLORING BEYOND YOUR STATE
THE WORLD AFTER WORLD WAR II

Following World War II, one of the most important changes in our world has been the advance of technology.

THE ADVANCE OF TECHNOLOGY

Over the last fifty years, there have been tremendous advances in scientific research and technology. **Technology** refers to the methods and tools a society uses to make and do things. Recent technology is based on the use of science to meet our everyday needs. The rapid changes and improvements of modern technology have become an important part of American life. The trend since World War II has been for machines and equipment to be able to do more and more marvelous things—better, cheaper and faster. The result has been an almost continuous stream of major inventions: jet airplanes, radar, antibiotics, nuclear energy, lasers and computers. Each of these has had a major impact on society.

THE COMPUTER REVOLUTION

Developments in **computers** have been leading the revolution in technology. Although computers have been around since 1945, each year new and more imaginative ways are found to use them. The computer led to many improvements in our quality of life. The computer has supplied us with many labor-saving machines and equipment. Today, a **computer chip** no larger than a person's thumbnail can power a computer that can process over 300 million instructions in a second.

    Computers are expected to become even more powerful in the future. One possible effect of this is that many jobs performed by people will be done by computers.

❖ CONTINUED

At the same time, many new jobs will open up in the computer field. New ways will be developed for using them. Computers will perform new services, such as giving medical advice. They will make possible new services and benefits that are impossible to predict today.

READING ABOUT TECHNOLOGY

For the next several days read your local newspaper. Find **one** article dealing with any aspect of technology. Briefly summarize the article, and explain how it might change the world we know today.

EXPLORING YOUR COMMUNITY
BECOMING A COMMUNITY ORAL HISTORIAN

Can you recall a time when you heard adult family members speak about what it was like when they were growing up in New York? Or can you remember when a family member spoke about living through an important event in New York's history?

BEING AN ORAL HISTORIAN

If you were to record this adult family member's story, you would be participating in a special process. Historians call this "oral history"—collecting memories of the past obtained through interviews of eyewitnesses.

THE IMPORTANCE OF ORAL HISTORY

People today seem to have less time to keep diaries or to write journals. As a result, there is a growing need to preserve the personal or human side of history for future generations. Fortunately, many people are living longer. They provide a rich resource for historians, because many of these people actually experienced the past events that historians are now interested in.

In this *Exploring Your Community,* you will be given an opportunity to become an oral historian. Remember that your oral interview only records a person's memories of the past. A person's memories are often not the whole story, but only that person's point of view. In addition, a person's memory of events often changes over time and may contain inaccuracies.

◆ CONTINUED

PREPARING TO BECOME AN ORAL HISTORIAN

Acting as an oral historian involves more than just turning on a tape recorder or video camera and letting someone talk. Careful planning and research are needed to conduct a successful interview.

SELECTING AN ORAL HISTORY PROJECT

The first step is to decide *who* to interview and *why*. The most common type of oral history involves interviewing a family member or friend. In this interview, gather as much information as you can about the person's life. Focus on how the person's culture (*attitudes, customs and beliefs*) has influenced his or her life.

DEVELOPING A QUESTIONNAIRE

Start by creating a questionnaire—an outline of topics you wish to cover during your interview. You should use "leading" words, such as **describe, explain** and **discuss.** Remember, you want to "open up" the memory of your interviewee. Here is a sample questionnaire about a person's reactions at the time of the Vietnam War—a war that involved U.S. soldiers fighting in a far-off Asian country during the 1960s.

SAMPLE QUESTIONNAIRE

Name: _____ Address: _____

- How old were you when the war in Vietnam was being fought?
- Were any of your family members involved in the war? If so, **identify** who they were and **describe** the role they played in the war.
- **Describe** your feelings about U.S. involvement in Vietnam.
- **Discuss** what you remember about the feelings of those around you.
- **Describe** any other memories from that period in your life.
- At the time, did you agree with the decision of the United States to participate in the Vietnam War? **Explain.**
- Have your ideas on this topic changed since the end of the war? If so, **describe** how they changed and **explain** what caused them to change.

American soldiers relaxing after a battle in the jungles of Vietnam

CONTINUED

CONDUCTING THE INTERVIEW

The success of the interview will depend in large part on how you behave during the interview itself. Here are some helpful hints to keep in mind:

- ❖ **Make an Appointment.** Make an appointment several days in advance. Allow at least 30 minutes for the interview. Bring along a good tape recorder with which you are familiar. Be sure to test it before going to the interview.

- ❖ **The Start of the Interview.** Start by chatting informally with the person being interviewed, to put yourselves at ease. Start recording the interview with a short introduction, such as:

> "This interview is being conducted with Ms. Barbara Neuman at her home. It is Thursday, April 3, 1997. It is 4:30 in the afternoon."

Begin the interview with easy questions. Avoid questions that require simple yes or no answers. Your questionnaire will help you to ask questions that call for descriptive answers.

- ❖ **Stay On The Topic.** If your subject strays from the topic, try to re-focus the interview as soon as possible. Follow up important information and details with new questions that may not be on your questionnaire.

- ❖ **Closing the Interview.** Always end the interview by thanking your interviewee. If you feel the interview has gone on too long, pick an appropriate time to end. If necessary, arrange another time for a follow-up interview. For example, you might say:

> I would like to end the interview now. However, this was so interesting I would like to come back and talk more about other things you remember about the Vietnam War. Is that all right?"

CREATING A COVER SHEET FOR THE TAPES

No one will understand what your tape is about just by looking at it. You will need to make a cover sheet that explains the themes and ideas discussed in your interview. Use the following guide to create your cover sheet.

❖ CONTINUED

COVER SHEET FOR THE TAPED INTERVIEW

Topic of the Interview: _____

Person Being Interviewed: _____

Signature Granting Permission: _____

RUNNING TIME AND IDEAS COVERED

Minutes: 1–4 General background information about the person

Minutes: 5–8 Immediate reactions to the Vietnam War

Minutes: 9–15 Personal opinions about the need to be involved in the war

SUMMARIZING YOUR UNDERSTANDING

Directions: Use your knowledge to fill in the blanks in the following graphic organizers.

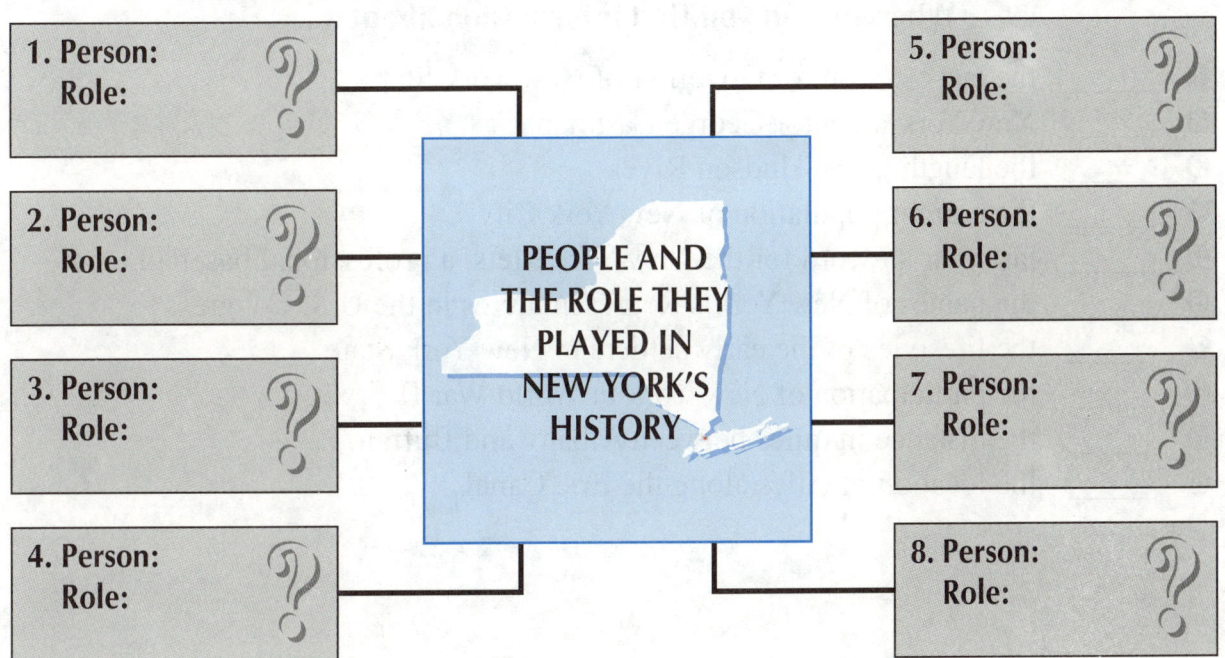

PEOPLE AND THE ROLE THEY PLAYED IN NEW YORK'S HISTORY

1. Person: Role:
2. Person: Role:
3. Person: Role:
4. Person: Role:
5. Person: Role:
6. Person: Role:
7. Person: Role:
8. Person: Role:

198 NEW YORK: ITS LAND AND ITS PEOPLE

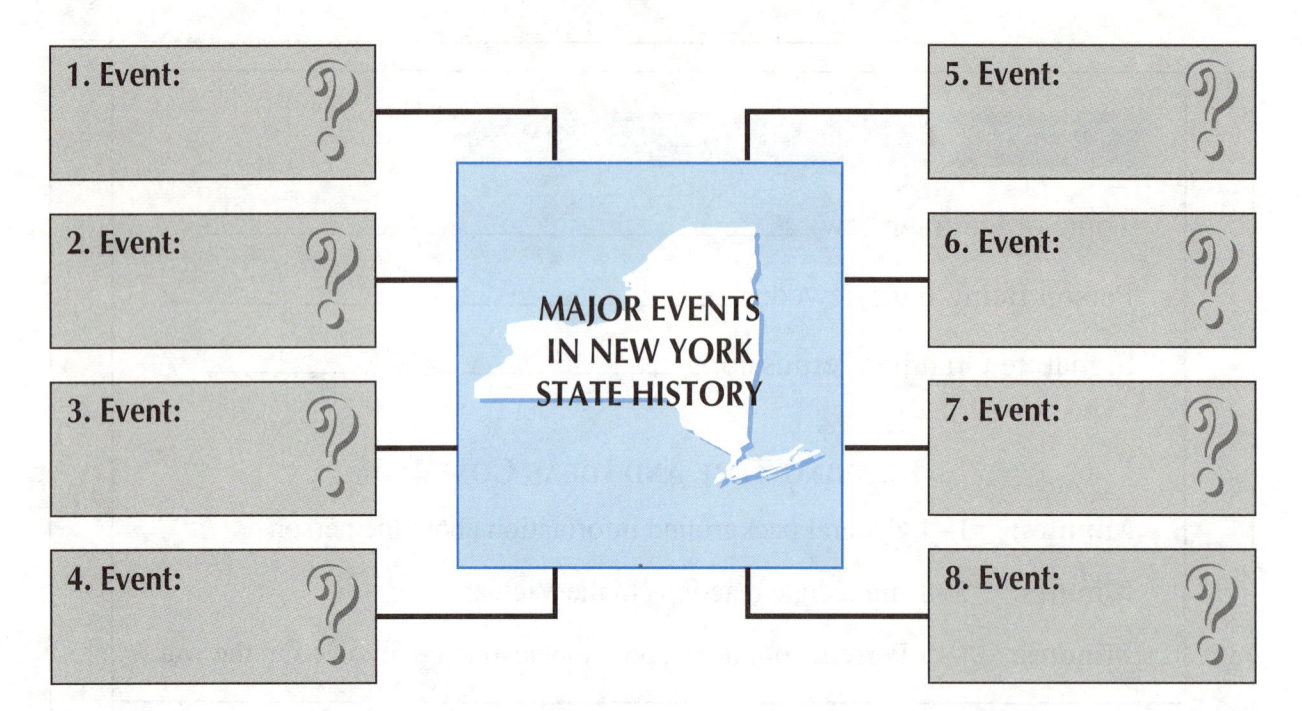

1. Event:

2. Event:

3. Event:

4. Event:

MAJOR EVENTS IN NEW YORK STATE HISTORY

5. Event:

6. Event:

7. Event:

8. Event:

FINDING INFORMATION IN DIFFERENT REFERENCE SOURCES

In the previous unit you learned about almanacs and atlases. In this unit you read about encyclopedias. Each reference tool is helpful in finding different kinds of information. See if you know when to use an **almanac, atlas** or **encyclopedia.**

Where would you find information about ....

❶ _____ the last election for Governor of New York State
❷ _____ New York inventor George Eastman
❸ _____ the length of the Hudson River
❹ _____ the current population of New York City
❺ _____ last year's record for the New York Mets, a professional baseball team
❻ _____ the names of New York's Representatives in the U.S. Congress
❼ _____ the lifestyles of the early settlers in New York State
❽ _____ the participation of New York in World War II
❾ _____ the distance in miles between Albany and Buffalo
❿ _____ the location of cities along the Erie Canal

INFORMATION SHEET #2: HISTORY

ITEMS FOR YOUR EXHIBIT

Following is a list of suggested tasks for your project. Feel free to add any others that you think portray the history of your neighborhood, village, town or city.

CREATING A BROCHURE FOR A HISTORIC SITE

Every community has interesting historic sites where people can step back in time and visit the past. If you have ever taken a trip with your family and stayed in a hotel or motel, you may have noticed brochures (*pamphlets*) in the lobby about interesting historic sites. Create a brochure about an interesting historic site in your community. Be sure that your brochure includes the following:

- **Clear and accurate directions for locating the place:** Indicate if public transportation is available. Also state how a person can use this transportation to get to the place. Provide a simple map that explains how to reach the historic site. Mention other unique or historic locations on your map.

- **Some photos of the site:** Current photographs are easy to obtain. Old-time photos may be available in your community library or museum.

- **The history of the site:** Explain what role the site played in the history of your community. Also, if it is a person's home, explain who lived there and why the site is important. Provide some interesting historical facts about the place or the person who lived there.

- **Information about the hours of operation:** State if there is an admission charge. Include the site's phone number in case someone has a question or needs to call ahead.

WRITING A COLUMN FOR A NEWSPAPER

Often, newspapers include feature stories about well-known personalities. These short articles tell us something about the person's background and character as well as his or her accomplishments. Imagine you are a famous columnist. Choose several individuals who influenced the history of your town or city. You should select people who are no longer living. For each person you select, write a short feature column. You will need to carry out some research about the person in your local library, museum or town historian's office. Be sure that your column contains such information as:

❖ CONTINUED

- ❖ **Birth/death:** Dates when the person was born and died.
- ❖ **Biography:** What were the main events in the person's life?
- ❖ **Character:** Include any interesting facts about the person's character.
- ❖ **Achievements:** Include a description of the person's major achievements.

HOLDING A HISTORICAL PAGEANT

Become an important historical character. Each student can then research his or her character and prepare a costume. On the day of the pageant, you and your classmates should walk around the classroom dressed in costumes. Each person should stop at the front of the classroom to say something about his or her character.

MODELING A HISTORICAL DIORAMA

Make a **diorama** (*miniature scene*) of an event in the local history of your community. The diorama can be made of paper glued to cardboard, or out of clay and other materials. For example, your diorama might show life among the Native Americans of your area, a famous battle from the American Revolution or an early factory.

DRAWING A SYMBOL AND FLAG FOR YOUR COMMUNITY

New York has a seal and a state flag. The **seal** appears on all official documents issued by the state and the flag flies over state buildings. In the center of the seal or flag are two boats on the Hudson River with the sun rising in the background. Two figures, Liberty on the left and Justice on the right, support the shield. On top of the shield is a globe with the American eagle on it. Below all of this is a ribbon with the state motto in Latin—"Excelsior"—this means "Ever Upward."

New York State Seal

What would a seal and flag for your village, town or city look like? Each item in New York's seal and flag represents something. For example, at the feet of the woman is a royal crown. The crown is used to show New York's opposition to living under a king's rule.

New York State Flag

In designing your village, town, or city seal and flag, remember that each item should symbolize (*stand for*) something related to your city or town. It can be something about your city or town's history, geography, government or economy.

UNIT 4
PEOPLE IN SOCIETY

Native Americans: The First New Yorkers

A Puerto Rican Day Parade in N.Y.C.

Immigrants Arriving at Ellis Island

Do you like pizza, tacos or egg rolls? Each of these foods was brought to New York by a different ethnic group. An **ethnic group** is a group that shares traditions, customs, beliefs and ancestors. New York's many ethnic groups have created a colorful mix of cultures that makes New York State an exciting place to live. In this unit, you will learn something about the different ethnic groups that live in our state. This will help you to appreciate how each group has contributed something special and unique to New York.

WHY DO PEOPLE HAVE DIFFERENT CULTURES?

- "BON JOUR" French
- "NA MAS TAY" Hindi
- "BUON GIORNO" Italian
- "GUTEN TAG" German
- "HELLO" English
- "DZIEN DOBRY" Polish
- "BUENOS DIAS" Spanish
- "NI HAU" Chinese
- "SHALOM" Hebrew

No matter how you say it, "hello" still means the same thing. Obviously, there are many ways to say any word. How did these differences in language and culture first come about?

One explanation for cultural differences can be found in a famous Bible story. Once upon a time, all people spoke the same language and followed the same customs. There were not many people, and they moved together from place to place. During their travels, the people of the world came upon a flat plain, where Iraq is now located. They settled there to build a city. First, they made bricks of straw and clay, which they baked to make them as strong as stone. With the bricks, the people built walls and buildings. After the city was built, they decided to build a very high tower. People hoped the tower would be high enough to reach up to heaven.

According to the Bible story, God looked down from heaven on the people busily building the tower and became angry. God decided to stop them from completing the tower by making them speak different languages. Suddenly, people could no longer understand each other.

Unable to communicate, people stopped their work on the tower. Those who could understand each other joined together. God scattered these people with their different languages to the four corners of the Earth. Since that time, people have had different languages and different ways of life. The abandoned tower became known as the **Tower of Babel**. "Babel" came to mean confusing sounds and voices.

The people of the world speak a variety of languages. *Do you know how these differences in language first developed?*

This story is one attempt to explain how languages and cultural differences developed throughout the world. Other societies have also tried to explain the development of different cultures. The Iroquois, for example, believed that the Great Spirit gave corn to the Mohawks, squash to the Onondagas and beans to the Senecas. They believed these different gifts explained the differences in language and customs among these three tribes. The ancient Greeks thought that different cultures were inspired by different gods and goddesses.

Cultural differences are a fascinating part of human life. At times, cultural differences have led to conflict, while at other times they have brought about cooperation and the spread of new ideas.

How did different cultures come about? What role have cultural differences played in the development of our nation, state and community? The answers to many of these exciting questions await you in the following unit.

HOW WOULD YOU CATEGORIZE YOURSELF?

4A

In this activity, you will see how people often identify themselves with groups based on race, nationality, ethnicity and religion. This activity will help you to understand what each of these terms means. Look for the following important words:

▶ Race   ▶ Nationality   ▶ Ethnicity   ▶ Religion

To help you, the ▶ symbol will appear in the margin where the **term** first appears.

One of the things that makes the United States very special is its people. Each American is a unique individual, with qualities, talents and abilities that make him or her special. Yet each of us also has some things in common with other Americans. For example, some people share the same customs or religious beliefs. The characteristics that people share sometimes lead them to identify themselves as part of a group.

HOW WOULD YOU GROUP YOURSELF?

In this activity, you will learn some of the ways Americans identify themselves. You will look at different racial, national, ethnic and religious groups. Before you start to look at other groups, let's first see how you might "group" yourself:

- ❖ What is your race?
- ❖ What is your nationality?
- ❖ What is your ethnic group?
- ❖ What is your religion?

Did you group yourself correctly? The answer really depends on how you define these words. Each of these words—race, nationality, ethnicity and religion—is a concept. A **concept** gives a name to things that, although different, have something in common. For example, the word "bird" is a concept. It applies to many different creatures: eagles, blue jays, ducks and chickens. However, all these animals share some common characteristics—they have feathers.

HOW PEOPLE ARE OFTEN GROUPED

You have probably heard people use the words **race, nationality, ethnic group** and **religion.** How well can you define them? Let's take a look at each of these terms.

RACE

Over the course of time, human beings in different parts of the world developed slight physical differences. For example, some people have a light skin color; others have a darker skin color. Sometimes these differences are used to identify groups of people.

Most people identify themselves with a racial group. A **race** is a group of people who are identified by the color of their skin or certain other physical characteristics. The Census Bureau lists six groups in classifying Americans by race:

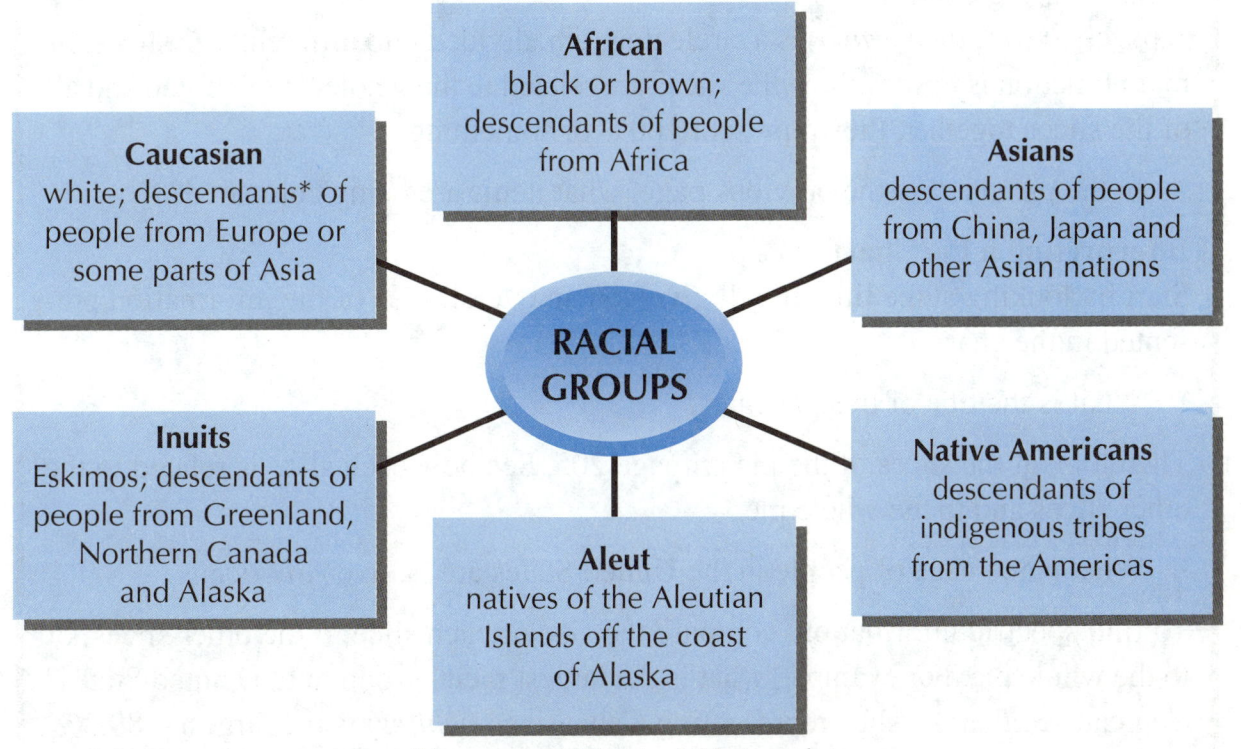

RACIAL GROUPS

- **African**: black or brown; descendants of people from Africa
- **Caucasian**: white; descendants* of people from Europe or some parts of Asia
- **Asians**: descendants of people from China, Japan and other Asian nations
- **Inuits**: Eskimos; descendants of people from Greenland, Northern Canada and Alaska
- **Aleut**: natives of the Aleutian Islands off the coast of Alaska
- **Native Americans**: descendants of indigenous tribes from the Americas

*people's descendants are their children, their children's children, and so on.

People from each of these racial groups have ancestors who came from different places. There are also many people who have mixed racial backgrounds.

> Which racial group (or groups) do you now think you belong to?

The United States is a **multi-racial society**, made up of people of many different races. The pie chart to the right shows the racial makeup of the United States in 1990:

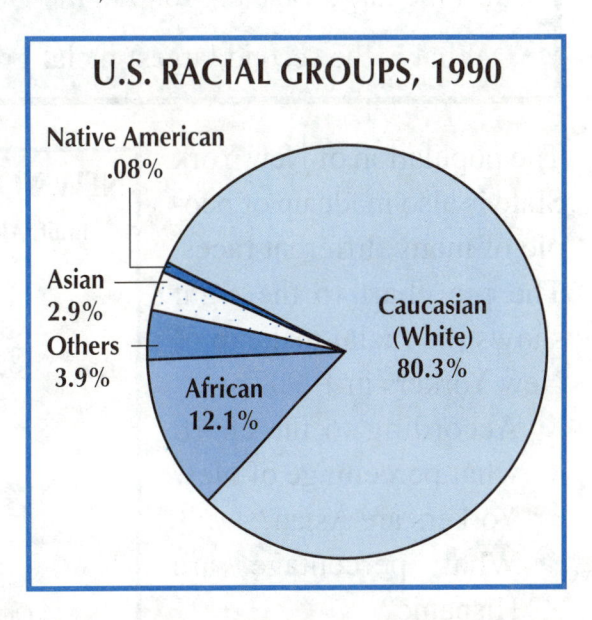

U.S. RACIAL GROUPS, 1990

- Native American .08%
- Asian 2.9%
- Others 3.9%
- African 12.1%
- Caucasian (White) 80.3%

206   NEW YORK: ITS LAND AND ITS PEOPLE

> Having trouble interpreting the information in this pie chart? If so, you should read the following Skill Builder on interpreting pie charts.

Skill Builder

INTERPRETING PIE CHARTS

What Is a Pie Chart?
A pie chart (*or circle graph*) is a circle diagram, divided into different size slices. Its main function is to show how the slices are related to the whole "pie." If you add all of the slices together, they represent 100% of something.

❖ In the pie chart on the previous page, what items are being compared?

Interpreting a Pie Chart
Start by looking at the title. It will give you an overall idea of the information presented in the chart.

❖ What is the title of this pie chart?

Then look at the slices of the pie on page 205. See how each slice is related to the other slices and to the whole pie.

❖ What percentage of people in the United States are Native Americans?

To find specific information, compare the size of each slice to the other slices, or to the whole pie. For example, what is the largest racial group in the United States? You can see that the slice representing Caucasians (*whites*) is the largest—80.3%. Thus, the largest racial group in the United States is Caucasian.

❖ What is the second largest racial group in the United States?

The population of New York State is also made up of people of many different races. The pie chart to the right shows the racial makeup of New Yorkers in 1990.

❖ According to the chart, what percentage of New Yorkers are Asian?

❖ What percentage are Hispanic?

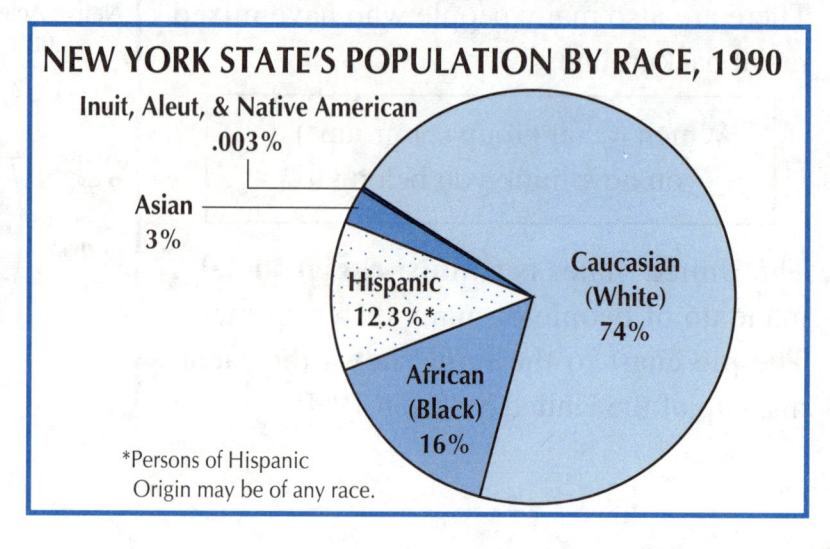

NEW YORK STATE'S POPULATION BY RACE, 1990

Inuit, Aleut, & Native American .003%
Asian 3%
Hispanic 12.3%*
Caucasian (White) 74%
African (Black) 16%

*Persons of Hispanic Origin may be of any race.

NATIONALITY AND NATIONAL ORIGIN

The word **nationality** refers to the country in which a person is a citizen. For example, if you were born in the United States or became a U.S. citizen, your nationality is American.

National origin sounds similar to nationality, but it means something different. National origin refers to the country where your parents, grandparents or ancestors came from. **Ancestors** are members of your family who lived a long time ago, such as your great-grandparents. For example, the national origin of one of your friends might be German. A German American is an American whose family (*parents, grandparents, or ancestors*) originally came from Germany.

THINK ABOUT IT

When you go home, ask your parents where your family's ancestors came from. What do you think they will say?

ETHNICITY

Ethnic groups are people who have the same national origin, language or race. For example, African Americans are of the same race. Irish Americans have the same national origin. In the United States, people's national origin often forms the basis of their ethnic identity. People who trace their ancestors back to Italy identify themselves as Italian Americans because of their national origin.

People who speak the same language may also be considered members of an ethnic group. **Hispanics**, sometimes known as Latinos, form one of New York's largest ethnic groups based on language. Hispanics may come from or have ancestors from the Caribbean area, Central America or South America. Most Hispanics in New York are from Puerto Rico or the Dominican Republic—two islands in the Caribbean.

✔ **CHECKING YOUR UNDERSTANDING** ✔

1. What percentage of New Yorkers trace their ancestry back to Italy?
2. From which continent do most New Yorkers trace their ancestry?
3. What ancestry groups might make up the category "other"?

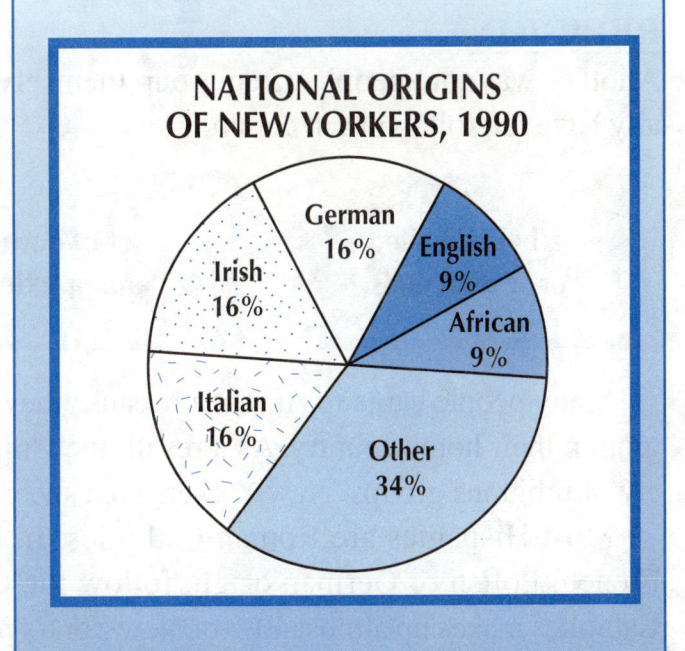

NATIONAL ORIGINS OF NEW YORKERS, 1990

- German 16%
- English 9%
- African 9%
- Other 34%
- Italian 16%
- Irish 16%

208 NEW YORK: ITS LAND AND ITS PEOPLE

Knowing someone's ethnic group may tell us something about that person's way of life. It may tell us what foods the person prefers. We may also be able to guess something about that person's other customs.

However, we also have to avoid the dangers of **stereotyping** (*assuming all people from one ethnic group are the same*). Individual differences are often just as important as ethnic identity. New York is well-known for its many ethnic groups. This is because many immigrant groups first settled in New York. We can see this ethnic diversity in the wide variety of foods New Yorkers enjoy and the many kinds of music they listen to. How many restaurants in your neighborhood serve ethnic foods? Do you also have radio and cable televisions stations that broadcast in foreign languages?

A sign in different languages in a New York City neighborhood. *Do you know which ethnic groups live in your community?*

✔ CHECKING YOUR UNDERSTANDING ✔

Name **three** ethnic foods popular with New Yorkers:

Food	This food comes from .....
❖ _____?_____	❖ _____?_____
❖ _____?_____	❖ _____?_____
❖ _____?_____	❖ _____?_____

RELIGION

▶ Another way that people often group themselves is by religion . Most religions usually have the following in common:

a belief in God or several gods	a set of customs and practices	an organization, such as a church, which sets rules for its members

Many people came to America because they were not allowed to practice their religion in their home country. As a result, the United States became a nation with a variety of religious groups. New Yorkers are especially proud of their religious diversity.

Most Hispanics are Roman Catholics. In addition, most New Yorkers of Irish, French, Polish or German origin follow the Catholic religion. As a result, Roman Catholics makes up almost 40% of New York's population—the religion with the largest number of members in the state. There are also many Protestant Christians in New York. These include Episcopalians, Methodists, Lutherans and Presbyterians.

About half of all American Jews live in New York State. Jewish New Yorkers make up about 15% of the state's population. Most of them live in New York City and its surrounding suburbs.

Muslims, Hindus and Buddhists are some of the other major religious groups found in New York. Muslims are one of the state's fastest growing groups. Immigrants from Asia, Africa and the Middle East and their descendants are often Muslim. So are many African Americans who have converted to Islam. More than half a million Muslims live in New York today. Hinduism is another religion common among New York's population. Many Hindu families trace their origins to South Asia. New York's Buddhist population tends to come from East and Southeast Asia, especially China, Japan, Korea, Vietnam, Cambodia and Thailand.

A Muslim house of worship.
What houses of worship exist in your community?

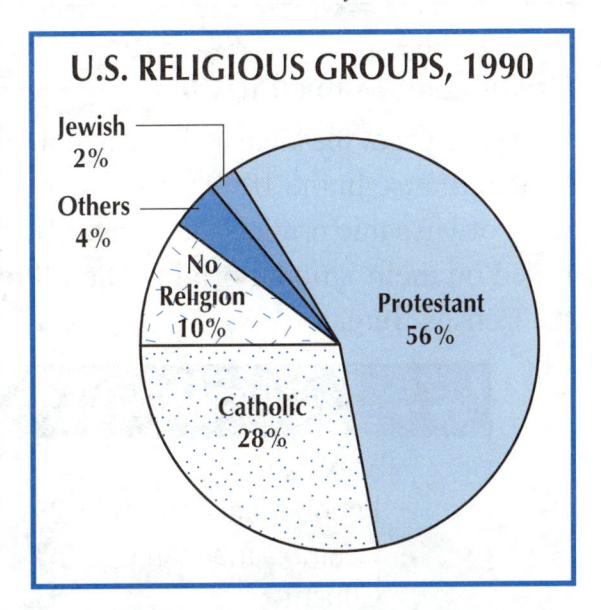

U.S. RELIGIOUS GROUPS, 1990

- Jewish 2%
- Others 4%
- No Religion 10%
- Catholic 28%
- Protestant 56%

✔ Checking Your Understanding ✔

Name two major religious groups in New York State.

Name a religious group in your community.

REVIEWING HOW YOU IDENTIFIED YOURSELF

At the start of this activity you answered some questions to "group" yourself. Review page 204 to check what you wrote when you first began this activity. How would you now group yourself?

- ❖ What is your race?
- ❖ What is your ethnic group?
- ❖ What is your nationality?
- ❖ What is your religion?

REVIEWING YOUR UNDERSTANDING

Creating Vocabulary Cards

Race

Define the term "race":

Give an example of a racial group:

Ethnicity

Define the term "ethnicity":

Give an example of an ethnic group:

Creating an Ethnic Pie Chart

Every 10 years the Census Bureau conducts a **census**—a count of every person in the United States. In the 1990 census, about 1 out of every 11 persons surveyed said they were of Hispanic origin. The Census Bureau also asked Hispanics to group themselves based on their national origin. The following chart shows what Hispanic people told the Census Bureau:

HISPANICS BY NATIONAL ORIGIN: 1990

Mexican	60%	South American	5%
Puerto Rican	12%	Dominican	3%
Central American	6%	Spaniard	3%
Cuban	5%	Others	7%

As you can see, about 6 out of every 10 Hispanics (60%) said they were of Mexican origin. This makes Mexican Americans the largest Hispanic group in the United States.

Often, converting information into a pie chart makes it clearer. Let's change this information into a pie chart. Make a copy of the circle to the right. Then take each item from the table and fill in its "pie slice." Use the markings around the circle to help you to divide the "pie." Each space between the marks represents 1% of the whole "pie." The pie chart has already been started for you.

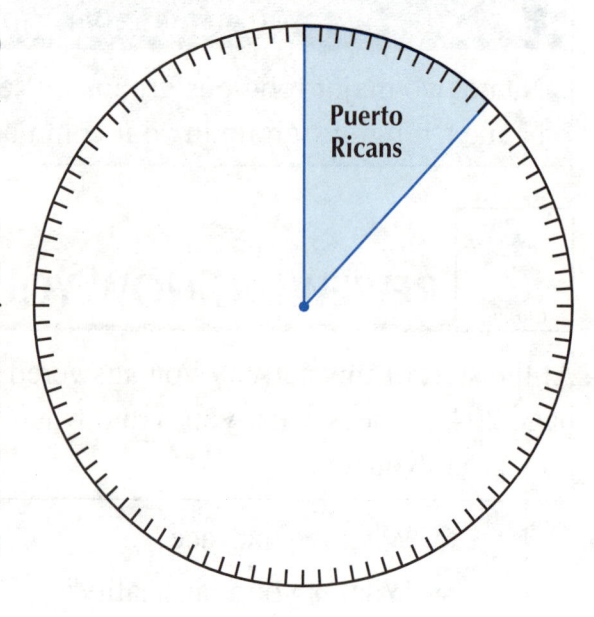

MAKING CONNECTIONS

EXPLORING BEYOND YOUR STATE
SOME MAJOR WORLD RELIGIONS

In this activity, you learned that New York is a state with many different religions. Many New Yorkers get their values and traditions from the world's major religions.

JUDAISM

In ancient times, the first people to believe in a single God were the Jews (*Hebrews*). The belief in a single God is called **monotheism**. Jewish people believe that God is the creator of the universe and is all-powerful and just. They also believe that God made a special promise to protect them, so long as they obeyed the **Ten Commandments**—a set of rules to live by. Jews believe these rules were given to **Moses** as he led them from slavery in Egypt back to Israel some 4,000 years ago. Much of Judaism is based on following the rules of the Ten Commandments and leading good lives. The Jewish house of worship is called a **synagogue**.

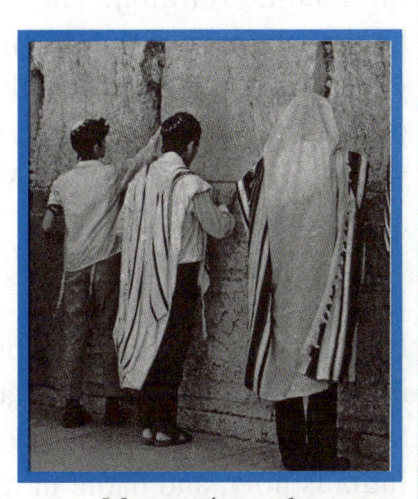

Men praying at the Wailing Wall in Jerusalem—one of the holiest sites for Jews.

CHRISTIANITY

Christians also believe in one God. They take their name "Christian" from **Jesus Christ** of Nazareth, who they believe was the son of God. Jesus taught his followers to be merciful and good to others. Christians believe Jesus sacrificed himself for the sins of humanity. They further believe Jesus returned from the dead and rose to heaven. They see this as proof that God opens heaven's gates to all those who have faith in Jesus and lead good lives. The Christian house of worship is called a **church**.

The Church of the Holy Sepulchre in Jerusalem was built in the place where it is believed Jesus rose to heaven.

❖ CONTINUED

ISLAM

Muslims follow the Islamic religion. They live mainly in the Middle East, Asia and Africa. Muslims also believe in one, all powerful God known as **Allah**. They believe that Allah has complete control over each person's actions. Muslims base their religious beliefs on the teachings of **Mohammed**, the founder of the Islamic religion. They believe he was the last of Allah's messengers. His teachings form the basis of their holy book, the **Qu'ran** (*Koran*). Muslims believe the Qu'ran contains the words of Allah, as told to Mohammed. The Muslim house of worship is known as a **mosque**.

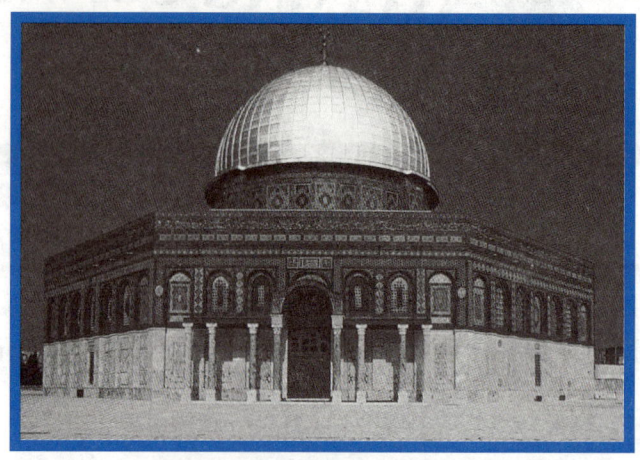

The Dome of the Rock, located in Jerusalem, is one of the holiest sites for Muslims.

HINDUISM

Hinduism began in India more than 3,000 years ago. Unlike religions with a belief in a single God, Hinduism has many gods and goddesses. Hindus consider the cow to be a holy animal, so they will not eat beef. They believe the **Ganges River** in India is holy, and bathe in it to wash away their sins. Hindus also believe that at death, a person's spirit leaves his or her body to be reborn in another living thing. If a person has acted well in his or her lifetime, that person will rewarded by having a better life when he or she is reborn. This process of being reborn in another living thing is called **reincarnation**. Hindus practice their religion at home or in a temple.

BUDDHISM

Buddhists trace their roots to India, where their religion first began. Buddhism is based on the teachings of **Siddhartha Gautama** (sid-dahr'-tuh gaw-tuh-muh). He was an Indian prince who searched for the true meaning of life. **Buddha**, as he became known, taught that excessive desires are the main cause of pain and suffering. Instead of being concerned with obtaining wealth, Buddhists believe that a person should try to discover the meaning of life. Buddhist places of worship are known as temples or shrines. Some Buddhists retreat into monasteries, where they **meditate** (*think deeply*) and study Buddhist teachings.

◆ CONTINUED

PEOPLE IN SOCIETY   213

EXPLORING RELIGIOUS BELIEFS

Name **three** major religious groups living in New York. List some of their religious beliefs.

Religion	Major Religious Beliefs
_____	_____
_____	_____

EXPLORING YOUR COMMUNITY
LEARNING ABOUT PEOPLE IN YOUR COMMUNITY

In this activity, we have learned more about ourselves. Now let's turn our attention to learning more about our neighbors and friends.

LOOKING AT OTHER RELIGIONS

Find someone in your class or neighborhood who belongs to a different race, ethnic group or religion than yourself. Compare your family's traditions and customs with theirs.

1. Do you celebrate any different holidays? If so, what are they?
2. Does your religion require that you eat or avoid any special kinds of foods? If so, what are they?
3. Do you both celebrate any of the same holidays?
4. Do you both share in any other common traditions or customs? If so, what are they?

WHAT GENERALIZATIONS CAN YOU MAKE ABOUT NEW YORK'S ETHNIC GROUPS?

4B

In this activity, you will learn about the different ethnic groups that have made New York their home. Look for the following important words:

- ▶ Generalization
- ▶ Anti-Semitism
- ▶ Harlem Renaissance
- ▶ Barrios

Generalizations are powerful organizing tools. They allow us to summarize large amounts of information in a more manageable form. In this activity, you will examine how generalizations are formed and practice making your own generalizations.

WHAT IS A GENERALIZATION?

Look at the following list:

- ❖ **New York City** borders the **Atlantic Ocean.**
- ❖ **Geneva** borders **Seneca Lake.**
- ❖ **Albany** is located on the **Hudson River.**
- ❖ **Buffalo** is next to **Lake Erie,** one of the Great Lakes.

It may be hard to remember all of these facts. But if you look at them as a group, you can see a pattern. These four facts about cities in New York have something in common. This pattern may actually be more important than any specific fact.

Rochester is located along the Genesee River.
What other cities are near large bodies of water?

THINK ABOUT IT

What do these four facts about cities in New York have in common?

HOW GENERALIZATIONS ARE FORMED

The list shows that *major cities are located near large bodies of water.* This general statement describes what all of the specific examples have in common. When a general statement identifies a common pattern, it is called a generalization. Let's see how this generalization might be presented in a diagram.

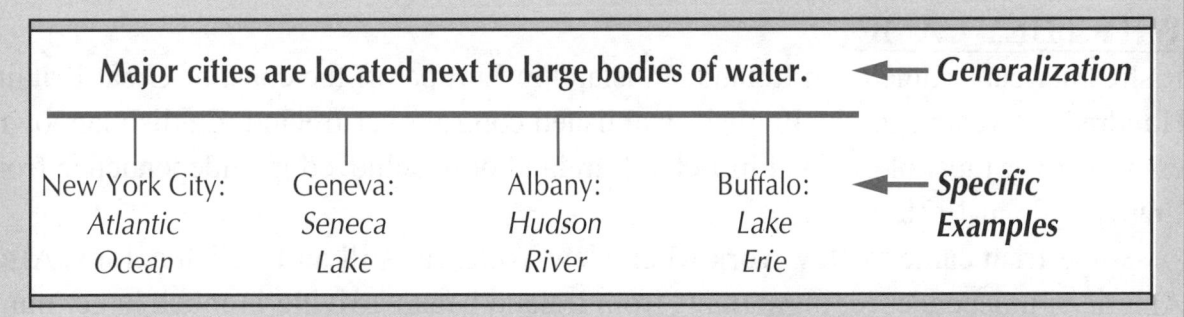

Major cities are located next to large bodies of water. ← *Generalization*

| New York City: Atlantic Ocean | Geneva: Seneca Lake | Albany: Hudson River | Buffalo: Lake Erie | ← *Specific Examples* |

A generalization shows what several facts have in common. A generalization can also help us to make predictions. Each of the previous examples showed a major city next to a large body of water. We might now guess or predict that if we look at any other major city, it will also be located next to a large body of water.

Although generalizations are useful tools, we must be careful in applying them. For example, is our generalization really true for all large cities? Suppose we applied it to Las Vegas. If you look at a map, you will find that Las Vegas is **not** located next to a large body of water. This means we have to change our original generalization. Based on all the facts we now have, we can say that *many*, but not all, major cities are located next to large bodies of water.

When you are asked if a generalization is true, you must find specific examples and facts for support. Remember, generalizations are always subject to change as new information is learned. Now let's see how this modified generalization might look when presented in a diagram:

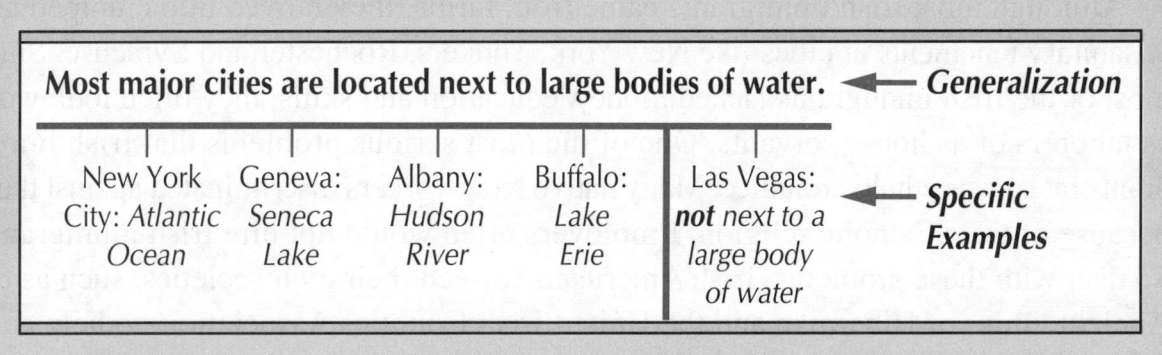

Most major cities are located next to large bodies of water. ← *Generalization*

| New York City: Atlantic Ocean | Geneva: Seneca Lake | Albany: Hudson River | Buffalo: Lake Erie | Las Vegas: **not** next to a large body of water | ← *Specific Examples* |

You have just learned how a generalization is formed and changed. How good are you at creating your own generalizations? Let's apply what you just learned to see if you can make generalizations about some ethnic groups in New York.

IMMIGRANTS COMING TO NEW YORK, 1820–1920

THE IRISH AMERICANS

WHY THEY CAME

Irish Americans came from Ireland, an island in Europe off the coast of Great Britain. Hundreds of years ago, the English established control over Ireland. English landowners took over most of the land in Ireland. Ireland only achieved its independence from English rule in 1921.

Some Irish came to New York when New York was still an English colony. After American independence, immigrants from Ireland began arriving in much larger numbers. Most of the Irish immigrants were poor, unskilled workers who followed the Catholic religion. They had few opportunities in Ireland. From 1820 to 1930, about $4\frac{1}{2}$ million Irish immigrants came to the United States, looking for a better way of life.

In 1845, a new disease struck the potato crop in Ireland. Since many people in Ireland lived on potatoes, they had no food. During this period, more than a million people starved to death in Ireland. The potato famine in Ireland led to a massive increase in Irish immigration to the United States. Even after the famine, Irish immigrants continued to come to America in large numbers. By 1870, one out of every five people in New York City had been born in Ireland. The same was true of many upstate cities such as Troy.

THE PROBLEMS THEY FACED

Irish immigrants faced a series of hardships that began with their journey across the Atlantic Ocean. On the overcrowded sailing ships, diseases spread quickly among the passengers. As many as one-tenth of the passengers died on the voyage.

Although most Irish immigrants came from farms, they moved into cramped and unsanitary tenements in cities like New York, Yonkers, Rochester and Syracuse. Since most of the Irish immigrants lacked money, education and skills, they often took work as laborers or as house servants. One of the most serious problems that Irish immigrants faced was ethnic prejudice. Many native New Yorkers discriminated against them because of their Catholic religion. Employers often would not hire Irish immigrants. To deal with these problems, Irish Americans formed their own societies, such as the Ancient Order of Hibernian and the United Irish Counties Association, to help each other. They published their own newspapers, started their own community libraries, and found support from the local Catholic Church.

CONTRIBUTIONS OF THE IRISH

Irish Americans made many important contributions to New York. Irish workers helped build the Erie Canal and the railroads that made New York economically successful. Irish Americans built St. Patrick's Cathedral in New York City. Irish-American politicians, like Robert F. Wagner, Robert F. Kennedy and Daniel P. Moynihan, worked to improve the lives of all New Yorkers. Irish folk music and theater enriched New York's entertainment scene. Some Irish New Yorkers, like James Cagney, became famous movie stars.

Young girls participating in a St. Patrick's Day Parade in upstate New York

ST. PATRICK'S DAY

St. Patrick is honored as the saint who brought Christianity to Ireland. Many Irish Americans celebrate March 17— **St. Patrick's Day**—with a parade. In New York it is a time when bands play and politicians march up Fifth Avenue. Students from all over New York head to Manhattan to take part in the parade.

> ✔ CHECKING YOUR UNDERSTANDING ✔
>
> 1. Why did the Irish immigrants come to America?
> 2. What problems did Irish immigrants face?
> 3. What contributions have Irish Americans made to American society?

THE ITALIAN AMERICANS

WHY THEY CAME

Italy is a country in Southern Europe. Very few Italians emigrated to the United States until the beginning of the 20th century. Then, between 1899 and 1910, almost two million Italian immigrants came to the United States. They came mainly to escape poverty. Italians were also attracted by transatlantic ships offering inexpensive fares to America for as little as $10. Steamship companies made it possible for immigrants in America to buy tickets for relatives still in Europe. Many of the Italian immigrants came here to work and save money to buy land back in Italy.

THE PROBLEMS THEY FACED

The voyage across the Atlantic in the early 1900s was difficult, but it was far better than only a few decades earlier. Steamships were larger and faster than before, making the crossing in only six days. Most immigrants still lacked fresh air and natural light while living below deck, but the risks of dying on the voyage were now low.

When they arrived, most Italian immigrants moved into crowded and unhealthy tenements in the major cities of New York State, especially New York City. Most lived in communities with fellow Italians who came from the same village and spoke the same language. Here, the residents could feel comfortable speaking their native language and following their own customs.

Hundreds of immigrants stand on the deck of the S.S. Patricia on its Atlantic crossing.

Most Italian newcomers came from rural areas. They lacked money, education and skills. Most of them could not even read and write. In addition, they did not speak English. For these reasons many of them found jobs with Italian-speaking bosses. Italians soon replaced the Irish as the main work force on railroads, streets and other public projects. They also began to develop their own small businesses. Some sold vegetables from pushcarts, while others opened small shops as barbers or tailors.

A major problem that Italian Americans had to face was ethnic prejudice from native-born Americans. Some people disliked the strange language, unusual clothes and Catholic religion of the Italians. In addition, some American workers disliked Italians because they worked for lower wages. To overcome these problems, Italian Americans formed their own societies, such as the "Sons of Italy."

CONTRIBUTIONS OF THE ITALIANS

Italian Americans made many important contributions to American society. They enriched the arts and music of New York. They introduced many delicious new foods, from spaghetti to pizza. Mario Cuomo, Rudolph Giuliani and Alfonse D'Amato are Italian Americans who became major political leaders. Most important of all, Italians have contributed to a strong work ethic and an emphasis on the importance of the family.

COLUMBUS DAY

Italians enliven the state with their many festivals, such as the **San Gennaro Festival** in New York City's "Little Italy." **Columbus Day** on October 12th celebrates Italian accomplishments. The festival honoring Columbus is observed with parades and parties in many cities in New York State. People wear "Italian Power" buttons, and floats in parades honor a wide variety of Italian groups and accomplishments.

FAMOUS NEW YORKERS

Fiorello La Guardia (1882–1947) was the son of an Italian father and a Jewish mother. Elected Mayor of New York City in 1933, at the worst of the Depression, he became the first Mayor to serve three straight terms one after the other. He was one of the most colorful and popular Mayors in the city's history. During a newspaper strike he read comic strips over the radio to the city's children. As Mayor, La Guardia fought corruption, modernized city government, balanced the budget and introduced improvements in health services, housing and recreation. La Guardia Airport in Queens is named after him.

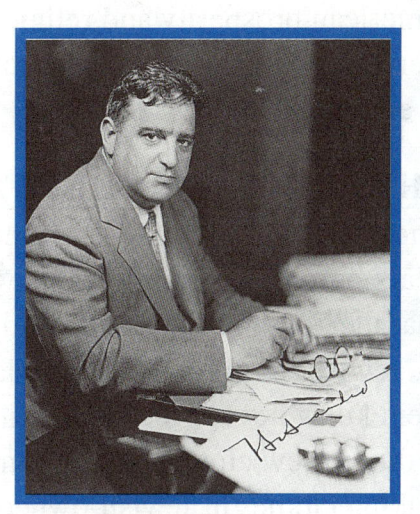

Fiorello LaGuardia

✔ CHECKING YOUR UNDERSTANDING ✔

1. Why did Italian immigrants come to America?
2. What problems did Italian immigrants face?
3. What contributions have Italian Americans made to American society?

THE JEWISH AMERICANS

WHY THEY CAME

The Jewish people who emigrated to the United States were united by a common religion, culture and history, rather than by coming from a single country. The first Jews arrived in New York as early as 1654. Up until the 1880s, most Jewish immigrants came from Germany. Between 1880 and 1920, over $1\frac{1}{2}$ million Jews left Russia and other Eastern European countries to settle in America.

In Russia, most Jews had lived in small towns in the countryside. They were not permitted to own land. Instead, they became craftsmen or traders, working as tailors, shoemakers or barbers. They spoke their own language, Yiddish, and had limited contact with other Russians. Beginning in the 1880s, the Russian government began restricting Jews even further. The government also encouraged mobs to attack and sometimes even to kill Jewish residents.

Jews fled Russia and other Eastern European countries to escape this harsh treatment and religious prejudice. They were attracted to the United States by news of American prosperity and religious freedom. In many cases, whole families emigrated. German steamship companies offered low fares to New York City, making it possible to emigrate.

THE PROBLEMS THEY FACED

The voyage across the Atlantic Ocean was unpleasant, but not as dangerous as fifty years before. The immigrants were usually crowded into bunks built in large rooms near the bottom of the ship. Many passengers became seasick during the voyage.

Jewish immigrants usually lacked money and did not speak English. But many of them knew how to read and write Yiddish. They often had other skills as well, like the ability to sew clothes. Many times they were recruited soon after they landed, to work making clothes in Jewish-owned workshops.

A major problem that Jewish immigrants faced was their terrible housing conditions. Most moved into the large Jewish community in the Lower East Side of Manhattan. There they lived in their own world, much as they had in Russia. They spoke Yiddish, read Yiddish newspapers, bought goods from Jewish shops, and rented rooms or tenement housing from Jewish landlords. The tenements were extremely crowded. Hundreds of thousands of people were crowded into a few square blocks. Most tenement dwellings lacked fresh air or natural light.

The lower East Side of New York City early in the twentieth century

Besides poor housing and working conditions, Jewish newcomers also faced religious and ethnic prejudice when they tried to leave their own neighborhoods and mix with other Americans. Prejudice against Jews is known as **anti-Semitism**. To overcome these problems, Jews often formed their own social organizations. They also found support from Jewish Americans already in New York for several generations.

CONTRIBUTIONS OF THE JEWS

Jewish Americans greatly enriched the life of New York. Jewish immigrants and their children became teachers, lawyers, bankers, doctors and artists. Among them were Irving Berlin, George Gershwin and Leonard Bernstein, noted Jewish-American songwriters and composers. Robert Moses, the son of German Jews, reshaped New York by designing Jones Beach and a network of highways and tunnels throughout the state. Two Jewish Americans who were important public leaders in New York were Governor Herbert Lehman and New York City Mayor Ed Koch.

SALUTE TO ISRAEL PARADE

On the first Sunday of each June, New York's Jewish population celebrates Israel's independence with a **Salute to Israel Parade**. New York's Jews use the parade to show their support for fellow Jews around the world.

FAMOUS NEW YORKERS

Irving Berlin (1888–1989) was born in Russia. He moved to New York City in 1893. As a young man, he sang in the streets of New York City and as a waiter in Chinatown. His first hit was *Alexander's Ragtime Band*. Berlin went on to write the words and music to over 1,500 songs. He also wrote songs for Broadway musicals and Hollywood films. Several of his musicals were made into movies. His most popular songs include *God Bless America*, *White Christmas* and *There's No Business Like Show Business*. He was awarded the Medal of Freedom in 1977 by President Ford.

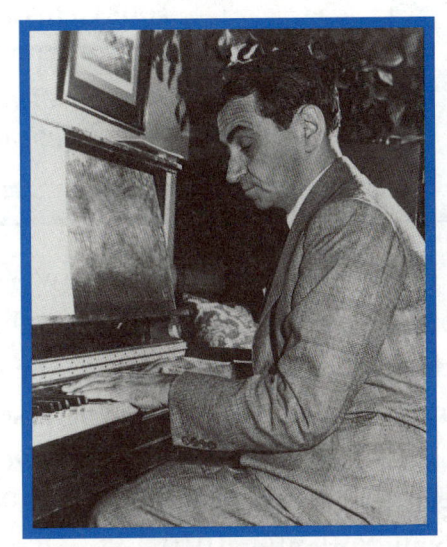

Irving Berlin

✔ CHECKING YOUR UNDERSTANDING ✔

1. Why did Jewish immigrants come to America?
2. What problems did Jewish immigrants face?
3. What contributions did Jewish people make to American society?

CREATING A GENERALIZATION

Can you think of a general statement that is true about all three of these immigrant groups? Recall that they all faced ethnic prejudice in America. Such a statement is a generalization.

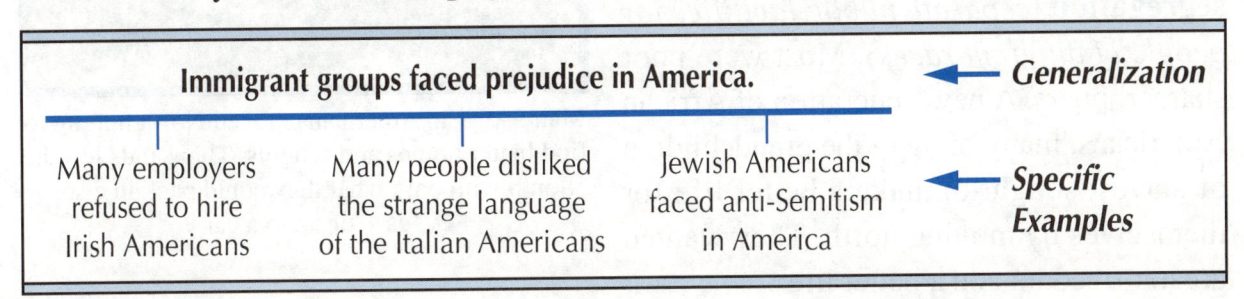

Immigrant groups faced prejudice in America.			← *Generalization*
Many employers refused to hire Irish Americans	Many people disliked the strange language of the Italian Americans	Jewish Americans faced anti-Semitism in America	← *Specific Examples*

✔ CHECKING YOUR UNDERSTANDING ✔

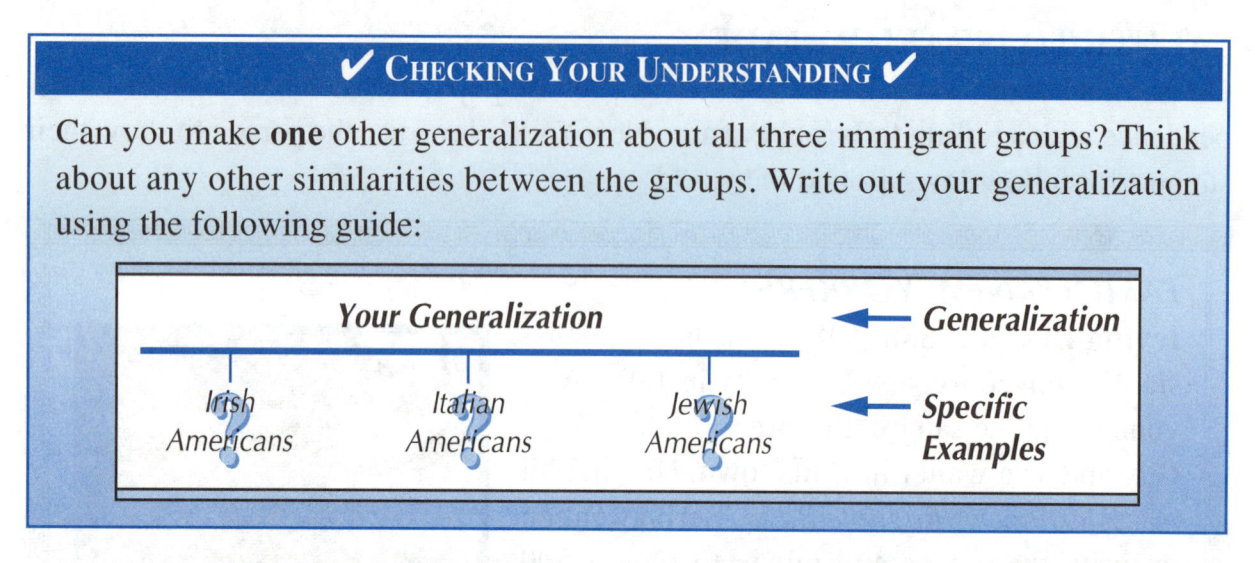

Can you make **one** other generalization about all three immigrant groups? Think about any other similarities between the groups. Write out your generalization using the following guide:

```
       Your Generalization              ← Generalization
    ───────────────────────────
      Irish      Italian     Jewish     ← Specific
    Americans  Americans   Americans       Examples
```

From its earliest days, New York has been a popular destination for immigrant groups. You have just read about three groups that emigrated to New York from Europe in the 1800s and early 1900s. The period following World War I brought several other groups to New York. In the next section, you will learn about three ethnic groups that came to New York State in these years. One group, the African Americans, was already present in New York long before 1900. However, many more African Americans moved to New York after 1910.

MIGRANTS AND IMMIGRANTS TO NEW YORK, 1910–1990

THE AFRICAN AMERICANS

Why They Came. Since its earliest beginnings, New York has been a home to African Americans. Between 1910 and 1930, a large number of African Americans living in the South began moving to New York and other Northern states. In the South, they had received little schooling and were often the target of violence. They also faced public **segregation** (*separate public facilities for people of different races*). Most were poor sharecroppers. A new generation of African Americans, many of them the grandchildren of slaves, sought to make a better life for themselves by moving north. They wanted greater freedom and a better life.

Many African Americans moved North hoping to find better homes and schools. Thousands left the South with only what they could pack in a suitcase or tie to a car.

In these same years, there was a great need for labor in the North. When the United States entered World War I, the supply of European immigrant workers was cut off. After the war, immigration continued to be limited by new laws. For the first time, many African Americans could find jobs in Northern factories. Many settled in Harlem, a neighborhood in Manhattan. A re-awakening of African-American music, dance, poetry and song at this time became known as the **Harlem Renaissance**. ◀

THE PROBLEMS THEY FACED

African Americans who moved north faced many problems. Most arrived with little money, education or skills. Although their wages were higher than in the South, they still received low pay. Another problem facing African Americans was housing. Most African Americans lived together in separate neighborhoods. Landlords frequently overcharged them. They could not find housing in other parts of the city.

One of the most serious problems they faced was **racial discrimination**. This means prejudice against someone because of race. African Americans were often refused jobs and were prevented from buying homes in many areas. As a result, they often experienced greater unemployment and poverty than some other groups in New York.

ADJUSTING TO LIFE IN NEW YORK

To deal with some of these problems, African Americans often formed their own neighborhood churches. As early as 1776, the first black church in New York was started. More recently, African Americans took other steps to fight discrimination. In the late 1930s, Adam Clayton Powell, Jr., organized African Americans to **boycott** stores in New York that would not hire them. This meant they refused to buy from these stores. Eventually, the stores gave in to this economic pressure and hired black workers. Powell later became the first African American to be elected to the New York City Council. He was also the first African American to head an important committee in the U.S. Congress. In the 1960s, African Americans organized the Civil Rights Movement to pass laws against racial discrimination.

CONTRIBUTIONS OF AFRICAN AMERICANS

African Americans have made many important contributions to New York. The Harlem Renaissance in the 1920s helped to re-awaken African-American pride in their culture and acheivements. Langston Hughes wrote poems and plays about the black experience. In addition, African Americans have contributed to the music, food, theater, sports and politics of New York.

Black leadership of the Civil Rights Movement not only ended discrimination against African Americans, but also encouraged new movements to end discrimination against women, Latinos, Asians, Native Americans, senior citizens and people with disabilities. Important African Americans from New York include former Mayor David Dinkins, baseball player Willie Mays, basketball star Kareem Abdul-Jabbar and Malcolm X.

AFRICAN-AMERICAN DAY

On the first Sunday in September, thousands of African Americans turn out for the **African-American Day Parade**. Hundreds of marchers move up the main boulevard in Harlem. Thousands of spectators line the streets as the parade moves along to the beat of African drums. Many of the marchers wear traditional African clothing such as a dashiki—an African-style shirt.

David Dinkins was the first African-American Mayor of New York City.

FAMOUS NEW YORKERS

James Baldwin (1924–1987) was born in Harlem. In 1947, he began to write about his experiences involving racism and segregation. In 1953, he published his first novel, *Go Tell It on the Mountain*. The story told of his difficulties growing up as a young child in Harlem. Baldwin also wrote *Notes of a Native Son* (1955), *Nobody Knows My Name* (1961), *Another Country* (1962), and *Blues for Mr. Charlie* (1964). His books helped make him an international celebrity. At his death in 1987, Baldwin was one of America's most popular novelists and an important critic of American society.

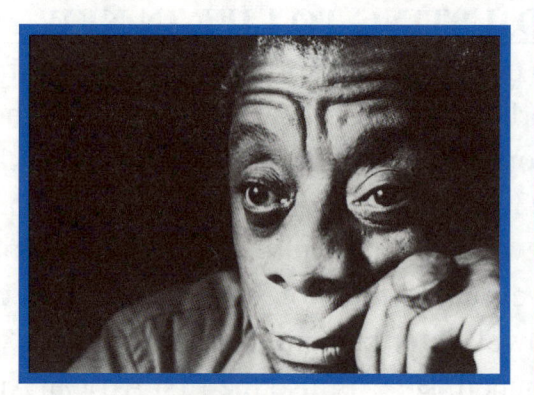

James Baldwin

✔ CHECKING YOUR UNDERSTANDING ✔

1. Why did African Americans come to New York?
2. What problems did African Americans face?
3. What contributions did African Americans make to New York society?

THE PUERTO RICANS

WHY THEY CAME

Puerto Rico is a small island in the Caribbean Sea, southeast of the United States. At one time, it was a colony of Spain. Because of Spain's influence, the main language spoken in Puerto Rico is Spanish. The United States took over the island in 1898. Puerto Ricans are American citizens and can travel freely to the U.S. mainland.

After the United States took over Puerto Rico, health care improved and the island's population grew. This eventually led to overcrowding and increased migration to the mainland United States. New industries opened in Puerto Rico in the 1940s and 1950s, but they did not create enough jobs. When the airlines introduced reduced fares to New York City, Puerto Ricans moved to New York in large numbers hoping to escape poverty and find a better way of life. Many came only for a short time, hoping to save money to take back to Puerto Rico.

THE PROBLEMS THEY FACED

Many Puerto Ricans arrived in New York with a background in farming and were unable to speak English. Men took low-paying jobs as laborers in factories, hotels and restaurants. Women worked as maids or sewed clothes in factories. Puerto Ricans competed with other groups for these jobs. More recently, the move of many manufacturing jobs out of New York City has hurt the Puerto Rican community. Unemployment and poverty remain serious problems.

Many of the new arrivals lived in **barrios**, neighborhoods, where Spanish was the main language. They often occupied some of the worst housing in the city. Landlords failed to repair many of these buildings. In the 1960s, Puerto Rican neighborhoods were often divided up by the construction of new highways and low-cost housing projects. Puerto Ricans also faced prejudice because of their use of the Spanish language and their different customs.

ADJUSTING TO LIFE IN NEW YORK

To deal with these problems, some Puerto Ricans formed neighborhood community groups. They published their own newspapers in Spanish. The Puerto Rican Association for Community Affairs and Puerto Rican Forum worked hard to promote a positive image and deal with problems. Some Puerto Ricans started their own businesses, while others promoted reform. They helped begin day care for working mothers, free health care clinics and free breakfast programs for poor children. Some Puerto Ricans started moving out of New York City to the suburbs and other parts of the state.

CONTRIBUTIONS OF THE PUERTO RICANS

The arrival of Puerto Ricans greatly enriched the culture and diversity of New York State. Puerto Rican cafés opened in different parts of New York City. Puerto Rican music was heard in night clubs and on the streets. The Puerto Rican Traveling Theater and Museo del Barrio encouraged a greater appreciation of Hispanic culture. Puerto Rican reformers like Herman Badillo drew attention to inner city problems and worked to improve conditions for all New Yorkers. Others, like talk-show host Geraldo Rivera and actor Raul Julia, became successful in the entertainment field.

PUERTO RICAN DAY

Puerto Rican Day, held on the first Sunday in June, is celebrated with parades, music and dancing. Puerto Rican politicians, celebrities and ordinary citizens march together up Fifth Avenue. The event has one of the largest turnouts of any ethnic parade held in New York City. Each year the number of participants increases.

The New York City Puerto Rican Day Parade

✔ CHECKING YOUR UNDERSTANDING ✔

1. Why did Puerto Ricans come to New York?
2. What problems did Puerto Ricans face?
3. What contributions have Puerto Ricans made to New York society?

THE KOREAN AMERICANS

WHY THEY CAME

Korea is a peninsula in northeast Asia. It is located in an area where China, Russia and Japan meet. Koreans have a unique culture, with their own language, history and traditions. At the end of World War II, Russian soldiers occupied North Korea, while U.S. troops occupied South Korea. Today, South Korea has a very successful economy and a democratic government. North Korea remains a dictatorship.

The first Korean immigrants to the United States were brought over by American missionaries. In the early 1900s, Japan conquered Korea. This led a handful of refugees to emigrate to the United States. By 1920, new immigration laws prevented Koreans from coming to the United States, except for a few who came to study at American universities. Many of them stayed here and became citizens.

In 1965, the United States passed a new immigration law that gave preferences to immigrants with skilled occupations and professions. This led to an influx of Korean doctors, nurses, accountants, chemists, engineers and technicians. Korean immigrants were often young. They came looking for economic opportunities and a better way of life. In a few years, tens of thousands of Koreans came to the United States. Many settled in New York.

THE PROBLEMS THEY FACED

The Koreans who arrived in the 1970s and 1980s faced fewer problems than earlier immigrants had. Instead of taking ships, they arrived in jet planes. Most were high school or college graduates. Many were professionals or managers. Although they spoke Korean, most had studied English in Korea. However, they did face the problem of starting a new life in New York. In addition, ethnic prejudice was directed against them by some Americans.

ADJUSTING TO LIFE IN NEW YORK

To overcome the problems of making a fresh start, many Korean immigrants moved to communities where other Koreans lived. This was especially true in neighborhoods of Queens like Flushing, Jackson Heights and Elmhurst. They formed religious and social clubs with other Koreans. They published newspapers and started radio and television stations in the Korean language. Many began their own businesses and professional organizations. These organizations, such as the Korean-American Association, provided support and help to newcomers, enabling them to open shops throughout New York City.

Korean immigrants formed organizations to keep alive their heritage while in New York. *Wearing ceremonial dress, Korean dancers perform a traditional fan dance.*

CONTRIBUTIONS OF THE KOREAN AMERICANS

The Korean-American community is relatively new to New York. Despite this, many Koreans have become very successful. The enthusiasm and involvement that Korean American parents show for the education of their children is widely admired. They are well represented in the professions and in universities. Korean Americans continue to make important contributions to all phases of life in New York.

KOREAN HARVEST FESTIVAL

On the third Sunday of September, Korean Americans celebrate the **Korean Harvest Festival** at Flushing Meadow. Participants wear traditional Korean clothing and perform traditional dances with fans and masks. Martial arts experts give exhibitions as spectators browse through arts and crafts displays.

> ✔ **CHECKING YOUR UNDERSTANDING** ✔
> 1. Why did Koreans come to New York?
> 2. What problems did Koreans face?
> 3. What contributions did Koreans make to New York society?

CREATING ANOTHER GENERALIZATION

MAKING A GENERALIZATION ABOUT ETHNIC GROUPS

Can you make **one** generalization about the three ethnic groups that you just read about? On a separate sheet of paper, write out your generalization using the following guide:

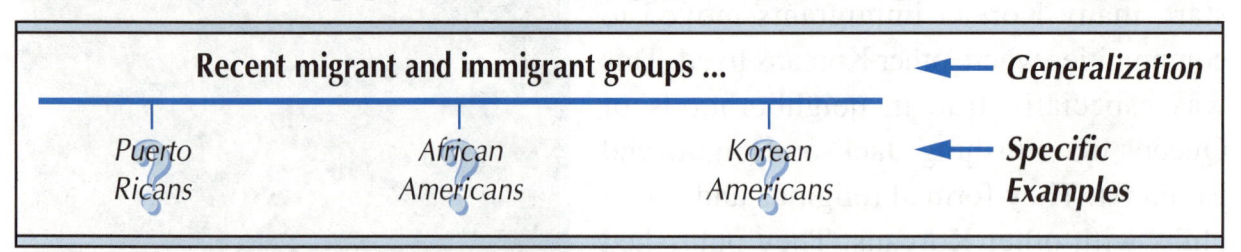

Recent migrant and immigrant groups ... ← Generalization

Puerto Ricans — African Americans — Korean Americans ← Specific Examples

REVIEWING YOUR UNDERSTANDING

Creating Vocabulary Cards

Generalization
What is a generalization?
Give an example of a generalization:

Harlem Renaissance
What was the "Harlem Renaissance"?
Name a writer of the Harlem Renaissance.

Making Further Generalizations About Some of New York's Major Ethnic Groups

In this activity, you learned about making generalizations. Can you make a generalization about **all** the ethnic groups you read about? Write your generalization on a sheet of paper, using the following guide:

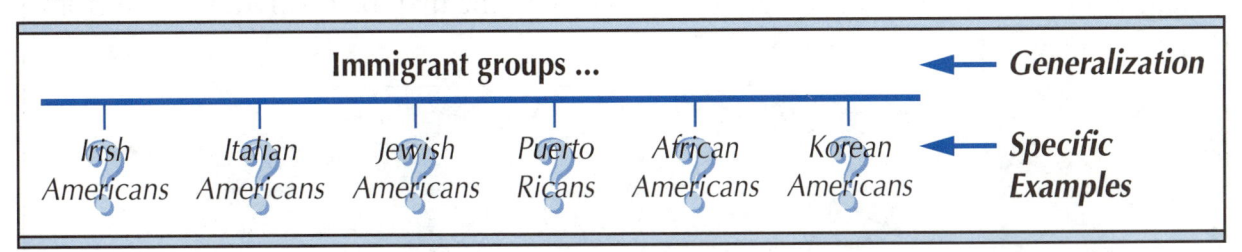

Immigrant groups ... ← *Generalization*

Irish Americans | Italian Americans | Jewish Americans | Puerto Ricans | African Americans | Korean Americans ← *Specific Examples*

MAKING CONNECTIONS

EXPLORING BEYOND YOUR STATE

THE UNITED STATES: A NATION OF IMMIGRANTS

The United States is different from other countries because most of our people are immigrants or the descendants of immigrants. There is no better way to show this than by looking at the people of New York State. The arrival of people from so many different cultures has greatly contributed to the diversity (*variety of differences*) of American life.

The table below shows where most recent immigrants to New York have come from:

Ellis Island as it looked in 1900. Today, immigrants are still attracted to New York, but Ellis Island has now become an immigration museum.

IMMIGRANTS SETTLING IN NEW YORK (1993)

Mexico	China	India	Vietnam	Russia	Haiti	Dom. Rep.
4,693	9,667	9,133	5,173	19,618	8,906	22,190

❖ CONTINUED

230 NEW YORK: ITS LAND AND ITS PEOPLE

Your Task: LEARNING ABOUT IMMIGRANTS

Use an atlas to find out where the countries listed in the table on page 229 are located. Then write the names of the countries on a copy of the map below. Draw a line from each country to New York State.

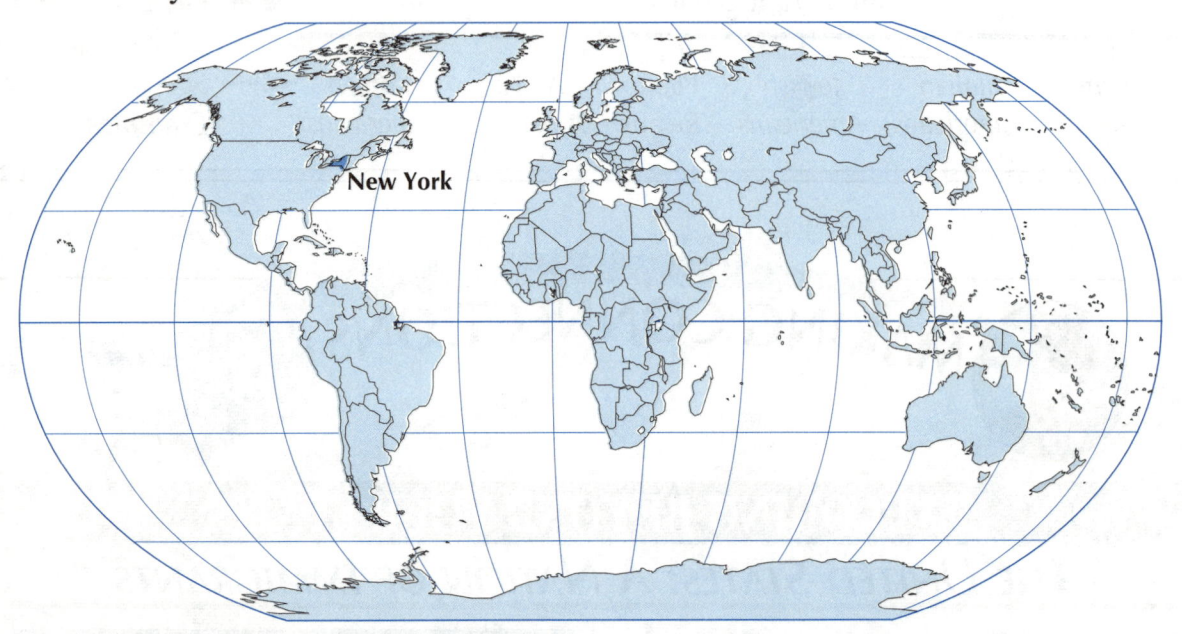

Do you have any friends who are immigrants to the United States?

❖ Which country did they come from?
❖ Find the location of the country in a world atlas.
❖ What things do your friends remember most about their former homeland?

EXPLORING YOUR COMMUNITY

LEARNING ABOUT ETHNIC GROUPS IN YOUR COMMUNITY

In this activity, you made several generalizations based on the experiences of six ethnic groups in New York.

Research: LEARNING ABOUT IMMIGRANTS

Would these same generalizations be true of New York's other ethnic groups? Let's find out.

❖ CONTINUED

Your class should divide into groups. Each group should research **one** ethnic group from the following list:

- Pakistani Americans
- Indian Americans
- Haitian Americans
- German Americans
- Greek Americans
- Chinese Americans
- Japanese Americans
- *You add one*

After the groups complete their research, they should decide on one generalization common to both this new group and the six they have just read about. One representative from each group should then report the generalization to the class. Finally, the class should decide which generalizations would be true for all these ethnic groups as well as the six others you read about in this activity.

Many New Yorkers enjoy eating food from foreign lands.
What generalizations can you make about your ethnic group?

FAMOUS NEW YORKERS

A. Philip Randolph (1889–1979) was one of the nation's most important labor and civil rights leaders. Born in Florida, he moved to New York City as a young man. It was while living in New York City that he emerged as the leading African American in the U.S. labor movement. In 1925, he organized the Brotherhood of Sleeping Car Porters—a group largely made up of African Americans. In 1937, following a long struggle against the railroads, he won a labor contract for his workers with the railroads. In 1941, he organized a "March on Washington." This put pressure on President Franklin D. Roosevelt to end racial discrimination in hiring practices in defense industries. Randolph was also a primary organizer of another "March on Washington" in 1963.

A. Philip Randolph

PEOPLE IN SOCIETY 231

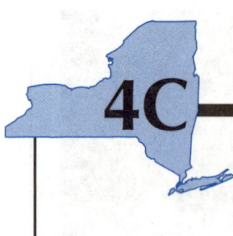

4C — WHAT IS CULTURAL DIFFUSION?

In this activity, you will examine different cultures. Look for the following important words:

▶ Concept ▶ Cultural Diffusion

▶ Earlier in this unit, you learned that a **concept** gives a common name to things that, although different, have something important in common. For example, each of the people who helps you to learn new things in school is called a "teacher." The idea of a "teacher" is a concept.

The concept "teacher" does not refer to any particular one of your teachers. Instead, it refers to all of your teachers. They all have certain characteristics in common.

- ❖ Each of your teachers works in a school.
- ❖ Each of your teachers helps you to learn new things.
- ❖ Each of your teachers is in charge of a class.

All of these characteristics help us to define the concept of "teacher."

Let's practice your ability to identify a concept. In this activity, you will look at several examples of events to find common characteristics. This will help you to identify an important concept: cultural diffusion.

CULTURAL DIFFUSION: A COMPLEX PROCESS

Introduction

Centuries ago, traveling was very difficult. Mountains, oceans and deserts were barriers that often prevented people of one area from meeting people in other areas. However, as time passed, people eventually came into contact with other groups. Sometimes this contact was brought about by trade. Other times, contact was created
▶ by war. Often, when these contacts took place, a process known as **cultural diffusion** occurred.

In this activity, you will read about four examples of cultural diffusion. As you read each example, try to figure out what characteristics each has in common with the others. At the end of the activity, you will be asked to define the concept of cultural diffusion on the basis of what you have learned from these examples.

FROM THE MIDDLE EAST TO EUROPE AND ASIA

Example #1. The wheel was invented about 6,000 years ago in the area we now call the Middle East. The wheel made it easier for people to carry heavy loads by using carts. Over the next thousand years, the use of the wheel spread west into Europe. It also traveled east across the center of Asia. Meanwhile, people in the Middle East improved the wheel to make it lighter and faster. With these improvements, they could build horse-drawn chariots. Soon, the use of the wheel had spread as far east as India. Each new group that started using wheels changed them slightly for their own purposes.

A chariot

✔ CHECKING YOUR UNDERSTANDING ✔

In this example of cultural diffusion, what happened to the wheel since it was first invented more than 5,000 years ago?

FROM CHINA TO EUROPE

Example #2. In the early 1200s, few Europeans had ever heard of China. In 1271, **Marco Polo** traveled to China in search of wealth. After 20 years of living in China, he returned home to Italy. He told of China's foods and inventions such as gunpowder, which the Chinese used for fireworks. Marco Polo also described China's copper coins, paper money and postal service. He spoke of magical black stones (*coal*) that provided heat when burned. Within 100 years, Europeans were using gunpowder to fire their cannons. Castles could be blown apart and the armor of soldiers could be destroyed.

Marco Polo arrives at Cathay (China).
Why were his travels important to Europeans?

✔ CHECKING YOUR UNDERSTANDING ✔

In this example, how did the Chinese invention of gunpowder affect the people of Europe?

FROM EUROPE TO AFRICA

Example #3. In most parts of Africa, Christianity was unknown until the 1800s. At that time, European nations became busy gaining control over much of Africa. Dutch, French, Belgian and British merchants in Africa were followed by Protestant and Roman Catholic missionaries (*people who try to convert others to their religious beliefs*). Today, the number of Africans that follow the Christian religion is about 160 million.

Africans in Mali pray at a mosque. What other religions are practiced in Africa?

✔ **CHECKING YOUR UNDERSTANDING** ✔

Which European religion was adopted by many of the peoples of Africa?

FROM THE AMERICAS TO EUROPE AND FROM EUROPE TO THE AMERICAS

Example #4. Five hundred years ago, Native Americans grew tomatoes, pumpkins, squash and potatoes. People in Europe had never seen these foods. In the early 1500s, Europeans first began exploring the Americas. They took back to Europe some of the foods they had eaten in the Americas. Soon, Europeans were eating tomatoes and potatoes. In the meantime, Europeans brought horses, sheep, goats, cattle and cats to the Americas. They also brought rats, mice and honey bees. All of these had been unknown in the Americas. Also, until the Europeans came, Native Americans had never suffered from smallpox, measles, chickenpox, or influenza. Europeans introduced all of these diseases to the Americas.

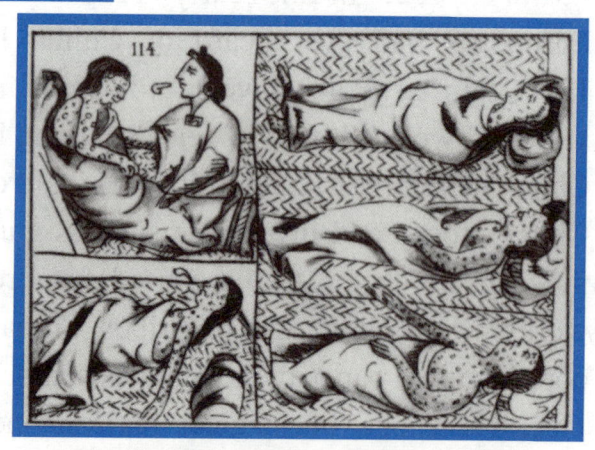

An illustration from a book printed in the 16th century, showing Aztecs suffering from smallpox.

✔ **CHECKING YOUR UNDERSTANDING** ✔

What exchanges took place between the Europeans and Native Americans?

PEOPLE IN SOCIETY 235

Closing: CREATING A DEFINITION FOR CULTURAL DIFFUSION

Now that you have finished reading about four examples of cultural diffusion, let's summarize what you have learned:

SUMMARY: FOUR EXAMPLES OF CULTURAL DIFFUSION	
Example	Description
#1	
#2	
#3	
#4	

Based on your summary, how would you define the concept of cultural diffusion?

REVIEWING YOUR UNDERSTANDING

Creating Vocabulary Cards

Concept
What is a concept?
Give an example of a concept:

Cultural Diffusion
What is cultural diffusion?
Give an example of cultural diffusion:

Creating an Ethnic Cookbook

British Americans love fish and chips; Chinese Americans like Szechwan pork; Greek Americans eat roast lamb. It may surprise you to learn that the foods you enjoy eating are examples of cultural diffusion. In fact, one of the best ways to learn about cultural diffusion is to study the spread of foods from one culture to another. Many of the foods we eat in New York were borrowed from other places.

In this section, the members of your class will create an "ethnic" cookbook, showing the origins of some common foods. To help put together this cookbook, each student will bring to school a recipe for **one** ethnic dish that they enjoy eating at home. You may want to ask your parent or some other adult from your ethnic group to help you write down your recipe.

Let's look at a recipe popular with one group of New Yorkers—Mexican Americans. Mexican cooking has a double heritage: Native American and Spanish. Corn, rice and beans are very common ingredients in the Mexican diet. These foods are used in a variety of ways to make different meals. Let's look at a recipe for **tortillas**, a food popular with Mexican Americans. Use this form as a guide for writing your own recipe.

The fajita (grilled steak rolled in a flour tortilla) is a favorite Mexican dish.
What foods are popular with your ethnic group?

TORTILLAS	
Ingredients:	1 cup tortilla flour
	1 1/4 cups warm water
Steps:	1. Put the tortilla flour into a medium sized bowl.
	2. Mix in the warm water to form a soft dough.
	3. Shape the dough into egg-sized balls.
	4. Flatten the dough into pancakes 4 inches wide on a tortilla press or floured board.
	5. Heat an ungreased griddle over medium heat.
	6. Cook tortillas for about 1 minute or until browned.
	7. Fill tortillas with various items, such as beef, or serve plain.
Serves:	This will make 6 to 8 tortillas.

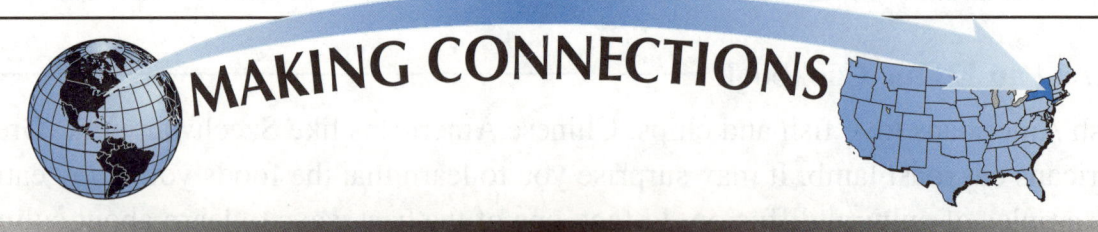

MAKING CONNECTIONS

EXPLORING BEYOND YOUR STATE
WORLD MYTHS AND LEGENDS

In this activity, you looked at how one society often influences another. Another way that societies influence each other is through myths and legends.

◆ CONTINUED

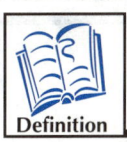

WHAT ARE MYTHS AND LEGENDS?

A **myth** or **legend** is a story that explains a fact of nature or tells about an event in history. Myths and legends are as old as humankind itself. In earliest times, people passed these stories down from one generation to the next. Later, many of these myths and legends were written down.

Myths and legends deal with people's innermost needs and fears. Where did the world come from? Why are we alive? The world's myths and legends are stories that attempt to provide an answer to these and other questions. They often tell how gods and goddesses control the world through their actions.

SOME POPULAR MYTHS AND LEGENDS

Most cultures have a myth or legend to explain the beginning of the universe. The following myth comes from ancient China.

THE BEGINNING OF THE WORLD

Once upon a time, the Chinese legend says, the universe was shaped like a huge egg. One day the egg split open. The top of the egg became the sky, while the bottom part became the Earth. From the center of the egg emerged the first man. For the next several thousand years, he grew a little each day. When he died, his head split open. Part of his head became the sun, the other part became the moon. His blood formed the seas, while his hair became the forests. His sweat became rain, his breath the wind and his voice became thunder.

Other cultures also have myths about the beginning of the world. The ancient Egyptians believed the first human was formed from the tears of the sun god. The Persians thought that their god created the first man out of light, while the Greeks believed that a giant formed the first man out of clay.

THE GREAT FLOOD.

Many cultures also have legends of a great flood. The Bible tells the story of Noah, who built an ark and brought two of every animal aboard. The ancient Sumerians also told of a flood, sent by the gods to destroy all living things. One person learned of the flood beforehand and built a large ship. Like Noah, he took his family and one male and female of all living creatures aboard.

◆ CONTINUED

The Greeks believed that the god Zeus, finding all people wicked, decided to destroy humanity by a great flood. Deucalion built a large wooden ark for himself, his wife and their sheep and cattle. Nothing survived the flood but a few mountain tops. However, the gods told him and his wife to throw stones behind their backs. As they did, the stones became men and women. In the Americas, Native American tribes like the Choctan also believed that the Great Spirit caused a flood to destroy all humans.

HOW MYTHS ARE SPREAD

Often, when one ancient people conquered another, they adopted some of their myths. Other myths were communicated by travelers, merchants or priests. The myths of ancient Rome were based on the myths of ancient Greece. Only the names of the gods and goddesses changed—for example, from Zeus to Jupiter, Kronus to Saturn, and Aries to Mars. The myths of the early Germanic peoples were adapted by the Vikings of Scandinavia. Because the Vikings were more warlike, they placed greater emphasis on the battles and struggles between the gods and heroes than the Germans had done.

LEARNING ABOUT OTHER MYTHS

Wouldn't it be interesting if you could learn about other popular myths and legends? One way of doing this is to speak to some of the adult members of your family.

❖ Ask them to tell you about a family myth or legend that has been handed down from one generation to another. Write a brief summary of this myth or legend.

❖ Come to school with your summary; compare and contrast it with legends that other members of your class have brought in.

❖ The class should try to select the **one** myth or legend that they feel is the most interesting.

❖ CONTINUED

PEOPLE IN SOCIETY 239

EXPLORING YOUR COMMUNITY
LOOKING FOR EXAMPLES OF CULTURAL DIFFUSION IN YOUR COMMUNITY

In this activity you learned about cultural diffusion. Cultural diffusion not only existed in the past. It happens every day throughout the world. For example, when Japanese students wear Western-style clothing, this is an example of cultural diffusion. When a Disneyland Theme Park opens in France or a McDonald's in Finland, that too is cultural diffusion.

PARTICIPATING IN A SCAVENGER HUNT

Let's have some fun by participating in a scavenger hunt. A **scavenger hunt** involves searching for examples that relate to a particular theme. For your scavenger hunt, your theme will be "cultural diffusion." You will need to find as many examples of cultural diffusion as you can in your community. For example, a Beatles record or CD would be an example of cultural diffusion, since the Beatles were a British rock and roll group in the 1960s. Their music became popular not only in the United States, but in most of the world.

EXAMPLES OF CULTURAL DIFFUSION IN YOUR COMMUNITY	
Example	How does this example illustrate cultural diffusion?
#1	
#2	
#3	
#4	
#5	
#6	
#7	
#8	

WHICH EVENTS WOULD YOU PLACE ON THE TIMELINE?

4D

In this activity, you will learn about and create a timeline using key events in history. Look for the following important words:

- Timeline
- Chronological Order
- Decade
- Century

Reading about history allows your imagination to wander back in time. It is exciting to read about the people and events of the past. Often, while important events are taking place in one part of the world, other important events are happening elsewhere. In order to see these connections, historians use a timeline.

TIMELINES AND THEIR MAIN PARTS

- A timeline is a type of chart. It shows a group of events arranged along a line in
- chronological order. "Chronological order" means the order in which the events actually happened.

A timeline can cover anything from a very short period to several thousand years. Its main purpose is to show a sequence of events. To understand a timeline, first look at its main parts—the title, events and dates.

TITLE → MAJOR EVENTS IN WORLD HISTORY

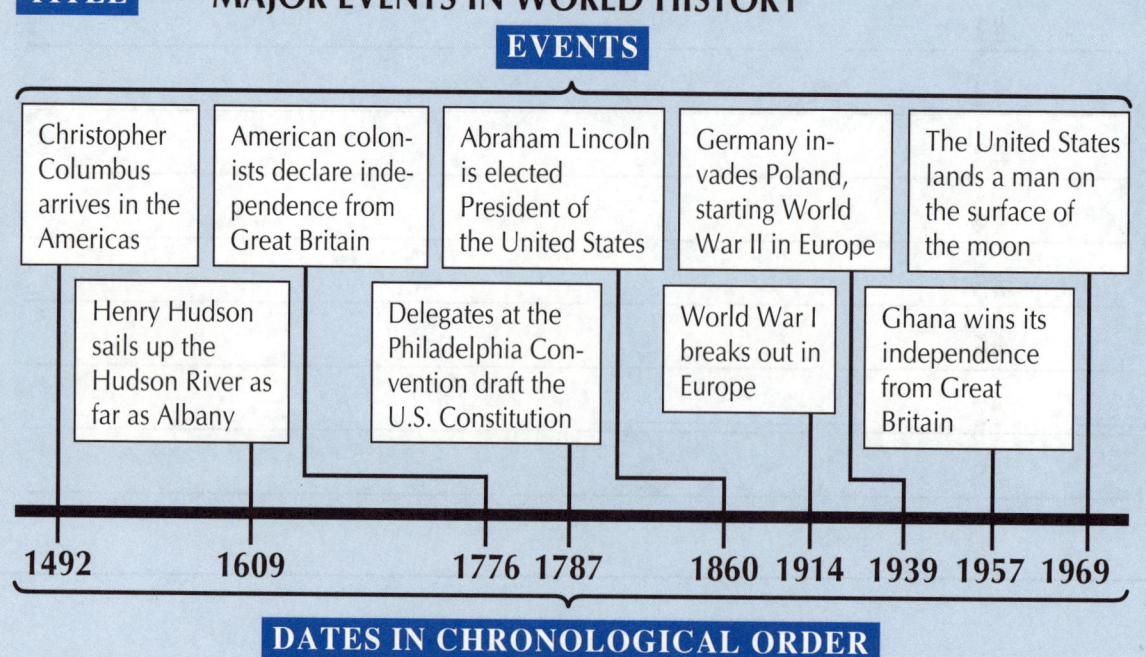

EVENTS

1492	1609	1776	1787	1860	1914	1939	1957	1969
Christopher Columbus arrives in the Americas	Henry Hudson sails up the Hudson River as far as Albany	American colonists declare independence from Great Britain	Delegates at the Philadelphia Convention draft the U.S. Constitution	Abraham Lincoln is elected President of the United States	World War I breaks out in Europe	Germany invades Poland, starting World War II in Europe	Ghana wins its independence from Great Britain	The United States lands a man on the surface of the moon

DATES IN CHRONOLOGICAL ORDER

TITLE

The title tells you the overall topic of the timeline. In the timeline on page 240, the title indicates that the items listed are major events in the history of the world.

> ✔ **CHECKING YOUR UNDERSTANDING** ✔
>
> **Selecting a title.** A series of events are listed below. What title would you give a timeline that had these events on it?
>
> - In 1777, **George Clinton** was the first person to be elected Governor of New York State.
> - In 1817, Governor **DeWitt Clinton** successfully pushed the State Legislature to spend public funds to build the Erie Canal.
> - In 1968, former Governor **Averell Harriman** became the chief U.S. negotiator at the Paris peace talks to end the Vietnam War.
> - In 1973, **Nelson Rockefeller** stepped down as Governor of New York to become Vice President of the United States. 
>
> Governor Nelson Rockefeller
>
> **Your Timeline Title:** _____?_____

TIMELINE DESIGN

On a timeline, the earliest event appears on the far left. The rest of the events are placed to the right of it, in the order in which they occurred.

First Event	Second Event	Third Event	Fourth Event	Last Event
1791	1792	1793	1794	1795

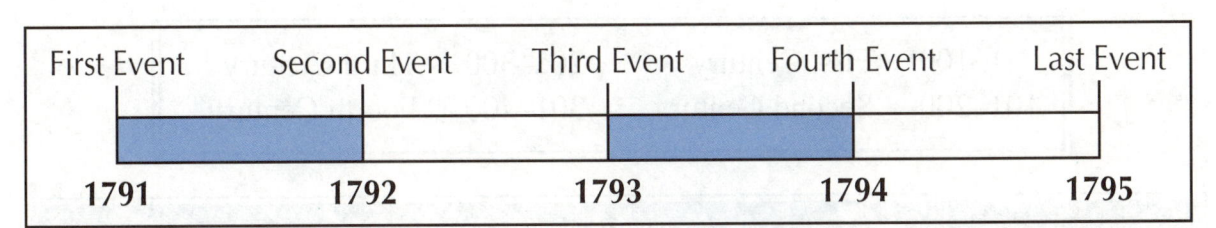

Sometimes timelines are drawn up and down (*vertically*) instead of left to right (*horizontally*). In that case, the earliest event is usually placed at the bottom of the timeline. The rest of the events are placed above the first event, in the order in which they occurred.

1794	— Last Event
1793	— Third Event
1792	— Second Event
1791	— First Event

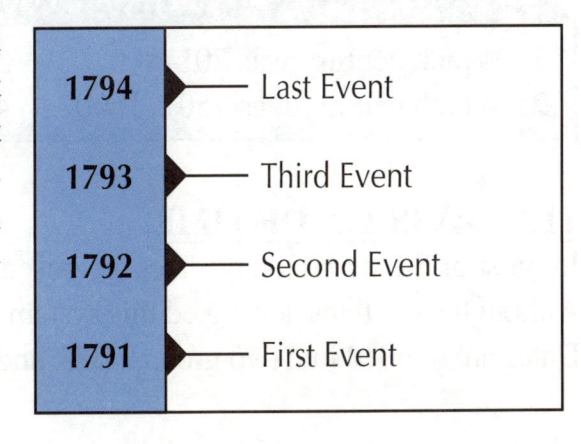

242 NEW YORK: ITS LAND AND ITS PEOPLE

PERIODS OF TIME

To fully understand timelines, you must also know about time periods. For short periods of time, you can divide a timeline into one-year intervals. For example:

| 1791 | 1792 | 1793 | 1794 | 1795 | 1796 | 1797 |

▶ For longer periods of time, you can divide a timeline into decades. A **decade** is a period of ten years. For example, the following timeline shows six decades of time:

| 1790 | 1800 | 1810 | 1820 | 1830 | 1840 | 1850 |

▶ An even longer period of time is a century. A **century** is a period of 100 years. For example, the following timeline shows seven centuries of time.

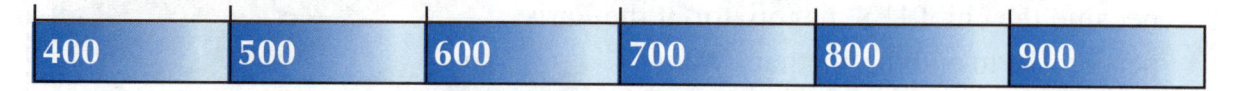

| 400 | 500 | 600 | 700 | 800 | 900 |

Now you try it. Make a copy of the timeline and put in the years from 1300 to 1800 by centuries:

How we identify centuries may seem confusing at first. The "20th century" means the 100 years from 1901 to 2000. The 1990s, therefore, belong to the 20th century. Let's see why.

| 1–100 | First Century | 201–300 | Third Century |
| 101–200 | Second Century | 301–400 | Fourth Century |

✔ CHECKING YOUR UNDERSTANDING ✔

1. Which century was 701–800?
2. Which century was 1501–1600?
3. What is the present century, 1901–2000?
4. What will the next century be called?

THE DIVISION OF TIME

In most of the world today, dates are based on when it is believed Jesus Christ was born. Although Christians developed this system of dates, many non-Christians also now use it. Dates are divided into two groups: B.C. and A.D. The dividing point is the birth of Christ.

PEOPLE IN SOCIETY 243

* **B.C.** (Before Christ) refers to any time before his birth. Sometimes B.C. is referred to as <u>**B.C.E.**</u>—<u>**B**</u>efore the <u>**C**</u>ommon <u>**E**</u>ra.

* **A.D.** refers to the time after the birth of Christ. A.D. stands for the Latin phrase *anno Domini*—"in the year of our Lord." Sometimes A.D appears as <u>**C.E.**</u>—meaning in the <u>**C**</u>ommon <u>**E**</u>ra.

Writers always add B.C. or B.C.E. to a date before the birth of Christ. However, we usually do not bother to write A.D. or C.E. if the date is after the birth of Christ. For example, if the present year is 1997, we generally write 1997—not 1997 A.D.

MEASURING THE PASSAGE OF TIME

To measure the number of years from one date to another, just subtract the smaller date from the larger date. Assume the year is 1997. How long ago was 1500? By subtracting 1500 from 1997, we arrive at 497 years ago.

```
  1997   (1997 years since the birth of Jesus)
− 1500   (1500 years since the birth of Jesus)
  ‾‾‾‾
   497   Years ago
```

✔ CHECKING YOUR UNDERSTANDING ✔

In 1825, the Erie Canal was completed in New York State. How long ago was that?

EVENTS

Each event on a timeline is related to the topic of the title. For instance, if a timeline has the title "The European Exploration of New York," Henry Hudson's voyage might appear as an event. Christopher Columbus' voyages should **not** appear, since Columbus never explored New York.

SELECTING EVENTS FOR A TIMELINE

Let's practice the skill of selecting appropriate events by choosing events for a timeline titled, "Key Events in the History of New York" **Hint:** Look for events that are related to the title. In the following list of events, you will notice that **not every** event is related to New York State history. Decide which events are related to the title of the timeline. Then, on a separate sheet of paper, make a timeline of these events in chronological order.

244   NEW YORK: ITS LAND AND ITS PEOPLE

KEY EVENTS IN THE HISTORY OF NEW YORK

- 1989   David Dinkins becomes N.Y.C.'s first African-American Mayor
- 1996   The Summer Olympics are held in Atlanta, Georgia
- 1959   The St. Lawrence Seaway opens, allowing ships to travel from Canada to the Great Lakes
- 1969   The New York Mets win the World Series
- 1945   An atomic bomb is dropped on Japan
- 1986   Celebration of the 100th birthday of the Statue of Liberty
- 1952   The United Nations building is completed in Manhattan
- 1992   Bill Clinton is elected President of the United States
- 1911   The Triangle Shirtwaist factory fire in N.Y.C. kills 146 workers

HINT: Often you will have to list a date that falls *between* two dates on a timeline. For example, the year 1903 is between 1900 and 1910. Since 1903 is closer to 1900 (3 years) than it is to 1910 (7 years), place it on the timeline closer to 1900 than to 1910.

REVIEWING YOUR UNDERSTANDING

Creating Vocabulary Cards

Timeline

What is a timeline?

What are timelines used for?

Chronological Order

What is chronological order?

Arrange the following dates in chronological order: 1903, 1864, 1987 and 1745.

Making a Timeline About Your Life

A few events that happen during a person's lifetime often stand out. For example, your parents or grandparents may remember what they were doing in July 1969 when **Neil Armstrong** and **Buzz Aldrin** first stepped onto the moon. In this section you will be looking at important events that happened to you in your lifetime. Choose the

PEOPLE IN SOCIETY   245

five most important events of your life and put them on the timeline. Make the first year the one in which you were born.

IMPORTANT EVENTS IN MY LIFE

Birth Year

Ask your parent or guardian for **three** important events that happened to them in the last ten years. Add those events to your timeline.

MAKING CONNECTIONS

EXPLORING BEYOND YOUR STATE
CREATING A PICTURE TIMELINE

Timelines can be used to show important developments in such fields as art, music, literature or technology.

Skill Builder

CREATING A PICTURE TIMELINE

On the following pages is a list of some of the world's leading developments in technology. By placing these developments on a timeline, it is easier to see how inventions and discoveries in one part of the world often affected other parts of the world.

These events are **not** in chronological order. Create a timeline in chronological order from this list of technological improvements. Decorate your timeline by drawing a picture above or below the timeline to illustrate each development. This type of graphic is known as a **picture timeline**.

◆ CONTINUED

- ❖ **The Invention of the Wheel.** The wheel was first developed in the Middle East, around 4,000 B.C. It is believed that the Sumerians, a Middle Eastern people, invented the wheel. Around 2,000 B.C. the first chariots appeared. From the Middle East, the use of the wheel spread to Persia, India, China and Europe.

- ❖ **Construction of the Roman Aqueducts.** By 40 B.C., the city of Rome had conquered most of the Mediterranean world. One of the greatest Roman accomplishments was the construction of **aqueducts**, pipelines carrying water from the countryside to the city. Between 312 B.C. and 226 A.D., the Romans completed many aqueducts in Italy. Often the aqueducts carried water for up to 50 miles, over high stone archways that crossed valleys and hills. The Romans built similar aqueducts in other parts of the Roman Empire.

- ❖ **The Invention of Simple Tools.** About 30,000 years ago, people began making knives, spears, bows, arrows and needles out of bone, antlers and wood. The same developments occurred in several places in the world. Scholars do not know if these improved tools spread from one place to another, or whether they were invented independently.

- ❖ **Muslim Discoveries in Astronomy**. Between 1000 and 1600, learning flourished in the Muslim world. Some Muslims understood that the Earth was round and accurately predicted its size. They developed the **astrolabe**, an instrument used to determine the position of the sun and stars. This invention gradually spread to Europe, where navigators used astrolabes to navigate the oceans.

- ❖ **Building of the Pyramids.** Ancient Egyptian rulers were buried in huge stone tombs called **pyramids**. Built around 2,500 B.C., the Great Pyramid at Giza is the world's largest pyramid. It is estimated that it took 100,000 men almost 20 years to complete. To build the pyramids, the Egyptians developed new principles of geometry and engineering. This knowledge was borrowed by other peoples. For example, smaller tombs resembling pyramids are also found in other parts of Africa.

One of the Pyramids at Giza
What did the Egyptians need to know to build pyramids?

❖ CONTINUED

- ❖ **Paper Making.** Around 100 A.D., the Chinese developed paper. Bamboo shoots and the bark of trees were chopped into pulp and mixed in tubs of water. A fine screen was lifted out of the tub carrying a thin layer of pulp. When this layer of pulp was pressed and dried, it became a sheet of paper. From China, paper making spread to Central Asia, the Middle East and eventually Europe. The development of paper also made the later invention of printing possible.

- ❖ **Advances in Metallurgy.** West Africa is rich in such minerals as copper, iron and gold. Hundreds of years ago, West Africans learned how to heat up rocks to pull out these minerals. As early as 200 A.D., coins were being made out of West African gold. Until the 1500s, most European gold came from West Africa. Craftsmen in West Africa became skilled at making sculptures and other items out of brass, bronze and gold.

- ❖ **The Steam Engine.** The steam engine was first used in the early 1700s. The inventor **James Watt** improved the steam engine in the mid-1700s, making it powerful enough to run machinery. Watt's invention was used to drive textile machinery, creating the first factories. It was also used to power steamboats and railroad trains. These new inventions led to an Industrial Revolution, which spread from England to the rest of Europe and the United States.

James Watt helped to dramatically improve the design and efficiency of the steam engine.

EXPLORING YOUR COMMUNITY
CREATING A COMMUNITY TIMELINE

In this activity, you learned about timelines and how to create them. As you now know, timelines can be about almost anything.

MAKING A COMMUNITY TIMELINE

Let's create a timeline of important events and dates in the life of your community. These dates can include anything of importance. For example, you might want to include the building of a new community park, the opening of a new shopping center or the start of construction of a new community hospital.

❖ CONTINUED

248 NEW YORK: ITS LAND AND ITS PEOPLE

To find such information, you may:

- ask your parents
- research old community newspapers in your public library
- talk to your town historian or museum curator

After you have located **six** events that you feel are important enough to include in your timeline:

A. List the date of each event in the first column of the chart, and name the event in the second column.

B. Arrange the events into chronological order. In the last column, write (1) next to the event that happened first. Then write (2) next to the event that happened second, and so on. Continue numbering each event.

C. Now create your community timeline. You may even want to convert it into a picture timeline. To do this, draw a picture above or below the timeline to illustrate each event.

Date	Important Events in My Community	Chronological Order
?	?	?
?	?	?
?	?	?
?	?	?
?	?	?
?	?	?

PEOPLE IN SOCIETY 249

WHO WOULD BE YOUR NOMINEE TO THE NEW YORK HALL OF FAME?

4E

In this activity, you will learn about some of the many people who have contributed to the greatness of New York. Look for the following important words:

▶ Biography ▶ Autobiography

New York Daily — Vol. 1.8 No. 21 — First Edition
Geraldine Ferraro Nominated for Vice President

New York Daily — Vol. 1.8 No. 45 — First Edition
Martin Van Buren Elected President

New York Daily — Vol. 1.9 No. 24 — First Edition
Shirley Chisholm Elected to House of Representatives

New York Daily — Vol. 1.9 No. 73 — First Edition
Walt Whitman Publishes his Book of Poems

THINK ABOUT IT

What do you think all of these newspaper headlines have in common?

250   NEW YORK: ITS LAND AND ITS PEOPLE

WHO ARE THESE PEOPLE?

You may have heard the names of some of these people. Each of them is famous in some special way:

❖ **Geraldine Ferraro** was born in Newburgh, New York. In 1984, she became the first woman ever nominated by a major political party as a candidate for Vice President of the United States. At the Democratic National Convention, Presidential nominee Walter Mondale selected her as his Vice-Presidential running mate.

❖ **Martin Van Buren** was born in Kinderhook, New York. He was elected the 8th President of the United States. He rose to the position of President after serving as a U.S. Senator, Governor of New York and Vice President under Andrew Jackson.

❖ **Shirley Chisholm** was born in Brooklyn. She became the first African-American woman elected to the U.S. House of Representatives. She served in Congress from 1969 to 1983.

❖ **Walt Whitman** was born on Long Island in 1819. Whitman's principal work was a book of poetry, *Leaves of Grass*. His poems celebrated nature, democracy and individualism. Crippled by strokes, at the end of his life he was better known in Europe than in the United States.

Martin Van Buren

Walt Whitman

QUALIFICATIONS FOR THE NEW YORK HALL OF FAME

Each of these individuals is unique. They come from different races, religions and ethnic backgrounds. However, they all have **one** thing in common—each one is a New Yorker who has made a lasting contribution to the development of New York State.

Many sports honor their best players in a Hall of Fame. For example, the Baseball Hall of Fame is located in Cooperstown. However, New York State does not have a Hall of Fame to honor its greatest citizens. Can you imagine if it did? Who would you recommend to include? In this activity, you will be asked to nominate a person to an imaginary New York Hall of Fame. Here are the qualifications for admission:

❖ Each nominee must have been born in or lived in New York.
❖ A nominee can come from any field—a sports figure, scientist, inventor, politician, president or corporate executive.
❖ A nominee can still be living or be a figure from the past.
❖ A nominee must have done something that would be considered "great."

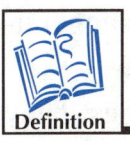

WHAT MAKES SOMEONE GREAT?

Notice the last item on the list of qualifications—"great." What does "great" mean? To help you answer this, you should create a list of criteria. **Criteria** are standards we use to evaluate something. For example, you might want to establish that the person must be well-known. If the person is not well-known, he or she would not meet your criteria for "greatness," and would not be admitted into the New York Hall of Fame.

Let's begin by creating some criteria for judging "greatness." Complete the first criterion by pointing out the letter of your choice. Then add two other criteria of your own.

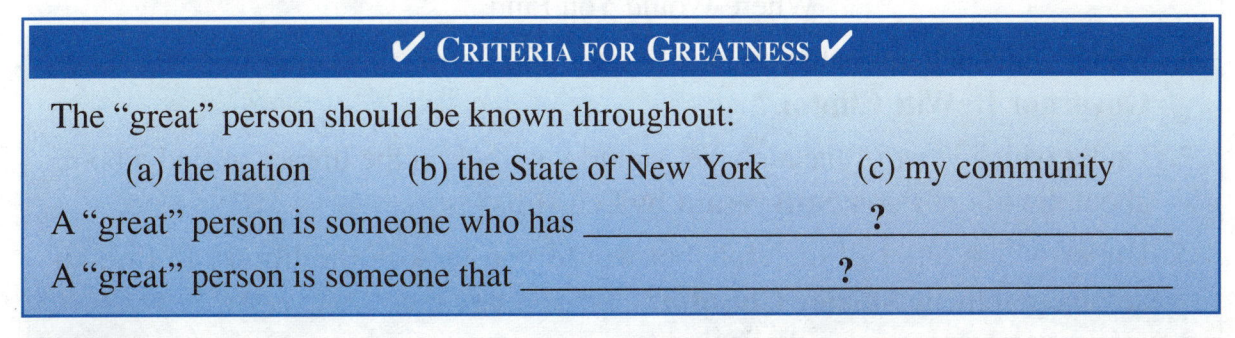

✔ CRITERIA FOR GREATNESS ✔
The "great" person should be known throughout:
(a) the nation   (b) the State of New York   (c) my community
A "great" person is someone who has _____?_____
A "great" person is someone that _____?_____

RESEARCHING YOUR NOMINEE

Your first task will be to research your nominee. You can find this kind of information in a number of sources.

ENCYCLOPEDIA

Encyclopedias have articles about many well-known people. These articles are arranged in alphabetical order. The encyclopedia has guide words or letters on the spine of each volume. These guide words help you to locate the name of the person you are looking up. In more recent times, many publishers of encyclopedias have made their sets available on computer programs. In fact, many libraries now allow you to search a topic on the library computer.

BIOGRAPHY

▶ A **biography** is a book about a person's life. A biography can be an excellent source of detailed information about a person. Some well-known people have had several biographies written about them by different authors.

AUTOBIOGRAPHY

Sometimes a person will write a book about his or her own life. This kind of book is
▶ called an **autobiography**. When reading an autobiography, you must remember that the person will usually build up the good things about his or her own life by exaggerating achievements. Likewise, the writer will usually play down any bad things.

Most libraries have entire sections devoted to biographies and autobiographies. They are not found on the library shelf by the name of the author. Biographies and autobiographies are listed in alphabetical order by the **last name of the person the book is about.** For example, a biography of Eleanor Roosevelt by Mary Wade would be under the letter **"R"** for Roosevelt and not under the letter **"W"** for Wade. You may also try searching the Internet for information about this person.

✔ CHECKING YOUR UNDERSTANDING ✔

Where Would You Find .....

1. Under which letter would you look to find information in an encyclopedia about **Governor DeWitt Clinton?**
2. Under which letter of the alphabet would you look in the library to find a book about the life of **Peter Stuyvesant** by Len Hills?
3. Under which letter of the alphabet would you look in the library to find an autobiography by **Shirley Chisolm?**

Now you are ready to go to the library to research your nominee. On a separate sheet, complete the following Research Guide:

NAME OF YOUR NOMINEE: _____

❖ **Source used:** Identify **one** source of information — the title of a book, the name of an article you read or the section of an encyclopedia you consulted.
❖ **Summary of the person's life.**
❖ **The person's major accomplishments.**
❖ **What makes this person great?**
❖ **Why should the person be in the New York Hall of Fame?**

PEOPLE IN SOCIETY 253

REVIEWING YOUR UNDERSTANDING

Creating Vocabulary Cards

Biography

What is a biography?

What information is found in a biography?

Autobiography

What is an autobiography?

How does it differ from an biography?

Locating Information in a Book

Imagine you want a book about George Eastman. In the library you select the biography, *George Eastman: Inventor.* Suppose you want to find information about his invention of paper-backed film that replaced bulky glass plates. You could search each page of the book, but this would be too time consuming. Information in a book can sometimes be found by scanning the **table of contents**. This is found in the first few pages. It contains a list of headings, broken into chapters, and the pages on which they can be found. In the book about George Eastman, you might find the following section from the table of contents:

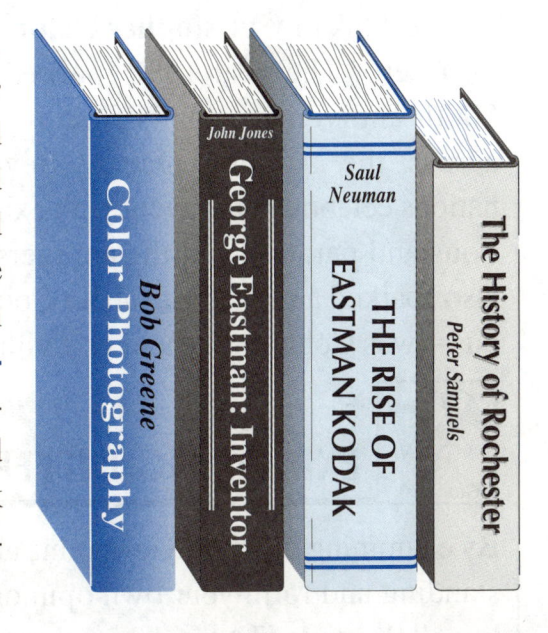

Chapter 5: The End of Glass Plates	102
Chapter 6: The Eastman Dry Plate Company Is Begun	123
Chapter 7: The Kodak Camera Is Introduced	137
Chapter 8: The Company Grows	154
Chapter 9: Color Photography Is Perfected	186

In which chapter would you look to find information about

1. how George Eastman invented paper-backed film?
2. the invention of the Kodak camera?
3. the year the company introduced color film for pictures?

MAKING CONNECTIONS

EXPLORING BEYOND YOUR STATE
WHAT MAKES SOMEONE A HERO?

A **hero** is someone who has helped others in an important way. A hero in battle may help save someone's life. Great people who help make history are also considered heroes. For example, many people think of **Christopher Columbus** as a hero. The year 1992 marked the 500th anniversary of his first voyage across the Atlantic Ocean. Several nations celebrated the event with exhibitions and parades. But the anniversary also sparked a new debate about Columbus—was Columbus a hero or a villain?

Christopher Columbus claims land in the New World for Spain.
Do you think he was a hero or a villain?

EXPLORING DIFFERENT POINTS OF VIEW

By examining different viewpoints about a person, you can often reach a better understanding and form your own opinion. The importance of looking at different views is well illustrated by the debate that took place over Christopher Columbus. Where do you stand on this issue?

> Based on what you know about Christopher Columbus, do you think he was:
> ☐ a **hero** or ☐ a **villain**? Explain the reasons for your opinion.

Imagine you could go back in time and hear from some of the people who actually knew Columbus in the past. Reports from eyewitnesses of past events are **primary sources**. Primary sources are the key means by which historians try to understand the past. Often different eyewitness accounts provide contrasting viewpoints of the same event. Here is what five eyewitnesses might have reported about Columbus.

❖ CONTINUED

Columbus came to us in 1486 with a plan to sail west to the Indies. He promised us wealth and power. After six years, we finally gave him the ships and supplies he needed. We agreed to give him part of all the riches if he kept his word. Columbus did obtain new lands for Spain. His discovery made us the richest nation in the world. We ate new foods and used new products because of him. Columbus widened our horizons. Because of him, we now realize the world is a larger place than we ever imagined.

King Ferdinand and Queen Isabella of Spain

What view do you have of Columbus after reading this source? Explain.

Columbus was feared and respected by our crew. We left Spain on August 3, 1492, sailing west. We had no idea what we would find or even if we would return. Many of the crew believed the world was flat. If you sailed far enough out on the ocean, you would fall off the edge. When we lost sight of land, many of the men cried because they feared they might never see land again. By early October, most of the crew were ready to kill Columbus and turn back. Luckily for Columbus, land was sighted just at this time.

Peralonso Niño, member of Columbus' crew

What view do you have of Columbus after reading this source? Explain.

Columbus was probably the greatest man who ever lived. His wisdom and courage allowed him to reach land by sailing west. His discovery of the Americas introduced its native peoples to our Christian teachings. These people were not believers in our Christian faith. They now have a chance to enter the heavenly gates. Columbus' discovery led to riches and power for our country. We have been able to teach the natives to grow new crops, to speak new languages and to lead their lives as good Christians.

Father Marchena, a Spanish priest

What view do you have of Columbus after reading this source? Explain.

CONTINUED

Columbus was a man without feelings for us. His arrival was a horrible event for our people. He claimed our homeland for his masters in Spain. When he returned to Spain, he left many of his men on our island. They bullied us. I finally led an attack of our warriors against them. We killed them all and burned down their settlement. But the next year, Columbus returned with 17 ships. He sent many of our people to Spain as slaves. His soldiers and cannons defeated us in battle. Soon we were all slaves. Meanwhile, thousands of my people died from mysterious diseases these invaders brought with them.

Chief Caonabo of the Taino Tribe

> What view do you have of Columbus after reading this source? Explain. Why do you think his view differs from those of the other three sources. Explain.

EVALUATING DIFFERENT VIEWPOINTS

Based on these different viewpoints, do you now think Christopher Columbus was: ❏ a **hero** or ❏ a **villain**? Explain your answer in a **one** page essay.

EXPLORING YOUR COMMUNITY
WHO IS A HERO IN YOUR NEIGHBORHOOD?

A hero does not have to be a person with a national or international reputation. In fact, someone in your community, school or family may be a hero. Almost everyone knows someone who might be called a hero. A local hero might be a community political leader, teacher, doctor, writer, judge, police officer or student.

DESCRIBING YOUR HERO

Who would your class select as a community hero? Let's find out. Use the following procedure to select **one** person as a local hero:

❖ Each member of the class should select **one** person whom he or she regards as a local hero. Each student will have **3 minutes** to present the name of his or her nominee to the class and explain why that person is a hero.

❖ CONTINUED

- ❖ The class should then select the top **three** nominees and discuss them.
- ❖ Finally, the class should vote for the person they think is the best community hero.

Now write an essay describing this person. Before you start, here are some notes about writing a descriptive essay.

HOW TO WRITE A DESCRIPTIVE ESSAY

Descriptive writing paints a mental picture of someone or something. It is used when you want to describe a person, an object or what a scene looks like. In effect, you provide "eyes" for your reader. Your description should create an impression in the reader's mind of a picture similar to the picture you "see." For example, you might describe what your hero looks like or the beauty of Niagara Falls.

Use words that appeal to the five senses. Describe how someone or something looks, smells, feels, tastes and sounds. Avoid vague and overused words such as "nice," "pretty," "good" and "great." A descriptive writing should proceed in some logical order. You might describe a nature scene by moving from left to right. You might describe a friend by discussing his or her qualities in the order of importance. Now write your essay about a local hero.

FAMOUS NEW YORKERS

Nathan Hale (1755–1776) A hero can be almost anyone. Nathan Hale, a school teacher from Connecticut, emerged as one of the greatest heroes of the American Revolution. Hale became an officer in the Continental Army during the American Revolution. He offered his services to General Washington. Washington asked him to take part in a dangerous mission—to sneak behind British lines on Long Island to learn about British plans. Disguised as a school teacher, Hale was quickly discovered and confessed to spying. He was hanged near the present-day corner of Sixty-sixth Street and Third Avenue in New York City. He is best remembered for his statement before being hanged—"I only regret that I have but one life to lose for my country."

Monument to Nathan Hale in Huntington, Long Island

258 NEW YORK: ITS LAND AND ITS PEOPLE

HOW WOULD YOU CLASSIFY THE LANDMARKS OF NEW YORK?

4F

In this activity, you will learn about many of the landmarks that reflect the rich and varied heritage of New York State. Look for the following important words:

▶ Museum   ▶ Classify

You are about to leave for school when the phone rings. Your older sister is calling from school. She says she forgot her report on "Landmarks to Visit in New York." She needs the report in school. "Can you get the report from my room and the notecards I left on top of the report?" she asks. "I need these notecards to finish writing my report. Meet me at the school library at 8:30." You agree to meet her.

Unfortunately, as you get off the school bus, you fall. You are not hurt, but the report and the notecards have scattered all over the ground.

Your sister will be furious. After picking the papers up, you realize that her notecards were not numbered. What are you going to do now? You don't want to disappoint your sister. Quickly, you start reading your sister's report to find out how to arrange the notecards. Here is what you find on the first page of her report:

NEW YORK: A FASCINATING STATE TO VISIT

New York is a wonderful place to live and a fascinating place to visit. Every year, millions of people make New York their vacation spot. It is a state that has just about every recreation a visitor could want—surfing and swimming along the Atlantic coastline, camping in the Adirondack wilderness, skiing in mountain resorts.

In addition to these natural wonders, New York has many important landmarks and historic buildings. The focus of my report will be on some of these unique landmarks. There are so many interesting places to visit in New York State that I have limited my report to four major categories.

❖ CONTINUED

These four categories are the following:

- Museums. **Museums** are places where works of art and other valuable objects are displayed. New York City has some of the most famous museums in the world. For example, the **Metropolitan Museum of Art,** located in Manhattan, is one of the world's greatest art museums. It has an ancient Egyptian temple, medieval armor and rooms with furniture from historic houses inside the museum. It also has famous paintings and sculptures. Its collection is so vast that only a small part of it can be displayed at one time.

    The Metropolitan Museum of Art

- Historic Sites. This type includes places tied to the history and heritage of New York. It includes places that have been restored or rebuilt to show what life was like in the past. In northeastern New York there is **Fort Ticonderoga,** located where Lake Champlain and Lake George meet. This fort is closely tied to the struggle for national independence. During the American Revolution, the fort changed hands many times. In 1775, it became the site of the first American victory over the British in the Revolution.

- Homes of Famous People. This group includes the birthplaces and homes of well-known New Yorkers. For example, in **Hyde Park** you can visit the home of Franklin D. Roosevelt—the 32nd President of the United States. After his death, Roosevelt's home and adjacent library were declared national historic sites.

- Unique Places. This group includes unusual and one-of-a-kind places known for their beauty or amusement. For example, in west-central New York is **Watkins Glen State Park.** The park, by Seneca Lake, is one of the best known of the eighteen parks in the region. There are 300 foot-high cliffs and nineteen waterfalls in the park. The park is enjoyed by many recreation-minded boaters, campers, swimmers and hikers. In winter, cross-country skiing is enjoyed by area residents.

Now you know what you must do. Your sister's notecards describe different landmarks in New York. You must classify her notecards into the types of landmarks she listed. Before you start, you need to understand what it means to classify.

HOW TO CLASSIFY

> To **classify** is to arrange, organize and sort information. When we classify, we group each piece of information together with other similar information. Classifying is especially helpful when we want to make sense out of many items that seem disorganized. Could you imagine shopping for sneakers in a department store if no one in the store knew in which department sneakers were sold? You would have to search through the entire store. To prevent this problem, store managers take each item and decide which department to sell it in. That is why, if you wanted to buy sneakers, you would know to look in the footwear department. If you needed a baseball glove, you would know to find it in the sporting goods section. Store managers classify goods by department. Grouping similar items together by department makes shopping easier.

THINK ABOUT IT
What other situations can you think of where classifying is used?

CATEGORIZING INFORMATION

Luckily for you, your sister has already set up a classification system for the different types of landmarks—historic sites, museums, homes of famous people and unique places. Your task is simply to place each card into its correct category. How can you do this? Here is the procedure you should follow:

1. Look through **each** card.
2. Try to identify the landmark's basic feature.
3. Categorize each card into the group where it belongs. For example, if a card is about the birthplace of a famous person, you should categorize that card in the group: "Homes of Famous People." At the end, all the cards in the same category should have similar features.

PEOPLE IN SOCIETY   261

Let's do the first card together:

> **A**
> *Landmark: Erie Canal Museum (Syracuse)*
> In 1825, the Erie Canal opened. This canal linked Lake Erie at Buffalo with the Hudson River at Albany. This allowed cargo to move by water from the Great Lakes to the Atlantic port of New York City. The building was originally a station along the canal that weighed boats and collected tolls.

Notice how the information on this card is about important events that occurred at this place in the past. Since it relates the place to the history of New York, it can be classified as a "historic site." Copy the following chart to help you keep track as you classify each card. Place a check mark (✔) in the appropriate column in which the card can be grouped. The first card has already been done for you.

Note: A few of the cards may fit into more than one category.

	Historic Sites	Museums	Homes of Famous People	Unique Places
Card A	✔			
Card B				
Card C				
Card D				
Card E				
Card F				
Card G				
Card H				
Card I				
Card J				
Card K				
Card L				
Card M				
Card N				
Card O				

NEW YORK: ITS LAND AND ITS PEOPLE

B. Susan B. Anthony House (Rochester):
Susan B. Anthony was a leader in the Women's Rights Movement. Opponents of women's rights often attacked her in the press. Today, her home has become a museum.

C. Hill Cumorah (Palmyra).
Each year Mormons visit the birthplace of Joseph Smith, founder of the Mormon Church. He discovered golden plates beneath a rock near Hill Cumorah. The Mormon bible is based on these plates.

D. Sunnyside (Tarrytown).
Washington Irving wrote "Rip Van Winkle" and "The Legend of Sleepy Hollow." After living overseas, he bought Sunnyside in 1835. He changed this old farmhouse into a fairy-tale like house.

E. Federal Hall Memorial (New York City).
In 1703 this building became the new city hall for New York City. It is also where John Peter Zenger's trial was held. George Washington was sworn in as President here. James Madison proposed the Bill of Rights in this building.

F. Sagamore Hill (Oyster Bay).
This was the home of President Theodore Roosevelt. It is located on Long Island, overlooking Long Island Sound. The home reflects Roosevelt's spirit and interests. It is furnished with many family mementos.

G. Ellis Island (N.Y.C. Harbor).
A facility was built in 1890 to receive immigrants to the United States. Over the next 62 years, millions of people passed through its doors. It was closed in 1954. In 1964, work was begun to restore it. Today it is a museum about the immigrant experience.

H. Niagara Falls (Niagara Falls).
The falls are one of the world's most spectacular views. Over 182 foot high, the falls are visited by over 11,000,000 people each year. 700,000 gallons a second flow through Niagara from Lake Erie into Lake Ontario.

I. Vanderbilt Mansion (Centerport).
Built in 1896, this 54-room mansion was the summer home of Frederick W. Vanderbilt, grandson of Cornelius Vanderbilt. The mansion is a symbol of the wealth held by many of America's industrialists.

PEOPLE IN SOCIETY

J. Baseball Hall of Fame (Cooperstown).
In 1839, Abner Doubleday invented baseball. One hundred years later, America's first sports hall of fame opened at Cooperstown. Visitors can see plaques dedicated to the players and managers of baseball.

K. United Nations Headquarters (New York City).
The United Nations was created in 1946 as a place for nations to discuss their problems. The headquarters occupies 18 acres alongside the East River. Many of the world's leading architects helped build the United Nations.

L. Museum of Natural History (New York City).
The museum is the world's largest natural history museum. It occupies 4 city blocks. Visitors can see dinosaur skeletons, meteorites and models of Native American villages.

M. Corning Glass Center (Corning).
This is one of the world's most complete museums devoted to the manufacture of glass. The museum's collection has more than 24,000 objects, with some dating back to 1400 B.C.

N. Fire Island National Seashore (Long Island).
Fire Island is a string-bean shaped barrier island formed by sand deposited beyond the reach of the tides. Much of its 32 miles are unpopulated. Today, there are seventeen communities on the island.

O. Brooklyn Bridge (Brooklyn/Manhattan).
When completed in 1883, the bridge was called the "Eighth Wonder of the World." At one time it was the longest suspension bridge ever built. It has been the subject of paintings, photos, posters, essays and stories.

Once you are finished categorizing the cards, you have only one task left—to get to the library to meet your sister!

264   NEW YORK: ITS LAND AND ITS PEOPLE

COMPARING CLASSIFICATION SYSTEMS
Closing

How does your method of classifying the landmarks compare with others? Compare how you categorized the landmarks with what your classmates did.

1. Were your categorizations of the landmarks the same as those of your classmates?
2. Did any of the landmarks fit into more than one category? If so, which ones?
3. Have you and your family ever visited any of these landmarks?

   ❖ If so, describe your visit to the landmark.
   ❖ If not, which one landmark would you most like to visit? Why?

REVIEWING YOUR UNDERSTANDING

Creating Vocabulary Cards

Museum
What is a museum?
Name two museums in New York State:

Classify
What does it mean to "classify"?
Give an example of a group of items that can be classified:

Locating Landmarks on a Map of New York

Make a copy of the outline map of New York on page 265.

   A. Find where each landmark mentioned in this activity is located on the map.

   > **HINT:** The town or city where each landmark is located may be found in parentheses next to its name.

   B. List the names of the landmarks on the outside border of the map. Then draw a line from the name of each landmark to the place where it is found.

   C. Lastly, make a map **legend** or key. Create a symbol for each type of landmark on your map. For example, the location of each museum might be shown as a large M inside of a circle. For places with several landmarks, put all of the symbols next to each other at that place's location on the map.

MAKING CONNECTIONS

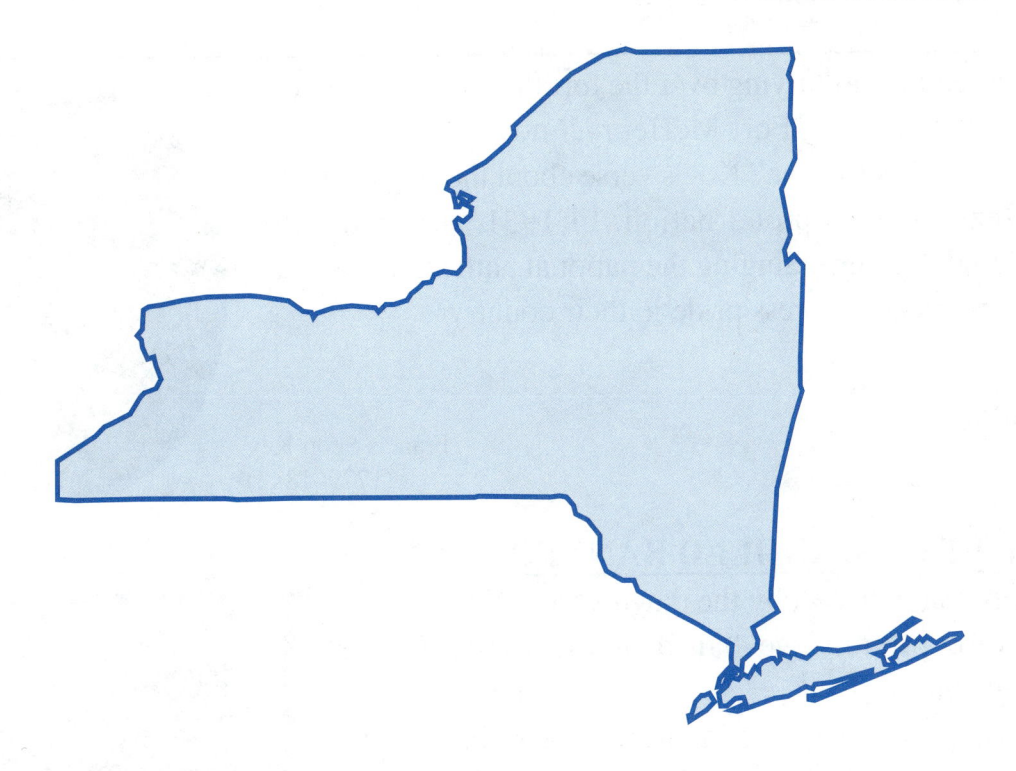

EXPLORING BEYOND YOUR STATE
OUR NATION'S SYMBOLS

Every country has what one French historian has called its "places of memory." These historic landmarks serve as symbols identifying the spirit of that nation and its people. A **symbol** is something that stands for something else. Symbols take many forms. Some symbols are visual. For example, a red light is a symbol meaning stop. Holidays, emblems, flags, songs and places can also be symbols.

Another example of something that has become identified with the spirit of the United States is "The Star Spangled Banner." During the War of 1812, **Francis Scott Key** was held captive on a British warship. The warship shelled Fort McHenry, an American fort. The next morning, Key was so happy to see the

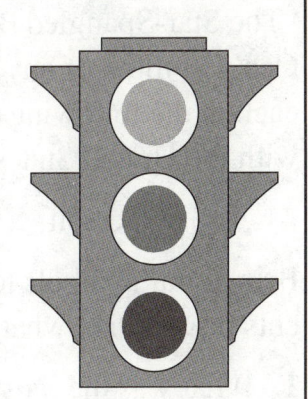

◆ CONTINUED

American flag still flying over the fort that he wrote a poem called "Defense of Fort McHenry," now known as "The Star-Spangled Banner." Key's verse about the flag captured the feelings of a proud nation. In 1931, it became the **National Anthem**. Singing the national anthem is one way that Americans express pride in their country.

Francis Scott Key
(1779–1843)

THE STAR-SPANGLED BANNER

Oh say, can you see, by the dawn's early light,
What so proudly we hail'd at the twilight's last gleaming,
Whose broad stripes and bright stars through the perilous fight,
O'er the ramparts we watch'd, were so gallantly streaming?
And the rockets' red glare, the bombs bursting in air,
Gave proof thru' the night that our flag was still there.
Oh say, does that star-spangled banner yet wave
O'er the land of the free and the home of the brave?

FINDING OTHER NATIONAL SYMBOLS

"The Star-Spangled Banner" is just one symbol that people identify with our country. Can you think of any other symbols that people identify with the United States? For each of the following categories, **name** or **draw** the symbol you most closely identify with the United States:

- person
- object
- event
- place

Bring your symbols to school and discuss them with your classmates. Ask your parents or guardian what symbols they associate with the United States.

1. What was the most popular national symbol among your classmates?
2. What is your parent or guardian's favorite symbol for the United States?

❖ CONTINUED

EXPLORING YOUR COMMUNITY
CREATING A PAMPHLET ABOUT YOUR COMMUNITY

How well do you know the major attractions in your community? Do you know what might interest someone visiting the area where you live? Let's put your knowledge to work.

MAKING A COMMUNITY PAMPHLET

Use your knowledge to create a pamphlet for a community "Visitor Information Center." Your pamphlet should have the following format:

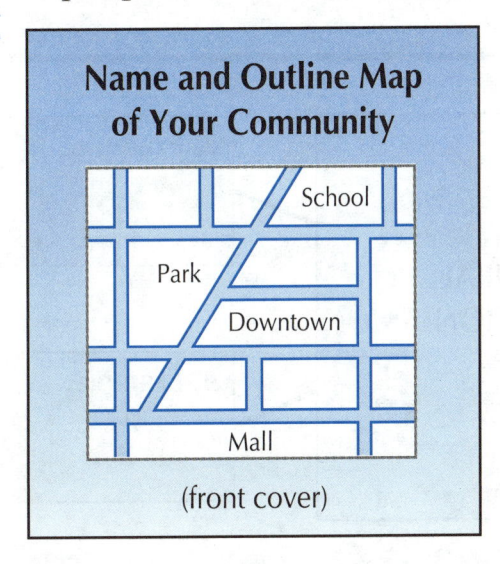

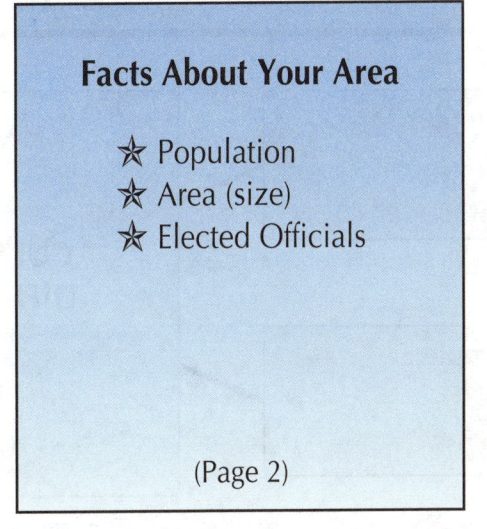

Name and Outline Map of Your Community

(front cover)

Facts About Your Area

★ Population
★ Area (size)
★ Elected Officials

(Page 2)

Special Attractions

★ Museums
★ State and Local Parks
★ Festivals
★ Historic Sites
★ Cultural Events
★ County Fairs

(Page 3)

Presented by

Your Name

(back cover)

SUMMARIZING YOUR UNDERSTANDING

Directions: Use your knowledge to fill in the blanks in the following graphic organizers.

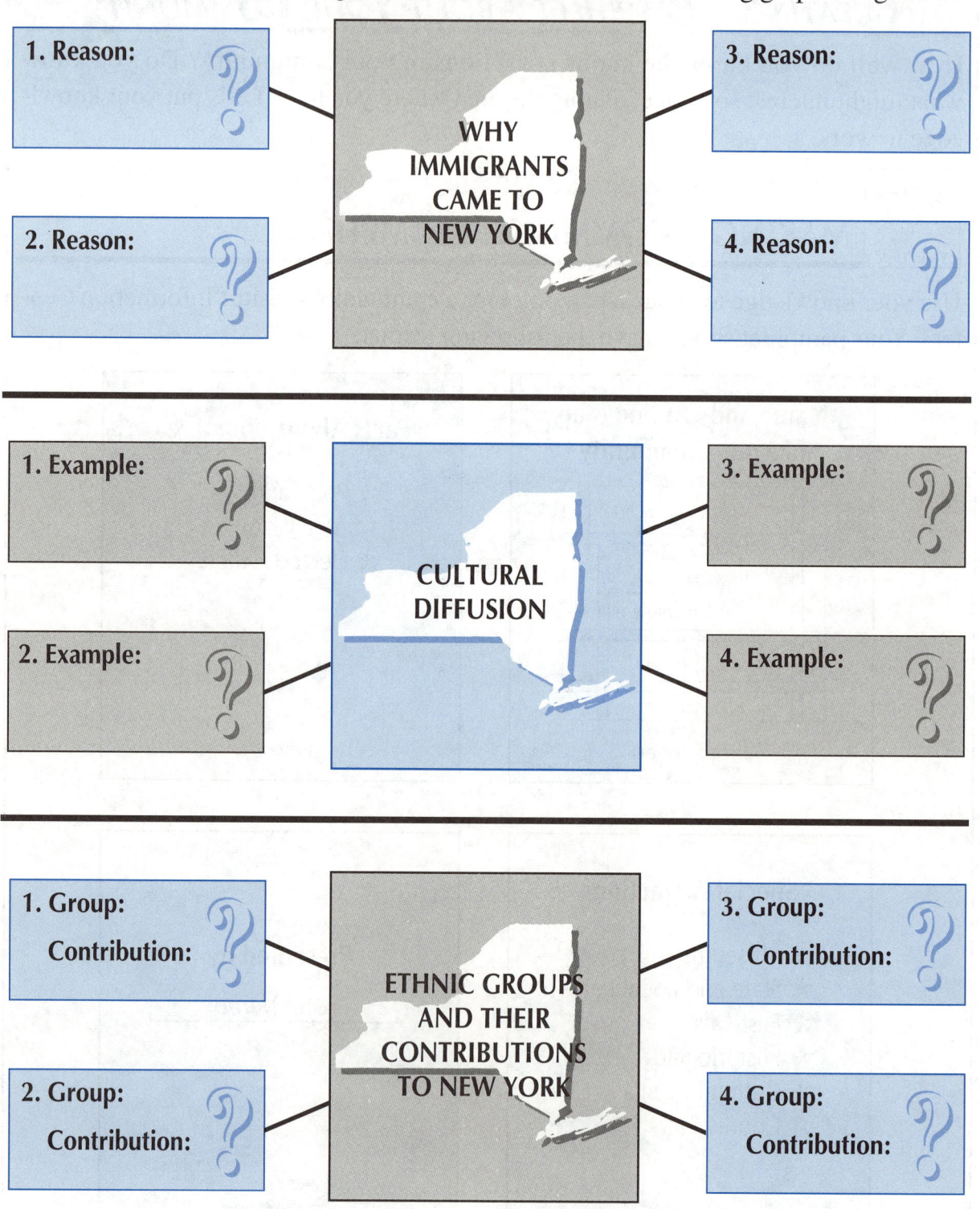

WHY IMMIGRANTS CAME TO NEW YORK
- 1. Reason:
- 2. Reason:
- 3. Reason:
- 4. Reason:

CULTURAL DIFFUSION
- 1. Example:
- 2. Example:
- 3. Example:
- 4. Example:

ETHNIC GROUPS AND THEIR CONTRIBUTIONS TO NEW YORK
- 1. Group:
  Contribution:
- 2. Group:
  Contribution:
- 3. Group:
  Contribution:
- 4. Group:
  Contribution:

INFORMATION SHEET #3: PEOPLE IN SOCIETY

CREATING ITEMS FOR YOUR EXHIBIT

Following is a list of ideas for your project. However, feel free to present anything else that you think does a good job of portraying the heritage of the people of your community.

CREATING A POSTCARD FROM AN INTERESTING SITE

Your village, town or city has interesting places to visit. Write a postcard that tells people about a place of interest in your community. On one side of the postcard, write an address and a message telling about the place. On the other side, place a picture of what you described on the message side of the card.

Dear Sal,
This postcard shows the front of the Guggenheim Museum in New York City. Designed by a famous architect, the museum is like a giant corkscrew. You start at the top and wind your way down without ever taking stairs. See you soon.
Tom

POSTCARD

To: Mr. Sal Smith
825 Jackson Avenue
Rome, NY 13440

MAKING A BUMPER STICKER

During World War II, someone came up with the idea of putting a personal message on the bumper of his car. Everyone who saw the car got the message, and the bumper sticker was born. Today, it would be hard to go for a ride and not see stickers on hundreds of car bumpers. For many Americans, the bumper sticker has become their "personal billboard." What better way to let people know about your community than a bumper sticker. Wherever your family car travels, people will learn about your town or city. Create a bumper sticker that tells people about your town or city.

◆ CONTINUED

HOLDING A MULTICULTURAL COMMUNITY FAIR

Your teacher should divide your class into teams. Each team will select a different group to learn about. Try not to choose your own ethnic group. Here are a few of the ethnic groups to choose from. Feel free to add others to this list.

- German Americans
- Polish Americans
- African Americans
- Dominican Americans
- Russian Americans
- *You Select One*

Each team will be assigned a section of the classroom to create a booth for a Multicultural Fair. Each booth will represent a different group. Booths will be decorated to reflect the cultures they represent. On the day of the fair, students should visit each team's booth.

To decorate the booths, each team should collect or make the items listed below. Teams will be awarded points for each item they can find, make or create:

- **Foods (20 points).** Students may display recipes and pictures of typical ethnic foods. These foods should be ones for which their group is well known.

> **NOTE:** *For each student who cooks the food from that cultural group for other students to sample, the team will receive a bonus of 10 points.*

- **History and Contributions (15 points).** Students may display posters, charts or pictures summarizing the history of their group and its major contributions.
- **Customs and Traditions (20 points).** Students may display posters or pictures showing some unique customs of the group they chose.
- **Music and Dance (15 points).** Students may bring in music or perform traditional dances that are popular among members of the cultural group they chose.
- **Holidays (15 points).** Students may display items, articles or signs showing which holidays the cultural group celebrates.
- **Costumes (15 points).** Students may display pictures, drawings or photographs of people dressed in traditional costumes of the group they chose.

> **NOTE:** *For each student who wears a traditional costume from his or her selected culture, the team will receive a bonus of 10 points.*

UNIT 5
ECONOMICS

Members of the Cloak-makers Union on strike (1916)

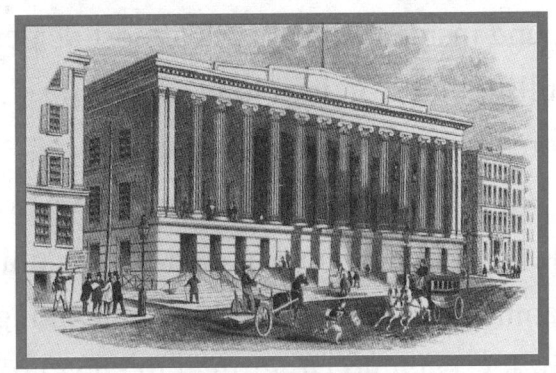

Wall Street, 1852

Consumer making a purchase in Woodstock

Economics is about how people earn money and what they buy. It is also about banks, factories, stores and farms, and how they work. In this unit, you will learn about the things that are needed to make goods and to provide services—natural resources, labor, capital goods and knowledge. You will also learn about starting a new business, conserving natural resources and trading with other countries.

PROFESSOR SMITH VISITS A FACTORY

The year is 1765. Adam Smith, a professor from Scotland, is wearing a handsome light coat, silk stockings, trousers that end at his knees and wide-buckle shoes. He has large eyes and his head shakes slightly when he speaks. He is visiting a factory to find the answers to several questions that confuse him.

"Step right this way, Professor Smith," says a tall, thin man who leads the professor through the doorway. "Thank you kindly, sir," Smith replies. The sound inside the factory is almost deafening. At one end of the room, men are pulling hot iron into long, thin wire. In another corner, a man hammers the wire to straighten it as it cools.

Smith's eyes dance around the workshop. He watches a number of men busily cutting and hammering the red hot iron, and making small circles, each no larger than the head of a pin. "Professor Smith, would you believe that there are 18 separate operations in this workshop for making pins?" says his guide.

"But wouldn't it be much simpler to have each man make the pins from start to finish?" Smith asks, with some excitement in his voice. "In my grandfather's day they would have done that," the tall man answers "but we've discovered that it is much faster to divide the work up among all the men. This division of labor allows each man to become more skilled at his own simple task. No time is lost by having the men switch from one job to another."

Adam Smith

Smith was greatly impressed by what he saw at the pin factory. The division of labor seemed to him to be the secret that made people more productive than at any other time in history. People were growing more food, making more cloth, and producing more glass and ironware than ever before. And all this from the simple idea of dividing up the work into separate tasks.

Indeed, it seemed to Professor Smith that the division of labor had spread through almost all of British society. Some people were doctors, others were carpenters, farmers or soldiers. Each person did what he or she did best. This seemed to make society more productive.

However, one thing continued to nag him. In the pin-factory, each man had a specialty. One man drew iron, while another straightened it into pins. The factory owner hired the workmen and told them what to do. The owner alone decided everything.

But what about society as a whole? What was the guiding force that told each person in society what to do? Who made sure that there were enough farmers to grow wheat for the bakers, and that the bakers baked enough bread for everyone who needed bread to eat? Society was like a huge pin-factory, but it miraculously ran without a factory owner telling everyone what to do. How did each person know what job to fill and what to do?

In olden times, people had carried on the same kind of work that their parents had done or obeyed the orders of their king or ruler. It was easy to see how those societies worked—everyone was told what to do. But society in Great Britain and America was quite different now. Each person did what he or she considered to be best for himself or herself, without a single thought about what was good for society. And yet, society was not falling apart. In fact, things were better than ever. Smith wondered, could there be some "invisible hand" guiding everyone?

Adam Smith spent many years pondering this question. In this unit you will learn the answers to some of the questions that had puzzled the old professor.

5A HOW WOULD YOU SPEND YOUR MONEY?

In this activity, you will make decisions about how to spend money. These decisions will introduce you to two key ideas in economics—scarcity and opportunity cost. Look for the following important words:

▶ Economics ▶ Opportunity Cost ▶ Consumption
▶ Problem of Scarcity ▶ Production ▶ Consumer

To help you, the ▶ will appear in the margin where the term first appears.

Today must be your lucky day! You have opened the mail and found a birthday card from your favorite aunt and uncle. Inside the card is a gift of one hundred dollars. Excitedly, you ask your mother, "What should I do with this money?" She says there are many things you could do. She suggests that you make a list of different ways of using the money.

WHAT SHOULD YOU DO WITH THE MONEY?

On a separate sheet of paper, list all of the things you would want to do if you had an extra $100:

I Want:	It Would Cost:
1.	$
2.	$
3.	$

What you want to buy will be influenced by your personal tastes and values. You will also be affected by the prices that different things cost. If you are like most people, the things you want probably cost more than $100. So you would have to choose between different things. Whenever you make choices about how to use your money, you are involved in economics.

THE PROBLEM OF SCARCITY

Economics is the study of how individuals, businesses and nations make things, buy things, spend money and save money. People who study economics are known as **economists**. Economists believe that the basic problem of economics is the problem of scarcity. Something is *scarce* when we do not have enough of it. The **problem of scarcity** involves two basic ideas:

1. People usually have unlimited wants. There are many things you probably want. Once you had them all, you would most likely find new things that you wanted.

2. A society can produce only a limited number of things at any one time. There is only a certain amount of available goods (*video games, cars, clothes*). There is only a certain amount of available services (*car-washing, banking services, restaurants*).

The problem of scarcity exists because (1) most people want an unlimited number of things, and (2) society does not have enough resources to produce an unlimited amount of goods and services. In other words, even with your birthday gift of $100, you would probably want more things than your $100 could buy. Your scarce resources cannot satisfy your unlimited wants.

✔ CHECKING YOUR UNDERSTANDING ✔

Suppose every person were given 5 million dollars a year. Do you think this would end the problem of scarcity? If yes, explain how. If not, explain why not.

Because of the problem of scarcity, economists point out that there is an **opportunity cost** to every economic decision. This "cost" is the opportunity one gives up to do other things. For instance, assume you have saved enough to buy either a radio or a book. You decide to buy the radio. The "opportunity cost" of your radio is the book you **might** have bought instead.

MAKING AN ECONOMIC CHOICE

Now it's time for you to make your decision.

1. How would you spend your $100?
2. What would be some of the opportunity costs of your decision?

REVIEWING YOUR UNDERSTANDING

Creating Vocabulary Cards

Economics

What is "economics"?

How is economics different from geography?

The Problem of Scarcity

What is the "problem of scarcity"?

Give an example you experienced of the problem of scarcity:

Dealing with the Problem of Scarcity

Let's see how the problem of scarcity might affect your school. Imagine that the following is a list of problems facing your school:

Problems	Amount Needed to Fix the Problem
The basketball team needs new uniforms	$3,000
New instruments are needed for the band	$4,000
The school wants to replace certain computers	$6,000
The school needs a new roof	$4,000
The school needs to be painted	$3,000

Your school has only $9,000 in its budget. How would you spend this money? Assume you are writing a letter to your school newspaper. Explain which problems you would attempt to solve by spending the $9,000.

Dealing with Opportunity Costs

Opportunity costs are not just something you read about in a school textbook. In fact, they create economic problems that you face each day of your life. Everything you do means giving up something else. Describe a situation in your life in which you dealt with the problem of scarcity and opportunity costs.

ECONOMICS 277

MAKING CONNECTIONS

EXPLORING BEYOND YOUR STATE
DIFFERENT TYPES OF ECONOMIC GROUPS

Our economy depends on two types of activities: production and consumption.

PRODUCTION AND CONSUMPTION

Production is the act of making or providing goods and services. For example, a farmer produces food and a doctor provides medical services. **Consumption** is the act of using these goods and services. **Consumers** are people who use goods and services to satisfy their needs and wants. A consumer uses foods by eating them, clothes by wearing them, and a barber's services by having a haircut.

A consumer shops for her family. What makes someone a consumer?

ECONOMIC GROUPS

An **economic group** is a group of people involved in some economic activity. Our society has many different kinds of economic groups. Each one produces and consumes goods and services.

FAMILY

Families are consumers as well as producers. A family often makes decisions about where its members live, what they eat or wear and what other things they buy. Decisions about productive activities are also often made by the family. Sometimes, family members work together on a farm or in a family business. More often, family members work at different jobs.

❖ CONTINUED

WORKERS

All products require some labor. Workers are the people that supply this labor. But a worker also needs food, housing and other goods and services in order to live. This means that workers are both producers and consumers.

LABOR UNIONS

Labor unions are organizations of workers whose goal is to get higher wages and better working conditions. At one time, there were no labor unions. Workers labored long hours often in unsafe conditions. If they complained, they would be fired. Workers found that by acting together in a labor union they had greater influence on their employer. As members of a labor union workers may strike. A

Airline workers strike at a New York airport. Why would workers want to join a union?

strike is when union members refuse to work until their demands are met. The United Auto Workers is an example of a labor union. Can you think of the name of any other labor unions?

SMALL BUSINESSES

A small business is a unit of production. Small businesses are usually owned by a single individual, a family or a small group of people. Small business owners run their businesses on a day-to-day basis. They usually specialize in providing local services or making unique products. Some small businesses that you might know are your neighborhood baker, dry cleaner or bicycle shop. What other small businesses exist in your neighborhood?

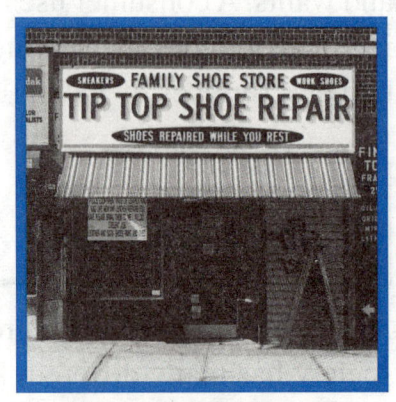

This shoe repair shop is an example of a small business.

LARGE CORPORATIONS

A **corporation** is a special type of business. People form a corporation by investing money in the business. In exchange, they are given a part (*share*) in the corporation. A large corporation has thousands of shareholders. Because corporations produce things in very large quantities their products are often less expensive. The cars we drive, the foods we eat and the clothes we wear are often made and sold by large corporations. For example, the Ford Motor Company is

❖ CONTINUED

a large corporation that makes both automobiles and trucks. What other large corporations can you name?

GOVERNMENT AGENCIES

A government agency is a part of the government that controls a particular kind of economic activity or public concern. For example, the **Environmental Protection Agency** protects the environment. It makes sure that individuals and businesses do not pollute our air or water. What other government agencies can you name?

Workers assemble a car at a Ford Motor Company plant.

CHOICES THAT ECONOMIC GROUPS MAKE

Each group in our economy must make economic choices. Often, each choice has both advantages and disadvantages. On a copy of the following chart, fill in those advantages and disadvantages that are incomplete.

Group	Decision	Advantages	Disadvantages
family	decides to buy a new house	the family will have a larger and roomier place to live	*you complete*
worker	decides to look for a new job	may find a job and earn more money	*you complete*
small business	decides to sell a new product	may become successful and make large profits	*you complete*
labor union	decides to strike for higher wages	*you complete*	striking members will receive no wages
large corporation	decides to make a new product	*you complete*	makes a large investment in developing it
government agency	requires detailed reports before allowing any new construction	makes sure no new buildings will harm the environment	*you complete*

FAMOUS NEW YORKERS

Samuel Gompers (1850–1924) was the son of working-class Jewish parents. His family moved from England to America when he was 13 years old. They settled on the East Side of New York City. Gompers followed his father's lead and became a cigar maker. However, Gompers felt that labor conditions for cigar workers were unfair. In 1886, he helped form the **American Federation of Labor** (*known as the A.F.L.*). The A.F.L was not a union itself, but a group of several unions with a national leadership. Its aim was to improve conditions for skilled workers. Gompers was elected the A.F.L.'s first president. Under his leadership, the A.F.L. grew and became successful. Gompers continued as president of the A.F.L. until his death in 1924.

Samuel Gompers

EXPLORING YOUR COMMUNITY
CONSUMPTION AND PRODUCTION IN YOUR COMMUNITY

We are all consumers in our society. However, not everybody consumes the same things. Usually, different groups use different things.

CONSUMPTION

On a separate sheet of paper, list **two** goods and services that you, your friends, teenagers and adults in your community buy and consume:

Items You Consume:
1. _____ ?
2. _____ ?

Items Your Friends Consume:
1. _____ ?
2. _____ ?

◆ CONTINUED

Items Teenagers Consume:	1. _____?_____	
	2. _____?_____	
Items Adults Consume:	1. _____?_____	
	2. _____?_____	

Are any of the goods and services you listed sometimes consumed by all four groups? If so, explain why this might happen.

PRODUCTION AND CONSUMPTION
Your Task

What things are produced and consumed in your community?

List two things that are produced in your community:

1. _____?_____   2. _____?_____

List two things that are consumed in your community:

1. _____?_____   2. _____?_____

FAMOUS NEW YORKERS

George Westinghouse (1846–1914) was born in Central Bridge, New York. His first invention came at age nineteen, and was followed by some 400 other inventions during his lifetime. One of his best known inventions, air brakes came in 1868. Air brakes for railroads permitted a trainman to stop an entire train at one time by using compressed air to stop the train's wheels. This helped provide greater train safety. Before the invention of air brakes, trainmen had to stop each car of the train separately—causing many passengers to be hurt by the jerking motion of the train as it stopped. Westinghouse was also a pioneer in introducing AC electricity—the alternating current system for transmitting electricity. Alternating current electricity can be sent over greater distances. This allowed the Westinghouse Electric Company to become one of the nation's largest and richest corporations.

George Westinghouse

HOW WOULD YOU ILLUSTRATE THE FACTORS OF PRODUCTION?

5B

In this activity, you will learn about the things that go into making a product. These items are called the factors of production. Look for the following important words:

- Goods and Services
- Factors of Production
- Land
- Labor
- Capital Goods
- Entrepreneurs

In the last activity, you learned about the "production" and "consumption" of goods and services. Let's take a closer look at how goods and services are produced and consumed.

WHAT ARE GOODS AND SERVICES?

▶ **Goods**. Goods are things that people make. For example, foods, toys, clothes, cars and houses are goods. Department stores, shoe stores, bakeries and supermarkets all sell goods.

✔ **CHECKING YOUR UNDERSTANDING** ✔

Name two other "goods" that people make.

▶ **Services**. Services are things that people do for others. People who provide services include electricians, plumbers, barbers and auto mechanics.

✔ **CHECKING YOUR UNDERSTANDING** ✔

Name two other "services" that people supply to others.

THE FACTORS OF PRODUCTION

The **factors of production** are all the things needed to produce goods and services. Think of a can of soda: what materials, labor, machinery and management skills came together to produce it?

There are four main types of factors of production: **l**and (*natural resources*), **l**abor, **c**apital goods and **e**ntrepreneurship. A useful mnemonic device to help you remember the factors of production might be C-E-L-L.

LAND (NATURAL RESOURCES)

Economists use the term "land" to mean the resources found in nature. These resources include metals and other minerals, water, plants and soil. For example, steel is needed to make a car. Iron and coal are needed to make steel. These resources—iron and coal—are taken from the Earth. No matter how advanced a society is or how skilled its workers are, it cannot produce new goods without natural resources.

Central New York State
How many natural resources can you identify in this photograph?

✔ CHECKING YOUR UNDERSTANDING ✔
List some of the natural resources that are needed to build a house.

LABOR

Labor is the work that people do to make goods or provide services. Labor includes the talents, training, skills and knowledge of the people who make things and provide services. Labor involves many kinds of workers: plumbers, bus drivers, welders, police officers, fire fighters, nurses, teachers, bankers and singers. All goods and services include some human labor. For example, even a completely automated (*machine-run*) factory needs workers to design, build, run and repair the machinery.

Old-time illustration of the Buffalo Forge Company
How has the role of labor changed with the use of automation?

✔ CHECKING YOUR UNDERSTANDING ✔
List some of the workers whose labor is needed to build a house.

CAPITAL GOODS

Capital goods are things that are used to make other goods and services. For example, machines and tools are capital goods. They are used to make other goods or to help perform other services. Buildings, railroads and trucks may also be capital goods if they are used to produce other goods or services.

> ✔ **CHECKING YOUR UNDERSTANDING** ✔
>
> List some of the capital goods you would need to build a house.

ENTREPRENEURSHIP

Land, labor and capital goods must be combined and organized to make something. People who bring these factors of production together are called **entrepreneurs**. They are the owners of businesses. They combine, coordinate and organize the other three factors of production. An entrepreneur risks his or her money in the hope of making a profit. A **profit** is the amount of money left over after the expenses of the business have been paid.

Often a business grows too large and complicated for one person to run. Then the business is run by people called managers. The **managers** work for the entrepreneur.

> ✔ **CHECKING YOUR UNDERSTANDING** ✔
>
> What is the person called who acts as the entrepreneur for building a house?

FAMOUS NEW YORKERS

John Jacob Astor (1763–1848). As a young man, he entered the fur trade. He invested his profits by shipping furs to China for silks and spices. By 1800, he was one of the richest New Yorkers. Astor then began investing in real estate. In the early 1800s, lands located just beyond the built-up areas of Manhattan were available at low prices. In 1803, Astor bought 70 acres of land located an hour's ride from the city limits for $25,000. By 1870, the land was worth $20 million. Today this area is known as Times Square. At age 85, Astor was asked if he would have done anything differently in his life. He replied that his only regret was that he didn't buy all of Manhattan. At his death, he was the richest man in America.

John Jacob Astor

ECONOMICS 285

Closing: "SEEING" THE FACTORS OF PRODUCTION

"Seeing" or "visualizing" is one of the best ways to understand something. By visualizing you connect an idea with a picture. For example, you have just learned about the four factors of production. Now let's tie these factors to a picture. This will make the factors easier to understand and remember. The following photograph shows three of the four factors of production. The fourth factor, entrepreneurship, was responsible for bringing these three factors together.

✔ CHECKING YOUR UNDERSTANDING ✔

Look carefully at the details in the above photograph. Then explain which items in the photograph illustrate each factor of production. Remember, only three of the four factors are shown.

Now it's your turn to find pictures that show the factors of production. Look through some newspapers or magazines. Find a photograph or drawing to show each factor of production. You may use one photograph or drawing to show more than one of the factors.

Generally, all four of the factors of production are needed to produce a good or a service. For instance, to grow a crop a farmer needs soil and water (*land*). In addition, fuel and machinery are necessary (*capital goods*). The farmer must also work hard at plowing, planting, fertilizing and harvesting (*labor*). Finally, the farmer must be able to put these three factors of production together in a reasonable way to get a good harvest (*entrepreneurship*).

REVIEWING YOUR UNDERSTANDING

Creating Vocabulary Cards

Goods and Services
What are "goods" and "services"?
Give two examples of each:

Factors of Production
What are the four "factors of production"?
Give an example of each factor:

Identifying the Factors of Production

Do you wear jeans? Imagine the different factors of production that were brought together to make this product. Jeans are made mostly from cotton. First, farmers must use natural resources like seeds and soil to grow the cotton. When it is ready to be harvested, the cotton is picked, cleaned and shipped to factories by workers. The factory uses spinning machines (capital goods) to turn the cotton into thread. The thread is then woven into cloth on other giant machines.

Once the cloth is dyed blue, it is cut into pieces following the patterns for jeans of different sizes. These pieces are then sewn together, a zipper is added and buttons and snaps are sewn on. The jeans are then labeled, packed and shipped to stores. Finally, you enter the store (owned by an entrepreneur) and try on one of the pairs of jeans. They fit! So your parent gives the cashier some money and you take them home.

Now it's your turn. Select any product. What things need to be done to produce it? Describe each process and explain how each of the factors of production are used to make the product. Use the numbered boxes below to help you explain each of the various steps. Add boxes if needed.

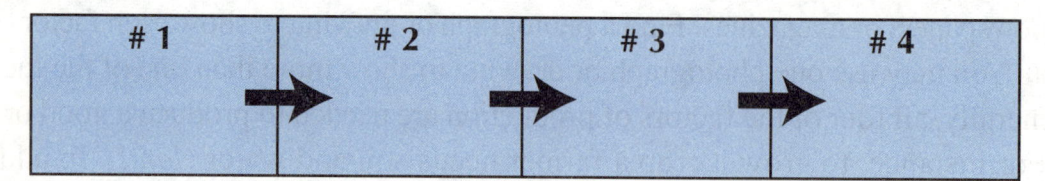

# 1	# 2	# 3	# 4
→	→	→	

Uses of the Factors of Production

In this activity, you learned how the factors of production are combined to make different goods and services. Any particular factor of production can be used in many different ways. For example, aluminum (*land/natural resource*) may be used to make a soda can, a bracelet or an automobile part.

1. What other things can be made of aluminum?
2. A carpenter (*labor*) may build furniture or a house with his or her labor. What other things can a carpenter build?
3. A truck (*capital goods*) may haul bricks or carry furniture. In what other ways can a truck be used?
4. A businessperson (*entrepreneur*) may decide to invest his or her money in starting a farm or a shoe store. What else can an entrepreneur invest in?

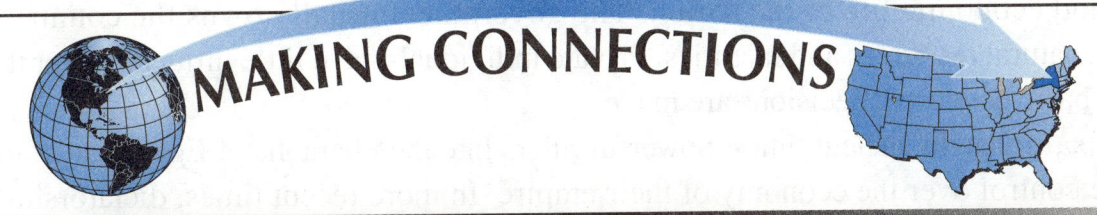

MAKING CONNECTIONS

EXPLORING BEYOND YOUR STATE
HOW SOCIETIES MEET THEIR ECONOMIC NEEDS

Everyone has wants and needs. But our wants are unlimited. They can never be fully satisfied. No nation, no matter how rich it is, has enough resources to make everything that its people want. As a result, every society must make choices in answering three basic economic questions:

- What should be produced?
- How should it be produced?
- Who should get what is produced?

TYPES OF ECONOMIC SYSTEMS

Societies usually answer these basic questions in one of three ways. The way that a society chooses is called its **economic system**.

TRADITIONAL ECONOMY
In a **traditional economy**, the three basic questions are answered by custom. People do things the way they were done in the past. A person's occupation is determined at birth. For example, if a boy's father is a sheep farmer, then he too will become a sheep farmer.

A rural village uses traditional methods.

◆ CONTINUED

Examples. Traditional economies are found mostly in rural, non-industrial areas. Today, traditional economies still exist among the Bushmen of the Kalahari Desert of South Africa, the Berber tribesmen of Algeria and the native tribes in the jungles of Brazil.

COMMAND ECONOMY

In a **command economy**, all important economic decisions are made by government officials. The central government often holds complete power over the political and economic life of the nation. The government usually owns the country's land, natural resources and factories. Private individuals have little influence over the way basic economic decisions are made.

Examples. In ancient times, powerful rulers like the Pharaohs of Egypt had complete control over the economy of their empire. In more recent times, dictatorships have often had command economies, such as Cuba and China. All countries have some features of a command economy. For example, even in the United States, the national government can influence production through its taxing and spending powers.

FREE MARKET ECONOMY

In a **free market economy**, people are free to produce whatever they wish and to consume whatever they can afford. People produce and sell goods and services in order to make a profit.

THE ROLE OF SUPPLY AND DEMAND IN A FREE MARKET ECONOMY

In a free market economy, basic economic questions are answered by the interaction of consumers and producers. Consumers determine the *demand* for a product. If a product becomes more expensive, fewer people are willing to buy it. For example, fewer people will buy a pair of shoes costing $100 than if the same shoes cost $10.

Producers determine the *supply* of a product. If the price that consumers will pay for a product increases, producers are willing to make more of that item. For example, manufacturers and merchants will be willing to make more shoes if they can sell them for $100 a pair rather than for only $25.

How does the supply and demand for apples affect their price?

CONTINUED

Through their buying decisions, consumers determine which products will sell and which will be available. What a consumer will pay and what a producer will sell determines what is produced. Here is how these two interact in a free market economy:

❖ If consumers are willing to pay more for an item, then producers will make more of it. This is done because producers are anxious to increase their profits.

❖ If consumers are not willing to pay as much for an item, then producers will have to lower their prices and will not sell as many of that item.

❖ If producers raise their prices, not as many consumers will be willing to buy the product.

THE ROLE OF GOVERNMENT

Even in a "free" market system, there is some government influence on the economy. The government provides stable conditions and a system of laws under which people can conduct business. The government also acts as a "policeman" in the marketplace. It tries to make sure that consumers and businesses treat each other fairly.

Examples. Most nations in the world today have a free market economy. The United States, Japan, Germany, Canada and Sweden are all examples of nations with free market economies. What other countries can you name that have a free market economy?

Consumers shopping in Canada
What type of economic system does Canada follow?

COMPARING AND CONTRASTING ECONOMIC SYSTEMS

Copy the chart below. Then list **one** advantage and **one** disadvantage of each type of economic system.

ECONOMIC SYSTEM	ADVANTAGES	DISADVANTAGES
Traditional Economy	?	?
Command Economy	?	?
Free Market Economy	?	?

❖ CONTINUED

EXPLORING YOUR COMMUNITY
GOODS AND SERVICES PRODUCED IN YOUR COMMUNITY

Let's find out more about how the factors of production come together to make some of the goods and services found in your community.

EXPLORING THE FACTORS OF PRODUCTION IN YOUR COMMUNITY

Choose any one item produced, manufactured or grown in your community. Then make a copy of the chart below. For the item selected, describe the factors of production involved in producing, manufacturing or growing it. For example, if your community produces cars, you might write that a natural resource used in making cars is iron ore. It is needed to make steel for the body of the car. If your community does not produce, manufacture or grow any particular item, then broaden your area to include your city or county.

Picking apples in one of New York's many apple orchards.
What factors of production go into growing apples?

ITEM: _____?_____

Natural Resources: _____?_____

Labor: _____?_____

Capital Goods: _____?_____

Entrepreneurship: _____?_____

WOULD YOU START YOUR OWN BUSINESS?

5C

In this activity, you will learn about the free enterprise system by imagining what it might be like to start your own business. Look for the following important words:

- ▶ Business
- ▶ Free Enterprise System
- ▶ Occupations
- ▶ Factory

We live in a society in which many people can own businesses. A **business** can be defined as an economic activity in which someone tries to make a profit. The ability to start a business is possible because America has a **free enterprise system** (*sometimes called the free market economy*). Under this system anyone can start a business.

STARTING A BUSINESS

If enough consumers buy the products of a business, the business can make a lot of money. No wonder that in 1995 almost nine million new businesses were started in the United States. What would it be like to be a young entrepreneur? In this activity, you will have an opportunity to **imagine** what it might be like to start your own business.

Every business begins with an idea. To start, you should choose some kind of work that you enjoy and think you would be good at. Here are some suggestions:

❖ **Pet Care:** Caring for household pets: feeding, walking and washing pets
❖ **Notebook Covers:** Making book covers with your own designs on them.
❖ **Lawn Service:** Raking lawns to gather up leaves.
❖ **Other (Your Idea):** _____?_____

This student earns extra money by mowing neighbors' lawns.
What business would you like to imagine trying?

Now it's time for you to make a choice. Which business would you like to imagine trying?

My business will be ____?____ because I like ____?____.

GETTING INFORMATION AND ADVICE

Before starting a business, it is important to get advice from other people. Talk with your parent or guardian. Explain that you would like to know some of the advantages and disadvantages of starting a business like the one you are imagining. Make a list of their suggestions.

Advantages	Disadvantages
1.	1.
2.	2.
3.	3.
4.	4.

Earlier in this unit you learned about the **factors of production**. On a separate sheet, list the factors of production you would need for your business:

Factors of Production for My Business:
- Land (Natural Resources)—
- Labor—
- Capital Goods—
- Entrepreneurship—

FINDING OUT IF THERE WILL BE A PROFIT

Starting a business takes money. You may need money to buy raw materials (*land*) and tools and equipment (*capital goods*). Sometimes you may need money to hire other workers (*labor*). About how much money would you need to start your new business?

ECONOMICS   293

Also think of a reasonable price to charge for each item or service you provide. With the following chart, estimate what the costs might be in your first month of business (*left side of the chart*). Then figure out how much money you might earn from selling your product or service (*on the right side of the chart*). The amount of money left after you pay all your bills is your profit.

My First Month of Business

A. Cost of Materials: ?	Selling price of the item or service: ?
B. Cost of Advertising: ?	
C. Other: ?	
(add A, B, C for monthly costs)	Number of items or services you can sell each month: ?
	Multiply selling price by number of items sold. This is your
Monthly Costs: ?	Monthly Income: ?

Subtract your monthly costs (*left column*) from your monthly income (*right column*):

Total Monthly Income: $?
− (minus) Monthly Costs: $?

Monthly Profit or Loss: $?

MAKING A DECISION
Closing

You now have some idea what you would need, as well as the risks of starting your own business. If your monthly costs amount to more than your monthly income, you will have a loss. If you lose money for too long, you will go out of business.

Based on what you have learned in this activity, do you think you would like to start your own business? ❏ Yes ❏ No   Explain your answer.

REVIEWING YOUR UNDERSTANDING

Creating Vocabulary Cards

Free Enterprise System
What is the "free enterprise system"?
What are some of the features of the free enterprise system?

Business
What is a "business"?
List two types of businesses.

Interpreting a Pie Chart About Occupations in New York State

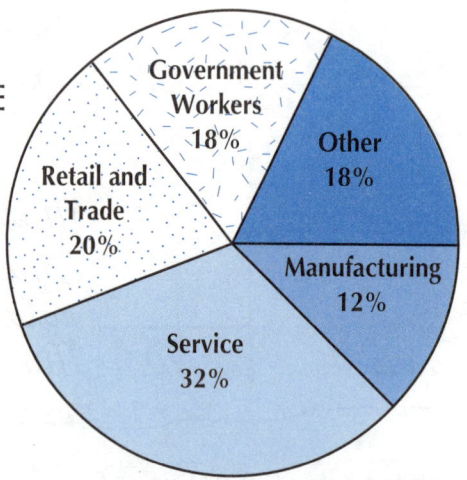

NEW YORK STATE OCCUPATIONS, 1994

- Government Workers 18%
- Other 18%
- Retail and Trade 20%
- Manufacturing 12%
- Service 32%

✔ Checking Your Understanding ✔

Use the information in the pie chart above to answer the following questions.

1. What is the title of the pie chart?
2. What percentage of people are employed by government?
3. In what type of occupation are the most New Yorkers employed?
4. In what type of occupation are the fewest New Yorkers employed?

Do you know anyone who has a job in government in New York State?

MAKING CONNECTIONS

EXPLORING BEYOND YOUR STATE
LEARNING ABOUT OCCUPATIONS IN NEW YORK STATE

You just learned about some of the things to consider in starting a business. Now let's look at some of the different kinds of **occupations** (*jobs*) from which you might choose when you get older. There are three general types of occupations:

- Using the land
- Making things
- Providing services

USING THE LAND: FARMING, RANCHING, FISHING AND MINING

Farming, ranching, fishing and mining are all occupations that use the land and its natural resources. **Farmers** are involved in **agriculture** (*growing crops*). To grow crops, farmers use **fertilizers** that add minerals and other nutrients to the soil. The number of people involved in agriculture has been declining. Over 80% of New York's farms have disappeared since 1900.

Harvesting on a modern American farm
What has been the trend in agriculture since 1900?

Despite the fact that the number of farms have declined, farming continues to be an important occupation in New York State. New York's main agricultural products include apples, grapes, strawberries, cherries, pears, onions, potatoes, cabbage, sweet corn, green beans, cauliflower, field corn, hay, wheat, oats and dry beans.

❖ CONTINUED

Ranchers are people who raise **livestock** such as cows, chickens and pigs. Livestock are often sold for meat. Some farmers in New York State raise cows for their milk. They process milk into dairy products such as cheese, butter, yogurt and ice cream. Many dairy farms are located in the Appalachian Plateau. The major livestock animals in New York are cattle, hogs, pigs, sheep and poultry.

People at work on a ranch raising livestock
What job do ranchers perform?

Fishermen catch fish from rivers, lakes and oceans. At one time fishermen worked on the Hudson River. However, fishing there has disappeared because of polluted waters. Fisheries now exist mainly along the coast of Long Island. The Great South Bay of Long Island is the nation's leading area for harvesting hard clams.

Miners dig or drill deep holes in the ground to find minerals such as coal. At one time, mining iron ore was an important occupation in the Adirondacks. However, the discovery of a better quality ore in the South and the Midwest of the United States led to a decline in iron mining in the Adirondack region. New Yorkers continue to mine salt, zinc, aluminum, talc and garnet (*a stone used in jewelry*).

MAKING THINGS: MANUFACTURING AND INDUSTRY

Many people work at making things. Economists call this type of occupation **manufacturing** or **industry**. Most people with jobs in industry work in factories. **Factories** are buildings in which goods are made. Manufacturing is important to New York. Aircraft, cameras, computers, medicines, furniture, glass, paper, television equipment, toys, and printing equipment are just some of the many goods manufactured here.

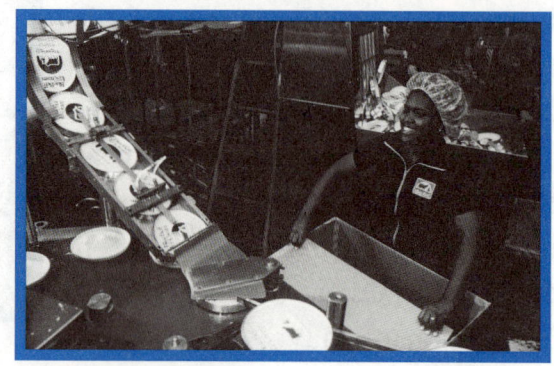

A factory where ice-cream is made
Are there factories in your neigborhood?

New York is one of the nation's largest producers of manufactured goods. Many important manufacturers have their factories in New York. These include I.B.M., General Electric, Kodak and American Telephone and Telegraph. Workers in New York work in such high-tech industries as computers, aircraft and medical instruments.

❖ CONTINUED

SERVICES: TRANSPORTATION, FINANCE EDUCATION, ENTERTAINMENT, SALES, NEW-MEDIA

Today, most people do not actually make goods. Instead, they work in **service industries**. These workers provide **services** to others.

Transportation. People who move goods from one place to another provide a service. The construction of the Erie Canal in the 1800s helped make New York a major transportation center. Buffalo, Albany, Ogdensburg, Oswego and Rochester became important trading centers. With over 110,000 miles of roads, truck transportation is a major occupation in New York. The state has over 500 airports. Kennedy and La Guardia are two of the busiest airports in the nation.

Finance. New York is the financial capital of the world. The New York Stock Exchange and American Stock Exchange are located in Manhattan. Many of the nation's largest banks are found in New York. In addition, more than 100 foreign banks have branches throughout the state. Along with the stock brokerage and insurance companies, they employ thousands of workers in the financial industry.

Higher Education. New York State has traditionally been a leader in education. There are two public university systems in New York State. The **State University of New York** has over 30 colleges and universities. The **City University of New York** has branches in each of the five boroughs. Together these systems help to educate thousands of students and employ thousands of teachers, administrators and support personnel. New York State is also home to many leading private colleges and universities—Columbia University, Cornell, Vassar, New York University and St. John's University.

Entertainment. The entertainment industry is also a major employer in New York State. All three major television networks—ABC, NBC and CBS—have their headquarters in Manhattan. Theaters, movies and the recording industry employ countless others. New York City has the nation's largest number of theaters for plays and musicals. New York State also leads the nation in producing books, magazines and newspapers.

Retail and Personal Services. Another type of service, retail sales, is provided by people who buy goods in large amounts and resell them to individual consumers. This is what a department store or grocery store does. Still others serve us by giving us information, teaching us, cleaning our clothes, cooking and serving our food, and watching after our health. Doctors, lawyers, grocery store cashiers, teachers, nurses, telephone operators, waiters and hair dressers all provide us with services.

◆ CONTINUED

New-Media. The new-media industry consists of small companies that develop and market Internet sites, multimedia software, on-line computer entertainment and other digital offerings. This industry is growing rapidly. It now employs more workers in New York than traditional media like television, book publishing and newspapers. New-media has grown in New York because of the large number of young designers, artists, writers and computer programmers living here who are skilled in computer technology and the Internet.

FINDING OUT ABOUT OCCUPATIONS

New York is a leading area for many different fields of work. What occupation do you think New York is best known for? Explain.

EXPLORING YOUR COMMUNITY
REPORTING YOUR LOCAL ECONOMIC NEWS

Entrepreneurs often try to create excitement about their business in order to increase sales. For example, a store may decide to carry a new national brand or a shopping mall may decide to modernize. Although reports of these events are not carried in national newspapers, they often make news locally.

FINDING LOCAL ECONOMIC NEWS

Let's find out what such an event might look like if it were turned into a newspaper story. In this section you will act as a news reporter. You will write about the economic life of your community. You may report about a recent event like the opening of a new store. Or you may focus on a particular occupation, like the work of a doctor, police officer, secretary or factory worker.

To find out more about the event or occupation, you should interview a member of your community who knows about it. For example, if you live in Corning, you might interview a glass blower. If you live in Rochester, you might take a tour of a Kodak factory.

◆ CONTINUED

WRITING A NEWSPAPER ARTICLE

Before you begin, let's look at some of the steps involved in writing a newspaper article.

❖ First, get your parent's permission to speak to **one** business person, government official or community member who is willing to help you with a class assignment. Then ask that person what is new and important in the economy of your community.

❖ A news reporter always writes an article in the "third person." This means using "he" or "she" rather than "I." The tone of the article should be neutral. You are reporting the news, not writing an editorial which expresses your opinions.

❖ Your article should have a headline to catch the reader's attention. For example, "New Store To Open In Main Street Mall."

❖ The article's first paragraph is known as the "lead." It gives readers an idea of what the article is about. The rest of the article spells out the details. News articles are written so that readers can learn the basic information quickly. Then, if they wish, they can continue reading the article to learn more details. The lead should be interesting, so that the reader will want to find out more. For example,

> To most people, Jones' Pharmacy on Main Street is just another store. Not so to Mark Williams, the man in the white coat behind the counter. As a pharmacist, his job is often filled with excitement. Mr. Williams recalled how one day he saved the life of a young child by ...

❖ A newspaper article reports facts to its readers. After reading your article, a person should have the answers to certain basic questions:

- **Who** was involved?
- **What** happened?
- **Where** did it happen?
- **When** did it happen?
- **Why** did it happen?

❖ Like all good writing, preparing for a news article requires careful work. First, a reporter uses reference tools to develop knowledge about the topic of the article. Then the reporter visits the place that the article is about, to interview the person involved.

❖ Once your article is completed, bring it to class. Compare your article with those of your classmates. Then put the articles together in a class newspaper devoted to some of the interesting economic news taking place in your community.

HOW WOULD YOU PROMOTE THE ECONOMY OF NEW YORK STATE?

5D

In this activity, you will look at New York's many important resources. Then you will design a campaign to help convince foreign businesses to locate in your state. Look for the following important words:

▶ Investments ▶ Natural Resources ▶ Minerals

New York Daily
Vol. 1.4 No. 7 — First Edition

Governor Meets With Foreign Officials In An Attempt To Attract Business To New York

New York Daily
Vol. 1.4 No. 7 — First Edition

Japanese Company Considers Opening New Plant In New York

You may have noticed similar headlines in your local newspaper. New York, like other states, tries to attract foreign companies to invest in New York State. These ▶ **investments** (such as building factories or relocating business to New York) can mean more tax dollars for the state treasury and more jobs for state residents.

Many factors attract foreign investors to a state. A key factor is the availability of educated and skilled workers. Another important factor is the existence of valuable ▶ natural resources. **Natural resources** are materials found in nature that are available for human use. They include both the water and land used to grow food and the minerals we use to make products. New York is a state rich in many natural resources.

As you read the following paragraphs, think about how these resources might attract potential investors to our state.

THE NATURAL RESOURCES OF NEW YORK

FORESTS

One of New York's most valuable natural resources is its forested land. More than 18 million acres of forested land cover half of the state. They provide recreation areas in which people can hike, fish, take nature walks and camp out. In addition, a major lumber industry has developed on these lands. New York's trees include sugar maples, red maples, white birches and pine. Some of these trees are cut down and used to make paper, lumber, plywood and other wood products.

MINERALS

▶ A **mineral** is something useful that is found in the ground. New York has many important minerals. During the Ice Age, receding glaciers left large amounts of gravel and sand throughout the state. Zinc is also mined in New York; so is gypsum for use in building materials. Salt is used for animal feed and for melting ice on roads. Iron ore is used to make iron and steel products. Garnets are used for jewelry and sandpaper, while talc is used in the production of paints and talcum powder.

Shipping logs from the Adirondacks (1919)
Are forests still an important resource in New York State?

WATER

New York's 70,000 miles of rivers and streams and 5,300 square miles of lakes provide a key resource. The Great Lakes and the waters off Long Island are centers of fresh and salt water fishing. Commercial fishermen in New York haul in millions of pounds of fish each year. New York is a major supplier of clams, lobsters, oysters, flounder and scallops to the nation. Water is also important in producing electricity. For example, dams at Niagara Falls produce much of the power for New York's homes and businesses.

Rowing on one of New York's many lakes
In addition to recreation, why are New York's waters an important natural resource for the state?

SOIL

Although many people think of New York as a great urban state, it is also important in agriculture. Its soils are fertile and much of its land is used for farming. New York farmers grow grapes, apples and vegetables. They also raise poultry, hogs, sheep and dairy cattle. Dairy products are an important part of the agricultural scene. Only Wisconsin produces more dairy products than New York.

✔ CHECKING YOUR UNDERSTANDING ✔

1. Describe some of New York State's many important natural resources.
2. List some of the products in your home that may come from New York State.

FAMOUS NEW YORKERS

Alfred E. Smith (1873–1944). One Governor who was very successful in promoting New York's economy was Alfred E. Smith. Born in New York City, in 1918 Smith became the first Roman Catholic to be elected Govenor of New York. He later won three more terms in office. Smith was a popular and forceful Governor. He sponsored many important public works around the state—building bridges, office buildings, hospitals, parks and prisons. He increased state money to aid schools. He introduced new laws to help workers injured on the job. Smith brought many new jobs to the state. To pay for these programs, Smith convinced the state legislature to pass New York's first income tax. In 1928, he ran unsuccessfully against Herbert Hoover for President.

Alfred E. Smith

CREATING AN ECONOMIC PROFILE OF NEW YORK STATE

The Governor of New York State has many responsibilities. One of the most important is to help the state's economy. Imagine that the Governor has asked you to design an advertisement to attract companies to New York State.

Before you can begin this task, you will need to gather information about the economy and resources of our state. Use an almanac or encyclopedia to conduct your research. On a separate sheet of paper, complete as much of the following information as you can find:

I. The Geography and People of New York State

Total Area: _____ Acres of Forest Land: _____
Climate: _____
Major Geographic Features: _____
Population: _____ Rank in Population: _____
Population Density: _____

II. The State's Economy

Major Natural Resources: _____
Major Industries: _____
Chief Agricultural Crops: _____
Major Ports: _____
State Taxes on Business: _____
Average Household Income: _____
Educational System: _____
Unemployment Rate: _____

III. Other Information about the State

Major Tourist Attractions: _____
New York State Motto: _____
Famous People Born in New York State: _____
Other Information About New York State: _____

DESIGNING YOUR ADVERTISEMENT FOR NEW YORK STATE

Closing

On a separate sheet of paper, create an advertisement to be read in a foreign country or another state. Which information should you focus on to emphasize New York's many advantages? Remember, as a member of the Governor's committee, your goal is to attract businesses to locate in New York State. In carrying out that goal, keep in mind that:

❖ artistic talent is **not** important for designing the ad
❖ creating an interesting advertisement is essential
❖ search magazines and newspapers for pictures to use in your advertisement
❖ you may want to ask your parent for help in taking photographs to use in your advertisement

304 NEW YORK: ITS LAND AND ITS PEOPLE

REVIEWING YOUR UNDERSTANDING

Creating Vocabulary Cards

Investments
What are examples of investments?
How can investments help the State of New York?

Natural Resources
What are "natural resources"?
Name three natural resources found in New York State:

Examining a Product Map of New York

As you have learned in Unit 2, maps come in different shapes and sizes. They can also provide different kinds of information. The following map is a type of theme map called a **product map**. Examine it and then read the Skill Builder on the following page. It will help you to interpret the map.

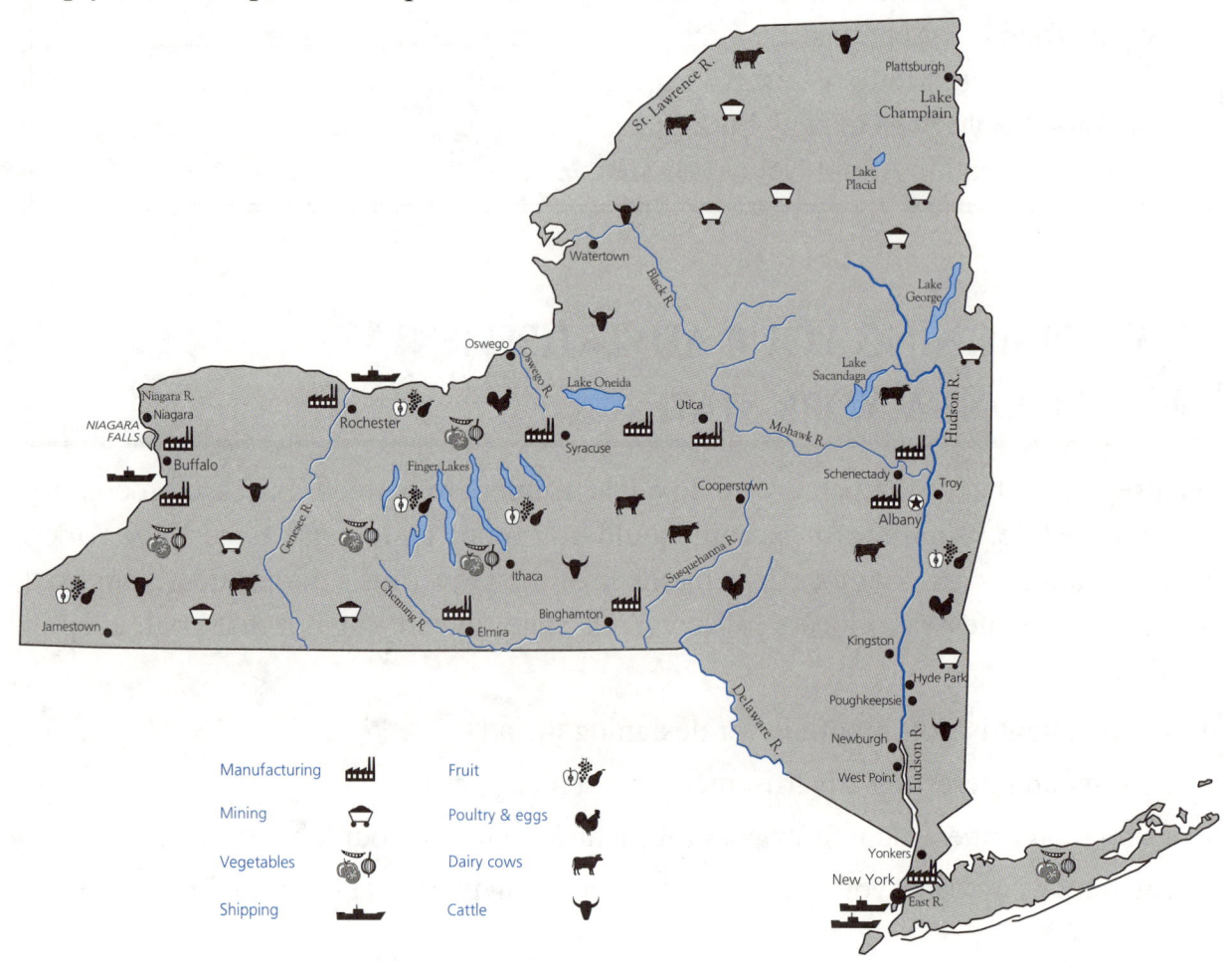

Manufacturing
Mining
Vegetables
Shipping
Fruit
Poultry & eggs
Dairy cows
Cattle

Skill Builder: INTERPRETING A PRODUCT MAP

WHAT IS A PRODUCT MAP?
On a product map, picture symbols are used to stand for various agricultural, mineral and manufactured products. Crops and animals are agricultural products. Valuable resources found in the soil are mineral products.

- Name **two** crops grown in New York State.
- Name **two** animals raised in New York State.
- Name **a** mineral found in New York State.

THE LEGEND OR KEY
The legend explains what each symbol represents. For example, each area in New York State that grows fruit is shown on the map with a small picture of different types of fruit.

- What does the 🛒 symbol stand for?
- What does the 🐄 symbol stand for?
- What symbol is used for poultry and eggs?
- What symbol is used for shipping?
- What city is located closest to where poultry is raised?
- In what parts of the state does mining take place?
- What two cities are located closest to where dairy cows are raised?

✔ CHECKING YOUR UNDERSTANDING ✔

Let's check your understanding of some of New York's natural resources and the products made from these resources. Make a copy of the following list. If the item is:

- **a natural resource**, mark **NR**
- **a product**, mark a **P**

1. forests	4. lumber	7. bricks	10. clothing	13. zinc
2. garnets	5. chemicals	8. books	11. plastics	14. talc
3. apples	6. plywood	9. calculators	12. paper	15. steel

MAKING CONNECTIONS

EXPLORING BEYOND YOUR STATE
THE RESOURCES OF THE UNITED STATES

In this activity, you learned about the variety of resources in New York State. However, New York is only one of the 50 states. What do you know about the resources of your country, the United States?

LAND

The United States has almost 5 million square miles of land. One-fifth of the land is fertile enough to grow crops. The Atlantic Coastal Plain, prairies, Great Plains and California's Central Valley are the main farming regions.

The United States is generally blessed with moderate temperatures, abundant rainfall and some of the world's richest soils. As a result, our nation grows enough food to feed its people. There is even enough food left over to export to other nations.

In California and Florida, great quantities of fruits and vegetables are grown. In Idaho, Maine and New York, potatoes are an important crop. Soybeans are raised in the Great Lakes region and in the Midwest. Tobacco, hogs and poultry are found in the Carolinas. In Texas, beef, poultry and wheat are among the main agricultural products. Cotton is grown in Texas, Louisiana, Mississippi and Alabama. Corn is grown throughout the Midwest. In the mountain areas of the West, farmers raise sheep and goats. In the Dakotas, Minnesota, Wisconsin and Iowa there are many dairy farms.

MINERAL RESOURCES

The United States is rich in mineral resources, including oil, gas, iron and coal. Other mineral deposits include gold, silver, uranium, phosphates, bauxite, mercury, nickel, potash, tungsten and zinc.

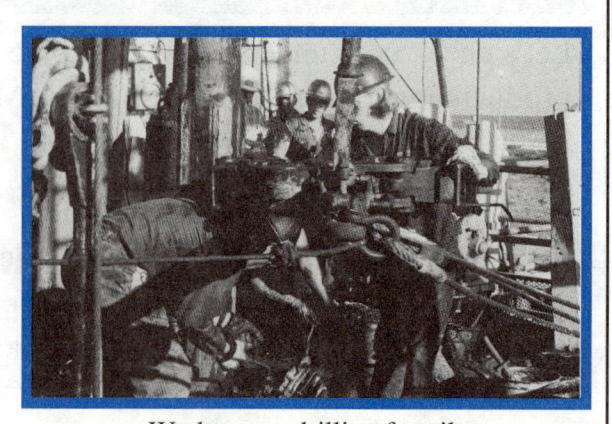

Workers are drilling for oil.

◆ CONTINUED

HUMAN RESOURCES (PEOPLE)

The skills and know-how of the American people have contributed greatly to the success of the American economy. Our system of public education has helped develop our skilled work force and our inventiveness. The United States is a leader in manufacturing and technology, producing such items as computers, electronic products, military hardware, automobiles and aircraft. The nation also has an advanced service industry. Americans specialize in scientific research, software development, medicine, banking, finance, entertainment and engineering. With all of these advantages, the United States is able to produce many goods and services.

CREATING A PRODUCT MAP OF THE UNITED STATES

Earlier in this activity you learned about a New York product map and how it is used. What would a product map look like for the United States? Using the information you just read on this and page 306, create your own product map. Make a copy of the map of the United States. Create your own legend. The symbols you create will be up to you. However, be sure you assign a symbol to each product mentioned.

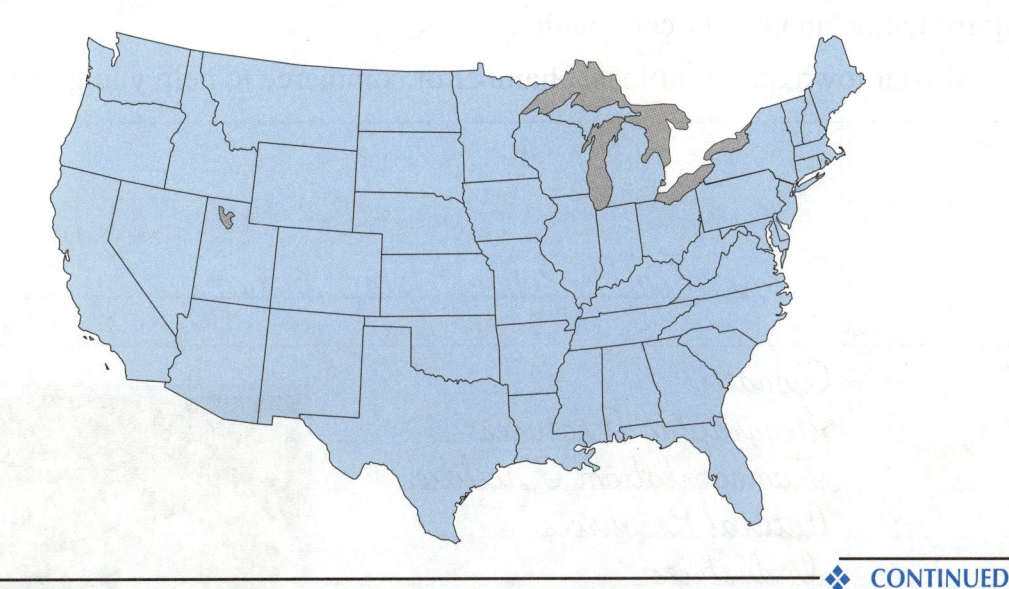

❖ CONTINUED

✔ CHECKING YOUR UNDERSTANDING ✔

1. Name **two** major crops grown in the United States.
2. Name **two** types of livestock raised in the United States.
3. Name **two** minerals mined in the United States.
4. Name **one** product manufactured in the United States.
5. Name **two** services that Americans perform.

EXPLORING YOUR COMMUNITY
AN ECONOMIC PROFILE OF YOUR COMMUNITY

In this activity you created an economic profile of New York State. What about the community where you live? What is it best known for? What are its chief crops, its major industries and most important businesses? In order to help you focus on the answers to some of these important questions, let's create an economic profile.

CREATING AN ECONOMIC PROFILE OF YOUR COMMUNITY

Where can you find the information you will need to complete your economic profile? There are several good sources of information at your fingertips:

- Talk to your parents and other adults about what information they can supply about the economy of your local community. Make a copy of the chart below on a sheet of paper. Then ask them to help you complete the chart.
- Visit your school or local library and ask the librarian to help you find economic information about your community.
- Call your town offices or local chamber of commerce to help you gather data.

Economic Profile of My Community: ___?___

Climate:
Geographic Features:
Transportation Facilities:
Natural Resources:
Industries:
Agricultural Products:
Service Industries:
Tourist Attractions:
Local Government Policies (such as local sales tax):

The Catskill Game Farm attracts many visitors each year.

HOW INTERDEPENDENT ARE WE WITH FOREIGN COUNTRIES?

5E

In this activity, you will learn how people in different countries have become economically interdependent (*they rely or depend on each other*). Look for the following important words:

▶ Interdependent ▶ Exports ▶ Imports ▶ Hypothesis

Technologies like the telephone, fax, television, jet planes and computer are said to be "shrinking" our world. Of course, the world isn't actually getting smaller; it just seems that way. Because of these new technologies, people now have more contact with distant places than they had earlier.

THE WORLD'S GROWING INTERDEPENDENCE

This increased contact has made people around the world much more interdependent. Nations are **interdependent** when they rely on trading with other nations for goods and services. For example, many American jobs are based on selling **exports**. Exports are goods and services sold from the United States to other countries.

A foreign ship unloads containers in New York.

> New York State accounts for almost 25% of the nation's exports. One out of every eight jobs in New York is related to exports. New York exports food, machinery, instruments, chemicals and transportation equipment.

The United States also relies on imports. **Imports** are products from other countries brought into the United States for sale.

> New York is a leading importer. It has two major areas for goods coming into the United States: New York City and the ports in the Great Lakes District. Like the rest of the nation, New York imports more goods than it exports.

Other countries also depend on importing products from America and exporting products to us.

310   NEW YORK: ITS LAND AND ITS PEOPLE

> How many goods in your house do you think come from foreign countries?
> ❏ less than half   ❏ about half   ❏ more than half

▶ At this point, your answer is only a hypothesis. A **hypothesis** is an educated guess; it may or may not turn out to be right. In this activity, you will find out if you "guessed" correctly. To do this, you will conduct an inventory of items in your house.

MAKING AN INVENTORY IN YOUR HOME

Let's begin by looking at the contents of any two rooms of your home. Examine only furniture, lamps and other objects that you can easily move.

❖ You will find that many things have the name of the **country of origin** (*country where they came from*) stamped or printed somewhere on them. For example, in the kitchen you might find a can of coffee. Look closely at its label. You will see that it probably came from Brazil or Colombia. If you cannot identify where an item came from, move on to another one.

❖ If an object is made in the United States, include it on your list. You are not just looking for foreign made items, but also things made in America. If an item has been partly made in two countries, list the names of both countries (Example: USA/Spain).

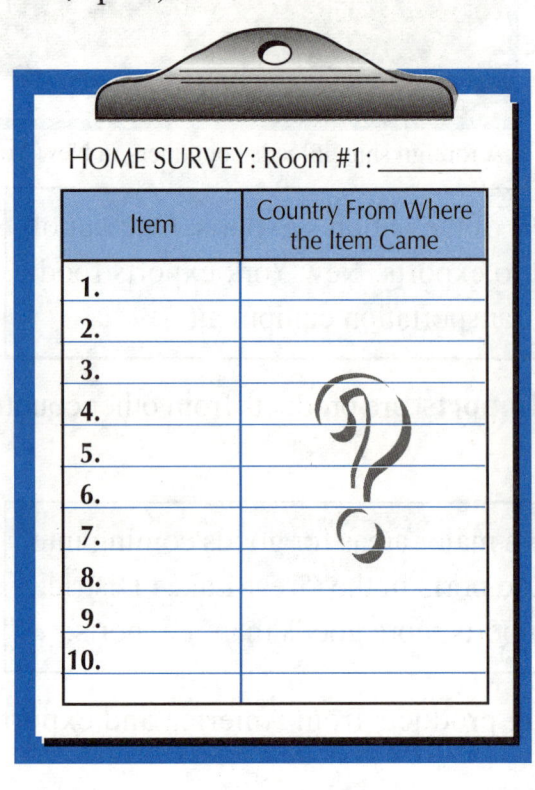

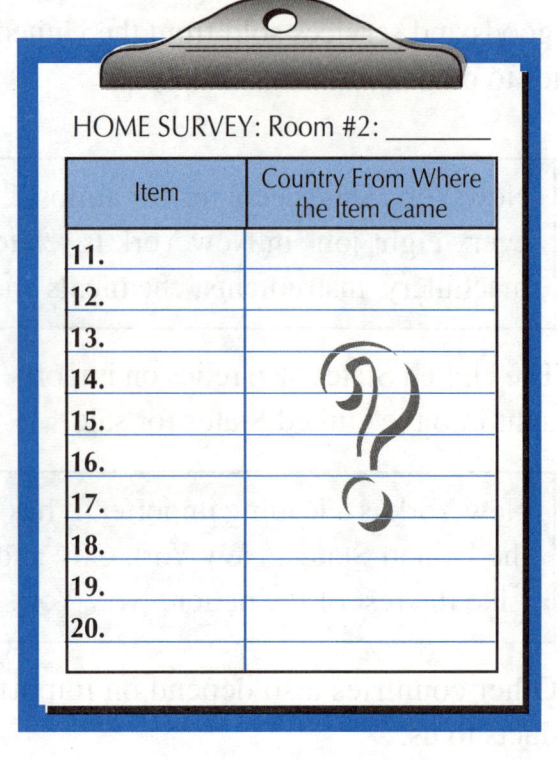

HOME SURVEY: Room #1: _____

Item	Country From Where the Item Came
1.	
2.	
3.	
4.	
5.	
6.	
7.	
8.	
9.	
10.	

HOME SURVEY: Room #2: _____

Item	Country From Where the Item Came
11.	
12.	
13.	
14.	
15.	
16.	
17.	
18.	
19.	
20.	

FIGURING THE PERCENTAGE OF IMPORTED PRODUCTS

Make a separate list of all the countries on your chart. Next to each country, write the number of items you found from that country in your two rooms. Convert that number into a fraction by dividing the number of items from each country by the total number of items in your survey. For example, if you found

$$\frac{2 \text{ items from Brazil}}{20 \text{ is the total number of items}} = \frac{2}{20} = \frac{1}{10}$$

In this case, one out of every ten (one-tenth, or 10%) of the items came from Brazil.

You may have studied **percentages** in your mathematics lessons. (*A percentage is a fraction with a denominator of 100.*) Percentages make it easier to compare different fractions. Turn each fraction into a percent by using a calculator. Divide the **numerator** (*top number of the fraction*) by the **denominator** (*bottom number of the fraction*). This method will show you the percentage of products in the two rooms that were made in the United States and that came from other countries. Use the following chart to help you keep track of your calculations.

Country	Number of Products	Fraction	Percent
1.			
2.			
3.			
4.			
5.			
6.			

THINK ABOUT IT

1. Was the percentage of products from the United States more than half (*over 50%*)?
2. Which country, other than the United States, supplied the most products in your inventory?

312   NEW YORK: ITS LAND AND ITS PEOPLE

MAPPING THE COUNTRIES OF ORIGIN

Get a copy of an atlas from your school or public library. Use the atlas to locate each country on your home inventory chart. Make a copy of the world map below. Then list the items around the outside margin of the map. Finally, draw a line from each item to the location of its country of origin. For example, if one item in your home inventory was coffee, you would write the word "coffee" in the margin surrounding your map. Then you would draw a line from that word to its country of origin—probably Brazil or Colombia.

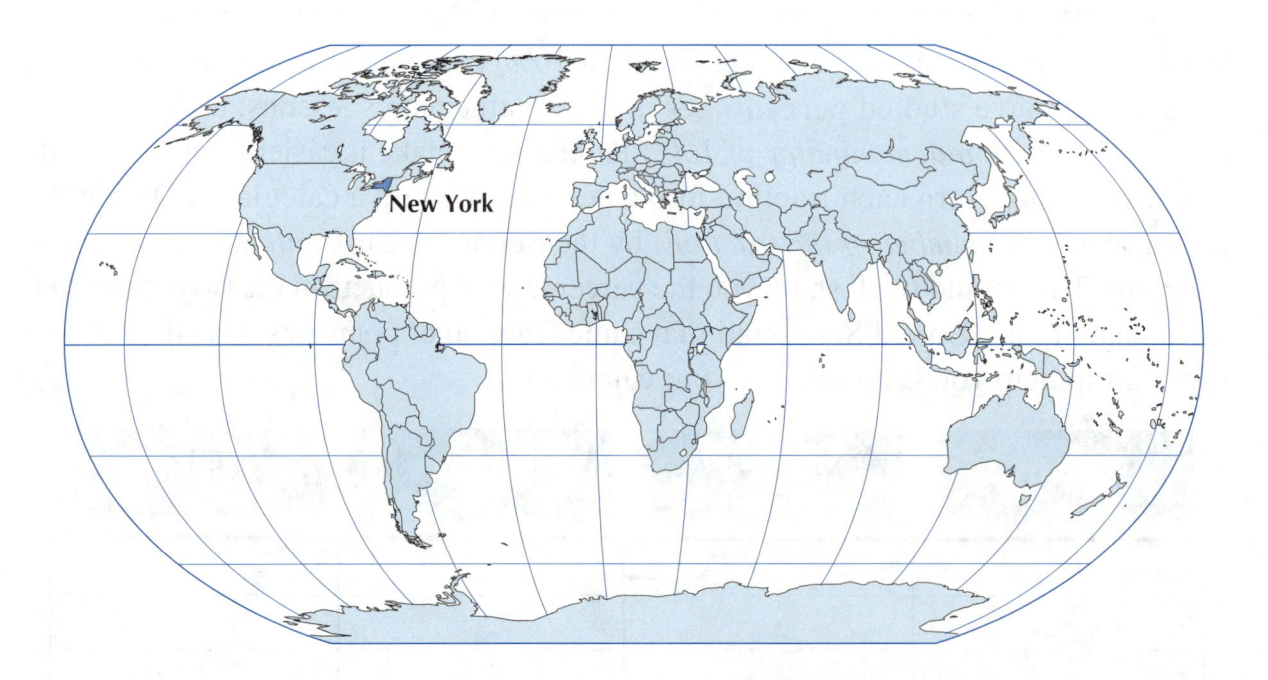

✔ CHECKING YOUR UNDERSTANDING ✔

1. How many items in your inventory came from foreign countries?
2. How accurate was the original hypothesis you made when you began this activity?
3. Were you surprised by the results of your inventory?   ❑ Yes   ❑ No
   If so, how? If not, why not?
4. What conclusions about global interdependence can you draw from the results of your inventory and those of your classmates?

ECONOMICS 313

REVIEWING YOUR UNDERSTANDING

Creating Vocabulary Cards

Exports
What is an export?
Name a product that is exported from the United States:

Imports
What is an import?
Name a product that is imported into the United States:

Learning About Our Major Trading Partners and What We Trade with Them?

In this activity, you learned about the interdependence of New York State and the United States with foreign countries. Which foreign nations does the United States trade with the most? What goods do we most often export? What do we most often import? In activity 2G, you learned how to use an almanac. Let's get some further practice in using this important reference tool. Use an almanac to find the answers to the following questions:

MAJOR TRADING PARTNERS OF THE UNITED STATES

1. Which nations do we export the most goods to?
2. Which nations do we import the most goods from?
3. What kinds of products do we sell the most to other nations?
4. What kinds of products do we buy the most from other nations?

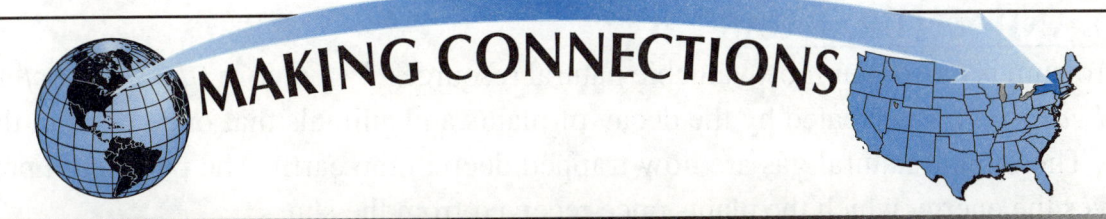

MAKING CONNECTIONS

EXPLORING BEYOND YOUR STATE
WHY NATIONS TRADE WITH EACH OTHER

In this activity, you learned how people in one part of the world often depend on trade with people in other parts of the world. One of the reasons that nations trade with each other is that natural resources throughout the world are unevenly distributed.

❖ CONTINUED

THE UNEVEN DISTRIBUTION OF RESOURCES

Because of the uneven distribution of natural resources, one nation often needs resources found in other nations. They get these resources by trading with each other. Japan, for example, has very little oil, but is a major producer of automobiles. Japan needs fuel for its factories, electricity, cars and heating needs. Saudi Arabia, on the other hand, has a lot of oil, but lacks a large automobile industry. As a result, Japan buys oil from countries like Saudi Arabia. Saudi Arabia uses the money it gets from selling oil to Japan to buy products such as cars from Japan and other manufacturing countries.

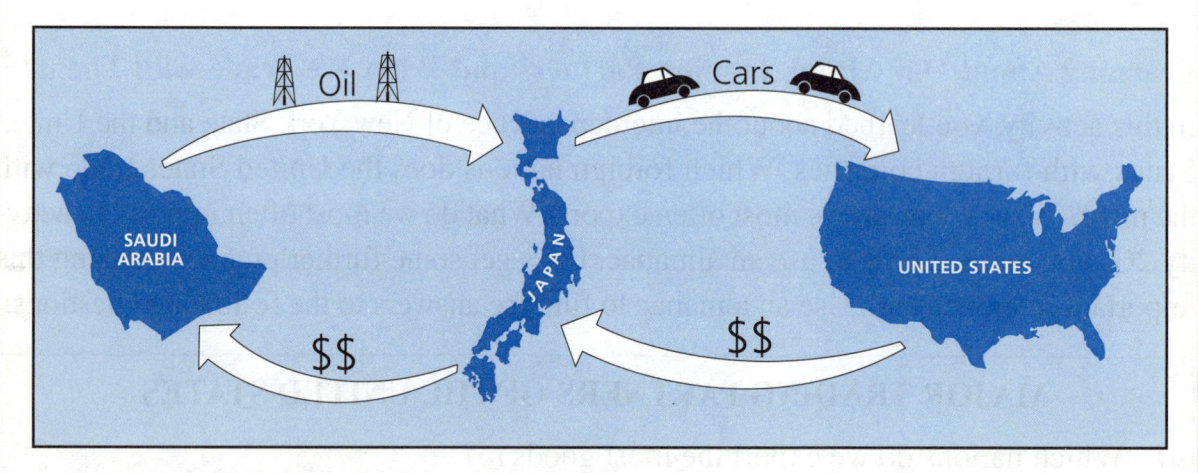

Through trade, the Japanese can concentrate on what they do best: manufacture products. They exchange these manufactured products (*such as cars*) for the natural resources they need (*oil*). The two maps on page 315 show the distribution of several important natural resources throughout the world.

OIL AND NATURAL GAS

Petroleum is one of our most valuable natural resources. **Petroleum** (*the source of oil and gasoline*) was created by the decay of plants and animals that once lived in the sea. The oil and natural gas are now trapped deep in the earth. The petroleum preserves the energy which the plants once received from the sun.

The energy from the petroleum is released when the oil and gas are burned. For this reason, oil and natural gas are used to meet our energy needs. They are valuable because modern countries burn billions and billions of gallons of these resources each year. However, oil and gas are found only in those areas where conditions have allowed them to be trapped. Finally, oil is more valuable than natural gas because it is easier to transport.

▸ CONTINUED

ECONOMICS 315

WORLD OIL AND NATURAL GAS DEPOSITS: 1995

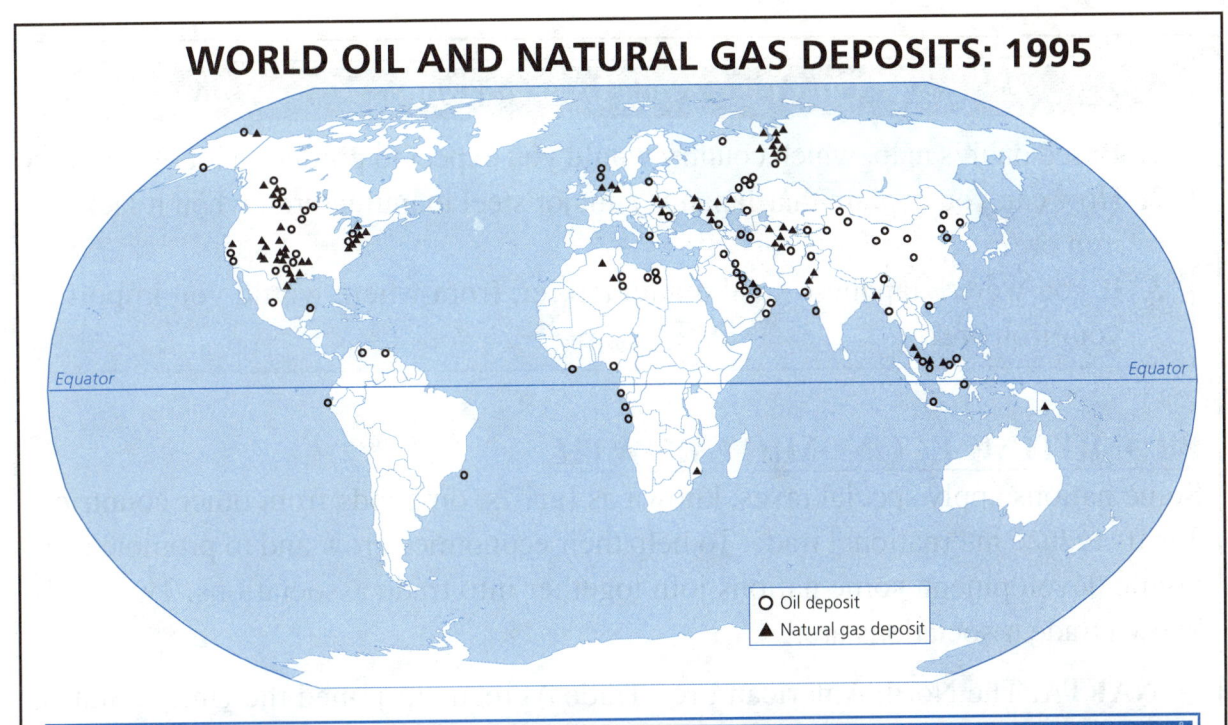

○ Oil deposit
▲ Natural gas deposit

✔ Checking Your Understanding ✔

1. Based on this map, which areas of the world do you think export the most petroleum?
2. Which areas of the world do you think need to import petroleum?

IRON ORE

Iron ore is necessary for making both iron and steel. Steel is used to make machinery, beams for buildings, automobiles, airplanes and a large number of other products.

WORLD IRON ORE DEPOSITS: 1995

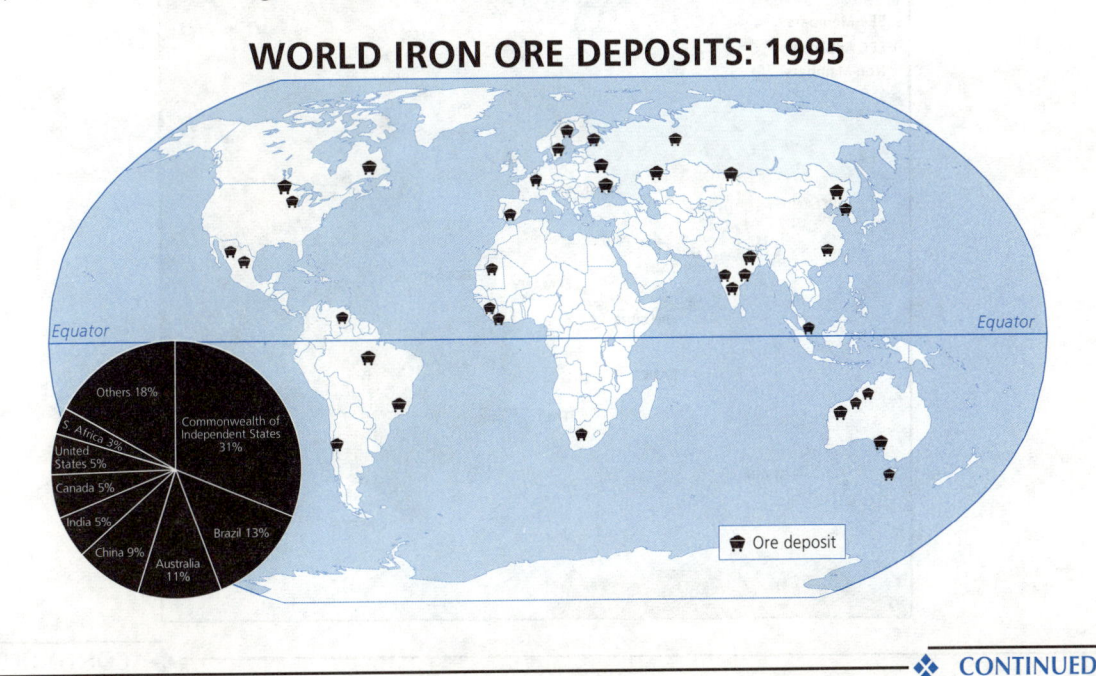

Ore deposit

- Commonwealth of Independent States 31%
- Brazil 13%
- Australia 11%
- China 9%
- India 5%
- Canada 5%
- United States 5%
- S. Africa 3%
- Others 18%

◆ CONTINUED

> ✔ **CHECKING YOUR UNDERSTANDING** ✔
>
> 1. Based on this map, which country would you expect to produce a lot of steel?
> 2. How can you explain that Japan is a major steel manufacturer, when it lacks iron ore?
> 3. If you were a Japanese steel manufacturer, from where would you import your iron ore?

PROMOTING ECONOMIC GROWTH

Some nations apply special taxes, known as **tariffs**, on goods from other countries. Tariffs reduce international trade. To help their economies grow and to promote economic development, some nations join together into trade associations. Two well-known trade associations are:

❖ **NAFTA.** The North American Free Trade Agreement joined the United States, Canada and Mexico together. In this trade association, each nation agreed to eliminate most tariffs on goods from the other two members.

❖ **The European Common Market or E.E.C.** Most countries of Western Europe now belong to this association. Member nations are allowed to trade goods freely among themselves without having to pay tariffs.

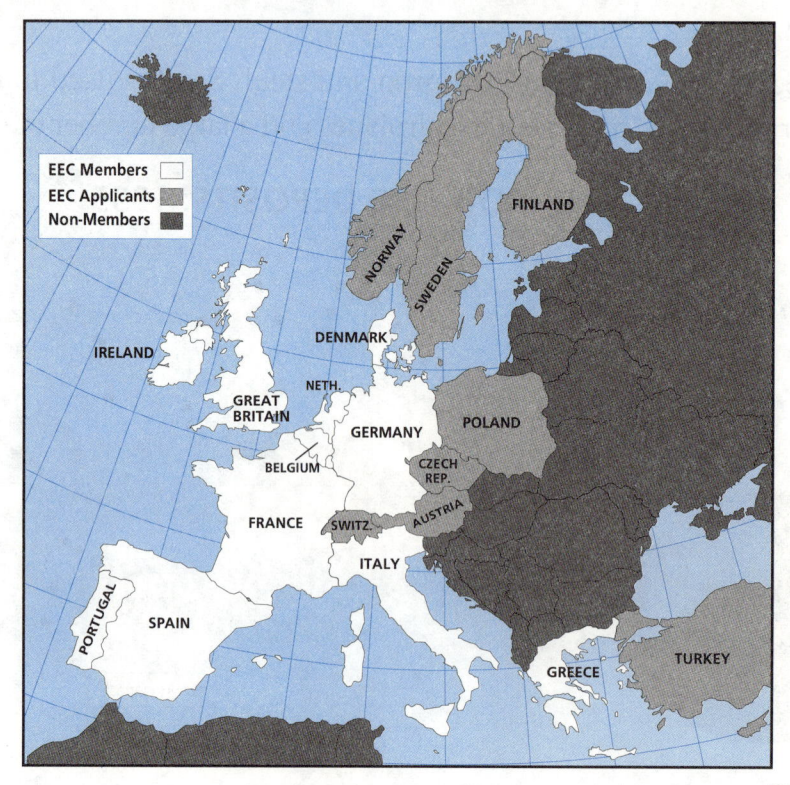

❖ CONTINUED

EXPLORING YOUR COMMUNITY
SHOPPING FOR FOREIGN GOODS IN YOUR NEIGHBORHOOD

Items made in far-off lands were once extremely rare. Today, they are common in many homes. To find such products often requires you to go no farther than your neighborhood stores.

LOOKING AT COMMUNITY STORES

Let's explore your neighborhood stores to see how many goods from distant lands can be bought there.

❖ The class should be divided into several groups. Group members should visit a neighborhood store. Once there, make a list of **four** items sold in the store that are produced in foreign countries. The best stores to explore are grocery stores, department stores and specialty shops.

❖ Remember to look for the "country of origin" label on each product (*or the store's labels on the shelf*) to find where the product originally came from. U.S. laws require foreign-made goods to be labeled. This shows consumers they are buying a foreign-made product. The product must have been made outside of the United States.

A neighborhood yarn shop
Do you think there are any goods in this store that have come from foreign lands?

Store in the Community Where the Product is Sold: _____?_____

Continent	Country	Description of Item
North America		
Europe		
Asia		
Africa		

318 NEW YORK: ITS LAND AND ITS PEOPLE

SUMMARIZING YOUR UNDERSTANDING

Directions: Use your knowledge to fill in the blanks in the following graphic organizers.

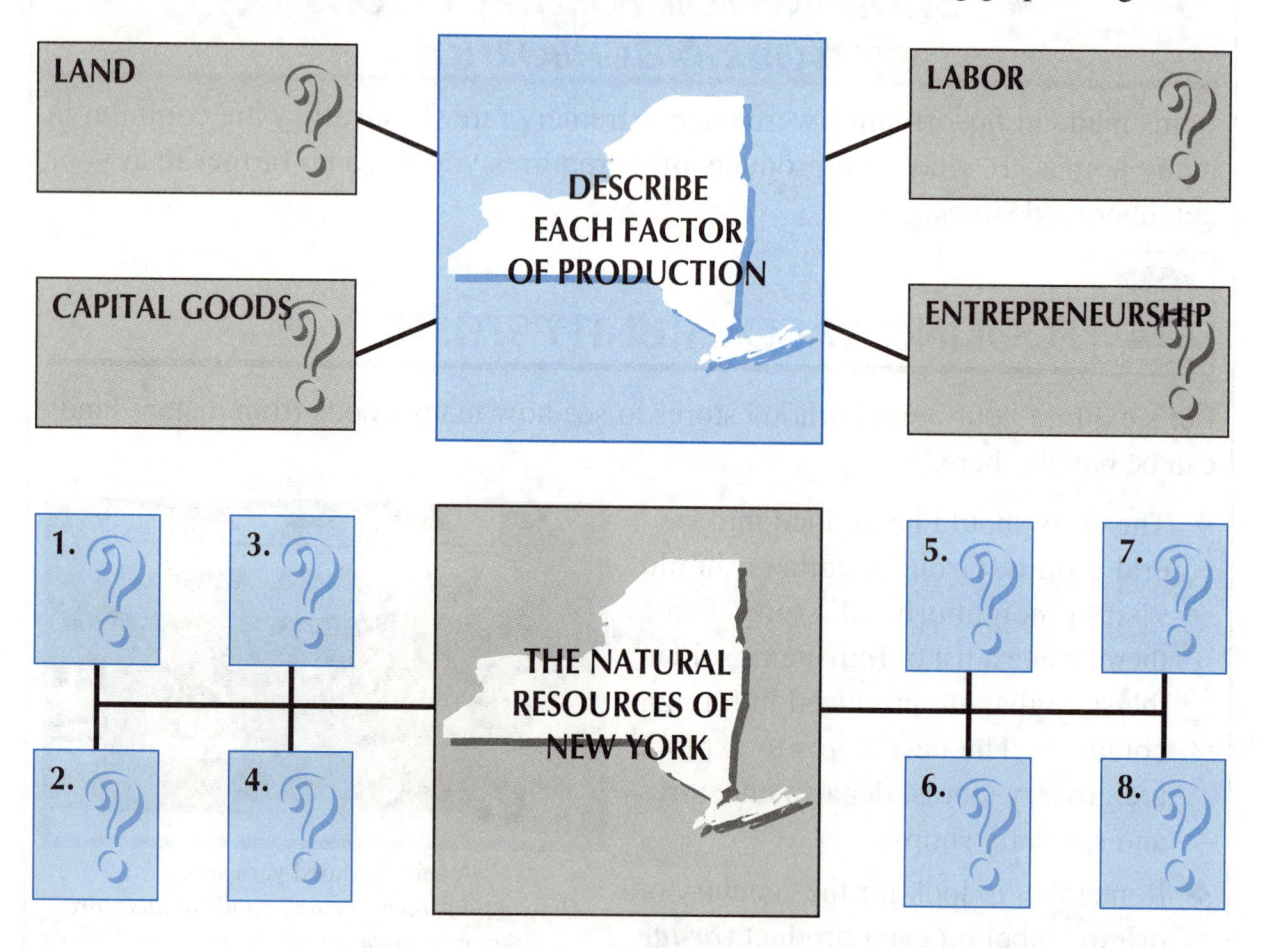

- LAND
- CAPITAL GOODS
- LABOR
- ENTREPRENEURSHIP

DESCRIBE EACH FACTOR OF PRODUCTION

THE NATURAL RESOURCES OF NEW YORK

1.
2.
3.
4.
5.
6.
7.
8.

THE DIFFERENCE BETWEEN A GOOD AND A SERVICE

Copy the chart below. Then write whether the person involved in each occupation sells a good *or* performs a service:

Does this Person <u>Sell a Good</u> or <u>Perform a Service</u>?			
Barber		Teacher	
Auto Mechanic		Pharmacist	
Doctor		Electrician	
Baker		Police Officer	
Grocer		Tailor	

ECONOMICS 319

INFORMATION SHEET #4: ECONOMICS

CREATING ITEMS FOR YOUR EXHIBIT

Following is a list of tasks for your project. These are suggestions, so feel free to add those others that you think would best show the economy of your town or city.

CREATING AN ECONOMIC MAP

Your town or city may have an industrial park where factories are located. It may also have a mall where people do their shopping. Create an economic map of your town or city. On your map show the following:

❖ Shopping malls
❖ Industrial parks
❖ Unemployment office
❖ New businesses
❖ Farms
❖ Banks

A neighborhood bank
What things will you include on your economic map?

CREATING A COMPANY STORE OR MUSEUM DISPLAY

Often, businesses are the driving force in the development of a community. You can learn a great deal about the history of your town or city by visiting a business that has its own museum or conducts tours of its plant. In Illion, near Utica, for example, you can visit the Remington Firearms Museum. In 1816, Eliphalet Remington, made a new type of barrel to improve the accuracy of rifle bullets. This was the start of the Remington Arms Company. The company museum displays a variety of old-time posters, typewriters and other memorabilia from the company's past.

Your town or city may have similar businesses tied to the history of the community. Choose a business whose history goes back to an earlier period of time. Create a museum display that shows the history of the company and how it parallels the history of your town or city.

❖ CONTINUED

MAKING A PICTURE PLATE

A few years ago, the Department of Motor Vehicles began selling custom designed license plates to New York motorists. These plates were created for eleven different regions in the state. In addition, plates were also created for fans of the New York Rangers, Buffalo Bills, and the New York Yankees. Design a "Picture Plate" for your town or city using a copy of the blank frame below. Your plate should demonstrate pride in your community. Also try to create an interesting saying on your license plate—using no more than seven letters or numbers.

NEW YORK

Your Town City or Name

CREATING AN ADVERTISEMENT

New York is home to many of the nation's largest advertising companies. Advertisements are an excellent means to inform and to motivate people to buy a new product. Towns and cities have also used ads. For example, New York City advertises itself as the "Big Apple." Create an ad for your own town or city. If you live in New York City, focus on your borough or neighborhood. Use pictures to get your message across. Also write the words to go along with the pictures.

CREATING A TOWN OR CITY EDUCATIONAL DIRECTORY

Public education is one of the most important responsibilities of government. Education has been handled by state and local governments throughout New York's history. New Yorkers take pride in their schools. On average, New York spends more than any other state on educating its students. Create a directory of your school district and two colleges in your area. You should provide:

- the official name and address of the school district's headquarters
- the name and address of one public and one private college
- the type of college: community college, four-year college or business school

UNIT 6
GOVERNMENT

President Clinton addresses Congress

Governor Pataki signs a bill

New York City's Mayor Giuliani delivers an address to the city

Every society has some kind of government. A government makes laws and has a system to punish people who break the laws. The government also provides a way for people to cooperate. They can work together through the government to make new laws or to change laws they believe are unfair. In this unit, you will find out how governments are organized. You will also learn some of the main features of your local, state and national governments.

A YOUNG AUTHOR STRUGGLES THROUGH THE NIGHT

Thomas Jefferson, a tall, red-haired Virginian, sat alone at his desk. Candles lit up the large, spacious room. It was a hot Philadelphia night in July 1776, and sweat rolled from his brow.

Thomas thought about the exciting events of the past few years. He remembered the taxes that the English Parliament had forced on the American colonists. The Americans had had no voice in deciding whether these taxes were fair. Then Thomas thought about his own role in leading the young representatives in the colonial assembly of Virginia against these policies. The dispute with England over taxes had quickly led to war.

Thomas had been one of Virginia's representatives to the Continental Congress in Philadelphia. George Washington, another Virginian, was appointed to lead the Continental Army. But the English had sent thousands of well-trained troops to fight the colonists. Thomas thought it would be hard for the colonists to win against such a well trained army. Perhaps he and the other members of the Continental Congress would be hanged as traitors if the colonists lost.

The Continental Congress knew that it needed the support of most colonists in order to win the war. A few key members of the Congress had formed a committee to write a public announcement. This announcement would explain to the colonists and to others around the world why the 13 American colonies should declare independence from England. The other members of the committee were older and more experienced than Thomas. But they thought that he would do the best job in writing the declaration. Now it was all up to him.

Thomas Jefferson

Thomas was only 33 years old. He was

an experienced writer and lawyer. However, the burden of his task was enormous. Could he write something so powerful that it would inspire his fellow countrymen to support independence? Could he also convince France to enter the war on the side of the Americans, against the English?

Thomas paced back and forth between the fireplace and the open windows of his parlor room. Again and again he wondered: What should he say in the declaration? What could he write that would inspire others to be willing to risk their lives for independence?

Thomas' thoughts went back to his days at college and his favorite teacher, Dr. William Small. Dr. Small had often spoke of the many types of governments. He had also discussed the great variety of views about which type of government was the best.

In recalling these ideas, many new questions entered Thomas' mind. What did the future hold for the American colonies? Would each colony break away and become a separate and independent country? Or would each of the colonists be willing to give up some power in order to unite the other colonies together into a single country? What kind of government should they pick? Should they become a democracy—a government in which the people choose their own government officials? Could such a system of government work in a new and inexperienced nation?

Thomas put down his feather pen on the desk and stared blankly out the window. A cool breeze entered the room. His mind was filled with conflicting emotions. He felt both fear and hope as he thought about the future. What could he write in the declaration that would make things easier for his fellow countrymen in the difficult years ahead?

As you read through this unit, you will learn the answers to these and other questions about the American system of government that raced through the mind of Thomas Jefferson on that warm summer night over two hundred years ago.

WHAT RULES WOULD YOU MAKE FOR YOUR CLASS?

In this activity, you will learn how governments work by writing a set of rules for your class. Look for the following important words:

▶ Rules ▶ Laws ▶ Penalty ▶ Charter

To help you, the ▶ appears in the margin where the **term** is first explained.

▶ In order to get along together, people develop rules of behavior. A **rule** tells people to do or not to do something. Good rules ensure decency, consideration and comfort in our dealings with others. With rules, we know how to behave and how we can expect others to behave. Good rules are fair. They make sure that everyone has equal rights and responsibilities.

LAWS AND PENALTIES

▶ **Laws** are rules that are made by the government. Once a law is made, there is a ▶ **penalty** for breaking it. For example, a law may state that cars must stop if a traffic light is red. If a car does not stop at a red light, the driver has broken the law. The penalty for breaking this law is that the driver must pay a fine.

✔ CHECKING YOUR UNDERSTANDING ✔

Can you list a "rule" in society that tells us something we **cannot** do? What is the penalty for breaking that rule?

CREATING RULES FOR A CLASS CHARTER

Imagine that it is the first day of school. Your teacher begins by talking about writing a ▶ class charter. A **charter** defines the rules of behavior for a group. Your teacher says these rules will be made up by the class. The class must keep in mind that the rules must protect the rights of class members and allow them to do their work without distraction. In addition, the rules must be accepted by both your teacher and principal. As an example, your teacher suggests the following rule about class tests: *all failing test papers must be signed by a parent or guardian.*

Now it's your turn. Let's see how good you are at making rules and penalties for your class. What rules and penalties can you suggest? Some topics for rules are listed below:

YOUR SUGGESTIONS FOR A CLASS CHARTER

Tests
Rule:
Reason:
Penalty for breaking the rule:

Classroom Behavior
Rule:
Reason:
Penalty for breaking the rule:

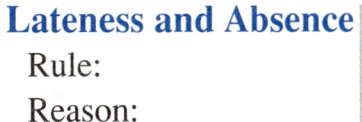

Homework
Rule:
Reason:
Penalty for breaking the rule:

Grades
Rule:
Reason:
Penalty for breaking the rule:

Lateness and Absence
Rule:
Reason:
Penalty for breaking the rule:

Other Topics
Rule:
Reason:
Penalty for breaking the rule:

REACHING AN AGREEMENT ON YOUR CLASS CHARTER

Are your rules and penalties similar to those of other students? Compare your list with those of your classmates and teacher. Try to come to a **consensus** (*agreement*) on a set of class rules. Be sure to include the penalty as part of the rule. List the rules below on a separate sheet of paper. Then submit them to your teacher for approval.

Rules for the Class Charter

Rule #1:

Rule #2:

Rule #3:

Rule #4:

Rule #5:

REVIEWING YOUR UNDERSTANDING

Creating Vocabulary Cards

Rules

Define the term "rules":

Give an example of a rule:

Charter

Define the term "charter":

Why would a society need a charter?

The Rules and Laws of Your Community

You may not realize it, but rules and laws affect how you live each day. This can be seen in many different ways. For example, look at the following pictures.

Picture #1

Picture #2

What do these pictures tell you about what you should and should not do? These signs are probably similar to some of the signs in your own community. Find **two** signs or notices of rules or laws in your community. For each sign or notice:

❖ write, draw or photograph what is written on it
❖ explain the meaning of the rule or law

MAKING CONNECTIONS

EXPLORING BEYOND YOUR STATE
THE RISE OF GOVERNMENTS

People are social creatures; they need to live with other people in groups or communities. Can you imagine what disorder would result if we could do anything we pleased without regard to other people? A community needs to protect its members against such disorder. As a result, communities must make rules to settle disagreements among members and to protect the community from those who violate the rules. A **government** is the organization that makes a community's rules, settles its disputes and protects its members from others who may be hostile.

THE FIRST GOVERNMENTS

The earliest societies were probably small tribes of people who wandered the countryside hunting animals and gathering plants to eat. We do not know how they governed themselves. Most likely, in some tribes a group of the oldest adults made the decisions. In other tribes, the strongest, wisest or bravest person may have enforced the rules.

About 10,000 years ago, peoples in the Middle East and North Africa learned how to plant seeds, make tools and grow their own food. This led to people settling in villages. These advances brought both benefits and problems. People now had more food, but faced attacks by neighboring groups. Some villages grew in size, and village life became more complex. There was a greater need for rules in order to settle disputes.

Primitive tribesmen making tools
How did planting seeds, making tools and growing food lead to the development of governments?

About 6,000 years ago, the first great civilizations arose in Egypt, Iraq, China and Pakistan. They are often called **city-states** because they usually centered on a single city. Each was governed by a ruler who claimed to be chosen by the gods. The

❖ CONTINUED

ruler controlled the lives of the people. He or she made laws, settled disputes, collected taxes and maintained an army.

Over the next several thousand years, this form of government spread. In the Middle East, Europe, India and China, powerful city-states conquered neighboring areas. Sometimes the conquered areas were added to the city-state. As a result, some city-states grew into vast **empires**, ruling over several areas. This happened, for example, in Egypt and China. In these empires, the central government made laws, collected taxes and built public buildings. Other places, like the cities of Greece, remained small city-states.

China's rulers built a wall to guard against invasions of their vast empire.

THE DEVELOPMENT OF DEMOCRACY

In ancient times, most areas were ruled by kings or emperors. But in a few places small groups of people made decisions. In the city-states of ancient Greece, a new system of government was born about 2,500 years ago. Instead of a ruler telling everyone what to do, the citizens of the city-state made decisions together by electing officials and voting on important issues. This system was called **democracy**—government by the people. This new form of government set a pattern for democracies that would develop many centuries later.

CREATING A TIMELINE

Based on this reading passage and what you have learned in earlier units, create a **timeline** showing when:

❖ the first city-states were established
❖ democracy developed in Greece
❖ New Amsterdam was settled by the Dutch
❖ the United States became independent from England
❖ the U.S. Constitution was adopted

❖ CONTINUED

EXPLORING YOUR COMMUNITY
HOW IS YOUR SCHOOL GOVERNED?

In many ways your school is like a community. Like every community, your school has a system of government. There are different groups—students, teachers, school administrators, parents and school boards—that work together to keep order, promote learning, protect people's lives and safeguard property. What role does each group play in governing your school? Let's find out.

COMPARING SCHOOL RULES

Do you know how your school "government" is organized? For example, who decides when students should eat lunch, or when teachers and students should go home? Who decides if your class can go on a school trip or what books you will use? To find out, work with your teacher to answer the following questions:

The James H. Boyd School on Long Island. Like every school, this one has a system of government to keep order and make decisions.

❖ Is there a student government in your school?

❖ How are the members of your student government chosen?

❖ Describe the procedure followed in your school for making rules.

❖ Who is in charge of carrying out the rules? Give an example.

❖ What does the principal do? Does the principal have any assistants?

❖ What part do parents and teachers play in making school decisions?

❖ How does your school's system of government allow one group of people to check (*prevent*) another group from making changes too quickly? Do you think a system of "checks and balances" is a good idea?

Now that you know the rules of your school, how do they compare with those of other schools? There are many ways to find out the rules that govern other schools. Your class can write a letter to students in other districts. Another way is to use the information highway—the **Internet**—to communicate with other schools.

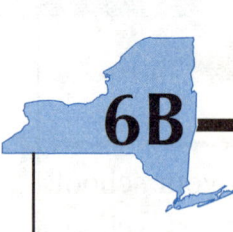

WHO REPRESENTS YOU IN THE NATIONAL GOVERNMENT?

6B

In this activity, you will learn who represents you in the national government. Look for the following important words:

- Government
- Democracy
- Federalism
- Legistlative power
- Executive power
- Judicial power

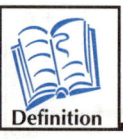

WHAT IS A GOVERNMENT?

In early times, when large numbers of people began living near each other, cities and nations emerged. A need quickly developed for an organization that would maintain order. The organization people set up to protect their community and to make rules for themselves is called a **government**. By making and enforcing rules, the government keeps order, protects people's lives and safeguards property.

TYPES OF GOVERNMENT

Throughout history, three main types of governments have existed. They are monarchy, dictatorship and democracy.

MONARCHY

A **monarchy** is a government in which a king or queen has political power. A king or queen is someone who has inherited power. Often, the king or queen claims to rule by "divine right"—being chosen by God to act as ruler. Sometimes the monarch shares power with an elected law-making body. When the king or queen dies, power passes to one of the monarch's children or relatives.

DICTATORSHIP

A **dictatorship** is a system in which all the powers of government are in the hands of one person or a small group. This person or group seizes power because they claim to know what is best for the society. Often, they use force and violence to maintain their rule. The ruler or group decides

King Louis XIV claimed that God chose him to rule France.

what everyone must do, and is not concerned about what others want. With power concentrated in the hands of a single person or group, people have no rights.

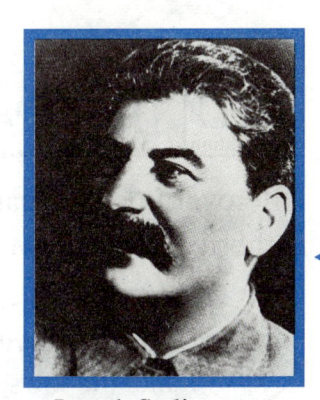

DEMOCRACY

In a **democracy**, the government's power comes from the permission of the people it governs. The people usually decide on important issues by electing officials, called **representatives**. This type of government, known as a **representative democracy**, exists in the United States as well as in other countries around the world.

Joseph Stalin was a dictator of the former Soviet Union.

> We live in a democracy where people elect their officials. Do you know the names of the people who represent you?

Like many Americans, you may not know the names of all the people who represent you. In this activity you will learn about some of these people. Let's begin by looking at how the government of the United States is organized.

THE DIVISION OF POWERS

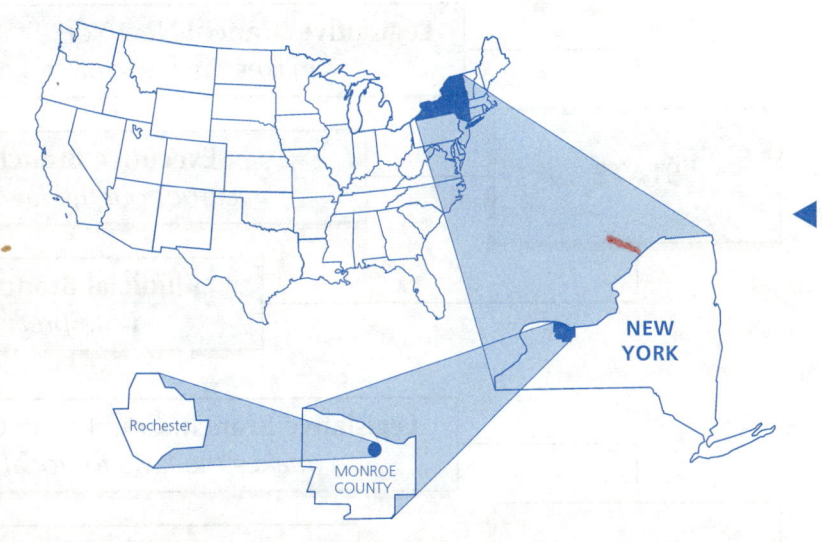

In our system of government, power is shared among several levels of government. This division of government powers is called **federalism**. One level is the **national** (*federal*) government. It deals with matters affecting the whole country, such as the defense of the nation. At another level are **state governments**. Each one handles matters occurring within their state. For example, states make laws about who may drive a car. **Local governments** are a third level. They deal with county, city, town and village matters. For example, local governments maintain and repair neighborhood streets.

THE SEPARATION OF POWERS

All governments—national, state and local—are given three powers to carry out their authority. These powers are:

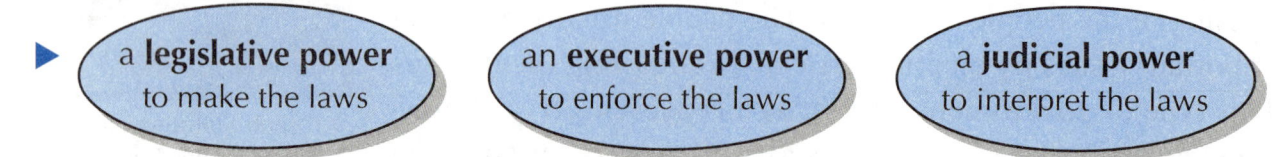

- a **legislative power** to make the laws
- an **executive power** to enforce the laws
- a **judicial power** to interpret the laws

Each level of our government—national, state and local—has created special institutions or **branches** to help carry out these powers. The following chart describes these different levels of government and their branches.

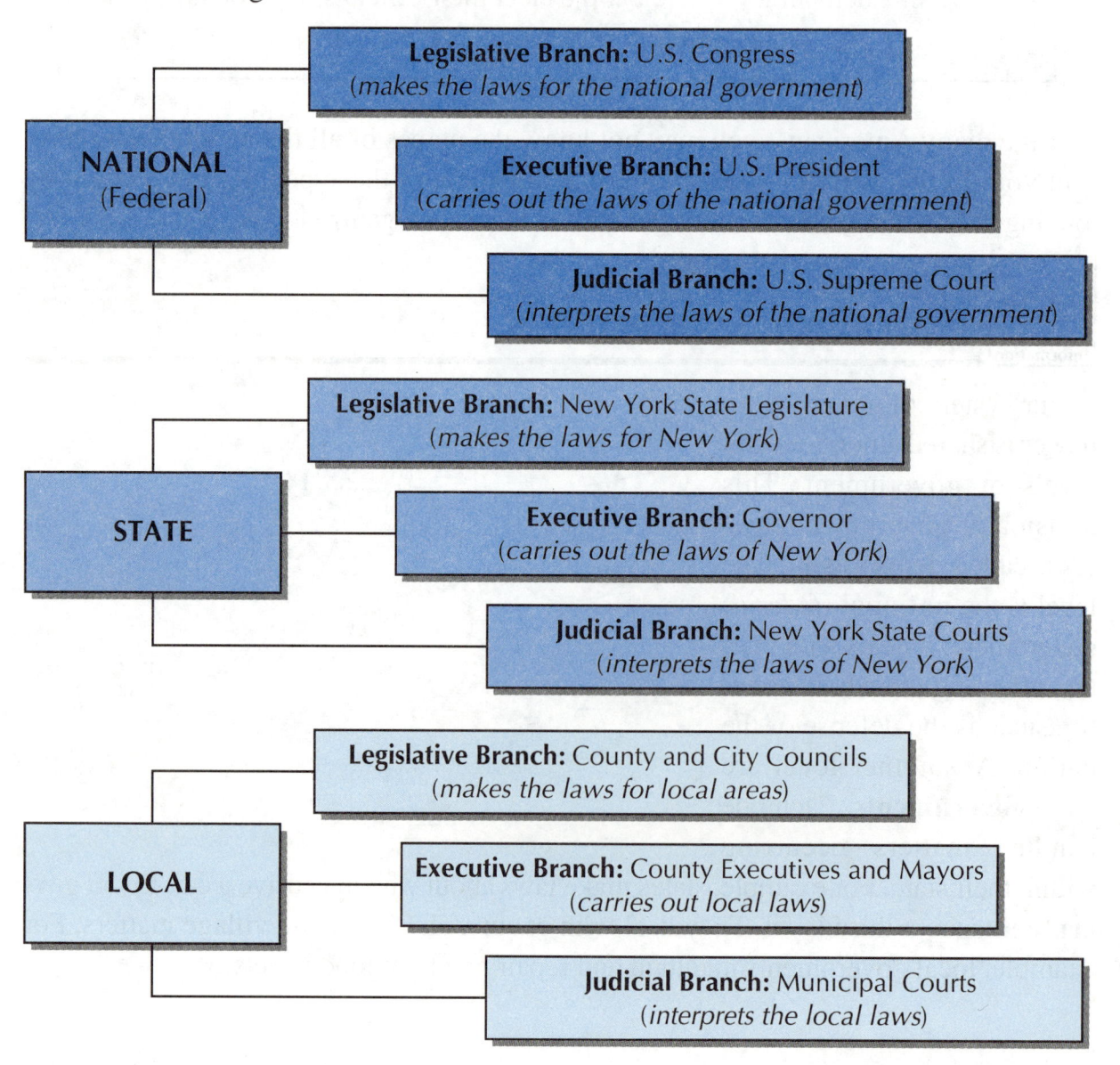

NATIONAL (Federal)
- **Legislative Branch:** U.S. Congress (*makes the laws for the national government*)
- **Executive Branch:** U.S. President (*carries out the laws of the national government*)
- **Judicial Branch:** U.S. Supreme Court (*interprets the laws of the national government*)

STATE
- **Legislative Branch:** New York State Legislature (*makes the laws for New York*)
- **Executive Branch:** Governor (*carries out the laws of New York*)
- **Judicial Branch:** New York State Courts (*interprets the laws of New York*)

LOCAL
- **Legislative Branch:** County and City Councils (*makes the laws for local areas*)
- **Executive Branch:** County Executives and Mayors (*carries out local laws*)
- **Judicial Branch:** Municipal Courts (*interprets the local laws*)

Now let's take a closer look at our national level of government.

OUR NATIONAL GOVERNMENT

LEGISLATIVE BRANCH

Our national government is located in Washington, D.C. The legislative or law-making branch is called **Congress**. The main job of Congress is to make laws for the nation. Congress has two parts, known as **houses** because they meet and vote separately: the **Senate** and the **House of Representatives**.

Each of the 50 states has **two** members in the U.S. Senate. In the House of Representatives, the more people a state has, the more representatives it has. Since 1990, New York State has had 31 representatives. Only California and Texas have more representatives in Congress than New York.

Members of the House of Representatives pose for a picture. How many representatives are there?

	House of Representatives	Senate
Number of members:	435	100
Length of term:	2 years	6 years
Representation is based on:	The size of the state's population	Two from each state
Elected by:	Voters from a particular Congressional district	Voters from the entire state

✔ CHECKING YOUR UNDERSTANDING ✔

How many people represent New York State in the U.S. Congress?

EXECUTIVE BRANCH

The main job of the **executive branch** is to carry out or enforce laws. Our nation's chief executive is the **President of the United States**. The President runs the agencies of the executive branch. For example, he or she is in charge of the Federal Bureau of Investigation (F.B.I.). The President also represents our country to other nations and serves as Commander-in-Chief of all U.S. armed forces. The President lives in the White House in Washington, D.C.

Bill Clinton being sworn in as President of the United States.
What is the main job of the President?

Length of term:	4 years
Number of terms:	A maximum of two full terms.
Qualifications	35 years old, a resident of the United States for 14 years and a native-born citizen

JUDICIAL BRANCH

The role of a **judicial branch** is to interpret the laws—applying them to individual cases that come before the court. The **U.S. Supreme Court** is the highest court in the nation. The Justices of the U.S. Supreme Court base their decisions on our national laws and the U.S. Constitution. There are also other federal courts to enforce our national laws.

Length of term:	Justices serve for life.
How Justices are selected:	Selected by the President, but must also be approved by the U.S. Senate
Number of Justices on the U.S. Supreme Court:	Nine (9)
Qualifications:	There are no qualifications mentioned in the U.S. Constitution for being a Supreme Court Justice.

WHO ARE YOUR REPRESENTATIVES IN THE NATIONAL GOVERNMENT?

Now that you know how the national government is organized, do you know the names and faces of the people who represent you? List the names of the officials who represent you in the national government. Also, try to provide a photograph for each. Use the following sources to help you:

- Visit or call your local office of the **League of Women Voters**.
- Look in your phone book, under government (often in the *Blue Pages*).
- Search local newspapers for pictures of your elected officials.
- Search electronic media, such as the **Internet**.

WHO REPRESENTS YOU AT THE NATIONAL LEVEL OF GOVERNMENT

A. President of the United States:
(name) _____ (photo)

B. Vice-President of the United States:
(name) _____ (photo)

C. U.S. Senators from New York State:
1. (name) _____ (photo)
2. (name) _____ (photo)

D. Your Representative in the U.S. House of Representatives:
(name) _____ (photo)

REVIEWING YOUR UNDERSTANDING

Creating Vocabulary Cards

Government

What is a government?

List one reason for having a government:

Democracy

What is a democracy?

List one characteristic of a democracy:

Identifying Buildings of the National Government

Look at the following photographs. How many of these national government buildings can you identify? Also, identify some of the people who work in each building.

Picture #1

OUR NATIONAL GOVERNMENT

Picture #3

Picture #2

MAKING CONNECTIONS

EXPLORING BEYOND YOUR STATE
OUR MODERN WORLD OF NATION-STATES

The system of **nation-states** first began in Europe. Several European countries were of similar size and strength. Each of these countries developed its own government. People within each country often spoke the same language and shared similar customs. Many people came to believe that each group of people with its own language and customs should have its own separate state and government. From this belief, our modern system of nation states developed.

❖ CONTINUED

IDENTIFYING A NATION'S GOVERNMENT

Our world is divided into almost 200 nations. Many of these nations are democracies, while others are monarchies or dictatorships. Make a copy of the following map showing New York State and the outlines of the countries in the world.

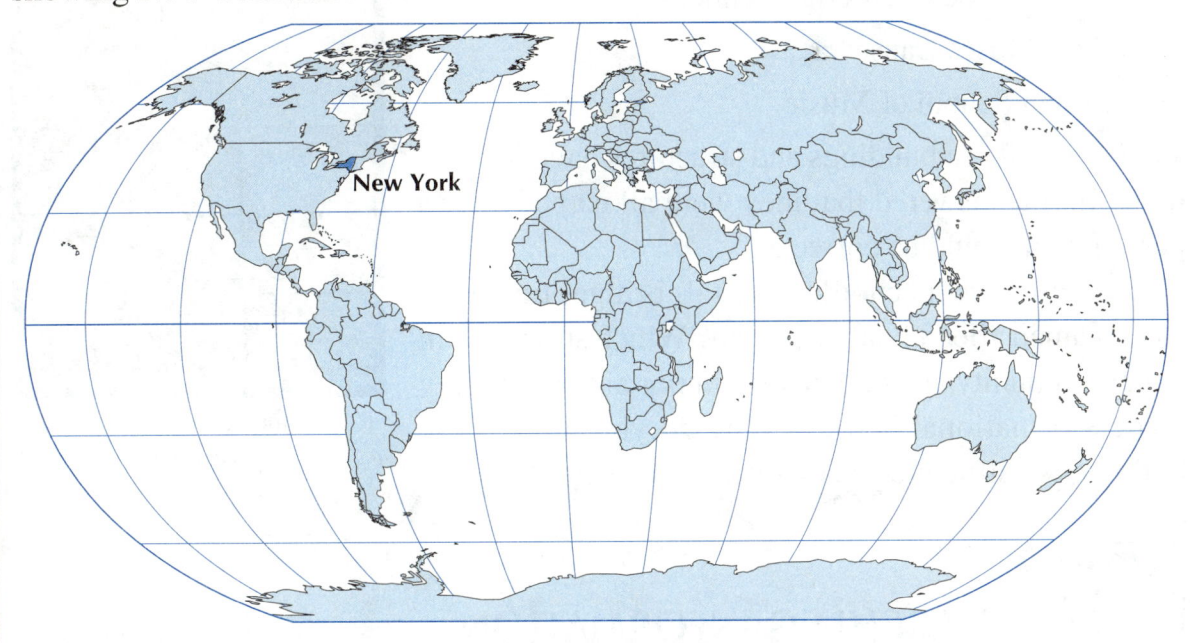

Select **one** country from each of the following areas:

(1) North America (3) Europe (5) Africa
(2) South America (4) Asia

For **each** country, look up its current type of government. This information can be found by looking at:

❖ an **almanac**. Look at a section called: "Nations of the World." The type of government can be found by finding the nation's name and looking under "Government: Type." Consider countries under military rule as dictatorships.

❖ an **encyclopedia** (*printed or electronic*). Look in an encyclopedia or an encyclopedia's current "Yearbook."

Next, find the location of the country on your copy of the map and write in its name. Create a map key or legend for the three types of governments. For example, you might use gray shading with a pencil to show **democratic** nations; black to show that the nation is a **dictatorship**; and blue to indicate that a nation is a **monarchy**. Then, fill in the five countries you have researched based on your coloring system.

EXPLORING YOUR COMMUNITY
WHO IS THAT BUILDING NAMED AFTER?

- Thomas E. Dewey Thruway
- George Washington Bridge
- Theodore Roosevelt High School
- Robert Moses Causeway
- Eastman School of Music

What do all these buildings and structures have in common? If you answered that they were all named after a person, you would be correct.

Do you have a school, hospital, bridge, tunnel or street named after a famous person? Which structures in your community are named after important community leaders or national heroes? Why do you think these buildings or structures were given these names?

Roy Mann Junior High School in Brooklyn

RESEARCHING INFORMATION

To help you find this information, make a copy of the following chart. For each type of building or structure in the chart, list at least **one** example. Then write a brief description telling something about the person who the structure was named after:

Building/Structure	Named After	Brief Description
School		
Hospital		
Government Building		
Street		
Other		

WHO REPRESENTS YOU AT THE STATE AND LOCAL LEVEL?

6C

In this activity, you will learn about our other two levels of government: state and local governments. Look for the following important words:

- New York State Legislature
- State Assembly
- State Senate
- Governor
- County Government
- Town and City Government

The United States is divided into 50 states. Each state has its own government. Each state government has three branches to carry out its powers.

THE GOVERNMENT OF NEW YORK STATE

New York's **state government** handles matters that affect people throughout the state. The state government provides money for schools, builds and maintains state roads, and provides a system of justice. It also protects the safety and health of its citizens. Like the national government, the state government is divided into legislative, executive and judicial branches. It is located in **Albany**, the state's capital. Let's begin our study of state government with a question:

New York State Capitol Building
Which branch of state government meets in this building?

> What are the names of the people who represent you in state government?

In this activity you will learn about the people who represent you in state government. First let's look at how New York State's government is organized.

LEGISLATIVE BRANCH

The legislative branch of New York State government is called the **New York State Legislature**. It makes the laws of New York. The state legislature consists of two houses (*parts that meet and vote separately*): the Assembly and the Senate. The **Assembly** has 151 members. Each member of the Assembly is elected for a term of two years.

340 NEW YORK: ITS LAND AND ITS PEOPLE

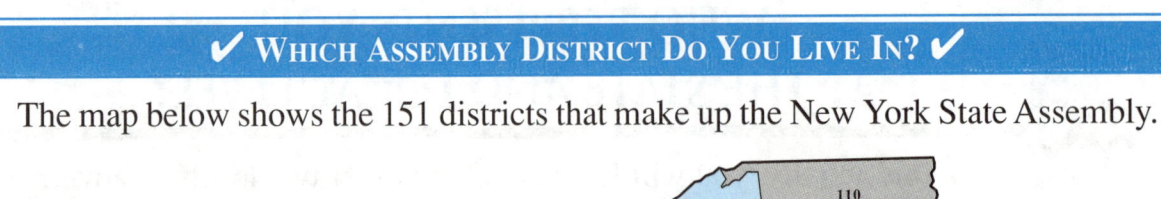

✔ WHICH ASSEMBLY DISTRICT DO YOU LIVE IN? ✔

The map below shows the 151 districts that make up the New York State Assembly.

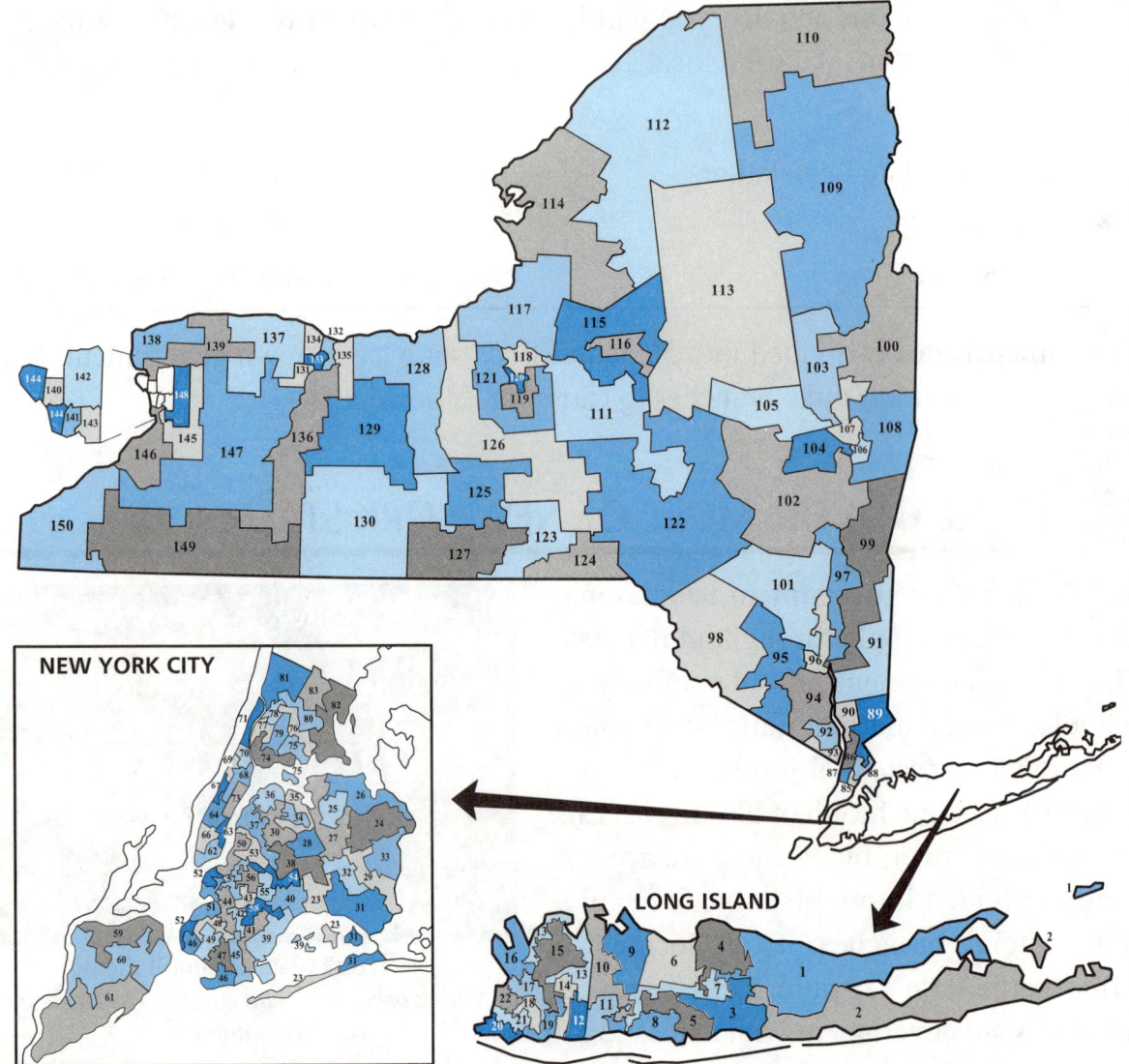

On a separate sheet of paper, answer the following questions:

1. In which assembly district do you live?
2. List the assembly districts that border your district.
3. Why do you think some assembly districts are larger than others?

▶   The second part of the New York State Legislature is the **Senate**. There are 61 members of the New York State Senate. Senators are elected by voters in 61 separate Senate districts. Members of the Senate also serve a two-year term.

✔ WHICH SENATE DISTRICT DO YOU LIVE IN? ✔

The map below shows the 61 districts that make up the New York State Senate.

On a separate sheet of paper, answer the following questions:

1. In which Senate district do you live?
2. Name the Senate districts that border your district.

EXECUTIVE BRANCH

The chief executive of New York's state government is called the **Governor**. The Governor's job is to enforce the laws that have been passed by the New York State Legislature. The chief duty of the Governor is to maintain order in the state. The

Governor is in charge of several departments, bureaus and agencies which help run the State government. He or she is also the Commander-in-Chief of the state's National Guard. In the event the Governor is away from the state or becomes ill, the **Lieutenant Governor** takes over some of the Governor's responsibilities. The Governor and Lieutenant Governor are both elected for a term of four years.

Many Governors of New York have used their position as a stepping stone to the White House. Martin Van Buren, Grover Cleveland, Theodore Roosevelt and Franklin D. Roosevelt were all New York State Governors before becoming Presidents of the United States.

President Van Buren was once Governor of New York. *Which other New York Governors became President?*

FAMOUS NEW YORKERS

George Pataki was born in Peekskill, New York on June 24, 1945. In 1981, he became the youngest Mayor ever of the City of Peekskill. He also served in the New York State Assembly and Senate. In 1994, Pataki was elected the 53rd Governor of New York State. In his first months in office he restored the death penalty, which had been rejected by other Governors for the past 18 years. Pataki also proposed stiffer penalties for people sent to prison several times, and cut state spending for the first time since 1943.

JUDICIAL BRANCH

The highest court in New York State is the **Court of Appeals**—the state equivalent of the U.S. Supreme Court. It is called the state's "highest court" since there is no further appeal from its decisions except to the U.S. Supreme Court. The Court of Appeals meets in Albany. It has seven members, including a Chief Judge. The judges are elected to fourteen-year terms.

New York State Court of Appeals
What does this court and the U.S. Supreme Court have in common?

Focus on Documents: *New York's Constitution*

A **constitution** is a written plan of government. New York State, like our national government, has its own constitution. In 1776, New York and the 12 other colonies declared their independence from Great Britain. The Continental Congress, the governing body during the American Revolution, asked each colony to write a constitution for itself. A convention of New Yorkers met in White Plains and then in Kingston to write such a constitution. On April 20, 1777, the constitution they developed was adopted.

Under New York's first constitution, only property-owners could vote. It also provided that every 20 years the voters of New York State would have a chance to decide if they wanted to revise their constitution. Since that first constitution, nine conventions have been held to revise the constitution.

The Constitution of 1821 added a Bill of Rights for the people of New York. Like the U.S. Constitution, it guaranteed citizens freedom of religion, speech and press, the right to a trial by jury and the right to protest peacefully in groups. The Constitution of 1821 also removed some property qualifications for voting. This made New York a more democratic state.

The Constitution was changed again in 1846. The Constitution of 1846 made our state government even more democratic. It gave the vote to all men over 21, whether they owned property or not.

In the 1890s, dishonesty and corruption in national and state governments became a major problem. New York delegates sought to solve the problem by changing the constitution yet again. The Constitution of 1894 provided a merit system for choosing government employees. The new system required applicants to pass a test to get their job. This constitution presently governs New York State.

LOCAL GOVERNMENT

COUNTY GOVERNMENT

Just as the United States is divided into 50 states, New York State is divided into 62 counties. **County government** dates back to the days when New York was a colony. Counties were first formed because there was a need to build courthouses, jails, poorhouses and orphanages. Today, county governments conduct elections, register voters, collect county taxes, operate courts and provide some health care services.

344 NEW YORK: ITS LAND AND ITS PEOPLE

Some counties are governed by a board of supervisors. Other counties are governed by an elected legislature. In most counties, the chief executive is called the **county executive** or **county manager**

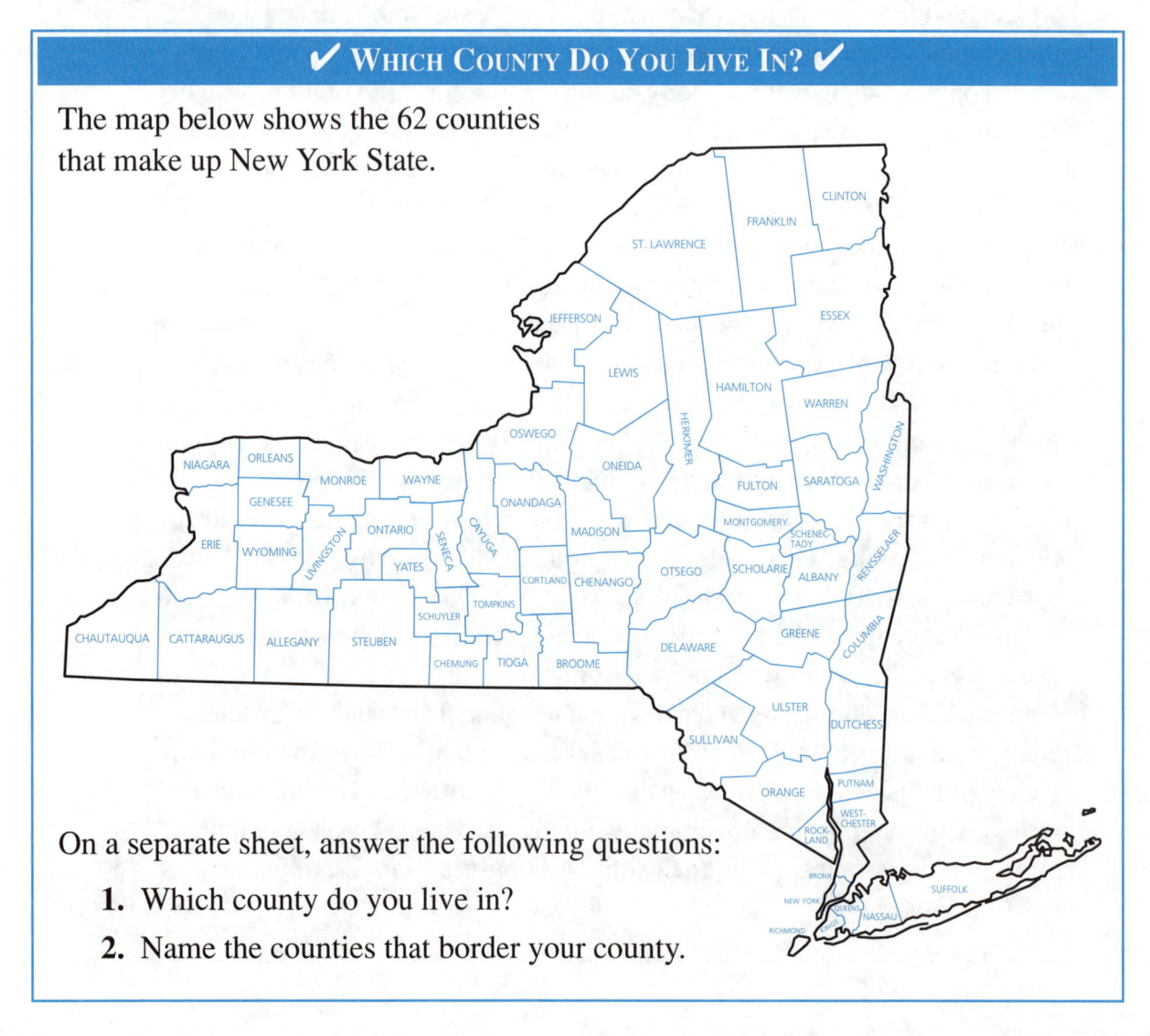

✔ WHICH COUNTY DO YOU LIVE IN? ✔

The map below shows the 62 counties that make up New York State.

On a separate sheet, answer the following questions:

1. Which county do you live in?
2. Name the counties that border your county.

Just as New York State is divided into counties, each county is further divided into cities, towns, villages and special districts.

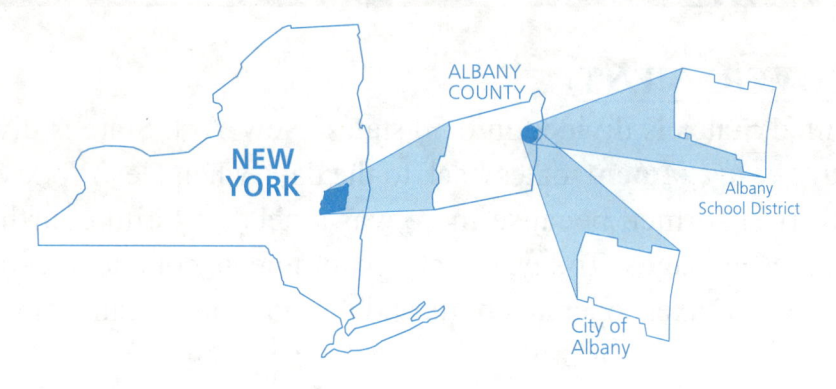

CITY GOVERNMENTS

City governments usually control an area with a large population. They date back to the time when New York was a colony. Today, there are 62 city governments in New York State. Their power extends to regulating and controlling property and managing local affairs.

One exception to the way counties are usually governed is New York City. The City's five counties, called **boroughs**, are governed differently from other counties in the state. All five boroughs are governed as part of New York City. Let's take a look at the four main parts of New York City government:

❖ **Mayor.** The **Mayor** is the chief executive of New York City. The Mayor is elected by all the city voters for a four-year term. The Mayor appoints three deputy mayors and the heads of several city agencies. These agencies perform various city-wide services, such as providing police protection, public transportation and garbage collection. The Mayor also prepares the city's budget along with the Comptroller. The **Comptroller** is the city's chief financial officer. Like the Mayor, the Comptroller is elected by all the voters of the city.

Mayor Guiliani at a ribbon cutting ceremony in New York City
What other jobs does the city's Mayor perform?

❖ **City Council.** The **City Council** serves as the city's law-making body. It is has one representative from each of its 51 districts. The **Public Advocate**, also elected by all the voters of the city, presides at meetings of the City Council. The Public Advocate only votes in case of a tie. The Public Advocate also reviews complaints and recommends improvements in city government services.

❖ **The Borough Presidents.** Each borough elects its own **Borough President**. The Borough Presidents appoint members of community school boards, the Board of Education and the planning commission.

❖ **City Courts.** The city has both civil and criminal courts to apply city laws.

In addition, local communities have their own community planning boards and community school districts. These give communities some "local" control.

FAMOUS NEW YORKERS

Rudolph Giuliani was born in Brooklyn. In 1970, he joined the U.S. Attorney's Office in New York. It was there that he jailed drug dealers, fought organized crime and prosecuted corruption in government. In 1993, he ran for Mayor of New York City. His victory made him the city's 107th Mayor. Since taking office, Giuliani has attacked crime, reformed the welfare system and reduced the city's workforce.

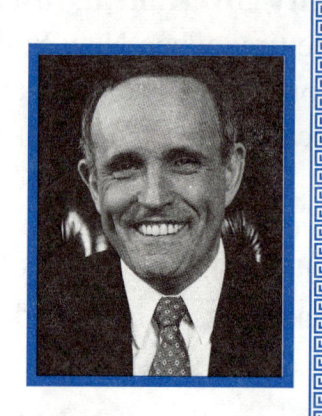

TOWN GOVERNMENT

In New York State, a "town" is a local area under a specific form of government—a township. There are over 930 towns in New York. The number of towns differs from one county to another. For example, there are three towns in Nassau County and 32 towns in Steuben County. **Town governments** usually handle such matters as water, sewage and drainage systems and local roads.

VILLAGE GOVERNMENT

Towns themselves are often further divided into **villages** or smaller units called **hamlets**. These first developed when people in an area wanted a specific service, such as fire protection or street lights. The almost 600 villages in New York vary in size from a few dozen people to more than 40,000 residents. Village governments handle law enforcement, operate water systems, sewers, parks and cemeteries.

DISTRICT GOVERNMENT

Sometimes a need arises for a service that is not provided by a city, town or village. In such cases, a **special district** is created to provide that service. Special districts often provide water, garbage disposal and snow removal. The largest number of special districts are school districts and fire districts.

WHO REPRESENTS YOU IN STATE AND LOCAL GOVERNMENT?

Earlier you identified the elected officials representing you on the national level. Can you also identify the officials who represent you in state and local government? Let's find out. Using the same sources of information from the previous activity, identify and provide a photograph of each of the following elected officials:

WHO REPRESENTS YOU AT THE STATE LEVEL OF GOVERNMENT

A. Governor of New York:
(name) _____ (photo)

B. Senator from your State Senate District:
(name) _____ (photo)

C. Representative from your State Assembly District:
(name) _____ (photo)

WHO REPRESENTS YOU AT THE LOCAL LEVEL OF GOVERNMENT

A. Mayor, City Manager or other local executive:
(name) _____ (photo)

B. County Supervisor or other local legislator:
(name) _____ (photo)

C. County, City or Town Judge:
(name) _____ (photo)

Think About It

Which government officials were the most difficult to find information about? Explain.

REVIEWING YOUR UNDERSTANDING

Creating Vocabulary Cards

New York State Legislature
What is the job of the New York State Legislature?
Which two houses make up the New York State Legislature?

County Government
Define county government.
What types of jobs are county governments responsible for?

348　NEW YORK: ITS LAND AND ITS PEOPLE

Interpreting a Bar Graph: The Governments of New York State

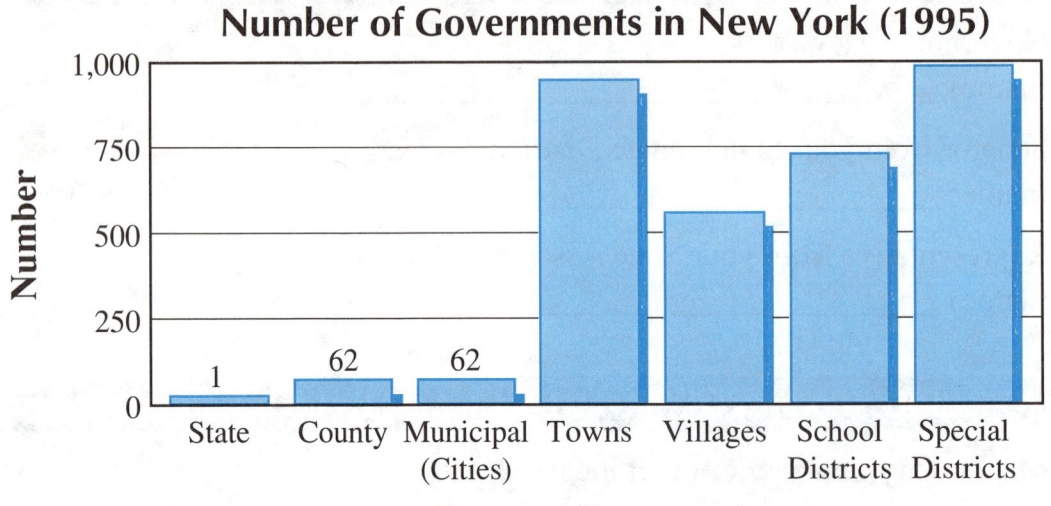

Number of Governments in New York (1995)

Type of Government	Number
State	1
County	62
Municipal (Cities)	62
Towns	~950
Villages	~560
School Districts	~735
Special Districts	~1,000

Types of Government

To better understand this graph, read the following Skill Builder:

INTERPRETING BAR GRAPHS

What Is a Bar Graph?
A **bar graph** is a chart that shows parallel bars of different lengths. It is used to compare several items.

❖ Do you know what items are compared in this bar graph?

Keys to Understanding a Bar Graph
Bar graphs have a vertical axis, which runs from top to bottom, and a horizontal axis, which runs from left to right.

❖ In this graph, what do the vertical and horizontal axes show?

Interpreting a Bar Graph
Start by reading the title. It gives you an idea of the information presented by the graph. To find specific information, look at each bar in the graph. For example, how many school districts were there in New York State in 1995? Slide your finger along the horizontal axis until you reach the bar marked "School Districts." Next, run your finger up to the top of the school district bar. If you look at the number scale along the vertical axis, you will see where the bar ends.

❖ About how many village governments were there in New York in 1995?
❖ What type of government in New York State has the most number of governments?

MAKING CONNECTIONS

EXPLORING BEYOND YOUR STATE
The U.S. Constitution

The division of power between our national and state governments is set forth in the **U.S. Constitution**. You will recall that a constitution is a written plan of government. It spells out how a government will make, carry out and judge the laws.

THE NEED FOR A NEW CONSTITUTION

Our first plan of national government after the colonies became independent was the **Articles of Confederation**. Many Americans felt that the central government under the Articles was too weak. In 1787, representatives from the 13 states met in Philadelphia to write a new constitution to replace the Articles. The U.S. Constitution established the powers and responsibilities of our new government.

The Rotunda at the National Archives where the U.S. Constitution is on permanent exhibit.

FINDING AMENDMENTS

Since it was first adopted in 1788, the U.S. Constitution has been amended (*changed*) several times to meet changing conditions. Do you know how many times the U.S. Constitution has been amended?

EXPLORING YOUR COMMUNITY
Writing to Your Elected Official

Most elected officials like to hear from their constituents. **Constituents** are the people who live in an official's home district.

◆ CONTINUED

WRITING A BUSINESS LETTER

Write a letter to one of your elected officials—your mayor, county legislator or supervisor. You may want to discuss:

- why he or she wanted to become an elected official
- what he or she finds most interesting and important about the job
- what advice he or she would give to young people about being a good citizen

Before writing your letter, let's review the proper form for a business letter:

Heading: Start your business letter with your address and today's date.

> 12 Main Street
> Buffalo, New York 14205
> December 14, 1996

Inside Address: Next list the name, title, organization and address of the person to whom you are writing.

> Honorable George Pataki
> Governor of New York State
> Executive Office Chambers
> Albany, New York 12201

Body: The body of a letter starts with a standard greeting. It is proper to address the person as: "Dear Mr." or "Dear Ms.," followed by the name. When writing to government officials, use their titles. If you are writing to a department or agency and you do not know the name of the person who will receive the letter, start with "Dear Sir or Dear Madam."

> Dear Governor:
>
> I am a fourth grade student at an elementary school in Buffalo, New York. I am writing to tell you that I think our state government should help children who do not have health insurance.
>
> My class has been studying some of the problems faced by these children. One very important problem is that parents take them to the emergency rooms of hospitals. This costs a lot of money and leads to long waiting periods in hospitals. To prevent this problem I think our state should set up a special health insurance program for children. Thank you for your kind attention. I look forward to hearing from you.

An introductory paragraph is used to tell who you are and what the letter is about.

The main part or body of your letter is where you discuss your message or need for information. The tone of your letter should be respectful. You should not be as casual as you would be if you were writing to a friend.

Signature: You may type your letter or write it by hand. Either way, sign the letter between the closing and your printed name.

> Yours truly,
> *Jesse Jones*
> Jesse Jones

Closing: It is proper to end with "Yours truly," or "Sincerely yours."

CONTINUED

MAILING YOUR LETTER

Now that you have written your letter, think about actually sending it to your representative. You might first want to get comments about your letter from parents, teachers and friends. Then make any changes you think are needed to your original letter.

After you have rewritten and signed your letter, mail it in an envelope addressed to your representative.

```
Your Name
Your Address
Your City, N.Y. Zip Code


            The Honorable (Name of Official)
            c/o Office of (Name of Official's Office)
            Local address
            City, N.Y.  Zip Code
```

FAMOUS NEW YORKERS

Robert Livingston (1740–1818) was born in New York City. Livingston spent his life serving his state and nation. He was one of the five people who helped draw up the Declaration of Independence. He then served as a member of the Continental Congress. Later, he helped write the New York Constitution of 1777. This document became New York's official instrument of government for the next 45 years. Livingston became the first U.S. Secretary of Foreign Affairs in 1781. In 1789, Livingston administered the official oath of office to President George Washington. Later, Livington was ambassador to France. He helped negotiate the purchase of the Louisiana Territory in 1803, almost doubling the size of the United States. Livingston then received a monopoly in steamboat navigation, after helping Robert Fulton build the steamship *Clermont* in 1807.

Robert Livingston

WHAT CHARACTERISTICS MAKE A PERSON A GOOD LEADER?

6D

Democratic society depends upon good citizens stepping forward to fill positions of leadership. In this activity, you will identify the characteristics that make a person a leader. Look for the following important words:

▶ Leader ▶ Dictionary ▶ Gettysburg Address

Throughout history, certain key individuals have had an especially important impact on the lives of others. These individuals are often called leaders. They possess certain qualities that others in society recognize and respect.

THINK ABOUT IT

Identify a person who you think is a leader. What qualities make him or her a leader?

WHAT MAKES SOMEONE A LEADER

▶ Most experts say that a **leader** must meet three requirements. A leader has to:

| have a vision for the future | be able to communicate that vision to others | have the ability to get others to act |

What personal characteristics do leaders need to meet these requirements?

LEARNING TO USE A DICTIONARY

A **characteristic** is a special trait or personal quality. Experts have identified several of the characteristics that they feel make someone a good leader. Which personal qualities below do you think most help someone to become a leader?

- fair
- unselfish
- compassionate
- courageous
- humane
- expressive
- honest
- popular
- skillful
- intelligent
- caring
- ethical

Note: You may not know the meaning of some words on the list. Use a dictionary to look up words you do not understand.

DICTIONARY

A **dictionary** is a reference book with many thousands of words arranged in alphabetical order. Dictionaries explain how to say each word correctly. This is done by dividing the word into syllables (*parts*) and showing which syllables in the word get accented. Some dictionaries tell you the origin of the word. Dictionaries also show the different parts of speech (*noun, verb. etc*) that the word might have. Finally, a dictionary lists the meaning of the word for each part of speech. Sometimes a dictionary gives a sample sentence to make the meaning of the word clearer.

> **fair** (fër). [Old English "foeger"] *Noun*. Gathering for sale of goods or display of goods or farm products, as in "state fair."
> *Adjective*. **1.** Beautiful, pleasing. **2.** Clear and sunny, as in "fair weather." **3.** With blond hair and light complexion. **4.** Just, unbiased, impartial, with equal treatment for all, as in "he received a fair trial."

There are often several meanings for a word. You have to pick the one that makes the most sense in the sentence you are reading. Which definition of "fair" would you choose for a possible characteristic of a leader? You would be correct if you selected definition #4: "Just, unbiased, impartial, with equal treatment for all."

Copy the following chart onto a separate sheet of paper. After you find the meaning of any new word you did not know, write it down. This will help you to build your vocabulary while learning about the characteristics of leadership.

	New Word	Definition of the Word
1.		
2.		
3.		
4.		
5.		
6.		
7.		
8.		

> Are there any other words you would add to the list of personal characteristics of a leader? If so, what are they?

Now that you have some understanding of all of the words, which personal characteristics do you think are most important in helping someone to be a good leader?

LOOKING AT TWO IMPORTANT LEADERS

Let's check your previous answer about the personal characteristics of a good leader. We can begin by looking at two people considered by many to have been good leaders. Each of them defended and promoted democratic principles and civil rights. Let's see what leadership characteristics each one possessed.

❖ **Abraham Lincoln** was the sixteenth President of the United States. He served as President from 1861 until his death in 1865.

❖ **Dr. Martin Luther King, Jr.,** was an important civil rights leader. This Baptist minister headed the Civil Rights Movement in the late 1950s and the 1960s.

Read the following account of Abraham Lincoln's career to find out which leadership characteristics he had.

ABRAHAM LINCOLN (1809–1865)

Many consider Abraham Lincoln to have been one of the greatest American Presidents. Lincoln was born in a log cabin. He struggled hard to become a lawyer. People liked his simple ways and plain style of speaking. He was known for his honesty. Lincoln soon went into politics. He was very intelligent and an excellent speaker. At that time, the most important issue facing the nation was the existence of slavery in the South. Lincoln helped form a new political party that opposed the spread of slavery to new states that were joining the United States.

Lincoln was elected President in 1860. People from the Southern states did not know of Lincoln's patience and understanding. In spite of his personal feelings, Lincoln promised he would not abolish slavery in the South where it already existed. But most Southerners did not believe him. Soon the Southern states declared they would leave the United States and form their own country—the Confederate States of America.

Abraham Lincoln

❖ CONTINUED

Lincoln believed it was important to keep all the states together in one nation. He also thought that the South could not beat the North in a war. He told the Southern states that he would not allow them to leave the United States. They did so anyway. Soon afterwards, the North and South went to war. Gradually, Lincoln came to the conclusion that the United States could not survive half slave and half free. In 1863, Lincoln issued the **Emancipation Proclamation.** This freed all enslaved people in the rebelling Southern states.

The Civil War lasted for four years and was the bloodiest war in American history. Many people doubted the wisdom of Lincoln's decision to go to war. But Lincoln thought the war was necessary. Eventually, the North won and the country was re-united. The **Thirteenth Amendment** to the U.S. Constitution was passed in 1865, abolishing slavery throughout the United States.

Near the end of the war, President Lincoln went to Gettysburg to dedicate a cemetery where thousands of Northern soldiers were buried. At the time, his **Gettysburg Address** attracted little attention. However, it is now recognized as one of the greatest expressions of the ideals of American democracy.

> *Four score and seven [87] years ago our fathers brought forth on this continent a new nation conceived in liberty, and dedicated to the proposition (idea) that all men are created equal ...*

Thinking about those who had lost their lives in the battle, Lincoln noted that nothing he could say could be more important than what those soldiers had already done by sacrificing their lives. He then ended his speech with these words:

> *We here highly resolve ... that this nation, under God, shall have a new birth of freedom; and that government of the people, by the people, and for the people shall not perish (be destroyed) from the earth.*

When the war was over, Lincoln was willing to forgive the South. He drew up plans to rebuild the South and was ready to welcome Southerners back into the Union as equals. However, Lincoln was assassinated (*murdered*) in 1865, just when the Civil War ended. It was left to others to reunite the country.

QUESTIONS ABOUT ABRAHAM LINCOLN

1. Go back to your list of personal characteristics of leaders. Did Abraham Lincoln possess any of the characteristics you thought were important? Explain.
2. It has been said that Abraham Lincoln helped to strengthen democracy in the United States. Would you agree? Explain.

Now let's take a look at another person considered to be a great leader.

DR. MARTIN LUTHER KING, JR. (1929–1968)

Nearly a century after the Civil War, the rights of African Americans were still being violated by the laws and practices of many states. For example, African Americans in the South were legally **segregated** (*separated by race*) in schools and forced to use separate public places such as restaurants, drinking fountains and buses. In addition, groups like the **Ku Klux Klan** committed violent acts against African Americans.

In the 1950s and 1960s, the **Civil Rights Movement** struggled to end racial segregation. Dr. Martin Luther King, Jr., a Baptist minister, became one of the leaders of that movement. King was a patient man who believed in non-violence. Unlike some other leaders, he opposed the use of violence to end segregation. If the government passed an unjust law, he felt people should oppose that law with non-violent actions, such as marches and strikes. He felt that peaceful resistance would eventually change most people's attitudes. King was very effective in using non-violent demonstrations and **boycotts** (*refusal to buy certain products or services*) against segregation.

Dr. Martin Luther King, Jr.

One of King's most important demonstrations brought hundreds of thousands of people together for a **March On Washington** in 1963. King was a gifted speaker who communicated his vision of future justice. It was during this rally that he delivered his **"I have a dream" speech**. In this speech he told Americans of his dream of a nation free of prejudice and discrimination.

Dr. King led the March On Washington in 1963. What methods did he use in his battle to win equality for African Americans?

> *I have a dream. It is a dream deeply rooted in the American dream. I have a dream that one day this nation will rise up and live out the true meaning of its creed [beliefs]. We hold these truths to be self-evident [clear], that all men are created equal. I have a dream that one day in the Red Hills of Georgia the sons of former slaves and the sons of former slave owners will be able to sit down together at the table of brotherhood.*

❖ CONTINUED

GOVERNMENT 357

Dr. King and his followers helped bring public segregation to an end. A new national law was passed that ended segregation in public transportation, hotels and restaurants. King also successfully fought to end unfair reading tests and other requirements that had been used to keep African Americans from voting.

In organizing demonstrations in the South, he risked imprisonment, violence and even death. Enemies threatened King and his family. They tried to blow up his house. They threw him in jail. Still, he refused to give up. Finally, in 1968, King was assassinated (*murdered*) by an opponent of civil rights.

Dr. King was a great social reformer who inspired people to act non-violently. He organized supporters of Civil Rights from all races. King and his followers achieved major social changes in America.

QUESTIONS ABOUT MARTIN LUTHER KING, JR.

1. Go back to your list of personal characteristics of leaders. Did Martin Luther King, Jr. possess any of them? Explain.
2. It has been said that Dr. King helped to strengthen the rights of all Americans. Would you agree? Explain.

RE-EXAMINING YOUR DEFINITION OF A LEADER

You just read about two people who many would consider good leaders. Create a Venn diagram showing the personal qualities of both leaders. Would you now change your list of characteristics that you think a good leader should have?

REVIEWING YOUR UNDERSTANDING

Creating Vocabulary Cards

Gettysburg Address	*I Have A Dream Speech*
Who delivered this address?	What qualities made Dr. King a successful leader?
What was its main message?	What was the main message of his "I have a dream" speech?

Using a Dictionary

Read the following definition and answer the questions below.

> **Cit·i·zen** (sit´i zen), *noun* **1.** a native or naturalized member of a state or nation who owes loyalty to his or her government and is entitled to its protection. **2.** an inhabitant of a city or town, especially one entitled to its privileges. **3.** an inhabitant: *The deer is a citizen of our woods.* **4.** a civilian, rather than a soldier or police officer.

1. What word is defined?
2. What part of speech is the word?
3. How is the word pronounced?
4. How many different definitions are given for the word?
5. Which definition of the word are you most familiar with?

MAKING CONNECTIONS

EXPLORING BEYOND YOUR STATE
LEADERS WHO STRENGTHENED DEMOCRACY

Abraham Lincoln and Dr. Martin Luther King, Jr. dedicated themselves to strengthening democracy in the United States. What other leaders can you think of who helped to strengthen democracy in this nation or some other part of the world?

RESEARCHING DEMOCRATIC LEADERS

On the next page you will find a list of leaders. Many of them come from New York State. Select **two** leaders. For each leader selected, write a **one** page summary of his or her life and accomplishments. Be sure to explain how their lives, writings or work helped to strengthen democracy here or in some other part of the world.

❖ **Where To Find Information**. To find information about these leaders, you will need to do some research. For your research use the following sources:

- **Encyclopedias**: Look for articles listed under the person's name.
- **History books**: Check the index for information about the person.

❖ CONTINUED

- ❖ **Biographies**: Find books written about the leader by other people.
- ❖ **Autobiographies**: See if the leader has written a book about himself or herself.

❖ **Presenting Your Information.** Before you write your summary, you should organize the information you find. To help you, use the following Research Guide:

> *Research Guide:*
> *Leader's Name: ?*
> *Summarize the life of the leader:*
> *Describe his or her major accomplishments:*
> *What characteristics made this person a leader?*
> *What were some effects of the leader's accomplishments?*

❖ **Organizing Your Notes.** Use your notes above to help you write a **one** page summary of the life and achievements of that person.

DEMOCRATIC LEADERS

- ❖ **Susan B. Anthony** (1820–1906) was a leader in the movements to abolish slavery and to achieve equal rights for women.
- ❖ **Elizabeth Blackwell** (1821–1910) was the first woman doctor in the United States. She was a leader in the movement to encourage women to become professionals—lawyers, doctors, ministers and teachers.
- ❖ **Winston Churchill** (1874–1965) rallied his country, Great Britain, against the threat of invasion by Nazi Germany during World War II.
- ❖ **Dorothea Dix** (1802–1887) was a social reformer who campaigned to improve conditions in prisons.

Susan B. Anthony (*standing*) and Elizabeth C. Stanton

❖ CONTINUED

- ❖ **Mohandas Gandhi** (1869–1948) used nonviolent civil disobedience to achieve independence from British rule for India and Pakistan.
- ❖ **Andrew Jackson** (1767–1845) encouraged the "common man" to participate in American politics. Many democratic reforms occurred during his Presidency.
- ❖ **Thomas Jefferson** (1743–1826) championed political and religious freedom.
- ❖ **Lyndon B. Johnson** (1908–1973) persuaded Congress to approve many programs to improve the quality of life for all Americans.
- ❖ **Nelson Mandela** (1925–present) helped lead the struggle to achieve equality for black South Africans. He became the first black South African to be elected president of his country.
- ❖ **José de San Martín** (1778–1850) helped to free Argentina, Chile and Peru from Spanish rule during the independence movements of 1816 to 1818.
- ❖ **Eleanor Roosevelt** (1882–1945) became an active spokesperson for human rights and social reform.
- ❖ **Elizabeth Cady Stanton** (1815–1902) was a leader in the Women's Rights Movement. She helped organize the first women's rights convention held at Seneca Falls in 1848.

Mohandas Gandhi
What did he and Dr. Martin Luther King, Jr. have in common?

EXPLORING YOUR COMMUNITY
IDENTIFYING A PERSON WITH LEADERSHIP QUALITIES

In this activity, you learned about some of the characteristics and qualities that identify someone as a leader. In addition, you researched several people who were important leaders in the past or present. However, leaders need not be in the national spotlight. In fact, a leader does not even have to be famous.

People with leadership qualities exist everywhere. Select **one** person in your own community who you think has shown leadership qualities. Then answer the following questions about that person:

1. What is the name of the person?
2. Identify at least two qualities that you think make that person a leader.
3. Describe an act by this person that illustrates his or her leadership qualities.

SUMMARIZING YOUR UNDERSTANDING

Directions: Use your knowledge to complete the following graphic organizer.

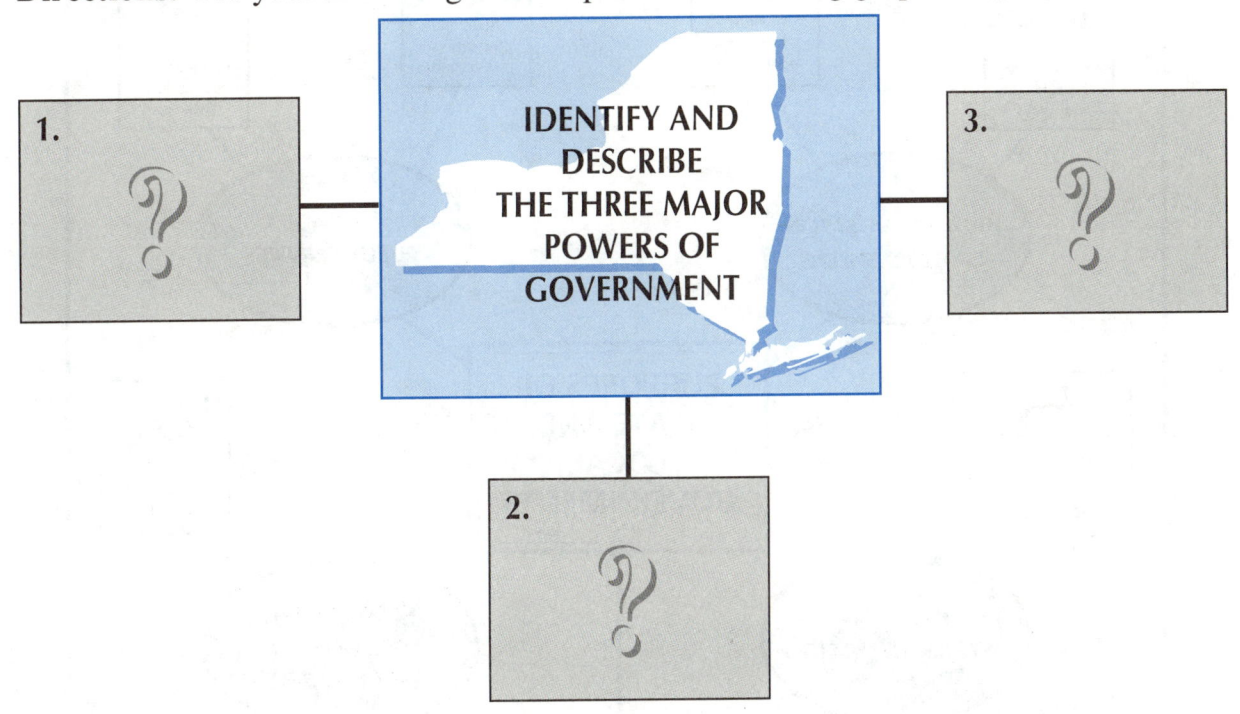

1. ?

IDENTIFY AND DESCRIBE THE THREE MAJOR POWERS OF GOVERNMENT

3. ?

2. ?

Directions: Complete the following chart about New York State government.

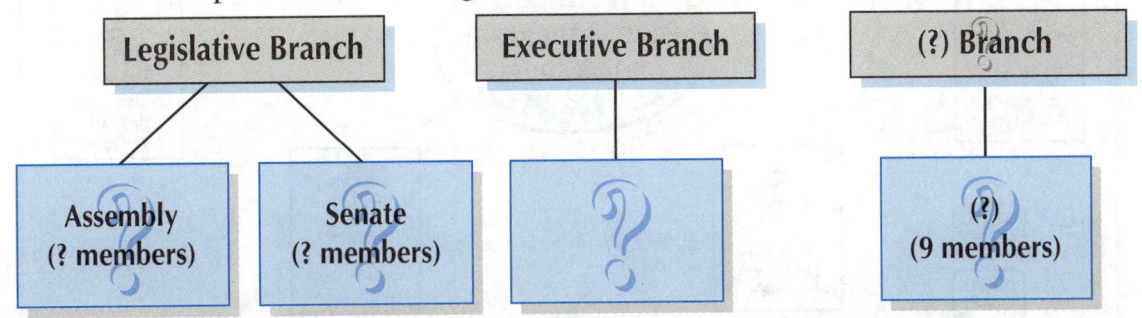

Legislative Branch	Executive Branch	(?) Branch
Assembly (? members) / Senate (? members)	?	(?) (9 members)

PURPOSES OF STATE AND LOCAL GOVERNMENT

Study the diagram on the next page. It shows some of the purposes of state and local governments in New York State. As you will notice in the diagram, state and local governments often have overlapping functions. For instance, local governments build, maintain and patrol local streets, while state government builds, maintains and patrols state highways.

Both state and local governments work to keep our roadways clean.

NEW YORK: ITS LAND AND ITS PEOPLE

PURPOSES OF STATE AND LOCAL GOVERNMENTS

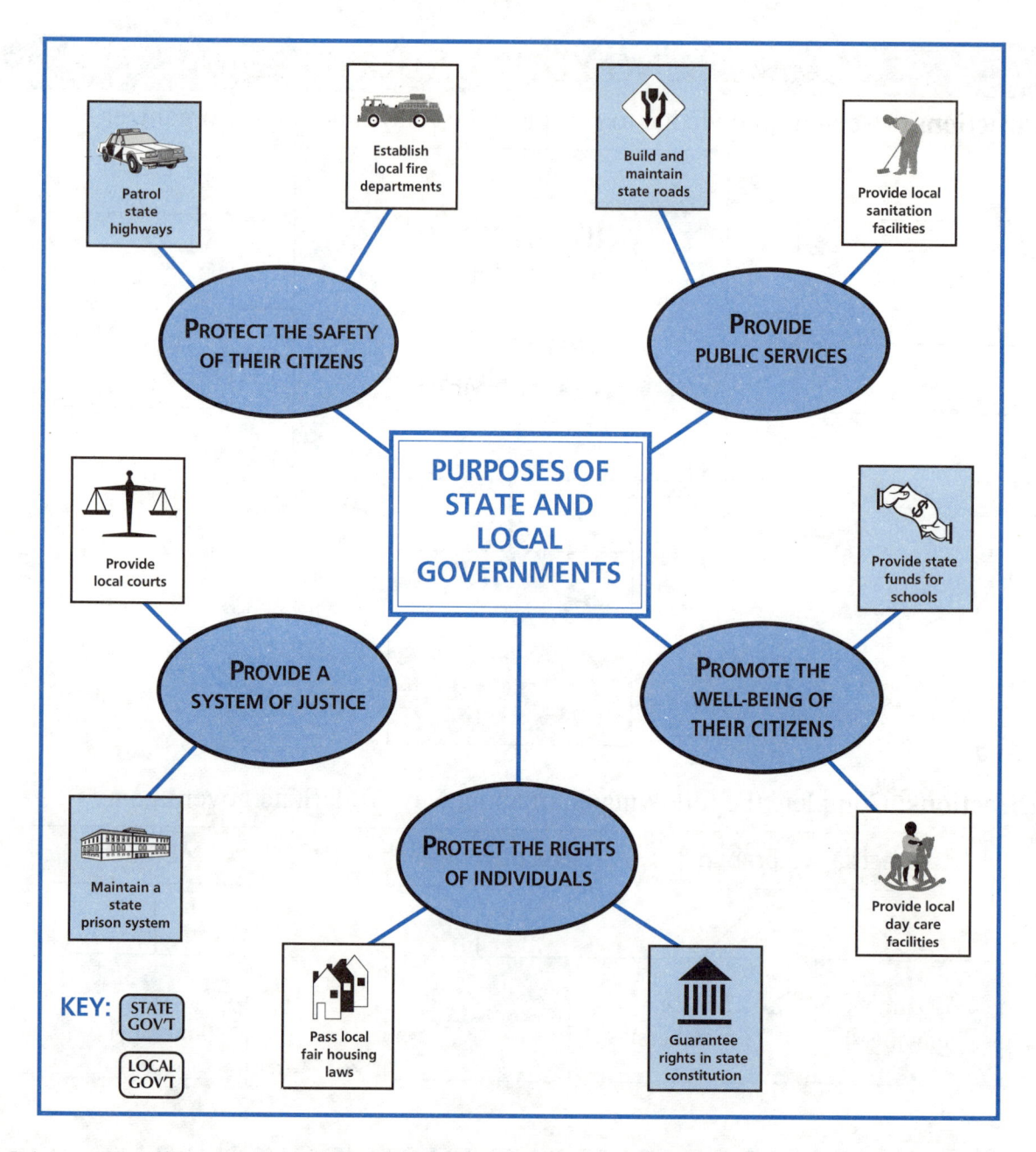

Protect the Safety of Their Citizens
- Patrol state highways
- Establish local fire departments

Provide Public Services
- Build and maintain state roads
- Provide local sanitation facilities

Provide a System of Justice
- Provide local courts
- Maintain a state prison system

Promote the Well-Being of Their Citizens
- Provide state funds for schools
- Provide local day care facilities

Protect the Rights of Individuals
- Pass local fair housing laws
- Guarantee rights in state constitution

KEY: STATE GOV'T / LOCAL GOV'T

Make a copy of the following chart. Then list the jobs that state and local governments have. Use the diagram above for this information.

Some of the Things That State and Local Governments Do

State	Local

INFORMATION SHEET #5: GOVERNMENT

GATHERING INFORMATION

There are many topics that you might gather information about for the government part of your class project. It may help you to begin by first finding the answers to the following questions. Write the information on a set of note cards.

- ❖ **government headquarters:** Where is your town or city government located?
- ❖ **elected officials:** Who are the important elected officials in your town or city?
- ❖ **terms of office:** How long are the terms of office for these officials?

CREATING ITEMS FOR YOUR EXHIBIT

The purpose of this part of your year-long project is to prepare materials that will show how your local government is organized and what it does. After looking at your project, people should better understand how your local government works. If you live outside New York City, you should focus on your town or village government. If you live in New York City, focus on the government of the city or of your borough. A list of suggestions for your project follows. Use these ideas or others that you think best show the structure and activities of your local town or city government

DRAWING A VILLAGE, TOWN OR CITY MAP

Start with an outline map of your county. On this outline map, draw the boundaries of the towns that make up your county, or one of the five boroughs if you live in New York City. Star the location of cities, villages and hamlets that are in **your** town. If you live in New York City, star the neighborhood where you live. Lastly, put a large dot where your **county seat** (*government headquarters*) is located. New York City residents should put a dot to show where the city's government is located.

TRACKING EVENTS IN YOUR TOWN OR CITY

For a period of several weeks, keep track of each time your village, town or city is mentioned in the newspapers. On a map of your town or city, draw a line to the location of the place mentioned in the news. On the border surrounding the place in the news, write a two-line description about why that particular place was in the news.

❖ CONTINUED

CREATING A GOVERNMENT SERVICES MAP

Local governments provide many different services to their residents. Draw a map of your village, town or city. On it, show the location of the following:

- government buildings
- offices of representatives
- police departments
- parks and playgrounds
- fire departments
- colleges and universities
- hospitals
- schools
- public skating rinks and pools

Fire protection is a service provided by local government.
What other local government services will appear on your map?

COMPARING THE IDEAS OF LOCAL POLITICIANS

In New York, the two largest political groups, known as "parties," are the Democratic and Republican Parties. Visit the headquarters of either of these parties, or ask politicians from these parties to visit your classroom. Find out why they are interested in serving in government, and what ideas they have about the future of your community. Then prepare a large chart comparing their ideas, suitable for display as part of your year-long project.

MAKING A CHART OF LOCAL GOVERNMENT

Prepare a chart showing the organization of your community government. Include photographs of officials who hold key positions in your local government. On your chart, indicate each person's name and what his or her role is in your government.

PROPOSING A REFORM

Identify a major problem in your community. Contact important local officials for their opinions on solving the problem. Then collect your notes from the interviews and place them in a binder or report folder. Prepare a title page and table of contents listing the names of the people you interviewed

UNIT 7
CITIZENSHIP

Political demonstration on the steps of the U.S. Capitol

Saluting the American flag

Governor Pataki speaks to the state legislature

In a democracy, ordinary citizens enjoy the most political power. They elect government officials and sometimes vote directly on issues. For our democracy to work effectively, American citizens must be well-informed. In this unit, you will learn what it means to be a citizen in a democracy. You will explore the ways in which citizens express their views. You will also examine the steps that citizens take to make well-informed decisions about public problems and issues. After you have completed this unit, you will better understand your rights and responsibilities as a citizen.

JASIEK BECOMES AN AMERICAN CITIZEN

Jasiek Wojczuk (Ya-shik Voy-chuck) was dressed in his best clothes. He gave one last look in the car mirror to straighten his tie. Then he and his family crossed the street and entered the Federal Building in Brooklyn. Jasiek was about to be officially sworn in as a new citizen of the United States.

Jasiek had gone through a great deal of trouble to become a citizen. Many years before, he had left his native Poland, a country in Eastern Europe. At that time, Poland was in a crisis. The neighboring country of Russia had forced an unfriendly system of government on Poland. People could not criticize their leaders. They were discouraged from going to church. The Polish economy was also not doing well. Almost everybody had a job, but the store shelves were almost always empty.

In 1981, Jasiek received a letter from a distant cousin inviting him to visit the United States. Jasiek traveled to New York City. There, his cousin showed him the Statue of Liberty, the Empire State Building and all the other sights he had read about while growing up in Poland.

During Jasiek's visit, something unusual was happening in his own country. Polish workers had organized themselves into a free union. Government officials had no control over this union and were very nervous. Finally, the government cracked down on the union. It also declared that people would no longer have public trials. Army leaders made many arrests.

Jasiek Wojczuk

The American government responded by allowing all Polish visitors to remain in the United States until the crisis in Poland came to an end. Jasiek decided to stay in America. Soon, he was taking English lessons and found a job helping to tear down old houses. He moved to a small apartment in a Polish section of Brooklyn.

Jasiek spent very little money on himself. Most of his earnings were sent to his young wife and two children who were still living in Poland. He missed his wife and children greatly. He decided to keep working while he thought of a plan to bring them to New York.

Jasiek started taking night classes at a local college. His English improved. He began to study computers. After two years, he quit his job tearing down houses and found work making technical designs with computers.

By 1984, Jasiek had saved enough money to bring his family to America. There were still some troubles getting govenment visas. Jasiek's American cousin had to help them out. Finally, Jasiek's wife and children arrived at John F. Kennedy International Airport in Queens. It was one of the happiest days of his life. Jasiek was surprised by how much his children had grown. Once Jasiek was re-united with his family, he decided to become an American citizen. He studied American history and learned about U.S. government. He passed the citizenship test with flying colors.

And now the great moment had finally arrived. Jasiek looked down, and saw his young son pulling at his sleeve. The family entered the courtroom, where the ceremony was about to take place. Jasiek's eyes focused on the judge who would lead the ceremony. He was told to raise his right hand and to take a pledge of allegiance to his newly adopted country—the United States. He smiled proudly as his wife and children looked on.

As Jasiek said the Pledge of Allegiance, he thought about what becoming an American citizen might mean. What rights and responsibilities would he now enjoy as an American citizen? Jasiek did not want to be just another citizen of the United States. He wanted to be a "good" citizen in his newly adopted country. He wondered what things he should do to achieve this.

In this unit you will find the answers to some of the questions that Jasiek asked himself as he took his pledge.

HOW WOULD YOU DEFINE A "GOOD" CITIZEN?

7A

We begin this activity by examining what citizenship is. Then you will conduct a survey of two adults in your community to find out what they think makes a "good" citizen. Look for the following important words:

- ▶ Citizenship
- ▶ Naturalized Citizen
- ▶ Survey
- ▶ Rights
- ▶ Duties
- ▶ Responsibilities

To help you, a ▶ appears in the margin where the term is first explained.

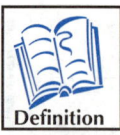

WHAT IS A CITIZEN?

▶ In some ways, citizenship is like a membership card. Citizenship means a person is a member of a particular nation. The idea of citizenship goes back to ancient Greece and Rome. In modern times, every nation has developed its own rules to define citizenship.

In the United States, you are an American citizen if you were born here or if your parents are American citizens. People who were not born here and whose parents are not American citizens can also become citizens. To do this, such a person has to live in the United States for a period of years and pass a citizenship test and take an oath. These
▶ people are called naturalized citizens.

CONDUCTING A SURVEY

Now that you know what a citizen is, what makes someone a "good" citizen? How do you think adults in your community might answer this question? In this activity, you will have the chance to find out. You will need to interview **two** adults to find out how they define a "good" citizen.

WHAT MAKES SOMEONE A GOOD CITIZEN?

In the interviews you are about to conduct, there are no right or wrong answers. The pur-
▶ pose of the survey is to find out how adults in your community define a "good" citizen. To carry out your survey, follow these steps:

❖ Ask your parent to suggest **two** adults who would be willing to participate in your project. One volunteer might even be your parent or guardian.

❖ Begin your survey by reading the following statement to each adult:

> As part of a school project, I am surveying two adults to find their answers to the question:
>
> *How would you define a good citizen?*

❖ After you have received a response to your question, thank your volunteer for his or her help in the survey.

COLLECTING DATA AND COMPARING ANSWERS

Make a copy of the following tally sheet to record the answers of your volunteers:

How would you define a good citizen?
❖ What did your first volunteer say?
❖ What did your second volunteer say?

After your survey is completed, share your answers with your classmates. The class should then choose the answers they feel best define what a "good" citizen is.

A good citizen is someone who …

HOW EXPERTS DEFINE A GOOD CITIZEN

How does your class definition of a good citizen compare with those of the experts? Following are qualities that some experts think a good citizen should have.

A good citizen is someone who is …

❖ **Respectful**. Good citizens treat others with respect, even when they disagree with other people's opinions.

❖ **Responsible**. Good citizens are responsible for their actions. They use self-control and follow the rules. They keep their promises and are willing to pay the penalty if they do something wrong.

❖ **Civic-Minded**. Good citizens sometimes donate their time and money to help improve the community.

❖ **Open-Minded**. Good citizens listen to others' opinions and sometimes change their minds. Good citizens will compromise in order to solve problems. They accept others with different traditions, customs and ways of living.

Now that you have read the views of the experts, would you change your definition of a good citizen? If so, how would you now define a good citizen?

A good citizen is someone who …

REVIEWING YOUR UNDERSTANDING

Creating Vocabulary Cards

Citizenship

What is "citizenship"?

What are some of the qualities of a citizen?

Naturalized Citizen

What is a "naturalized citizen"?

How is a naturalized citizen different from a native-born citizen?

Creating a "Good Citizen" Scrapbook

Have you ever read a newspaper story about a person who rushed into a burning building and saved a family? That person was not only performing an act of bravery, but was also being a good citizen.

Your daily newspaper will often have stories of people who are outstanding citizens. In order to focus on these deeds of good citizenship, let's create a scrapbook of good citizenship stories appearing in your daily newspaper. Over the next 10 days:

❖ cut out **two** articles dealing with acts of "good citizenship"
❖ paste each of these articles in a scrapbook
❖ write a brief summary about each article for your scrapbook
❖ Finally, briefly explain why you think each article represents an example of good citizenship.

Classifying Different Activities

You learned about classifying in several activities in this book. Being able to classify various common activities is a necessary part of good citizenship. Let's test your knowledge of classifying. On the next page are ten items that deal with social, political, economic, cultural and religious activities. Classify each item according to its type.

Note: Some activities may fall into more than one category. The first activity has been done for you.

Activity	Social	Political	Economic	Cultural	Religious
Attending a baseball game	✔				
Going to church services	?		?		?
Buying groceries in a supermarket		?		?	
Watching Spanish dancers do a tango	?		?		?
Joining a citizen's action group		?		?	
Baptizing a newborn child	?		?		?
Marching in an ethnic parade		?		?	
Selling items at a garage sale	?		?		?
Voting in a school board election		?		?	

MAKING CONNECTIONS

EXPLORING BEYOND YOUR STATE

THE RIGHTS, DUTIES AND RESPONSIBILITIES OF CITIZENSHIP

All U.S. citizens enjoy certain rights. They also have duties and responsibilities. Let's look more closely at a citizen's rights, duties and responsibilities.

A **right** is something that everyone in a society is entitled to do or allowed to do. For example, in America everyone has the right to practice his or her religion. This right is protected by the U.S. Constitution and cannot be taken away by government.

❖ CONTINUED

Duties are the "musts" of citizenship—things that the law says you must do. Performing your duty is something that is expected of a citizen in a democracy. If you refuse to perform your duties, you may have to pay a fine or even go to jail. Here are some of the duties required of American citizens:

Military service is an important duty of American citizens.
What other duties do American citizens have?

DUTIES

- ❖ Obey the laws of local, state and federal government
- ❖ Serve on a jury if called upon
- ❖ Help to defend the nation by serving in the armed forces if called upon
- ❖ Pay taxes to help support the government
- ❖ Testify in court if called upon to present evidence
- ❖ Attend school in order to receive an education

Besides the duties required of a citizen, there are also responsibilities. **Responsibilities** are the "shoulds" of citizenship. A citizen is not punished for failing to meet these responsibilities, but they are things a good citizen should do. The success of our democratic system depends on people taking the time and effort needed to be responsible citizens. Here is a list of some common responsibilities of American citizens:

RESPONSIBILITIES

- ❖ Vote in local, state and national elections
- ❖ Inform elected representatives about issues of concern
- ❖ Stay informed about the activities of local, state and federal government
- ❖ Serve in the government if elected or appointed
- ❖ Join a political party or work as an independent voter
- ❖ Help enforce laws by cooperating with the police

❖ CONTINUED

EVALUATING YOURSELF

Now that you have examined the duties and responsibilities of citizenship, would you call yourself a good citizen? Explain why or why not.

EXPLORING YOUR COMMUNITY
LEARNING ABOUT COMMUNITY NEWSPAPERS

In 1733, **John Peter Zenger** began to publish the *New York Weekly Journal* in New York. He printed a series of articles about the British governor of New York. The articles criticized the governor for taking advantage of Native Americans. The Governor responded by burning the newspapers and having Zenger arrested for libel (*printing harmful stories about someone*).

After sitting in jail for six months, Zenger was finally brought to trial. He hired a well-known Philadelphia lawyer, Andrew Hamilton, to defend him. Hamilton argued before the court that people should not be prevented from printing truthful articles about the government—no matter how critical they might be. The jury agreed and freed Zenger. The decision was very important because it upheld Zenger's right to print the truth. It also supported a key principle of democracy—**freedom of the press**.

Copies of Zenger's *Weekly Journal* were burned by British troops. *Why was the decision in the Zenger case so important?*

READING A NEWSPAPER

The tradition of free and independent newspapers lives on in New York State. In fact, in your community there is probably a local newspaper in the tradition of Zenger's *Weekly Journal*. Let's see what you can learn about this newspaper:

❖ What is the name of one local newspaper in your community?
❖ How often is the newspaper published, and what does it cost?
❖ What are some of the local news stories covered in the newspaper?
❖ What special features, such as cooking or health care appear in the newspaper?

7B YOU BE THE JUDGE!

In this activity, you will examine some of the rights that citizens in a democracy enjoy. Look for the following important words:

▶ Bill of Rights   ▶ U.S. Supreme Court

In the United States, we enjoy the benefits of a government dedicated to protecting the rights of its citizens. The Declaration of Independence stated that the main goal of any government should be to protect the people's rights to "life, liberty and the pursuit of happiness."

The **Declaration of Independence** did not spell out what *specific* rights Americans should enjoy. The U.S. Constitution originally listed only a few rights. When the Constitution was sent to the states for approval, many Americans believed it should be rejected because it failed to list each citizen's basic rights. The Constitution created a new government so powerful it was feared the national government might abuse the rights of citizens.

The Declaration of Independence being read to a Philadelphia crowd

THE BILL OF RIGHTS AND OTHER PROTECTIONS

The new U.S. Constitution was finally approved after its supporters promised that a "Bill of Rights" would be added. The first ten amendments were adopted only a few years later in 1791. These amendments are known as the **Bill of Rights**. Since then, seventeen additional amendments have been approved. Many of these later amendments also focus on defining and protecting the rights of citizens.

The Bill of Rights guarantees each individual special rights that cannot be denied or taken away by the government. These special rights generally fall into two categories:

❖ **rights that protect our freedom of expression**. For example, the First Amendment guarantees individuals the freedom of speech.

❖ **rights of people accused of a crime**. For example, the Sixth Amendment guarantees individuals the right to a fair and impartial jury trial.

Some of the amendments written after the Bill of Rights go even further in protecting our rights than the Bill of Rights itself. These amendments guarantee such rights as the right to vote and the right to the "equal protection" of the laws.

Often, disputes have developed over how the language of a particular constitutional right is to be interpreted. This is because no general rule can ever be so exact that it can tell in advance all of the situations that might arise. For this reason, we need courts to apply our laws to specific situations. The courts determine if a particular situation falls within the rule. For example, look at the sign to the right:

THINK ABOUT IT

We are fairly certain that the sign means no cars or trucks in the park. But what about bicycles, baby strollers and wheel chairs? Are they "vehicles" in the sense intended by the sign? Explain.

A court must interpret the words of a law to decide just what the law means. A court might say that the purpose of the rule prohibiting vehicles in the park is to avoid danger to pedestrians. Since wheel chairs and baby strollers pose no danger to pedestrians, they are not "vehicles" in the sense intended by the rule.

Because we live under the "rule of law," we want each person to be treated fairly. In every court, each party has certain rights. These rights include the right to have a lawyer, the right to hear opposing evidence and the right to present one's case. In criminal cases, the defendant also has the right to have the case tried by a panel of unbiased citizens known as a **jury**.

After a trial, the losing side will often ask a special court, known as a court of appeals, to reconsider the decision. The court of appeals will only change the decision if there has been an error in interpreting or applying a law. The **U.S. Supreme Court** is the nation's highest court of appeals. The Supreme Court often hears appeals in which it must interpret what is written in the U.S. Constitution.

THE EXERCISE OF JUSTICE

What would it be like to be a Justice on the U.S. Supreme Court? In this activity, you will have a chance to act as a Supreme Court Justice. You will review a famous case that once appeared before the Supreme Court. Like a real judge, you will weigh the evidence presented by both sides. Then, you will make a decision based on your understanding of the law. Good luck on your first case—your Honor!!!

SCHENCK V. UNITED STATES (1919)

THE FACTS OF THE CASE

Schenck was a member of a political party that opposed U.S. participation in World War I. When the government called up men to serve in the military, Schenck mailed leaflets telling these men that the war was both immoral and against the law. However, the pamphlet never directly told the men to refuse to serve, since such advice would have been against the law.

Schenck was accused of preventing the government from calling up men for the army. He was also accused of encouraging soldiers to disobey their officers. He was found guilty at his trial, but appealed his decision to the U.S. Supreme Court. Schenck claimed that his conviction violated his right to free speech.

ARGUMENTS USED BY SCHENCK

Schenck's lawyers argued that Schenck's right to free speech had been violated. The purpose of free speech is to allow people to criticize their government. Schenck's leaflet was clearly within this right. His lawyer admitted that it would be wrong to use free speech to call for an armed uprising against the government. But Schenck had done nothing of the kind. He had merely given his readers a different viewpoint about the war, and asked them to act for themselves.

The lawyer concluded that the government should not be allowed to imprison Schenck merely for questioning its decision to go to war. What other things might the government then attempt to do without allowing citizens to engage in free debate? Schenck was clearly not guilty and should be freed from prison.

ARGUMENTS USED BY THE U.S. GOVERNMENT

The lawyers for the United States argued that Schenck's pamphlet had only one purpose: to encourage men to disobey the law by refusing to serve in the armed forces. Failure to serve when called upon is against the law. People have a right to discuss whether or not to go to war, but they do not have a right to refuse to serve when called on. Telling people not to serve is disobeying the law.

The government's lawyers recognized that the First Amendment guarantees the right to free speech. But this freedom does not mean we can encourage people to break the law. There are some limits to free speech. For example, a person cannot shout "fire" in a crowded theater as a joke and then claim he or she was exercising free speech. A person has the right to free speech, but not the right to create a dangerous situation. No one has a right to use words that would create an *obvious* and *immediate* danger.

▸ CONTINUED

> Schenck's pamphlet clearly created an immediate danger, and should not be protected as free speech. If people had listened to Schenck, they would have refused to serve in the armed forces or even disobeyed their officers by refusing to fight. This would have caused chaos in the military. Schenck deserves to be in prison.

HOW WOULD YOU DECIDE THIS CASE?

You have now heard all of the evidence. It is time for you to decide the case. Before doing so, let's review what you learned in this case:

1. Summarize **two** arguments used by Schenck's lawyers.
2. Summarize **two** arguments used by the lawyers for the United States.
3. Based on the facts and your understanding of the law, how would **you** decide the case? Explain your decision.

REVIEWING YOUR UNDERSTANDING

Creating Vocabulary Cards

Bill of Rights
What is the "Bill of Rights"? List some of the rights mentioned in the Bill of Rights.

U.S. Supreme Court
What is the U.S. Supreme Court? Why is the U.S. Supreme Court such an important voice in interpreting our laws?

Classifying Constitutional Rights

The rights that Americans enjoy can be classified based on whether they protect a person's political, social, economic or religious rights. Here is what each of these rights is concerned with:

- ❖ **Political rights** allow a citizen to participate in government.
- ❖ **Social rights** deal with our ability to live in a community.
- ❖ **Economic rights** concern our ability to function in the economy.
- ❖ **Religious rights** protect our freedom of worship.

Listed below are several rights enjoyed by citizens in the United States. Try to classify these rights to see if they are political, social, economic or religious rights. You might first want to review the information about classifying found on page 260.

- The government cannot set up an official religion or limit people's freedom of religion.
- Citizens have a right to assemble peacefully and to send their complaints to government officials.
- The government will not send soldiers to live in a citizen's home in times of peace without first getting the citizen's permission.
- Police and other government officials cannot arrest people without good reason.
- The police cannot search a person's home, business or body without a search warrant (*special permission from a judge*). A judge will only issue the warrant if the search seems reasonable.
- No citizen can have his or her life, liberty or property taken away without proper legal procedures being carried out, such as a fair trial.
- An accused person has the right to be informed of the charges against him or her.
- A state government must give its citizens all of the privileges and liberties that citizens of the United States are entitled to.
- The right to vote cannot be denied to a person because of his or her race, or the color of his or her skin.
- All persons 18 years or older can vote.

A mosque is used by Muslims to pray. How might you classify the right to worship enjoyed by Islamic Americans?

Make a copy of the following chart. Then classify the rights above by putting a check mark (✔) in the appropriate column. (*The first one has already been done for you.*)

Description of the Right	Political Right	Social Right	Economic Right	Religious Right
Government cannot set up an official religion or limit people's freedom of religion				✔

MAKING CONNECTIONS

EXPLORING BEYOND YOUR STATE
HUMAN RIGHTS IN THE REST OF THE WORLD

The United Nations was created in 1945 as an international peace organization. One of its main goals is to promote human rights and freedom. **Human rights** are basic rights that all people need to enjoy life and live in a fair society.

In 1948, the United Nations adopted a document known as the **Universal Declaration of Human Rights**. It attempted to define those basic rights that members of the United Nations felt should be guaranteed to citizens of all countries. The rights included many rights that were similar to those spelled out in our own Bill of Rights. For example, the Universal Declaration of Human Rights said that everyone has a right to be free, and that no one should be enslaved or abused by other people.

Unfortunately, certain governments in the world have not always lived up to the ideals expressed in the Declaration of Human Rights. One example of a violation of human rights occurred in China in 1989.

View of the United Nations headquarters at sunset

PROTESTS IN TIANANMEN SQUARE

In 1989, large numbers of college students peacefully demonstrated in Tiananmen Square in Beijing, the capital of China. The students demanded greater personal freedom and a democratic form of government. The Chinese government told the demonstrators to go home, but they refused to do so. Then the government sent in soldiers and tanks to end the demonstrations. Government leaders feared the peaceful demonstrations might lead to a revolution. Some soldiers opened fire on the unarmed demonstrators in the square, killing hundreds of them. Student leaders were arrested and brought to trial. Many protesters were sent to prison for long periods, while others were executed. These events demonstrated that the Chinese people were not really free to criticize their leaders.

❖ CONTINUED

Chinese soldiers on their way to stopping demonstrations

READING A NEWSPAPER

Newspapers are often filled with stories about governments violating the human rights of their citizens. For the next several days, look through a newspaper. Choose **one** article from your newspaper that deals with a possible human rights violation. Explain how the government involved is denying a basic human right to its citizens.

EXPLORING YOUR COMMUNITY
COMMUNITY ORGANIZATIONS THAT HELP PEOPLE

Ten years after issuing the Declaration of Human Rights, the United Nations decided to provide special protection to young people. They issued the **Declaration of the Rights of the Child**. This declaration focused on the need to protect the rights of children. It stated that all children should be free from discrimination, and should be allowed to develop normally, both physically and mentally. It also stated that children are entitled to nourishing foods, a decent house, proper clothing and adequate medical care.

FINDING OUT ABOUT AN ORGANIZATION

Most communities have special public and private organizations that help children faced with problems. These organizations provide care for those who suffer from mistreatment, illness, accidents or other problems. Which organizations in your community help children? To find out:

❖ CONTINUED

- ❖ speak to adult members in your community
- ❖ look in the government pages of your community phone book
- ❖ call your local Chamber of Commerce

After you find this information, make a copy of the chart and complete it:

Name of the Organization	Address	How It Helps Children
?		
?		
?		
?		
?		

FAMOUS NEW YORKERS

Eleanor Roosevelt (1884–1962) was married to Franklin Delano Roosevelt. In 1921, her husband became ill with polio, a crippling disease. When he was elected President in 1932, his advisors encouraged Mrs. Roosevelt to serve as her husband's "eyes, ears and legs." She became one of the nation's most widely admired women. She advised her husband about legislation, spoke out on public issues, held press conferences for women reporters and fought for improved housing, education and other services. In 1945, Eleanor Roosevelt became Chairperson of the United Nations Commission on Human Rights. She played a key role in drafting the Universal Declaration of Human Rights and made sure it protected women as well as men. Throughout her life, Eleanor Roosevelt dedicated herself to making government a positive and caring force.

Eleanor Roosevelt

7C HOW DO PEOPLE PARTICIPATE IN A DEMOCRACY?

In this activity, you will learn about the differences between "direct" and "representative" democracy. You will also explore the many ways in which citizens participate in a democratic form of government. Look for the following important words:

▶ Democracy   ▶ Direct Democracy   ▶ Representative Democracy

Imagine that each year your school library sponsors a poster contest on a topic students are studying in school. This year, the library is sponsoring a poster contest about democracy. A section of the library has been set aside for the winning posters.

Introduction: CITIZEN PARTICIPATION IN A DEMOCRACY

You want to enter this poster contest, so you ask the librarian for the details. The librarian hands you a packet that describes the contest. Here is what it contains:

CONTEST PACKET

History of Democracy

In ancient times, most societies were governed by one ruler or a small group of rulers. About 2,500 years ago, the people of Athens, Greece, made a change from this system. They organized their government into a democracy. A **democracy** is a form of government in which the citizens rule themselves. In a such a government, the people hold the power.

In Athens, citizens took part directly in important government decisions. Of course, not everyone was a citizen. This system of **direct democracy** worked well because Athens was a small city-state. However, sometimes there are too many people in a society for everyone to decide and vote on every issue. As a result, another form of democracy developed. In an indirect or **representative democracy**, such as the United States, citizens elect people known as **representatives** to serve in their place and to make important government decisions for them.

Characteristics of Democracy

Democracy is an extraordinary form of government. It is admired by people all over the world for some of its unique characteristics:

❖ Democracy recognizes the worth and dignity of each person. For example, each person, no matter how rich or poor, is a valued and important member of society and is treated equally before the law.

❖ CONTINUED

- ❖ Democracy stands for **majority rule**, but it also protects the rights of those not in the majority. In a democracy, decisions are made by a majority of the people. A **majority** is more than half the voters. Members on the side with less than half, called the **minority**, have the right to disagree. People in the minority are allowed to object and to criticize. One day they may even convince enough people that they are right, and their opinions will become the majority opinion.

- ❖ Democracy allows more individual freedom than any other form of government. For example, people are free to express their opinions. The right to vote would have no meaning if people did not have the right to communicate and exchange ideas.

Ways to Participate in a Democracy

A citizen in a democracy should actively participate in his or her community. Here are some of the many ways in which citizens participate actively in our democracy.

Participation in your Community

- ❖ Participate in a school service project
- ❖ Pay taxes
- ❖ Serve on a jury
- ❖ Join a school club or organization, such as the P.T.A.
- ❖ Run for office in a school club or community organization
- ❖ Act directly to solve some local community problem
- ❖ Write letters to a local newspaper about community issues
- ❖ Help people in the community who are in trouble
- ❖ Contribute time or money to a local charity
- ❖ Speak at community meetings on public issues
- ❖ Serve as a volunteer firefighter or a hospital volunteer

Participation in your State and National Government

- ❖ Discuss issues of statewide and national importance with other people
- ❖ Help in an election campaign
- ❖ Serve in the armed forces of the United States
- ❖ Vote in statewide and national elections
- ❖ Join a political party
- ❖ Send letters to a representative, the President, or other policy-makers
- ❖ Publish articles on issues of state or national importance
- ❖ Run for election to public office
- ❖ Attend public meetings or demonstrations

❖ CONTINUED

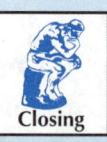

CONTEST RULES

Closing

Students who wish to enter the contest can do so by creating a poster about democracy. Your poster should:

- illustrate some of the actions that people do when they participate in a democracy.
- contain at least **three** illustrations. These illustrations can be drawings or pictures from newspapers or magazines, or your own drawings.

The person who makes the most creative poster will be declared the winner. May the best contestant win!

REVIEWING YOUR UNDERSTANDING

Creating Vocabulary Cards

Direct Democracy

What is "direct democracy"?

In what kind of society does direct democracy work best?

Representative Democracy

What is "representative democracy"?

In what kind of society does it usually work best?

Defining Democracy

A dictionary defines "democracy" as a government in which power is in the hands of the people. However, democracy means different things to each of us. Ask **two** adults how they define "democracy" and what they think is its most important characteristic.

DEMOCRACY

Person #1	Person #2
Definition: ?	Definition: ?
Main Characteristic: ?	Main Characteristic: ?

Interpreting a Line Graph: Voting Patterns of Americans

Most observers agree that for a democracy to work, its citizens must vote. But how often do Americans come out to vote on election day? Are Americans taking their voting responsibility seriously? The following line graph provides some answers:

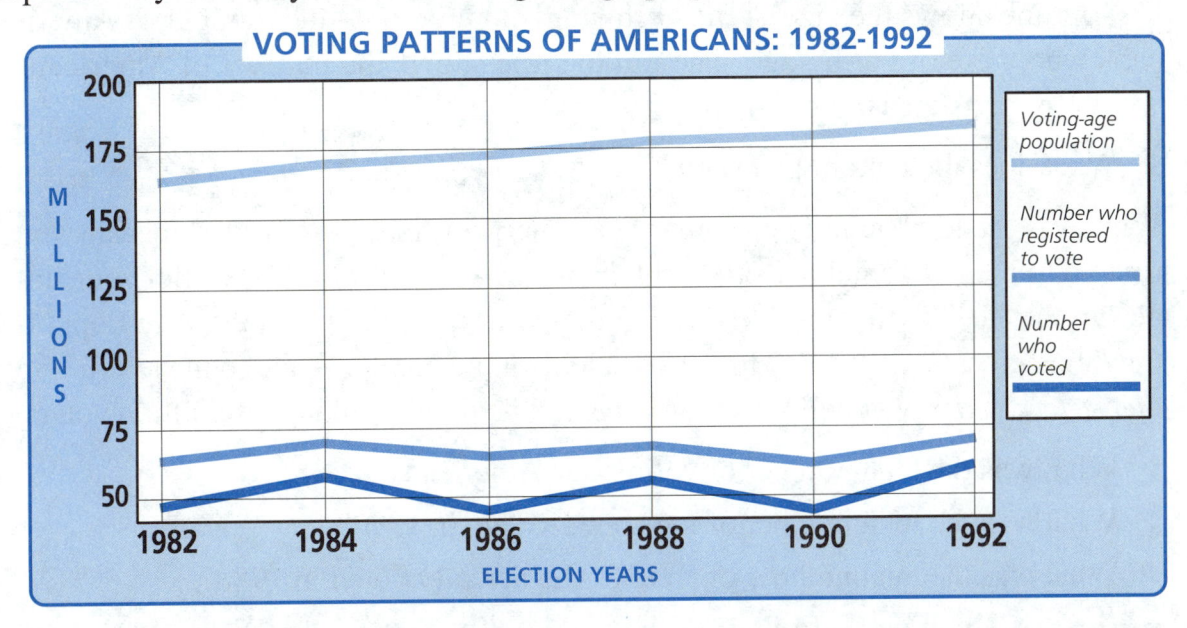

VOTING PATTERNS OF AMERICANS: 1982-1992

[Line graph showing three lines from 1982 to 1992 on election years. Vertical axis shows MILLIONS from 50 to 200. Lines represent: Voting-age population (rising from ~165 to ~188), Number who registered to vote (fluctuating around 65-75), Number who voted (fluctuating around 45-65).]

Are you having trouble understanding this line graph? If so, it will help if you first read the Skill Builder that follows.

Skill Builder: INTERPRETING LINE GRAPHS

What Is a Line Graph?
A line graph is a chart made up of a series of points connected by a line. It is used to show how something has increased, decreased or remained the same.

❖ What three items are shown in this line graph?

Keys to Understanding a Line Graph
Line graphs have a vertical axis, which runs from top to bottom. They also have a horizontal axis, which runs from left to right.

❖ In this graph, what does the vertical axis show?

❖ What does the horizontal axis show?

Interpreting a Line Graph
Start by reading the title. It will give you an idea of the information presented.

❖ CONTINUED

386 NEW YORK: ITS LAND AND ITS PEOPLE

❖ What is the title of this line graph?

If the graph has more than one line, a "legend" is usually needed. Like the legend of a map, the legend of a line graph shows what each line represents. In this graph, the top line shows the size of the voting age population—the number of Americans who were of voting age. The middle line shows the number of Americans who were registered to vote.

❖ What does the bottom line show?

What was the total number of voting-age Americans in 1984? To find this answer, first go to the horizontal axis and find the line marked "1984." Next, run your finger up the "1984" line until you reach the point where the "Voting Age Population" line crosses the "1984" line. If you look at the number scale to the left (*along the vertical axis*), you will see the number at this point is about 170 million voters.

❖ What was the total number of voting-age Americans in 1986?

❖ What was the total number of registered voters in 1990?

❖ What was the total number of people who actually voted in 1988?

Looking for Trends in a Line Graph
Sometimes a line graph can be used to identify a trend. A **trend** is the general direction in which things are moving. You can find a trend by following the direction of the points on the line graph. For example, one trend in the graph is that the voting-age population has continued to increase from 1982 through 1992.

❖ What has been the trend for the number of people who registered to vote?

❖ Do you see a trend for the number of people who actually voted?

❖ How might you explain any one of these trends?

Finding Your County Vote in the Last Presidential Election

Many people consider the U.S. President to be the most important elected official in the world. Every four years voters determine who will be the next President. In 1992, **Bill Clinton**, a member of the Democratic Party, ran against **President George Bush**, a member of the Republican Party.

Which candidate do you think voters in your county supported in that election? One way to find the answer is to look in an almanac. Check the index under the heading "Elections." Under this heading you will find the category "Presidential." Turn to the page listed. When you have located the information, complete the following chart:

In the 1996 Presidential race, President Clinton was challenged by Robert Dole, a

NUMBER OF VOTES	1992 PRESIDENTIAL ELECTION: CANDIDATES' NAMES
?	(D) Bill Clinton
?	(R) George Bush

member of the Republican Party. Which Presidential candidate do you think the voters in your county supported in that election? Check your answers in an almanac.

NUMBER OF VOTES	1996 PRESIDENTIAL ELECTION: CANDIDATES' NAMES
?	(D) Bill Clinton
?	(R) Robert Dole

FAMOUS NEW YORKERS

Franklin Delano Roosevelt (1882–1945) In 1928, Roosevelt was elected Governor of New York. Four years later, he was elected the 32nd U.S. President. Once in office, he was faced with the Great Depression. During the Depression, the American economy almost collapsed and millions of people were thrown out of work. Roosevelt restored the nation's spirit and remolded American life with his "New Deal" programs. His policies made the national government responsible for restoring the nation's economic well-being. His program provided work for the unemployed, health care for the elderly and protection for the nation's resources. Roosevelt also led the country during World War II and was re-elected to a second, third and fourth term. He died in April 1945. You can visit where he once lived at Hyde Park, close to Poughkeepsie, New York.

Franklin D. Roosevelt

388 NEW YORK: ITS LAND AND ITS PEOPLE

MAKING CONNECTIONS

EXPLORING BEYOND YOUR STATE
PARTICIPATING IN A DEMOCRACY—VOTING

In a democracy, citizens usually express themselves by voting. **Voting** is the way citizens tell their representatives how they feel about a particular candidate or issue.

EXPANDING THE NUMBER OF POTENTIAL VOTERS

The U.S. Constitution allows each state to set its own qualifications for voting. Our modern ideas about who should vote are different from those of the Constitution's authors 200 years ago. In those days, race, gender (*sex*), and property ownership affected who could vote. Only a small group of people actually voted in each state.

Property Ownership. The first restriction to be eliminated was the requirement that a man had to own property in order to vote. As cities and towns grew, the number of working men who did not own property also grew. These men paid taxes and took an interest in government, but they could not vote. New York eliminated most property qualifications for voting as early as 1821. By the 1850s, all the states had eliminated property ownership as a basis for voting.

Race. After the Civil War, the **Fifteenth Amendment** was passed. This amendment guaranteed the right to vote to men of all races. However, in some states it was not enforced until the 1960s.

Gender. For the first 130 years after the formation of the United States, women could not vote. As early as the 1840s, women reformers began demanding the right to vote. The struggle went on for many years. During World War I, many men went off to Europe to fight for democracy. Millions of women took their places on the "home front," working in factories, mills and mines. After the war, it was hard to

On May 6, 1912. Women in New York City marched to gain the right to vote.

❖ CONTINUED

deny that women were the equals of men. It also seemed odd to many Americans to fight for democracy in Europe, while opposing it at home. As a result, the **Nineteenth Amendment** was passed in 1920. It gave women the right to vote.

Age. As recently as the 1960s, most states set the age for voting at 21 years old. During the Vietnam War, 18-year-olds were considered old enough to fight and die for their country, but were told they were not old enough to vote. Most people believed this was unfair. As a result, the **Twenty-sixth Amendment** was passed in 1971. It gave 18-year-olds the right to vote.

DECIDING WHO SHOULD BE ALLOWED TO VOTE

The table below lists several proposals to change voting requirements. For each proposal, indicate whether or not you agree with it and explain your answer.

PROPOSAL	YOUR VIEW
1. Homeless people should be allowed to vote.	
2. People who cannot read or write should not be allowed to vote.	
3. Immigrants who are not yet citizens should be allowed to vote.	
4. People found guilty of a serious crime should be allowed to vote.	
5. Sixteen and seventeen-year olds should be allowed to vote.	

EXPLORING YOUR COMMUNITY

WHAT WOULD YOU SUGGEST FOR A COMMUNITY CITIZENSHIP PROJECT?

In this activity, you learned about some of the roles citizens play in a democracy. Citizen involvement in a community project is an important part of a democracy. There are many ways citizens can help their community. One idea now being used in many New York State communities is to have a person or business "adopt" a section of a highway.

❖ CONTINUED

THE ADOPT-A-HIGHWAY PROGRAM

The Long Island Expressway is a 65-mile highway that runs through Queens, Nassau and Suffolk Counties. The State Department of Transportation is responsible for keeping the highway litter-free. However, with budget cuts, pot-hole repairs and other maintenance costs, the department is often short of money.

To help keep the expressway clean, some businesses have started "adopting" a one-mile section of the highway. For a typical one-mile section, the "adoption" cost is from $5,000 to $10,000 a year. This money is used to clean up litter. The same practice is being carried on with other highways across the state.

A highway sign along the Long Island Expressway

At first that might seem like a lot of money—and for most of us it is. However, businesses often spend $100,000 a year on radio commercials. Some spend $7,000 for a full-page ad in a newspaper. Radio ads are heard once and often forgotten. Newspaper ads get thrown away each day. But a company that "adopts" a highway section gets to put up their own sign on the roadway. The sign is read by every person who drives past it, day in and day out.

FINDING A COMMUNITY PROJECT

The adopt-a-highway program is just one idea for a community project. Now it's your turn to design a project that will help improve your community. Maybe its cleaning up a vacant lot, boarding up an abandoned building or painting over a wall that has graffiti. Whatever your project, here are some things to keep in mind:

PROJECT TITLE: _____

Idea of the Project: _____?_____

Estimated Costs: _____?_____

Number of Volunteers Needed: _____?_____

How To Do It: _____?_____

HOW WOULD YOU REDUCE POLLUTION IN YOUR COMMUNITY?

7D

Informed decision-making is one of a citizen's most important responsibilities. In this activity, you will look more closely at pollution and use a problem-solving approach to help deal with this problem. Look for the following important words:

- Environment
- Pollution
- Acid Rain
- Problem Solving
- Criteria
- Brainstorming

One problem that frequently occurs in a community is pollution. Just think of the large number of people in your community who drive cars, cook food, throw things into the garbage and use products made in factories. These activities are innocent enough, but each one can cause pollution—the introduction of harmful materials into the environment. It is no wonder that protecting the environment has become a major concern for Americans in every community.

Factories pour dirt, fumes and chemicals into the air, polluting the environment.

DANGERS TO THE ENVIRONMENT

Our **environment** is made up of the Earth and all the resources that surround us, including air, water soil and wildlife. People used to think that because the world was so large, the actions of human beings could not damage the environment. People made fires or put their garbage in rivers without thinking much about it. However, the rise of industry and the growth of the world's population over the last 200 years has greatly changed our thinking.

Today, a major danger to our environment comes from pollution. **Pollution** is made up of the dirt, fumes, chemicals and other substances that make our environment unclean. Pollution is in the air we breathe and the water we drink. It kills plants and animals. It also causes disease among humans. Many people fear that if pollution is not controlled, it could eventually make our planet unlivable.

TYPES OF POLLUTION

Pollution has a number of causes. For example, **pesticides** are chemicals used by farmers to kill insects. However, they can be harmful to people. The rain sometimes washes these chemicals into our rivers and streams. Another source of pollution is from cars that pour exhaust fumes into the air. Many cities burn garbage. Some factories dump chemical **toxins** (*poisons*) into our rivers, lakes and oceans. Accidents involving off-shore drilling sites and large ships carrying oil result in **oil spills**. Such spills often cover hundreds of miles of ocean. They have made some seashores unusable and have killed plants and wildlife.

▶ Still another type of pollution is **acid rain**. Factory smokestacks and automobile exhaust fumes rise high into the air. These form new chemicals in the atmosphere that return to the Earth in the form of acid rain or snow. Acid rain is poisonous. It causes damage to forests, lakes, fish and even to people.

Oil drilling in the Gulf of Mexico. Why are companies searching for oil in the ocean a danger to our environment?

LOCAL POLLUTION

Pollution is not somebody else's problem. We are all affected by it. That means even the community you live in must take some steps to reduce pollution and protect the environment.

> **THINK ABOUT IT**
>
> What do **you** think is the greatest environmental danger to your community?

Are you correct? Compare your answers with those of your classmates. The class as a whole should then decide what is the most serious danger to the environment in your community.

> **THINK ABOUT IT**
>
> What does **your class** think is the greatest environmental danger to the community?

Now that you have identified the problem, what can be done about it? First, let's consider the appropriate steps to follow when **solving a problem**

AN APPROACH TO PROBLEM-SOLVING

STEP 1: IDENTIFY THE PROBLEM

Begin by identifying the problem. For example, as our population continues to grow, a problem has developed: where should we put the billions of tons of garbage thrown away each day? Some communities have tried towing their garbage out to sea to dump it. Other communities burn their garbage. However, both burning and dumping garbage can harm the environment.

> **A helpful hint**: Go through a mental checklist—*who, what, where, when*—when you try to identify or define the problem.

STEP 2: STATE THE CAUSES

Next, you will need to state **how** the problem came about. "Causes" are the different things that led to the problem. For example, many products we buy come wrapped in elaborate packaging. All the packaging eventually gets thrown away. This material simply adds to the mountains of garbage that must be gotten rid of every day.

STEP 3: CREATE CRITERIA

Before you look at ways to solve the problem, you must establish your criteria for a good solution. Criteria are standards for making a judgment about something. We use criteria to measure whether a solution is acceptable or not. For example, to evaluate suggested solutions to the garbage problem, you might consider the following criteria:

- ❖ What will it cost?
- ❖ What effect will it have on the environment?
- ❖ Will it be acceptable to most members of the community?

A "good" solution will be inexpensive, will reduce pollution to acceptable levels and will be something people agree to do.

STEP 4: PROPOSE POSSIBLE SOLUTIONS

Now you will need to explore possible solutions to the problem. First, list all the ways you can think of that the problem might be solved. You should brainstorm ideas with your classmates, listing as many solutions as you can.

❖ CONTINUED

BRAINSTORMING

Through brainstorming, people express their thoughts about a problem and develop new ideas to solve it. The excitement of hearing other people's ideas often helps the members of a brainstorming group to think of new ideas of their own. People in business and government often use brainstorming to help solve difficult problems. In this activity, you and your classmates might use the brainstorming technique to see what possible solutions you might come up with.

For example, one possible solution to the garbage problem is **recycling**—creating new products from garbage in the form of bottles, paper and plastic. Another solution could be putting the garbage in a **landfill** (*a huge hole in the ground*).

Second, for each proposed solution, find the information to answer the criteria you selected in Step 3. Here is a what a sample chart might look like that deals with the two solutions suggested here:

Deciding what to do with garbage is a serious problem faced by many communities.

	Recycling	Landfill
• What are the costs?	high	low
• What will be the effect on the environment?	good	bad
• Is it acceptable to the community?	yes	maybe

STEP 5: MAKE A CHOICE

Now you are ready to make a choice. You must compare the proposed solutions. Look at the advantages and disadvantages of each. Often there is no perfect answer. You may have to decide which advantages are more important, based on your own values. Since people value different things, reasonable people may disagree about what should be done.

APPLYING A PROBLEM-SOLVING APPROACH

Closing

Now it is your turn. Use the problem-solving approach you just learned to come up with some possible solutions to the main environmental dangers facing your community. Your teacher will divide your class into groups. Each group should do the following:

- Identify an important local environmental problem.
- State the causes of the problem.
- Create criteria for judging solutions.
- Propose possible solutions to the problem.
- Make a choice. Which solution does your group prefer?

REVIEWING YOUR UNDERSTANDING

Creating Vocabulary Cards

Problem Solving

What 5 steps are involved in solving a problem?

What kinds of problems can you use this approach with?

Acid Rain

What is "acid rain"?

What causes acid rain?

Interpreting a Pie Graph on Pollution

The pie graph to the right deals with the types of pollution found in the United States. Study the information in the graph. Then answer the questions that follow.

1. What was the main cause of pollution in the United States in 1994?
2. Which types of pollution listed in the pie chart might be examples of air pollution?
3. How might one type of pollution listed in the graph be reduced?

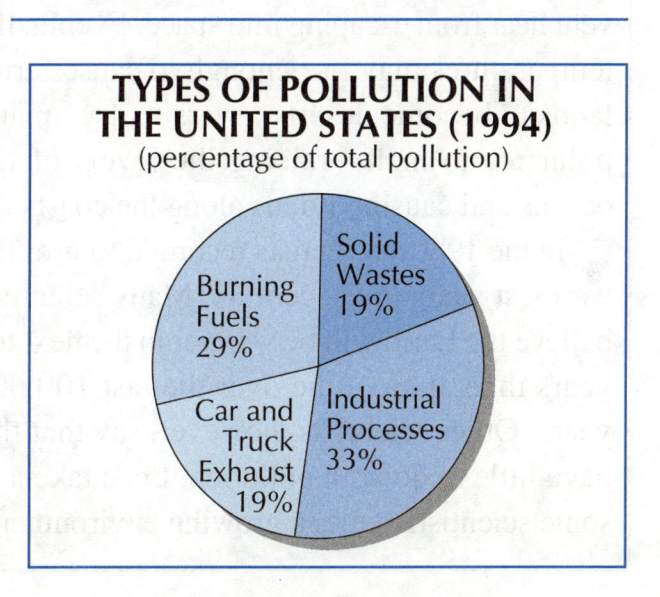

TYPES OF POLLUTION IN THE UNITED STATES (1994)
(percentage of total pollution)

- Solid Wastes 19%
- Burning Fuels 29%
- Car and Truck Exhaust 19%
- Industrial Processes 33%

MAKING CONNECTIONS

EXPLORING BEYOND YOUR STATE
CHANGES IN THE EARTH'S ENVIRONMENT

Over the last 100 years changes have been affecting the Earth's atmosphere at a rapid rate. Community environmental problems are part of a larger trend that knows no local or national boundaries. For example, pollution in Russia can now affect the United States.

WORLD-WIDE ENVIRONMENTAL PROBLEMS

There is great concern that some of the chemicals we use are gradually destroying the **ozone layer**. This layer is a band of gas that surrounds the Earth. It prevents harmful rays of the sun from reaching us. These rays can cause skin cancer and injure other parts of the body. Scientists have discovered a huge hole, as large as the United States, in the ozone layer above Antarctica.

A second world-wide change is **global warming**—a general rise in the Earth's temperature. Pollution in the air and increasing amounts of gases such as carbon dioxide prevent heat from escaping into space. Eventually, temperatures may rise enough to cause farmlands to become deserts, rivers to dry up and polar ice to melt—raising the levels of the oceans and causing floods along the coasts.

In the 1980s, scientists recorded four of the warmest years in the century. Many scientists believe the Earth will be warmer in the next ten years than at any time over the last 100,000 years. Other scientists, however, say that these changes in climate are natural and have little to do with pollution. Let's take a look at a line graph that examines what some scientists see as a growing environmental problem.

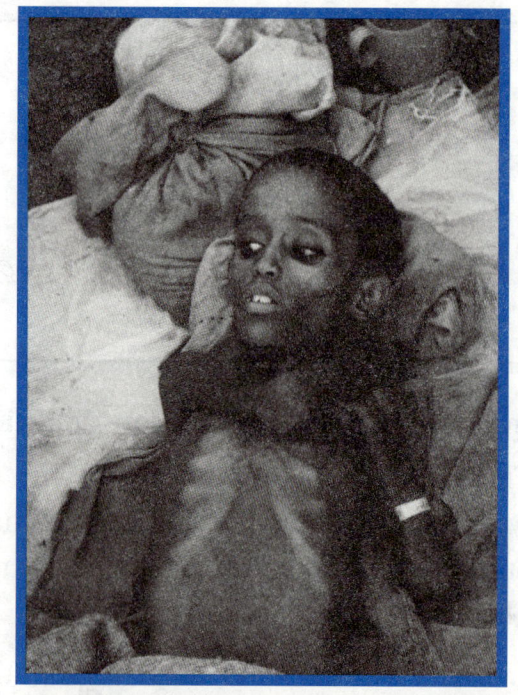

Changes in the Earth's environment lead to droughts. Future droughts may cause millions to starve.

❖ CONTINUED

Your Task

INTERPRETING A LINE GRAPH

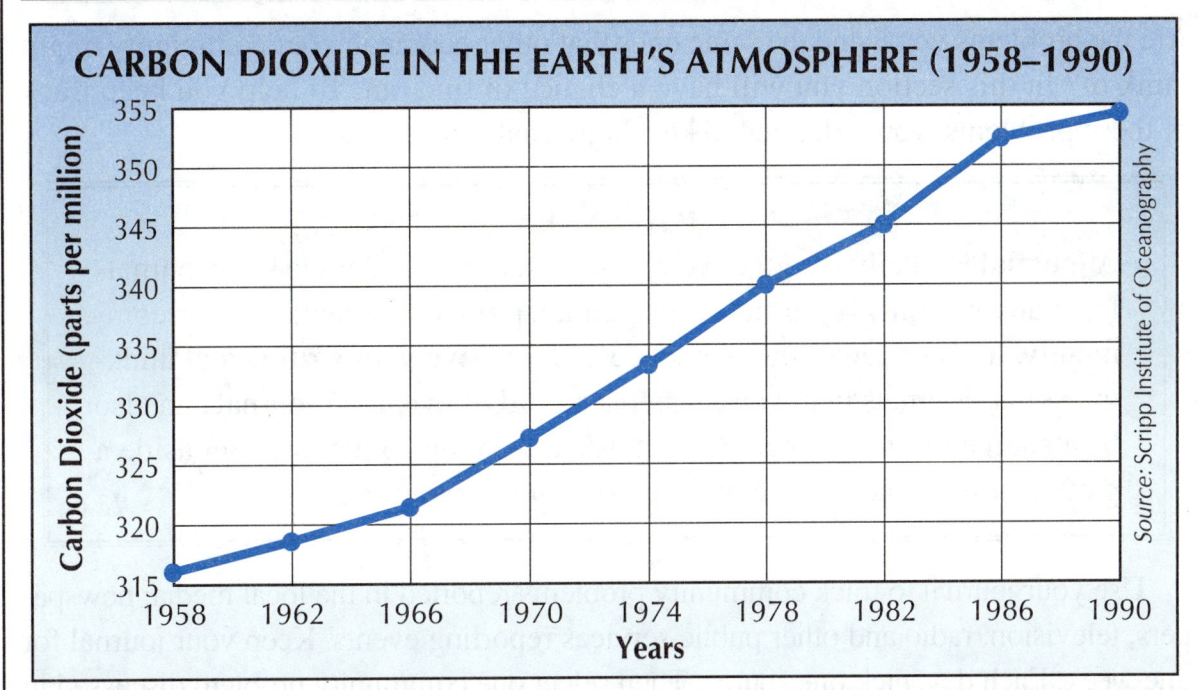

CARBON DIOXIDE IN THE EARTH'S ATMOSPHERE (1958–1990)

Carbon Dioxide (parts per million) vs *Years* (1958–1990), rising from about 315 ppm in 1958 to about 355 ppm in 1990.

Source: Scripp Institute of Oceanography

✔ Checking Your Understanding ✔

❖ What is the title of this line graph?
❖ In this graph, what does the vertical axis show? the horizontal axis?
❖ How much did carbon dioxide in the atmosphere increase from 1958 to 1990?
❖ What trend does the line graph show from 1960 to 1990?
❖ What might be some of the effects of this trend?

EXPLORING YOUR COMMUNITY
KEEPING A JOURNAL ABOUT COMMUNITY PROBLEMS

It is sometimes said that people know more about problems in other parts of the world than those around their own corner. Do you know about the problems facing your community? List **two** of the major problems you think your community faces. Discuss your answer with your classmates.

1. _____?_____
2. _____?_____

❖ CONTINUED

CREATING AND KEEPING A JOURNAL

Are the problems you listed the same ones that other people in your community might think of? In this section you will have a chance to find out. To help you keep track of these problems, you will need to keep a journal.

> ### ～ JOURNALS ～
> A **journal** is a daily record of your own observations. People keep journals for many reasons. A journal helps you keep track of events in your community. It also allows you to practice and improve your writing and thinking skills. Journals help you to keep a record of events. A journal can also be a source of ideas, when you are asked to write something. Set aside a particular time each day to make entries in your journal.

Use your journal to track community problems reported in the local media: newspapers, television, radio and other public services reporting events. Keep your journal for one week. Each day, pick one source. Then select one community problem discussed in that source. Once you choose your problem, you are ready to start entering information in your journal. There are many ways of keeping a journal. Here is one suggested method:

Date	Source of Information	Problem	Description or Recommendation
?	?	?	?

INTERPRETING YOUR JOURNAL

1. Which community problems were mentioned most frequently in the news? Compare your answer with those of your classmates.
2. Which of these problems do you think is having the greatest impact on your community? Explain your answer.
3. Do you have any suggestions for solving some of these problems? Compare your answers with those of your classmates.

SHOULD WE LIMIT THE AMOUNT OF VIOLENCE SHOWN ON TELEVISION?

7E

In this activity, we will look more closely at the citizen's task of decision-making: deciding whether or not the community should do something. In the pages that follow, you will be asked to take a stand on a public issue by reading several different sources. Then you will form your own conclusions and write a letter explaining your views. Look for the following important words:

| Should the President send soldiers to other countries to protect U.S. citizens there? | Should your state lower the age for driving a car? | Should your county raise taxes to build a homeless shelter? |

These are the kinds of public issues that citizens often think about and discuss. When you are 18 years old you will be able to take a stand on these and other important issues by voting. To be an informed voter, you must learn to make wise decisions on public issues. In this activity, you will have a chance to practice this important skill.

~ WHAT ARE ISSUES? ~

Issues are different from problems. An **issue** is something that people disagree about. It often concerns whether or not the government should do something, such as pass a law. There must be at least two different viewpoints for it to be an issue.

THE FIVE STEPS TO MAKING AN INFORMED DECISION

Skill Builder

In making **informed decisions** on public issues, you will need to:

Identify the issue	For example, you might be concerned that watching violence on television leads people to become violent in real life. Others may say that people are not affected by what they watch.
Get information from several sources	The more sources you look at, the more information you will find to help you learn about the issue. You will also get the benefits of seeing different points of view.

❖ CONTINUED

400 NEW YORK: ITS LAND AND ITS PEOPLE

3 Evaluate the information — You should compare what each of your sources of information has to say about the issue. When you evaluate information be sure to separate facts from opinions.

4 Compare different viewpoints — You should think of all the possible ways of dealing with the issue. Then you should compare these different viewpoints.

5 Make your decision — Finally, you should choose the view you think is best. You may come up with a view of your own. This could be a compromise of several views. A **compromise** is a solution in which each side gives up something, but also gets something in return.

When you need to make an informed decision, try to think of the illustration below. Recall that each step is part of the process of reaching a decision on a public issue. Now that you understand this, let's look at a real-life example in which you are asked for your opinion about a public issue. This example will help you to better understand these five steps and how they can help you to make an informed decision.

- Make your decision
- Identify and compare viewpoints
- Evaluate the information
- Get information from several sources
- Identify the issue

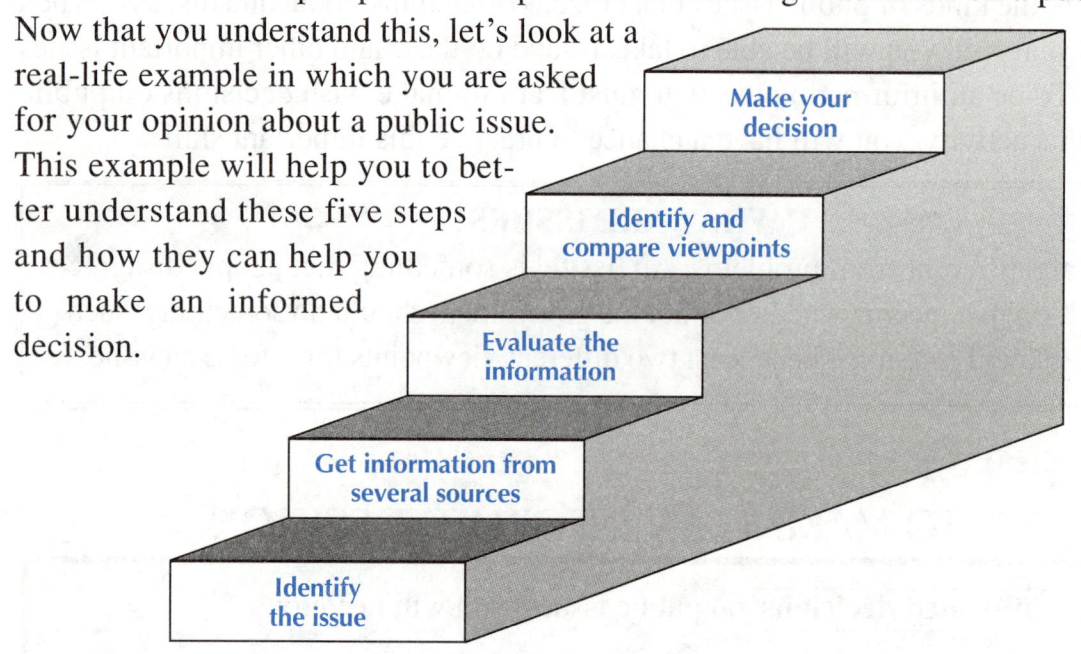

WOULD YOU SIGN A PETITION TO LIMIT VIOLENCE ON TELEVISION?

One evening at dinner, you are telling your parent what you learned in school about making informed decisions. Just then, the doorbell rings. It is one of your neighbors. He is holding some pamphlets and a **petition** (*a request or demand for action, sent to someone in authority such as a government official*).

STEP 1: IDENTIFYING THE ISSUE

Your neighbor reads the petition to both of you. It is addressed to your representative in Congress. The petition states that violence shown on television is one of the major reasons for rising crime throughout the nation. The petition states:

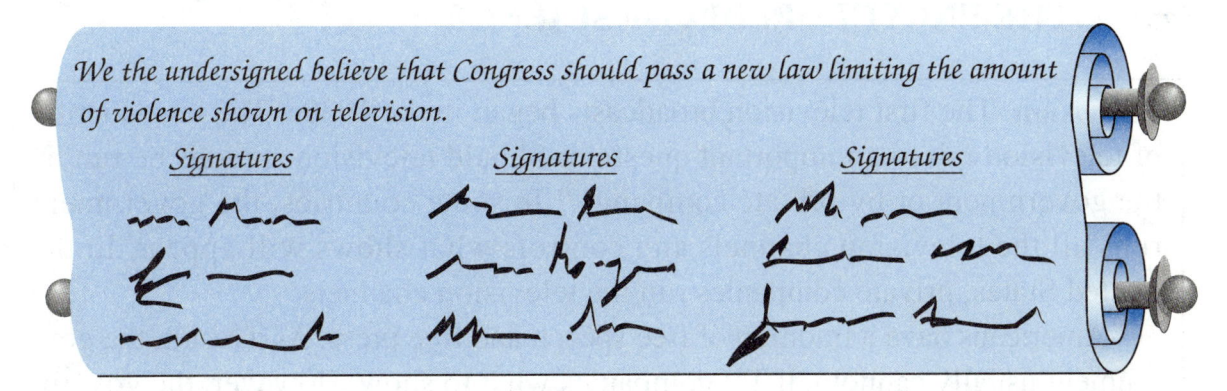

> *We the undersigned believe that Congress should pass a new law limiting the amount of violence shown on television.*
>
> *Signatures   Signatures   Signatures*

Your neighbor asks your parent to sign the petition. Signing the petition would mean that your parent agrees that this law is needed. Your parent says, " I would like more time to think about it."

After your neighbor leaves, your parent turns to you and says: "This is an important public issue. I don't know enough about it yet to make up my mind. Why don't we use the method you learned in school today to help me make an informed decision?"

✔ CHECKING YOUR UNDERSTANDING ✔

The first step towards making an informed decision is to identify the issue. What issue has your neighbor raised?

STEP 2: OBTAINING INFORMATION FROM SEVERAL SOURCES

In order to make an informed decision, you should gather information about the issue from different sources. Using special reference sources is a good place to begin. They give you basic information about the issue. Also, they can tell you where to find other information, such as articles written by experts.

Encyclopedias and almanacs are good starting points for any investigation. As you learned earlier, you must be careful to separate **facts** from **opinions**. Your parent suggests visiting the library together to find material.

✔ CHECKING YOUR UNDERSTANDING ✔

More information about the issue can be found in a variety of other sources. Name **three** other sources you might look at to find more information about the issue.

STEP 3: EVALUATING THE INFORMATION

Bringing together different sources of information is only the first step in making an informed decision. Next, you have to read and compare the different sources. Let's take a look at the first of several sources you might find in the library.

Source: THE ENCYCLOPEDIA OF SCIENCE

Television. The first television broadcasts began in the 1930s. The introduction of television raised an important question: Should television stations be run by the government or by private companies? In some countries, the government runs all the television channels and controls what shows will appear. In the United States, private companies run the television channels.

Americans have a tradition of free speech and free press. As a result, the government usually cannot tell TV companies what to show. However, the government does not let private television stations do just anything they want. The government still has the power to refuse to allow some shows to be aired. It rarely uses this right, but it always can.

Many critics believe the government should exercise this right more often, such as to curb violence on television. They propose that the government should at least rate all television shows for violence, just like the film industry rates the movies. Others say America would have much better programs if the government simply took over running the television stations.

✔ CHECKING YOUR UNDERSTANDING ✔

1. What question did the introduction of television raise?
2. How was this question answered in the United States?
3. What powers does the government have in the United States when it comes to television?

Now that you have some knowledge about the background of television, let's look at a second source of information you might use: a newspaper article.

Source: THE NEW YORK DAILY

The New York Daily

First Edition   Friday

TWO TEENS DIE IN HIGHWAY "DARE"

It all began as a joke. On Thursday night, Channel 3 was showing the latest action-adventure picture. In the movie, several teenagers lie down on the center divider line of a highway to show their friends they are not afraid.

After watching the movie, teenagers living near Albany began daring each other to lie down on the center line of the highway, just as the teenagers in the movie had done. Two teenagers took the dare, and now they are dead—run over by a driver who could not see them in the dark.

This is part of a growing number of violent, senseless deaths in America. Movies and television shows often influence us. Sometimes, we imitate what we see, as these teenagers did. Other times, we are influenced without even knowing it.

Parents, teachers and doctors across the nation are becoming alarmed at the growing amount of violence shown on television. Children watching television see thousands of acts of violence before they are old enough to go to school. Even cartoons often show violence between the cartoon characters. Some experts believe television violence may be partly responsible for the increasing violence in America. They are calling for Congress to pass new laws to ban all violence shown on television before 10 o'clock at night.

✔ CHECKING YOUR UNDERSTANDING ✔

1. What did this newspaper story have to say about violence on television?
2. Why are some people alarmed about the growing amount of violence on television?

Next, let's look at the third source of information you might use: a newspaper editorial.

NEWSPAPER EDITORIAL

Editorials are opinions written in newspapers and magazines. They are not news articles, which report facts. They usually represent the opinions of the editors. This allows them to speak out about a topic that concerns them. When trying to make an informed decision, it is a good idea to read editorials in several different newspapers and magazines. This allows you to learn about the opinions that different people have on the topic.

Source: EDITORIAL IN THE NEW YORK WORLD REPORT

WHERE WE STAND ON TELEVISION VIOLENCE

A growing number of people are seeking a new law to limit the violence shown on television. They think that violence on television is the main cause of violence in America. They are wrong. Poverty and the large number of guns are the main causes of violence.

Have the people in favor of this new law thought about the dangers of government control? Who in the government will decide which television programs are violent and which are not? Will the government also prevent stations from reporting violent stories on the news? Once the government controls some subjects on television, it may try to control others. Soon, the government will control everything we see. This violates our rights of free speech and a free press.

We believe it is better to let television stations show what they want. Parents should decide what their children can watch. If parents don't want their children to watch a show because it is too violent, there is a simple remedy: change the channel or turn off the set. If we allow the government to control what we watch, who can say where government controls will end?

✔ Checking Your Understanding ✔

What does this editorial tell you about allowing the government to control what private television stations can show?

A final source of information you might locate is a book about raising children.

Source: "HOW TO RAISE CHILDREN: ADVICE FOR PARENTS"

Page 231

Nightmares. As we all know, nightmares are terrifying dreams in which the dreamer feels helpless, afraid or sad. Tests show that children are the ones most likely to suffer from nightmares. Children may seem to enjoy television programs that show violence. However, once they are asleep, they often suffer from nightmares caused by these programs. For this reason, many parents and educators support the use of a special computer chip in televisions to prevent children from watching violent programs.

Educational Television. Since the 1960s, there have been many attempts to create interesting television programs. There are many shows that are both educational and fun to watch. The most successful of these has been "Sesame Street." Tests show that three-year olds watching Sesame Street regularly do better in learning some skills than those who do not watch the program. For this reason, many parents are asking the government to sponsor more educational programs.

CITIZENSHIP 405

> ✔ **CHECKING YOUR UNDERSTANDING** ✔
> 1. What does the book say about nightmares?
> 2. What does the book say about how television can shape our behavior?

STEP 4: COMPARE DIFFERENT VIEWPOINTS

You have just completed reading several sources. Now go back to the original issue:

> *Should the government limit the amount of violence shown on television?*

Think of all the different opinions you have read for dealing with this issue. They range from having the government do nothing to banning all the violence shown on television. After reading all of these different viewpoints, you may also have developed a solution of your own.

The following is a list of possible recommendations based on your reading. Make a copy of the chart. For each proposal, write down its advantages and disadvantages.

Views You Have Found— The government should:	Advantages	Disadvantages
❖ make no changes	?	?
❖ rate television shows like movies based on the violence they show	?	?
❖ place microchips in television sets to block violent programs	?	?
❖ ban all violent television shows before 10:00 at night	?	?
❖ *(you provide a possible solution)*	?	?

STEP 5: MAKING YOUR DECISION

Now that you have listed the advantages and disadvantages of each proposal, it's time to make an informed decision. Begin by comparing the disadvantages and advantages of each proposal. Decide which advantages and disadvantages are most important to you. There is usually no "correct" answer. All views have some advantages and disadvantages. Use a copy of the chart on page 406 to rank the possible actions, from the best (#1) to the worst (#5).

Possible Actions — The Government Should:	Number
❖ make no changes	?
❖ rate television shows like movies based on the violence they show	?
❖ insert microchips in television sets	?
❖ ban violent television shows before 10:00 at night	?
❖ (your solution)	?

Remember where we first began when your neighbor asked your parent to sign a petition? Now that you have made an informed decision, would you recommend that your parent sign it? ☐ Yes ☐ No Explain.

Did you make the right decision? If you think so, maybe you should try to persuade others to adopt your point of view. Write a letter to a newspaper, television station or your elected representative.

WRITING A PERSUASIVE LETTER OR ESSAY

A letter or essay that seeks to win someone over to your point of view is called a **persuasive essay**.

WHEN IS A PERSUASIVE ESSAY USED?
You use a persuasive essay to get a person to change his or her mind on a particular issue. For example, let's assume you wanted others to adopt the view that it is necessary to limit the amount of violence shown on television. You would use a persuasive essay to win them over to your point of view.

HINTS WHEN WRITING A PERSUASIVE ESSAY
You should clearly state your viewpoint. Then present logical reasons why the reader should adopt your view or suggested course of action. Avoid appeals to emotion. Instead, focus on presenting logical arguments and conclusions through the use of examples and comparisons.

❖ CONTINUED

WRITING A PERSUASIVE LETTER

In writing your letter, follow the "cheeseburger" format you learned about on pages 8 and 9. Let's review some of the steps you might take to write such a letter.

- **Introductory Paragraph.** Your introductory paragraph should state the purpose of your letter. In this case, your purpose is to convince the reader to limit the amount of violence shown on television.

- **Body of the letter.** Present as many reasons as you can to convince the person to support your viewpoint. Follow a clear and logical order. Each reason, for example, might be in a separate paragraph. Mention specific facts whenever you can to support your point of view. For example, you might mention that some young people are known to have acted in a "copycat" way after they saw violence on television or in the movies.

- **Closing the letter.** End with a summary of your main points. Try to impress your reader by concluding with some key fact or a memorable quote by someone about the subject. For example, point out how many people in our nation die each year from senseless violence. Conclude that this tragic situation cries out for immediate action.

MAILING YOUR LETTER

If you think you have written a strong persuasive letter, consider actually mailing it to your Congressperson in Washington, D.C. To do so, put your letter in an envelope addressed to your representative. You may want to review the proper form for writing a business letter discussed on pages 350 and 351

```
Your Name
Address
City, New York  Zip Code




                        The Honorable (name of representative)
                        c/o The United States House of Representatives
                        House Office Building
                        Washington, D.C.  20515
```

REVIEWING YOUR UNDERSTANDING

Creating Vocabulary Cards

Issue

What is an issue?

Name two issues facing Americans today:

Editorial

What is an editorial?

How are editorials helpful in making an informed decision?

Finding Information in an Almanac

The following is part of an index from an almanac. Review the topics in this index. Then answer the questions that follow.

ALMANAC

New York
- Area, capital 426
- Altitudes (high, low) 425
- Budget 150
- Cities 185
- Congressional Representation 360
- Debts 105-106
- Governor 89
- Mineral Production 428
- Population 360
- Presidential elections 583
- Schools 354
- State officials 91
- Unemployment benefits 142

1. The almanac gives information about New York State. List two pieces of information you could learn about New York in this almanac.

2. On which page of the almanac might you look to find:
   A. the name of the Governor of New York State?
   B. some minerals found in New York State?
   C. the highest and lowest points in New York State?

3. This almanac provides information about New York's schools. Name two types of information that you might find about New York's schools.

MAKING CONNECTIONS

EXPLORING BEYOND YOUR STATE
IMPORTANT ISSUES FACING AMERICANS TODAY

Throughout our history, Americans have been divided over certain issues. In the 1770s, Americans were divided over whether or not to declare independence from Great Britain. In the 1850s, Americans were divided over the practice of slavery. In the 20th century, Americans were divided over whether women should vote or whether the country should be involved in overseas wars.

READING A NEWSPAPER

Your Task

This tradition of disagreement continues today. The belief that reasonable individuals may hold different views about an issue lies at the core of our democracy. Let's look at a key issue facing our nation today. Over the next several weeks, read a national newspaper. Make a copy of the chart below to keep track of a major issue facing the nation:

DATE	SOURCE OF INFORMATION	DESCRIBE THE ISSUE

What do you think is the most important issue facing the nation today? Compare your answer with those of your classmates. Do their findings agree with yours? Explain.

EXPLORING YOUR COMMUNITY
WHAT ISSUES DIVIDE YOUR COMMUNITY?

The idea that people have different views on certain issues is not something that applies only in school. There are probably several issues today that people in your community disagree about.

❖ CONTINUED

For years community residents in Long Island City in Queens complained about the need for a park. Recently, New York City built a new Hunters Point Community Park with basketball courts, handball courts, water fountains, steel benches and a row of newly planted trees. This modern park even won an award for "design excellence" from the American Institute of Architects.

Hunters Point Community Park

Despite this, community residents are sharply divided over the park. Opponents of the park say it lacks grass and flowers, and has too much concrete. They want a traditional park with old-fashioned wooden benches, flowering gardens and shady trees to sit under in the summer. Other people love the park. They point to the many awards that it has received. They say some people oppose the park just because it is "different."

Long Island City is not alone in having local issues that divide people. Just about every community has some issues that most people have an opinion about. Is your community concerned about a new highway being built too close to a school? Is a new business opening up that many people in your community are against? What are the local issues dividing your community?

FINDING OUT ABOUT AN ISSUE

To find out, start by speaking to your parents and other adults in your community. Ask these people to suggest **one** issue that is a "hot" topic in your community. Have them tell you the pros and cons of each side. Also look at your community newspaper. Consult the "Letters to the Editor" and editorials, as well as news articles. Then make a copy of the following chart. Use it to record information on the issue:

THE ISSUE: _____?_____

Arguments of Those in Support	Arguments of Those Opposed
?	?

SUMMARIZING YOUR UNDERSTANDING

Directions: Use your knowledge to complete the following graphic organizer.

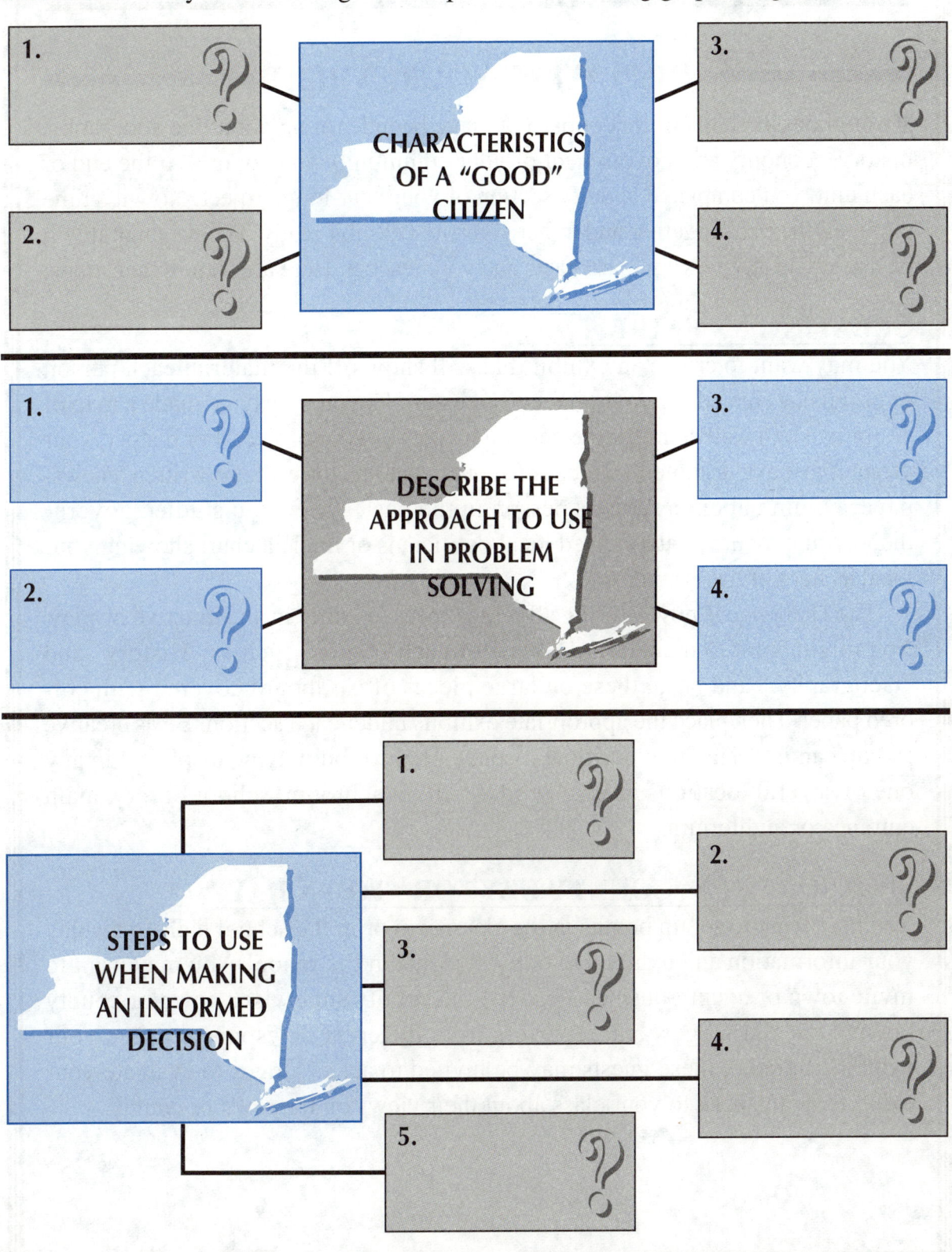

CHARACTERISTICS OF A "GOOD" CITIZEN
1.
2.
3.
4.

DESCRIBE THE APPROACH TO USE IN PROBLEM SOLVING
1.
2.
3.
4.

STEPS TO USE WHEN MAKING AN INFORMED DECISION
1.
2.
3.
4.
5.

INFORMATION SHEET #6: CITIZENSHIP

DISPLAYING YOUR EXHIBIT

Throughout the units of this book, you have been learning about the geography, history, economy and government of your community and county. At the end of each unit, you completed another section of your year-long project. Now it's time to put all the parts together and to get your final exhibit ready. The way that it will be done is up to you, your classmates and your teacher. Here are some suggestions:

CREATING AN EXHIBIT

You may want to create an exhibit that will show off the material each person or group has created for your project. For example, you may have made a map of your town or a wall chart for the geography part of your project. For history, your group may have designed a brochure about a local historic site or written a newspaper column about a famous person in the past. When you studied government, you may have interviewed local politicians or made a chart showing your local system of government.

The challenge is now to bring all these pieces together in an attractive display. You might want to make large labels for each section, such as "History" and "Geography," and paste these on large pieces of cardboard covered with colored paper. Then place the appropriate exhibits under each section. Be as creative as you can in designing your final display. The exhibit may be displayed in any one of several locations in your school—the lunchroom, school library, main entrance or auditorium.

SPONSORING A "COUNTY DAY" OR "TOWN DAY"

You may want to set up booths in the classroom or in the school halls to display your information and exhibits to other students in the school. You may want to invite town or county business leaders, the county supervisor, town or county lawmakers and judges, and reporters from different newspapers to see your exhibits. Some of these guests may be invited to act as judges to evaluate your exhibits, or to speak to your class about their views on the town or county.

CLOSING ACTIVITY: THE IMAGE I NOW HAVE OF NEW YORK IS ... ?

At the beginning of this book, you were invited to take a journey through New York—its land and its people. When you started out, you wrote what New York meant to you. Your trip through New York has covered its geography, history, people, economy and government. We hope you have learned a great deal about New York and your community.

WHAT DOES "NEW YORK" MEAN TO YOU NOW?

Your journey is about to come to an end. You should think once again about what New York means to you. One way to do this is to create an "ABC" book about New York:

❖ Each page should have one letter of the alphabet at the top.

❖ Each page should describe something different that you have learned about New York's geography, history, people, economy or government. What you describe should start with the same letter that is written on the top of the page.

❖ Each page should have a different illustration. These illustrations can be drawings you make yourself, pictures you cut out or photocopy from a newspaper, magazine or book. Each illustration should have a description or explanation.

Here is a sample of how one page dealing with the letter "A" might look:

Aa Albany

Albany is located near where the Hudson and Mohawk Rivers meet. Originally called Fort Orange, its first settlers were Dutch. It soon developed into a city because of the fur trade. Its population grew after the Erie Canal was built. Although the city is small in area, it is the capital of New York State.

Albany skyline

NEW YORK: ITS LAND AND ITS PEOPLE

To help you to organize your ABC book about New York, copy the following chart:

LETTER	WORD OR NAME	DESCRIPTION	ILLUSTRATION
A			
B			
C			
D			
E			
F			
G			
H			
I			
J			
K			
L			
M			
N			
O			
P			
Q			
R			
S			
T			
U			
V			
W			
X			
Y			
Z			

GLOSSARY

A

abolitionists. A group of people who opposed slavery before the Civil War. [146]

acid rain. Chemicals in the atmosphere from factory smokestacks and automobile exhaust fumes that return to the Earth in the form of rain or snow. [392]

Adirondack Mountains. The highest mountains in New York State, found in the northeastern part of the state. [69]

almanac. A book of facts published each year. Almanacs cover a wide range of subjects. They often list movie stars, explorers, musicians, writers, Nobel prize winners and athletes. [83]

ancestors. Members of your family who lived a long time ago, such as great-grandparents. [209]

Articles of Confederation. The agreement creating the first United States government. The government created by the Articles was unusually weak. The Articles were soon replaced by the U.S. Constitution. [133]

atlas. A book of maps and geographical information. [27]

autobiography. A book written by a person about his or her own life. [253]

automation. The use of machines to replace human labor. [283]

axis of the Earth. The imaginary line that the Earth spins on. [17]

B

Bill of Rights. The first ten amendments to the U.S. Constitution, guaranteeing individual rights. [374]

borough. One of the five counties of New York City: Manhattan, the Bronx, Queens, Brooklyn and Staten Island. [345]

Buddhism. A religion based on the teachings of an Indian prince who spent his life searching for the true meaning of life. [212]

C

capital goods. Goods that are used to make other goods and services. [283]

cartographers. People who make maps. [47]

Catskill Mountains. Mountains in southwestern New York State. [71]

cause. The reason why something happened. [165]

charter. A document defining the rules of behavior for a group. [324]

Christianity. A religion whose members believe Jesus died to save humanity. Christians believe that after his death, Jesus returned from the dead and rose to heaven. [211]

chronological order. The order in which events actually happened. [240]

citizen. A person who is a member of a particular nation. [368]

Civil Rights Movement. Movement in the 1950s and 1960s aimed at ending racial segregation. [356]

classify. To arrange, organize and sort information belonging to a certain group or category. It is especially helpful when trying to make sense out of many items that seem disorganized. [260]

climate. The average weather condition of a place over a long period of time. [45]

command economy. A system in which important economic decisions are answered by government officials. [288]

Common Market. An association of Western European countries formed to allow its members to freely trade goods among themselves. [316]

compass rose. A drawing on a map which shows the four basic directions: north, south, east and west. [49]

concept. A name given to a group of things that, although different, have something in common. [204]

constituents. The people who live in an elected official's home district. [349]

constitution. A written plan setting up how a government will work. [343]

consumers. People who use goods and services to satisfy their needs and wants. [277]

consumption. The act of using goods and services. [277]

continents. The world's seven major land masses: Asia, Africa, North America, South America, Antarctica, Europe and Australia. [18]

counties. Except for Louisiana, every state is divided into these smaller units. New York State is divided into 62 counties. [21]

country. A place that has borders separating it from neighboring places and has its own government. People in a country often speak the same language and have similar customs and traditions. [19]

criteria. The conditions we create to allow us to define and classify something. [251]

cultural diffusion. Exchange of ideas and customs between different peoples by trade, war and other contacts. [232]

culture. The way of life shared by a group of people. [80]

D

Declaration of Independence. A document issued in 1776 that explains why the colonists decided to seek independence from Great Britain. [125]

Declaration of the Rights of the Child. A declaration by the United Nations meant to focus world attention on the special need to protect the rights of children. [379]

democracy. A form of government in which citizens rule themselves. In a such a government, the people hold the power. [325]

demography. The study of population. [83]

depression. An economic downturn that occurs when many businesses fail and large numbers of people are unemployed. The Great Depression occurred in the 1930s. [170]

dictatorship. A system of government in which all power is concentrated in the hands of a single person or a small group. [330]

direct democracy. A form of democracy in which citizens take part directly in important government decisions. [382]

duties. Things that the law says you have to do. If you refuse to perform your duties, you may have to pay a fine or go to jail. [372]

E

Eastern Hemisphere. Name given to the half of the Earth east of the Prime Meridian. [17]

economics. The study of how nations, businesses and individuals make things, buy things and use money. [271]

editorial. A statement written in a newspaper that gives opinions of the newspaper's editors about important issues in the news. [403]

effect. What happens as a result of a situation, action or event. [165]

Emancipation Proclamation. Issued by Abraham Lincoln in 1862, it stated that enslaved people in the Confederacy would be freed on January 1, 1863. [355]

encyclopedias. Books that contain articles with information on many topics. Encyclopedias usually have many volumes. Their articles are arranged in alphabetical order. [251]

entrepreneurs. People who bring the factors of production together in the hope of making a profit. [284]

environment. The Earth and the natural resources that surround us. [391]

equator. An imaginary line drawn around the middle of the Earth. [17]

Erie Canal. Canal built in the 1820s to connect Lake Erie to the Hudson River. [136]

ethnic group. A group whose members share traditions, customs, beliefs and ancestors. Often members of the same ethnic group have the same national origin, culture, language or race. [201]

executive branch. The branch of government with the power to enforce the laws. [334]

exports. Exports are goods and services sold from one country to other countries. [309]

F

fact. A statement that can be checked for accuracy by looking at several sources to see if it is correct or incorrect. [100]

factories. Buildings in which goods are made. [296]

factors of production. All the things needed to produce goods and services. [282]

federalism. The division of government power between the national government and state governments. [331]

free market economy. An economic system in which the government allows people to produce whatever they can, and to consume whatever they can afford. [288]

G

gazetteer. A geographical dictionary that provides some information about each of its listings. [28]

generalization. A general statement identifying a common pattern in a group of things. [215]

geography. The study of different places around the world, including a study of people, where they live and how they are linked to the world around them. [31]

glaciers. Huge sheets of ice that once covered most of New York State. [60]

global warming. A general rise in the Earth's temperature caused by increasing amounts of gases such as carbon dioxide, which prevent heat from escaping into space. [396]

goods. Items people make or grow, such as food, toys, clothes and cars. [282]

government. The organization that makes a community's rules, settles disputes and protects members of the community from hostile groups. [327]

governor. The chief executive of a state government. [341]

Great Lakes: Five major lakes located between the United States and Canada: Lake Huron, Lake Ontario, Lake Michigan, Lake Erie and Lake Superior. [59]

H

hemisphere. Geographers divide the Earth into halves; each one is known as a hemisphere because each one is half of a sphere. [17]

hero. Someone who is known for his or her achievements. Heroes and heroines are the people who make history. [254]

Hinduism. A religion from India whose followers believe in many gods and goddesses. Hindus also believe that at death, a person's spirit leaves the body to be reborn in another living thing. [212]

Hispanics. An ethnic group whose language is Spanish. Hispanics may come from or have ancestors from the Caribbean area, Central America, South America or Spain. [207]

Homespun, Age of. The years 1800–1860 in which pioneer farmers in Western New York made by hand most of the things they needed to survive. [134]

Hudson Valley. Valley running northward from New York City to Albany. [72]

human rights. Basic rights that all humans need to enjoy life and live in a fair society. [379]

human-environment interaction. The way in which the physical features of a place affect its people, and how the people affect their environment. [33]

I

immigration. The movement of people into a country. An immigrant is someone who goes to a country with the intention of living there. [166]

imports. Products from other countries brought into the United States for sale. [309]

index. The final pages of a book listing the information in the book and page numbers where information in the book can be found. [28]

Industrial Revolution. A change in the way of making things that began in England in the late 1760s. Instead of being made by hand at home, goods were made by machines in workshops and factories. [154]

interdependent. Nations that rely or depend on trading with other nations for goods and services. [309]

Islam. The religion of Muslims. Muslims follow the teachings of Mohammed and believe in one all-powerful God, Allah. [212]

issues. A topic or question that people have two opposing viewpoints about. [399]

J

Judaism. The religion of the Jewish people. It is based on the belief that a single all-powerful and just God is the creator of the universe. [211]

judicial branch. The branch of government that interprets the laws. [334]

L

labor. The work that people do to make goods or provide services. This includes the talents, training, skills and knowledge of the people doing this work. [283]

land. In economics, this refers to resources such as metals, minerals, water, plants and soil found in nature. [283]

Latin America. A geographic area that includes Mexico, the Caribbean area and the countries of Central and South America. [80]

latitude. Imaginary horizontal lines that run across the Earth. They are sometimes called parallels because they run parallel to each other. [53]

laws. Rules made by a government. Violation of a law is usually punished with a penalty. [324]

leader. A person with three basic characteristics: a vision for the future, an ability to communicate his or her vision to others and the ability to get others to act. [352]

League of Five Nations. An alliance of five Iroquois tribes formed in 1570 to end the constant fighting among themselves. [109]

legend. The part of a map that is used to unlock the meaning of the map's symbols. The legend is sometimes called the "key." [49]

legislative branch. The branch of government that makes laws. [333]

line graph. A chart made up of a series of points connected by a line. Line graphs often show how something has increased, decreased or remained the same. [385]

location. Where something can be found in relation to other things. [31]

Long Island. A large island in southeastern New York. [75]

longitudes. A set of imaginary lines that run up and down a map or globe. They are drawn as lines connecting the North Pole to the South Pole. [54]

M

majority rule. A majority is more than half. In a democracy, decisions are made by a majority of the people. [383]

maps. A small picture, diagram or model of a place, showing where things are located. [47]

mayor. The chief executive of a city government. [345]

minerals. Valuable resources found in the Earth, such as iron ore or gold. [301]

Mohawk Valley. Valley cutting between the Adirondacks and Appalachian Plateau. [73]

monarchy. A government in which a king or queen holds power. A king or queen is a ruler who inherits his or her power. [330]

multi-racial society. A society made up of many different races. [205]

museum. Places where works of art and other valuable or interesting objects are displayed. [259]

myths. A story about a fact of nature or an event in history. They are as old as human civilization itself. [237]

N

NAFTA. The North American Free Trade Agreement was signed by the United States, Canada and Mexico. All three nations agreed to eliminate most tariffs among themselves. [316]

national origin. The country where your parents, grandparents or ancestors came from. [207]

nationality. The country in which a person is a citizen. [207]

Native American. The first people to live in the Americas. [101]

natural resources. Plants, animals and minerals found in nature used to grow food, supply energy, make clothing, provide housing and serve as raw materials. [45]

naturalized citizen of the United States. People who were not born in the United States and whose parents are not American citizens become citizens by living in the United States for a period of time and passing a citizenship test. [368]

New Amsterdam. The first settlement of Dutch people on Manhattan island from 1624 to 1664. [119]

New Deal. A program created by President Franklin D. Roosevelt to provide work and bring relief to Americans during the Great Depression. [171]

New Netherland. The early Dutch colony in New York. [119]

New York Court of Appeals. The highest court in New York State. It is the state equivalent of the U.S. Supreme Court. [342]

New York State Legislature. The legislative branch of our state government. It makes the laws for New York. The state legislature consists of two houses: the Assembly and the Senate. [339]

new-media. An industry of small companies that develop and market Internet sites, multimedia software, on-line computer entertainment and other digital offerings. [298]

Nineteenth Amendment. An amendment passed in 1920, giving women the right to vote. [389]

Northern Hemisphere. Name given to the half of the Earth north of the equator. [17]

O

opinion. A statement of personal beliefs, which cannot be checked for accuracy. [100]

opportunity cost. The "cost" of every economic decision measured by the opportunity someone gives up to do other things. [275]

oral history. Collecting and recording memories of the past obtained through interviews of eyewitnesses. [194]

orbit. The path made by the Earth as it travels around the Sun. [16]

ozone layer. A band of gas that surrounds the Earth. The ozone layer acts as a shield that prevents the harmful rays of the sun from reaching us. [396]

P

per capita income. The average amount of money each person earns. [83]

pesticides. Chemicals used by farmers to kill insects and other animals that eat crops. [392]

petition. A request or demand for change, sent to a government official or someone in authority. [400]

physical regions. Areas with similar geographical features or climate. Physical regions can can be large or small. [7]

pie chart. A circle diagram that is divided into different size slices in order to show how the parts are related to the whole pie. [206]

pollution. Dirt, fumes and other substances that make our environment unclean. [391]

population density. The average number of people living in an area. [83]

precipitation. Moisture that falls to the Earth as rain, snow, hail and sleet. [61]

President, United States. The chief executive officer of our national government. [334]

primary source. The original records of an event. [176]

Prime Meridian. An imaginary line drawn from the North Pole to the South Pole, through Greenwich, England. [17]

problem of scarcity. The chief problem in economics: that society has limited resources to satisfy people's unlimited wants and needs. [275]

problem solving. The five-step process someone goes through in order to find a solution to a problem. [393]

product map. A specialized type of map that identifies where agricultural products are grown and industries and resources are located. [304]

production. The act of making or providing goods and services. [277]

profit. The amount of money left in a business after expenses have been paid. [284]

R

race. A group of people identified by some common physical characteristics, such as the color of their skin. [205]

recycling. Creating new products from used cans, bottles, paper and plastic that would otherwise be thrown out. [394]

reform. To change a policy or way of life in order to make it better. [143]

regions. Areas near each other that have similar characteristics or features. [20]

religion. A system of belief about the existence of God or several gods. Each religion usually also has a set of customs and practices and an organization, such as a church, which sets the conduct of its members. [208]

representative democracy. A system of government in which citizens elect representatives to serve in their place and to make important government decisions for them. [382]

representatives. Elected officials, in a democracy, who carry out the will of the people. [382]

responsibilities. Things a good citizen should do, such as voting. [372]

revolution. A change of government by force. A revolution can also refer to a very rapid economic or social change, such as the Industrial Revolution. [124]

right. Something everyone in society is entitled to or allowed to do. Our rights are generally protected by the U.S. Constitution. [371]

S

scale. A device used by mapmakers to show what distance the measurements on a map stand for in real life. [50]

secondary source. The writings and viewpoints of historians and other authors written after an event. [176]

sectionalism. A feeling of greater loyalty to one's own section of the country, such as the North or South, than to the country as a whole. [150]

segregation. Separation of people by race. [356]

Seneca Falls Convention. A meeting held in 1848 at Seneca Falls, New York, by a group of women reformers who sought equal rights with men. [144]

service industries. Jobs in which workers provide services to others. [297]

services. Acts that people do for others. People such as electricians, plumbers and barbers provide services. [282]

Southern Hemisphere. The name given to the half of the Earth south of the equator. [17]

special district. A unit of government providing a service that is not provided by a city, town or village government, such as water supply or garbage and snow removal. [346]

sphere. An object that is shaped like a giant ball or globe. [17]

state government. The level of government that handles matters affecting people throughout the state. [339]

states. Most countries are divided into smaller political units known as states or provinces. The United States is divided into 50 units known as states. [21]

suburb. A residential community lying outside a city. [188]

symbol. Something that stands for or represents something else. A stop sign and the American flag are both symbols. [49]

T

table. An arrangement of words or numbers in columns used for organizing large amounts of information so this information can be easily located and compared. [85]

table of contents. A list found in the first few pages of a book with the main topics of the book, broken into units, and the pages on which they can be found. [253]

tariffs. Special taxes on goods from other countries. [316]

tenements. Apartment buildings built in New York City and other cities to house low income families. Tenements squeezed many families into a tight living space. [159]

Thousand Islands. A group of more than 1,000 islands in northern New York State that stretch for 50 miles along the St. Lawrence River. [68]

timeline. A chart that shows a group of events arranged along a line in chronological order. [240]

topography. The land forms of the Earth, such as mountains and plains. These forms were created by different processes throughout the Earth's history. [60]

traditional economy. A type of economic system in which the three basic questions are answered by tradition and custom. [287]

U

U.S. Congress. The legislative branch of our national government, making laws for the nation. Congress is made up of two houses: the Senate and the House of Representatives. [333]

U.S. Supreme Court. The highest court in the nation. The court bases its decisions on the U.S. Constitution and federal laws. [334]

underground railroad. A way for enslaved African Americans to escape from slavery in the South, until they reached a place where slavery was illegal. [146]

United Nations. An international organization whose goal is to keep world peace, promote international cooperation, and end hunger and disease in the world. [263]

Universal Declaration of Human Rights. This U.N. document defines basic rights that should be guaranteed to the citizens of all countries. [379]

urban. Relating to a city. New York City is an example of an urban area. [40]

urbanization. The movement of people from the countryside into cities. [158]

W

weather. An area's current temperature, wind and amount of sunshine. [61]

Western Hemisphere. The name given to the half of the Earth to the west of the Prime Meridian. [17]

World War I. A war that started in Europe in 1914. The United States entered the war in 1917. [168]

World War II. A war started in Europe in 1939, when Hitler's armies invaded Poland. [177]

PICTURE GAZETTEER

I. MAJOR LAND FORMS

Canyons. A canyon is a deep, narrow valley with very steep sides. Canyons are formed by running water that has eroded the ground over thousands of years.

Coastline. The land that lies next to a large body of water forms a coastline. The coastline of part of New York is next to the Atlantic Ocean.

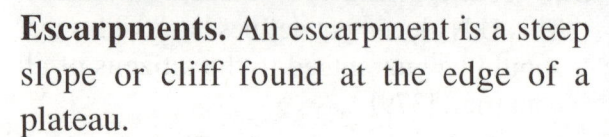

Escarpments. An escarpment is a steep slope or cliff found at the edge of a plateau.

Hills. Masses of earth and rock that are not as high as mountains are called hills. One example of hills in New York State is the Hudson Hills. They are found east of the Hudson River, mainly in Putnam and Dutchess counties.

Mountains. Huge masses of earth and rock that rise at least 1,000 feet above the land are called mountains. A group of mountains is called a mountain range. In New York State, two of the most famous mountain ranges are the Adirondack Mountains and the Catskill Mountains. The Adirondacks range in the height from 2,000 feet above sea level to 5,344 feet at Mt. Marcy—the state's highest point

Plains. A plain is a large area of flat or slightly hilly land. Plains are often used by people to build cities and farm crops because their land is flat.

Plateau. A plateau is an area of flat, level land that is raised higher than the regions around it. In New York State, the Appalachian Plateau is an example of a plateau. This plateau is New York's largest land region. This plateau is where many of the state's farms can be found.

Valley. A valley is an area of low land that runs between hills and mountains. In New York State many people live in the Hudson-Mohawk valley. The Hudson Valley is bounded by the Catskill Mountains to the west and the Taconics to the east.

424 NEW YORK: ITS LAND AND ITS PEOPLE

II. MAJOR BODIES OF WATER

Barrier Island. A barrier island is created when waves push up rock and sand to form pieces of land that rise above the surface of the ocean. A barrier island may be small or large enough to build homes. Fire Island, off the southern coast of Long Island, is an example of a barrier island in New York State.

Gulfs. A gulf is part of an ocean or sea, that is surrounded on three sides by land. On the southern border of the United States is an example of a large gulf—the Gulf of Mexico.

Harbors. A harbor is a protected body of water usually located along a coastline. Usually a piece of land stands between a harbor and the larger body of water. The economic success of New York City is due, in part, to its excellent harbor.

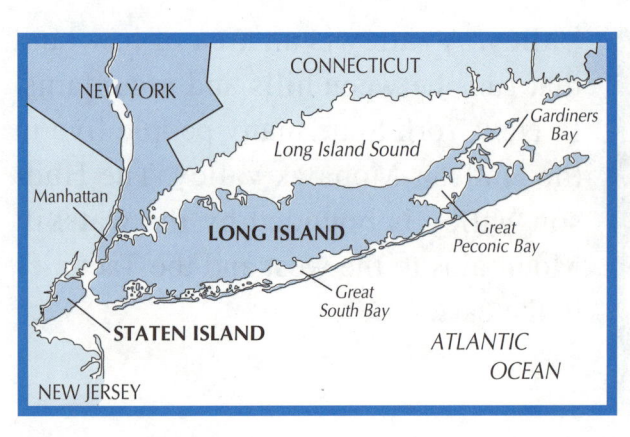

Islands. An island is a piece of land that is surrounded by water on all sides. Staten Island and Long Island are examples of islands in New York State. In upstate New York there are also many islands, such as the Thousand Islands.

Lakes. A lake is a body of water that is surrounded by land. In the United States there are five major lakes called the Great Lakes. Two of these lakes border New York State: Lake Erie and Lake Ontario. New York also has the Finger Lakes, Lake George and 8,000 smaller lakes.

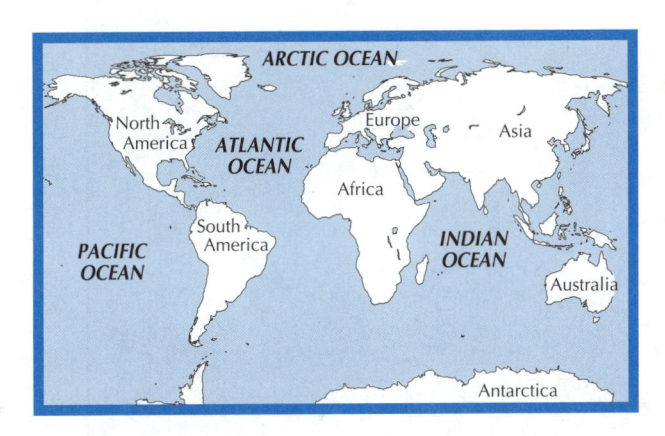

Ocean. An ocean is an extremely large body of salt water. There are four main oceans: the Atlantic Ocean, the Pacific Ocean, the Arctic Ocean and the Indian Ocean. New York State is located near the Atlantic Ocean.

Peninsula. A piece of land that is surrounded by water on three sides and is connected to a larger piece of land is called a peninsula. Much of the state of Florida forms a peninsula.

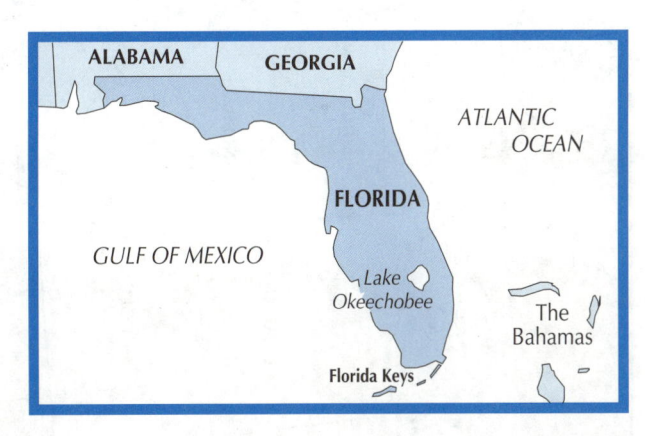

Rivers. They are long, narrow bodies of fresh water that flow into other rivers or the ocean. New York State has many rivers. Its two main rivers are the Hudson River and the Mohawk River. Other important rivers in New York include the Genesee, the Oswego, the Seneca, the Susquahanna, the Allegheny and the East River.

426 NEW YORK: ITS LAND AND ITS PEOPLE

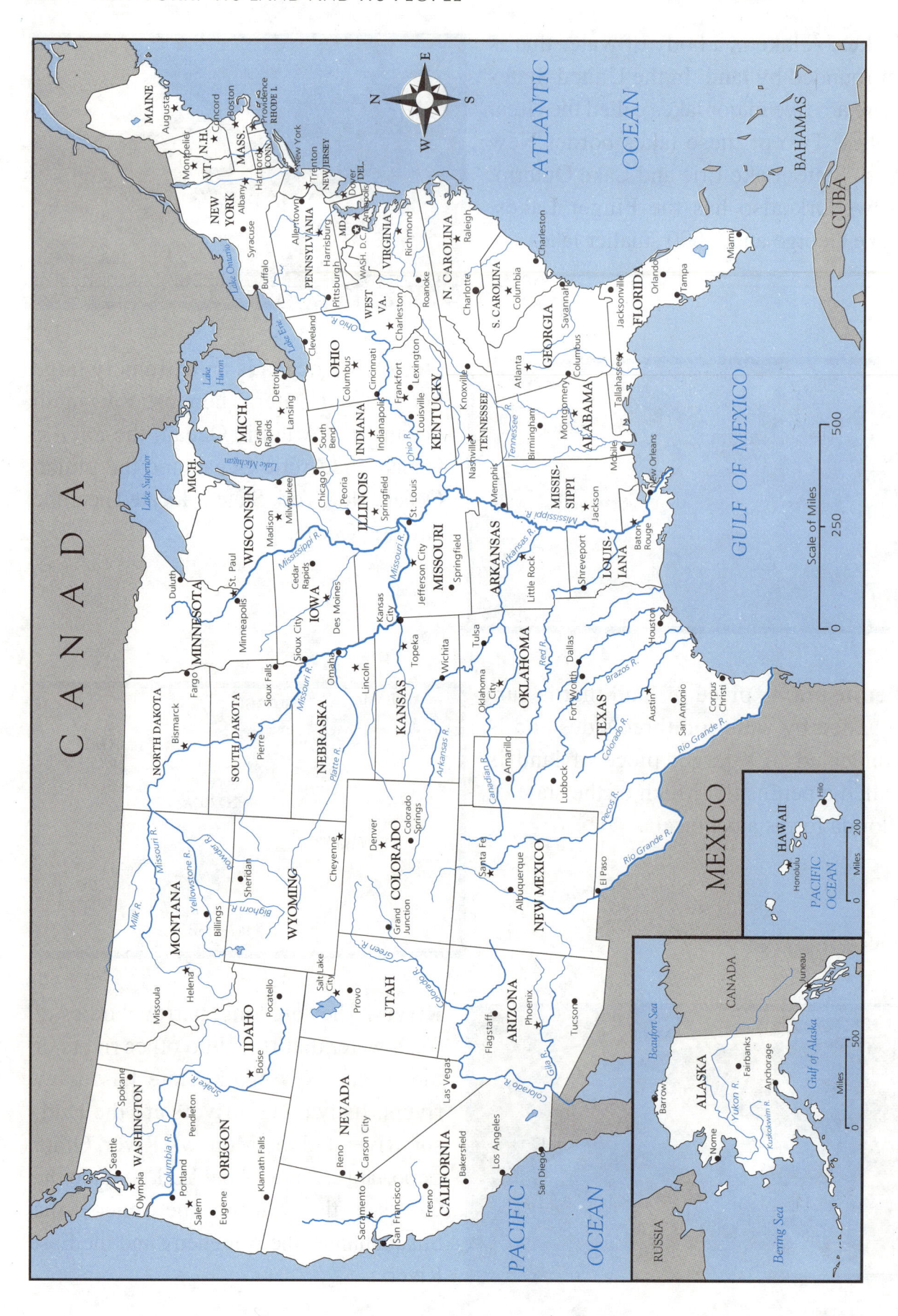

NEW YORK: ITS LAND AND ITS PEOPLE

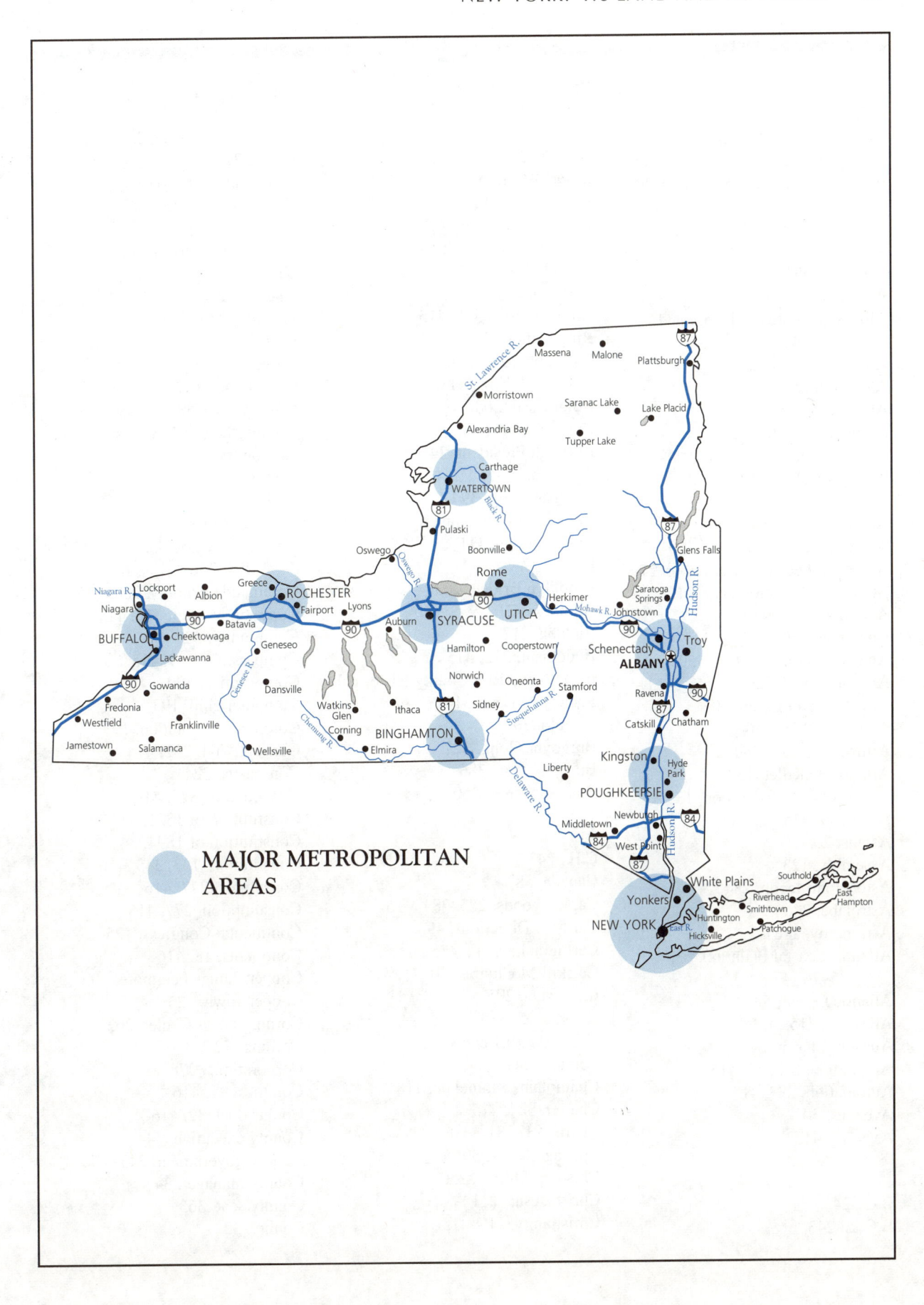

MAJOR METROPOLITAN AREAS

INDEX

A

A.D., 243
Abolitionists, 146, 415
Acid rain, 392, 415
Adirondack Mountains, 60, 69–70, 415
African-American Day Parade, 224
African Americans, 222–224
African, 205
Agriculture, 295
Albany Institute of History and Art, 141
Albany, 73, 339, 413
Aldrin, Buzz, 244
Aleut, 205
Algonquians, 102–111
Allen, Ethan, 126
Allegheny River, 59
Almanac, 83–86, 415
Amazon Rain Forest, 20
American Civil War, 149–150
American Federation of Labor, 279
American Revolution, 123–128
Ancestors, 207, 415
Anchorage, 39
Anthony, Susan B., 144, 359
Anti-Semitism, 220
Appalachian Plateau, 60
Aqueduct, 158, 246
Armstrong, Neil, 244
Arnold, Benedict, 132
Articles of Confederation, 133, 349, 415
Asians, 205
Assembly, 123
Astor, John Jacob, 284
Astrolabe, 246
Astronomy, 246
Atlantic Coastal Plain, 60, 63, 75–76
Atlantic Ocean, 59
Atlas, 27, 415
Ausable Chasm, 69
Autobiography, 253, 415
Automation, 283, 415
Avenues, 30
Axis, 17, 415

B

B.C., 243
B.C.E., 243
Baldwin, James, 224
Bar graphs, 348–349
Barrier Island, 76, 424
Barrios, 225
Baseball Hall of Fame, 250, 263
Battle of Long Island, 126
Battle of Oriskany, 127
Battle of Saratoga, 127–128
Bausch, John, 156
Berlin, Irving, 221
Bill of Rights, 374, 415
Binghamton, 71–72
Biography, 252
Blackwell, Elizabeth, 359
Boldt Castle, 68
Boldt, George, 68
Borough President, 345
Boroughs, 345, 415
Brainstorming, 394
Branches of government, 332
Brant, Joseph, 111
Bronx, 77
Brooklyn Bridge, 263
Brooklyn, 77
Buddha, 212
Buddhism, 212, 415
Buffalo and Erie County Historical Society Museum, 141
Buffalo, 70
Burgoyne, John, 127
Bush, George, 386
Business letter, 350

C

C.E., 243
Canada, 58
Capital goods, 283–284, 415
Cardinal Directions, 49
Cartographers, 47, 415
Catskill Mountains, 20, 71, 415
Caucasian, 205
Cause, 165, 415
Cause-And-Effect, 7
Century, 242
Champlain, Samuel de, 118
Charter, 324, 415
Charts, 91, 181
Chenago River, 59
Chisolm, Shirley, 250
Christ, Jesus, 211
Christianity, 211, 415

Chronological order, 240, 415
Church, 211
Churchill, Winston, 359
Cities, 22
Citizenship, 368, 415
City Council, 345
City-states, 324
Civil Rights Movement, 356, 415
Civil War, 148
Clans, 102
Classify, 260, 415
Clermont, 136
Cleveland, Grover, 159
Climate, 45, 61, 415
Clinton, Bill, 386
Clinton, DeWitt, 135
Clinton, George, 133
Coastline, 422
Collage, 129
Columbus Day, 218
Columbus, Christopher, 14, 117, 254–256
Command economy, 288, 415
Common Market, 316, 415
Community, 32
Compass rose, 49, 415
Compromise, 400
Computer chip, 193
Computer Revolution, 193
Concept, 204, 232, 415
Consensus, 324
Constituents, 349, 416
Constitution of 1821, 343
Constitution of 1894, 343
Constitution, 133, 343, 416
Consumers, 277, 416
Consumption, 277, 416
Continental Congress, 125
Continents, 18, 416
Cooper, James Fenimore, 102
Cooperstown, 72
Corning Glass Center, 263
Corning, 72
Corporations, 278
Counties, 21, 416
Country, 19, 32, 416
County executive, 344
County government, 343
County manager, 344
County seat, 363
County, 32

Criteria, 251, 393, 416
Cultural diffusion, 232–235, 416
Cultural region, 80–81
Culture, 80, 416
Cuomo, Mario, 192
Curtiss Museum of Local History, 141

D

D-Day, 179
Decade, 242
Declaration of Independence, 125, 374, 416
Declaration of Sentiments and Resolutions, 144
Declaration of the Rights of the Child, 379, 416
Degrees, 53
Delaware River, 59
Democracy, 325, 331, 382, 416
Demography, 83, 416
Denominator, 311
Depression, 170, 416
Descriptive essay, 257
Dewey, Thomas E., 191
Diary, 178
Dictatorship, 330, 416
Dictionary, 352–353
Diorama, 200
Direct democracy, 382, 416
Direction indicator, 49
Dix, Dorothea, 145, 359
Douglass, Frederick, 146
Draft riots, 148
Drafting, 9
Dutch East India Company, 14
Duties, 372, 416

E

E.E.C., 316
Eastern Hemisphere, 17, 416
Eastman, George, 156
Economic groups, 277–278
Economics, 271, 275, 416
Economic systems, 287–289
Edison, Thomas, 156
Editorial, 403, 416
Effect, 165, 416
Ellis Island, 166, 262
Elmira, 72
Emancipation Proclamation, 151, 355, 416

Encyclopedia, 113, 251, 416
Endicott, 71
Entrepreneurs, 284, 416
Environment, 391, 416
Environmental Protection Agency, 279
Epitaph, 151
Equator, 17, 53, 416
Erie Canal, 98–99, 135–136, 416
Escarpments, 422
Ethnic group, 201, 207, 416
Ethnicity, 207
Everglades, 40–41
Executive branch, 334, 417
Executive power, 332
Exports, 309, 417
Expressways, 29

F

Fact, 100, 401, 417
Factories, 296, 417
Factors of Production, 282, 417
Farmers, 295
Farnham, Eliza, 143
Federal Hall Memorial, 262
Federalism, 331, 417
Ferraro, Geraldine, 250
Fertilizers, 295
Fifteenth Amendment, 388
Finger Lakes, 59, 71
Fire Island, 76
Fire Island National Seashore, 263
Fishermen, 296
Flood, The Great, 237–238
Forests, 301
Fort Orange, 121
Fort Stanwix, 121
Fort Ticonderoga, 69, 126, 259
Free enterprise system, 291
Free market economy, 288, 417
Freedom of the press, 373
French and Indian Wars, 123
Fulton, Robert, 136

G

Gandhi, Mohandas, 359–360
Gardner, Lion, 198
Gates, Horatio, 127
Gautama, Siddhartha, 212
Gazetteer, 28, 417
Gender, 388
General Electric, 156
Generalization, 215, 417

Genesee River, 59
Geography, 31, 417
Gettysburg Address, 355
Giuliani, Rudolph, 346
Glaciers, 60, 417
Global warming, 396, 417
Globe, 48
Goethals, George, 91
Gompers, Samuel, 280
Goods, 282, 417
Government agencies, 279
Government, 327, 330, 417
Governor, 123, 341, 417
Gravestone rubbing, 151–152
Great Basin, 64
Great Lakes Plain, 70–71
Great Lakes, 59, 64, 417
Grid, 47
Gulf, 424

H

Hale, Nathan, 257
Half Moon, 14–15
Hamilton, Alexander, 134, 138
Hamlets, 346
Harbor, 424
Harlem Renaissance, 223
Hemisphere, 17, 417
Hero, 254, 417
Hill Cumorah, 262
Hills, 422
Hinduism, 212, 417
Hiroshima, 184
Hispanics, 207, 210, 417
Hogans, 115
Homespun, Age of, 134, 417
"How-To" Letter, 22–24
Howe, William, 127
Hudson River School, 81
Hudson River, 59
Hudson Valley, 61, 72–73, 417
Hudson, Henry, 14–15, 118
Human rights, 379, 417
Human-environmental interaction, 33, 36, 417
Hyde Park, 73, 259
Hypothesis, 310

I

"I Have A Dream" Speech, 356
Ice Age, 60
Immigration, 166–167, 417

Imports, 309, 418
Index, 28, 84, 418
Indigenous People, 101
Industrial Revolution, 154, 418
Industry, 296
Information
    Irrelevant, 88–89
    Relevant, 88–89
Informed decisions, 399
Interdependence, 309, 418
Internet, 329, 335
Interstate Highways, 30
Inuits, 205
Investments, 300
Irish Americans, 216–217
Iroquois, 102–111
    Confederacy, 109
    Constitution, 109–110
Islam, 212, 418
Island, 424
Issues, 399, 418
Italian Americans, 217–218
Ithaca, 72

J

Jackson, Andrew, 360
Jay, John, 134
Jefferson, Thomas, 125, 322–323, 360
Jewish Americans, 219–221
Johnson City, 71
Johnson, Lyndon B., 360
Jones Beach, 76
Journals, 398
Judaism, 211, 418
Judicial branch, 334, 418
Judicial power, 332
Jury, 375

K

Key, Francis Scott, 265
King, Martin Luther, Jr., 356–357
Kingston, 73
Kodak, 156
Kodak, Eastman, 253
Korean Americans, 226–228
Korean Harvest Festival, 228

L

Labor Unions, 278
Labor, 283, 418
LaGuardia, Fiorello, 219
Lake, 425
    Champlain, 59
    Erie, 58

    George, 69
    Oneida, 59
    Ontario, 58
    Placid, 69
Land (*Natural Resources*), 283, 418
Latin American, 80, 418
Latitude, 53, 418
Laws, 324, 418
Lazarus, Emma, 168
Leader, 352, 418
League of Five Nations, 109, 418
League of Women Voters, 335
Legend, 49, 264, 418
Legends, 237–238
Legislative branch, 333, 418
Legislative power, 332
Lieutenant Governor, 342
Lincoln, Abraham, 354–355
Line graph, 385, 418
Livestock, 296
Livingston, Robert, 351
Local government, purpose, 362
Location, 31, 35, 418
    Absolute, 32
    Relative, 32
Logo, 87
Lomb, Henry, 156
Long Island Expressway, 390
Long Island, 75–77, 418
Longhouse, 103
Longitude, 54, 418

M

Main idea, 142
Majority rule, 383, 418
Majority, 383
Managers, 284
Mandela, Nelson, 360
Manhattan, 39–40, 78
Manufacturing, 296
Maps, 47, 418
March on Washington, 356
May, Samuel, 146
Mayor, 345
Meridians, 54
Metallurgy, 247
Metropolitan Museum of Art, 259
Middle Colonies, 131
Mileage charts, 92
Minerals, 301, 418
Miners, 296
Minority, 383
Minuit, Peter, 119

Mnemonic devices, 4–5
Mohammed, 212
Mohawk River, 59
Mohawk Valley, 61, 73–74
Monarchy, 330, 418
Mount Marcy, 69
Mountain, , 423
Movement, 33, 36
Multi-racial society, 205, 419
Museum of Natural History, 263
Museums, 259, 419
Myths, 237–238, 419

N

NAFTA, 316, 419
Nagasaki, 184
Narrative Essay, 182–183
Nassau County, 76
Nation-states, 336
National Anthem, 266
National origin, 207, 419
Nationality, 207, 419
Native Americans, 101–111, 205
Naturalized Citizen, 368, 419
Natural Resources, 45, 300, 419
New Amsterdam, 119, 419
New Deal, 171, 419
New England Colonies, 130
New England Uplands, 74–75
New Netherland, 119, 419
New York City, 77–78
New York Court of Appeals, 342, 419
New York State Assembly, 339
New York State Flag, 200
New York State Legislature, 339, 419
New York State Seal, 200
New York State Senate, 340
New York Stock Exchange, 170
New York Thruway, 188
New-media, 298, 419
Newburgh, 75
Niagara Falls, 1, 60, 70, 262
Niagara River, 58
Nightmares, 404
Nineteenth Amendment, 389, 419
North Pole, 17
Northern Hemisphere, 17, 419
Numerator, 311

O

Ocean, 18, 425
Oil spills, 392

Old Bethpage Village, 141
Opinion, 100, 401, 419
Opportunity Cost, 275, 419
Oral history, 194–197, 419
Orbit, 16, 419
Oswego River, 59
Outline, 187
Ozone layer, 396, 419

P

Parallels, 53
Parker, Eli, 112
Parkways, 29
Pataki, George, 342
Patriots, 124
Patroons, 120
Pearl Harbor, 177–178
Penalties, 324
Peninsula, 425
Per Capita Income, 83, 419
Percentages, 311
Persuasive writing, 406–407
Pesticides, 392, 419
Petition, 400, 419
Petroleum, 314
Physical maps, 27, 419
Picture timeline, 245
Pie chart, 206, 210, 419
Place, 32, 35, 38–40
Plain, 423
Plateau, 71, 423
Plattsburgh, 69
Political Maps, 28
Pollution, 391, 420
Polo, Marco, 233
Population density, 83, 420
Posters, 181
Poughkeepsie, 73
Powell, Colin, 185
Prairies, 64
Pre-reading hints, 10
Precipitation, 61, 420
President of the United States, 334, 420
Pre-writing, 8
Primary Source, 176, 420
Prime Meridian, 17, 54, 420
Problem-solving, 393, 420
Product map, 304–305, 420
Production, 277, 420
Profit, 284, 286, 291, 293, 420
Proofreading, 10
Public Advocate, 345
Pueblos, 115

Puerto Rican Day, 226
Puerto Ricans, 225–226
Pyramids, 246

Q

Qu'ran (Koran), 212
Queens, 78
Quota System, 167

R

Race, 205, 420, 388
Ranchers, 296
Randolph, A. Philip, 231
Recycling, 394, 420
Reform, 143, 420
Region, 20, 67, 32, 35, 420
Reincarnation, 212
Religion, 208, 420
Remington, Eliphalet, 319
Representative democracy, 382, 420
Representatives, 382, 420
Reservations, 163
Responsibilities, 372, 420
Revolution, 124, 420
Right, 371, 420
Riis, Jacob, 159
Rivers, 59, 425
Robinson, Jackie, 87
Rochester, 70
Rockefeller, Nelson, 192, 241
Rocky Mountains, 64
Roosevelt, Eleanor, 360, 381
Roosevelt, Franklin D. 170–171, 177–178, 387
Roosevelt, Theodore, 174
Routes, 30
Rules, 324

S

Sachem, 103
Sagamore Hill, 262
Salute To Israel Parade, 221
San Gennaro Festival, 218
San Martín, José de, 360
Saratoga Springs, 74
Scale, 50, 420
Scarcity, problem of, 275–276
Schenck v. United States, 376
Schenectady, 73
Secede, 150
Secondary source, 176, 420
Sectionalism, 150, 420
Segregation, 356, 420

Seneca Falls Convention, 143, 420
Service industries, 297, 420
Services, 282, 420
Sierra Nevada, 64
Smith, Adam, 272–273
Smith, Alfred E., 302
Soil, 301
Solar system, 16
Songs, 180
South Pole, 17
Southern Colonies, 131
Southern Hemisphere, 17, 420
Spanish-American War, 172
Special districts, 346, 421
Sphere, 17, 421
St. Lawrence Lowlands, 60, 68–69
St. Lawrence River, 58–59
St. Leger, Barry, 127
St. Patrick's Day, 218
Stanton, Elizabeth Cady, 144, 360
Star-Spangled Banner, 266
State government, 339, 421
State government, purposes, 362
Staten Island, 78
States' Rights, 150
States, 21, 32, 331, 421
Statue of Liberty, 168
Street, 30
Strike, 278
Stuyvesant, Peter, 120
Suburb, 188, 421
Subways, 159
Suffolk County, 77
Sunnyside, 262
Supporting details, 143
Survey, 368
Susan B. Anthony House, 262
Symbol, 49, 421, 265, 266
Synagogue, 211
Syracuse, 71

T

Table, 85, 421
Taconic Mountains, 60
Tappan, Arthur and Lewis, 146
Tariffs, 316, 421
Taughannock Falls, 60
Technology, 193
Ten Commandments, 210
Tenements, 159, 421
Theme maps, 28
Themes of geography, 31, 37
Thirteenth Amendment, 355
Thousand Islands, 68, 421

Tiananmen Square demonstrations, 379
Time capsule, 177
Timeline, 240–247, 421
Title, 48
Topography, 60, 421
Tories, 124
Tortillas, 236
Tower of Babel, 203
Town government, 346
Towns, 22
Toxins, 392
Trade, foreign, 313–16
Traditional economy, 287, 421
Trends, 386
Triangle Shirtwaist Factory, 163
Tributary, 73
Trolleys, 158
Tubman, Harriet, 147
Tughill Plateau, 68
Turnpikes, 29, 136
Twenty-sixth Amendment, 389

U

U.S. Congress, 333, 421
U.S. Constitution, 349
U.S. House of Representatives, 333
U.S. Senate, 333
U.S. Supreme Court, 334, 375, 421
Underground Railroad, 146–147, 421
United Nations, 184–185, 263, 421
Universal Declaration of Human Rights, 379, 421
Urban, 40, 421
Urbanization, 158, 421
Utica, 74

V

Valley, 61, 423
Van Buren, Martin, 250
Vanderbilt Mansion, 262
Venn diagram, 113–114
Verrazano, Giovanni Da, 117
Veteran's Day, 186
Veteran, 186
Vietnam War, 195
Village government, 346
Villages, 22, 346
Vocabulary cards, 2–4

W

War of 1812, 135
Washington, George, 126
Water, 45, 90–91, 301
Watkins Glen State Park, 259
Watt, James, 247
Weather, 61, 421
West Point, 75
Western Hemisphere, 17, 421
Westinghouse, George, 281
Whitman, Walt, 250
Wigwams, 103
Wojczuk, Jasiek, 366–367
Workers, 278
World War I, 168, 174, 421
World War II, 177–180, 421
Wyandanch, 108

Y–Z

Yonkers, 75
Zenger, John Peter, 373

PHOTO CREDITS

This book includes written material and pictures from many different sources. Occasionally it is not possible to determine if a particular source or picture is copyrighted, and if so, who is the copyright owner. If there has been a copyright infringement with any material produced in this book, it has been unintentional. We extend our sincerest apologies and would be happy to make immediate and appropriate restitution upon proof of copyright ownership.

(LOC) Library of Congress; (NA) National Archives; (U.N.) United Nations; (N.Y.S.A.) New York State Archives; (N.Y.S.E.D.) New York State Department of Economic Development; (T.D.T.) Texas Department of Transportation; (t) top; (m) middle; (b) bottom; (r) right; (l) left; (c) center

COVER: New York City skyline: S. Milstein, Photographer.

OPENING ACTIVITY: Pg. 1: S. Milstein, Photographer.

UNIT 2: Page 14: N.Y.S.A.; 29: N.Y.S.A.; 30: S. Zimmer, Photographer; 32: S. Milstein, Photographer; 33: N.Y.S.E.D.; 35: Japanese National Tourist Office; 36: U.N.; 37: N.Y.S.E.D.; 38: N.Y.S.A.; 40: (t & b) NY Convention and Visitors Bureau; 41: T.J. Zimmer, Photographer; 45: U.N., Ray Witlin, photographer; 46: N.Y.S.E.D.; 59: S. Zimmer Photographer; 60: N.Y.S.E.D.; 61: (t) N.Y.S.E.D., (b) N.Y.S.E.D.; 63: NY Convention and Visitors Bureau; 64: M. Jarrett, Photographer; 65: LOC; 68: (t & b) N.Y.S.E.D.; 69: N.Y.S.E.D.; 70: N.Y.S.E.D.; 72: (t & b) N.Y.S.E.D.; 73: (t) N.Y.S.A., (b) N.Y.S.E.D.; 74: N.Y.S.E.D.; 75: N.Y.S.E.D.; 76: (t) N.Y.S.E.D., (b) Theodore Roosevelt Presidential Library; 77: (t) NY Convention and Visitors Bureau, (l) LOC, (r) N.Y.S.A.; 78: (l & r) NY Convention and Visitors Bureau; 79: N.Y.S.E.D.; 81: LOC; 83: N.Y.S.E.D.; 87: Schomburg Center For Research In Black Culture; 90: N.Y.S.E.D.; 91: LOC.

UNIT 3: Page 97: (t) LOC, (m) N.Y.S.A., (b) N.Y.S.A.; 98: LOC; 99: LOC; 102: N.Y.S.A.; 103: N.Y.S.A.; 104: (t & b) N.Y.S.A.; 105: (t) NA, (b) N.Y.S.A.; 106: N.Y.S.A.; 108: LOC; 110: N.Y.S.A.; 111: N.Y.S.A.; 112: LOC; 115: (t) LOC, (b) NA; 117: LOC; 118: LOC; 119: (t & b) LOC; 120: (t & b) LOC; 122: LOC; 123: LOC; 124: LOC; 125: LOC; 126: (t) LOC, (b) NA; 128: LOC; 130: LOC; 132: (t & b) LOC; 134: LOC; 137: (t) N.Y.S.A., (b) California State Railroad Museum; 138: NA; 139: National Portrait Gallery, Smithsonian Institution; 142: N.Y.S.A.; 144: LOC; 146: (t) NA, (b) LOC; 148: LOC; 152: S. Zimmer, Photographer; 154: NA; 155: N.Y.S.A.; 156: (t &b) LOC; 158: LOC; 159: N.Y.S.A.; 159: NA; 163: (t) S. Milstein Collection; (b) LOC; 164: (l, m. r) LOC; 166: (t) LOC, (b) S. Milstein Collection; 168: NA; 169: LOC; 170: (t) S. Milstein Collection, (b) NA; 171: Franklin D. Roosevelt Library; 174: LOC; 175: S. Zimmer, Photographer; 180: (l, m, r) NA; 181: (l & r) NA; 184: NA; 185: (t) U.N., (b) U.S. Army; 186: NA; 188: NA; 189: S. Milstein, Photographer; 191: NYS Executive Department, Office of General Services; 192: (t & b) NYS Executive Department, Office of General Services; 195: Schomberg Center For Research in Black Culture; 200: (t & b) N.Y.S.A.

UNIT 4: Page 201: (t) LOC, (m) G.A.L.O.S. Corporation, (b) LOC; 203: LOC; 208: S. Milstein, Photographer; 209: S. Milstein, Photographer; 211: (t & b) Israeli Department of Tourism; 212: Isreali Department of Tourism; 214: N.Y.S.E.D.; 217: N.Y.S.E.D.; 218: LOC; 219: N.Y.S.A.; 220: Milstein Collection; 221: LOC; 222: LOC; 224: (t) Office of the Mayor: Joan Vitale Strong, Photographer, (b) LOC; 226: G.A.L.O.S. Corporation; 227: Korea National Tourism Corporation; 229: LOC; 231: (t) Texas Dept. of Transportation. (b) NA; 233: LOC; 234: (t) National Museum of African Art, (b) LOC; 236: Texas Dept. of Transportation; 241: LOC; 246: U.N.: John Isaac, Photographer; 247: LOC; 250: (t) Bureau of Engraving and Printing, (b) NA; 254: U.S. Capitol Historical Society; 257: S. Zimmer, Photographer; 259: NY Convention and Visitors Bureau; 266: (t) LOC; (b) Six Flags Adventure Park.

UNIT 5: (t) LOC, (m) N.Y.S.A., (b) N.Y.S.E.D.; 272: LOC; 277: S. Zimmer, Photographer; 278: (t) S. Zimmer, Photographer, (b) S. Milstein, Photographer; 279: Ford Motor Company; 280: LOC; 281: LOC; 283: (t) N.Y.S.E.D., (b) N.Y.S.A.; 284: N.Y.S.A.; 285: Ford Motor Company; 287: U.N.; 288: Texas Department of Tranportation; 289: S. Zimmer, Photographer; 290: F. Greene, Photographer; 291: S. Milstein, Photographer; 294: LOC; 295: Texas Dept. of Transportation; 296: Texas Dept. of Transportation; 297: Texas Dept. of Transportation; 301: (t) N.Y.S.A., (b) N.Y.S.E.D.; 302: LOC; 306: Texas Dept. of Transportation; 308: N.Y.S.E.D.; 309: S.Milstein, Photographer; 317: S. Milstein, Photographer; 319: S. Milstein, Photographer.

UNIT 6: Page 321: (t) The White House, (m) NYS Governor's Office, (b) Mayor's Photo Unit: Edward Reed, Photographer; 322: NA; 326: (l & r) S. Milstein, Photographer; 327: LOC; 328: Pitlik Collection; 329: S. Zimmer, Photographer; 330: LOC; 331: LOC; 333: United State Capitol Historical Society; 334: The White House; 336: (l) LOC, (c) The White House, (r) Collection of the Supreme Court of the United States; 338: S. Milstein, Photographer; 339: S. Zimmer, Photographer; 342: (t) LOC, (m) NYS Governor's Office, (b) S. Zimmer, Photographer; 345: Office of the Mayor: Edward Reed, photographer; 346: Office of the Mayor: Edward Reed and Scott Foster, photographer; 349: NA; 351: N.Y.S.A.; 354: LOC; 356: (t) LOC, (b) NA; 359: LOC; 360: Consulate General of India; 361: S. Milstein, Photographer; 364: S. Milstein, Photographer.

UNIT 7: Page 365: (t) S. Zimmer, Photographer, (m) NA, (b) NYS Governor's Office; 366: Mark Jarrett, Photographer; 372: Hanna Kisiel; 373: LOC; 374: NA; 378: S. Milstein, Photographer; 379: U.N., Y. Nagata, Photographer; 380: Amnesty International; 381: Franklin D. Roosevelt Library; 387: LOC; 388: LOC; 390: S. Zimmer, Photographer; 391: LOC; 392: T.D.T.; 394: S. Milstein, Photographer; 396: U.N., John Isaac, Photographer; 410: S. Milstein, Photographer.

CLOSING ACTIVITY: Page 413: N.Y.S.E.D.

GAZETTEER: Page 422: (t, ml, mr, b) T.D.T.; 423: (t, mr) Department of Transportation, (m, l) S. Zimmer, Photographer, (b) T.D.T.; 424: (t & m) T.D.T.; 425: (t) NYS Arhives, (b) T.D.T.